Mill's *A System of Logic*

John Stuart Mill considered his *A System of Logic*, first published in 1843, the methodological foundation and intellectual groundwork of his later works in ethical, social, and political theory. Yet no book has attempted in the past to engage with the most important aspects of Mill's *Logic*. This volume brings together leading scholars to elucidate the key themes of this influential work, looking at such topics as his philosophy of language and mathematics, his view on logic, induction and deduction, free will, argumentation, ethology and psychology, as well as his account of normativity, kind of pleasure, philosophical and political method and the "Art of Life."

Antis Loizides teaches in the Department of Social and Political Sciences at the University of Cyprus

Routledge Studies in Nineteenth-Century Philosophy

Mill's *A System of Logic*
Critical Appraisals

Edited by Antis Loizides

Routledge
Taylor & Francis Group

LONDON AND NEW YORK

First published 2014
by Routledge

2 Park Square, Milton Park, Abingdon, Oxfordshire OX14 4RN
711 Third Avenue, New York, NY 10017

*Routledge is an imprint of the Taylor & Francis Group,
an informa business*

First issued in paperback 2017

Library of Congress Cataloging-in-Publication Data

Mill's a system of logic : critical appraisals / edited by Antis Loizides. —
1 [edition].
    pages cm. — (Routledge studies in nineteenth-century philosophy ; 6)
    Includes bibliographical references and index.
 1. Mill, John Stuart, 1806–1873.   2. Mill, John Stuart, 1806–1873.
 3. Logic, Modern—19th century.   I. Loizides, Antis, editor of compilation.
    B1608.L6M55 2014
    160—dc23
    2014001677

ISBN: 978-0-415-84124-5 (hbk)
ISBN: 978-0-8153-7194-6 (pbk)

Typeset in Sabon
by Apex CoVantage, LLC

Contents

Foreword

Mill's reputation as a philosopher—as against a noble figure and public thinker—went through a very bad batch in the earlier half of the twentieth century. In contrast, it has been recovering remarkably over the last forty years or so. The pattern is not particularly unusual. *Post mortem* slides of reputation, typically accompanied by severe or even perverse misunderstandings, seem to happen quite regularly to influential philosophers, especially to great philosophers who have a comprehensively worked-out view across the whole of philosophy. Locke, Hume, Kant and Hegel all come to mind. There is something in the sheer scale and breadth of their work, the daunting demand to grasp it as a whole, that discourages and dispirits a reader. Moreover, when vast comprehensiveness combines with great influence it is bound to annoy in some respect or other across the range of topics of which it treats—especially if it incorporates active political polemicism and attracts an admiring crowd, as in the case of Mill.

Still, even though Mill's reputation has been recovering for some time, the recovery has not yet reached the full range of his philosophy. There are signs of change, there is interest in Mill's treatment of a few disconnected topics outside moral and political philosophy, yet, overall, contemporary interest in Mill remains too one-sidedly restricted to his ethical and political writings. This is unfortunate. It is important to develop and familiarize an accurate picture of Mill as a *philosopher*, a philosopher who sought to integrate his interests in ethics and politics into his overall philosophy, rather than as a primarily political thinker with somewhat unaccountable side interests in philosophy. Mill worked out quite fully a naturalistic liberal humanism. Its epistemological side is just as important as its ethical side, today as in his own time. Critics as well as proponents should aim to understand it accurately and in detail. Nor is this just about understanding Mill. A balanced understanding of how philosophy developed in the nineteenth century must take proper account of the substance and point of the *A System of Logic* and the *Examination of Sir William Hamilton's Philosophy*.

These two works took up a large amount of Mill's time and thought. Coming toward the beginning and towards the end of his career, they are the groundwork of his standing as a philosopher. In them he expounds his philosophy of language, his naturalistic epistemology, his account, within that naturalistic and semantic framework, of induction, logic and mathematics, his conception of the moral sciences, his view of aprioricity and necessity, his phenomenalistic metaphysics. Both works have to be studied to get a full view of Mill as philosopher—nonetheless, all the topics just mentioned apart from the last can be found in the *System of Logic*. I would not want to condone neglect of the *Examination*, since behind its unappetizing title there lies some of Mill's most penetrating and probing thought. Still, the *System of Logic* is the work to which he gave the most time in his years of first maturity, and it is, as it says it is, a systematic treatise, whereas in the *Examination* Mill's own views are set out in the context of a sometimes strident polemic against Hamilton.

Mill himself thought that his two longest surviving works would be the essay on *Liberty* and the *System of Logic*. But whereas work on *Liberty* never comes to an end, and can sometimes seem to be multiplying *praeter necessitate* (I am, I admit, one of the culprits), work on the *System of Logic* cries out to be done. There is scholarly work to do—and the time is ripe to do it. For one thing, the history of philosophy has begun to move on, having fully caught up with Kant, to the fascinating complications of the nineteenth century. For another, current pluralism and diversity in philosophy makes it much easier to appreciate Mill, along with other nineteenth century philosophers, than was possible fifty or more years ago, when philosophical orthodoxy was so strongly at odds with most of their views, and certainly with Mill's.

It is extremely encouraging to see this renewal taking place. Mill's reputation as a philosopher who dealt comprehensively with the questions of philosophy is important even for his reputation as a moral philosopher. A just estimate will I believe show his philosophy to be one of the cornerstones of nineteenth century thought, still fresh and interesting today. I hope and believe that this excellent collection of papers will move his reputation strongly forward, and as one of the admirers of Mill I am grateful to the editor and contributors for the hard work they have devoted to a very worthwhile task.

—John Skorupski

Preface

John Stuart Mill's *A System of Logic* (1843) established him as a leading figure among his peers, dominating university education in the second half of the nineteenth century. He himself considered the *Logic* as the methodological foundation or intellectual groundwork for his later works in economic, ethical, social and political theory. And for the past sixty or so years Mill's ethical, social and political philosophy has been reassessed, rediscovered and even reinvented in light of it. It is a book that Mill saw through the press several times, each time making substantial revisions. Since Mill claimed, while in the process of writing it, that he was a "Logician" rather than anything else, the *Logic* became more than just a book—it was the book that would set the terms of the intellectual renovation he sought. As the Introduction to this volume discusses, the *Logic* was greeted as a monumental contribution to philosophical studies of the time, by friends and foes alike. Criticism was almost never absent, but no one ever questioned that they were "in the presence of a master."

A conscious effort has been made to enlist to this project individuals who have worked previously on Mill, could give a good look at Mill's *Logic* from the inside and could make connections between the *Logic* and other aspects of Mill's thought (and influence), as well as scholars with expertise on subjects with which Mill engaged in the *Logic* but who could have a critical look on Mill from the outside and make connections between Mill and contemporary analytical philosophy. The benefits of such a combination of expertise seemed to outweigh the costs—but whether it indeed did or not, remains to be seen. Moreover, as Mill's *Logic* touches upon an immense range of subjects, the contributions to this volume do not attempt to cover, or uncover, all of its aspects. Although much remains to be done—both philosophically and historically—for a full exploration of Mill's *Logic*, the volume does pay particular attention to some of its most important themes.

In Chapter 1, Stephen P. Schwartz critically examines Mill's theory of names, especially Mill's theory of proper names and of general terms. Schwartz brings out both the advantages and the shortcomings of Mill's theories compared with contemporary theories in the philosophy of language. In Chapter 2, Steffen Ducheyne and John P. McCaskey explore the sources and highlight the traditions that were important for Mill's *Logic*; they discuss how Mill reacted against certain traditions and trends as far as his views on ratiocination and

induction are concerned. In Chapter 3, Mark Balaguer shows that Mill's philosophy of mathematics cannot account for contemporary mathematics or
even the mathematics of his own day and attempts to offer an explanation for
what Mill should have said about mathematics, given his background philosophical commitments. In Chapter 4, Elijah Millgram examines the famous
exchange between Mill and William Whewell. The Mill-Whewell debate has
traditionally been cast as a disagreement about whether inference to the best
explanation has a place in science, but Millgram suggests that it is best understood as the clash of competing views in the philosophy of logic. In Chapter 5,
Frederick Rosen highlights the philosophical tradition, associationist psychology and utilitarian logic, in which Mill wrote by focusing on his thirty-year
relationship with Alexander Bain, which is depicted in terms of a double
helix, linking Mill's *System of Logic* of 1843 with Bain's *Logic* of 1870. In
Chapter 6, Bernard Berofsky examines Mill's theory of free will, comparing it
to that of David Hume. Berofsky suggests that an adequate defense of the regularity theory, which has failed to satisfy critics, resting on a revised account of
systematization may be found in the comments of Mill himself. In Chapter 7,
Christopher Macleod compares Mill and Kant as regards their appeal to the
validity of our spontaneous propensities as reasoning agents; Macleod offers
an interpretation of Mill's account of theoretical and practical reason that
attempts to do justice to the neglected fact that Mill's demonstration of the
principle of utility runs parallel to his demonstration of the principle of induction. In Chapter 8, Jonathan Riley makes use of Mill's *System of Logic* to
clarify what Mill means by different kinds of pleasures, and to confirm that,
for him, a difference of quality is an infinite difference, that is, an intrinsic
difference irrespective of quantity. In Chapter 9, Hans V. Hansen takes the
view that Mill's contributions to informal logic and the study of argumentation are considerable. Not only did Mill's work, Hansen argues, contribute
to the practice of argumentation, it was also an important precursor of the
development of informal logic in the late twentieth century. Chapter 10 examines whether the method of politics Mill sketched in *Logic* corresponds to the
one employed in his *Considerations of Representative Government*; to this
effect, the discussion draws on Mill's discussion of the method appropriate
to arts and sciences and his criticisms of the traditional methods of politics,
either deductive or inductive. Finally, Chapter 11 forms Alan Ryan's "second
sailing" with Mill's "Art of Life," revising some ideas on this aspect of Mill's
thought that originally appeared fifty years ago, when he first engaged with
Mill's architectonic *technê* of living.

I would like to express my gratitude and indebtedness to all contributors
for their willingness to participate in this project, their hard work preparing
their chapters (and related tasks) and their patience with unforeseen delays.
I am especially indebted to John Skorupski, Alan Ryan, Jonathan Riley, Fred
Rosen, Stephen Schwartz, Elijah Millgram, Georgios Varouxakis and Kyriakos Demetriou for advice and guidance during the completion of this project.
Hopefully, this volume will prove to be useful and interesting to all students
of John Stuart Mill, of the history of philosophy and of philosophy in general.

Introduction

Antis Loizides

Twenty two years after its original publication in 1843 a sixth edition of John Stuart Mill's *A System of Logic* appeared in bookstores and on bookshelves. By then Mill was confident, though reluctant to admit it publicly, that all that he had to worry about was "how to make the best use of my influence during such years of life & work as remain to me."[1] Already by 1847, the *Logic*'s success had given Mill much "capital," i.e., much leeway with publishers, that he could spend by promulgating radical opinions which would offend and scandalize "ten times as many people as" they pleased[2] and which would eventually establish him as "one of England's greatest sons."[3] Two more editions of the *Logic* appeared before his death on 8 May 1873, twelve days short of his sixty-seventh birthday. Surveys of Mill's life and works would soon parade through the press. For some, Mill was "[t]he great intellectual pointsman of our age"; he was "the man who has done more than any other of this generation to give direction to the thought of his contemporaries." "[W]e are left," the commentator added, "to measure the loss to humanity by the result of his labours."[4] The two works selected by Mill himself to survive longer than anything else he had labored on were *On Liberty* (1859) and *A System of Logic*.[5]

Seldom do students of Mill's works pause and think just how much Mill had worked on *A System of Logic*, taking fifteen years from inception to completion.[6] For most, at the time, Mill's *Logic* was "inestimable" and "a revolution."[7] Some were not so generous; according to Abraham Hayward, Mill's *Logic* was "a book which no one would read for amusement, hardly, indeed, except as a task; his style, always dry, is here at its driest." However, Hayward did note that "the circumstance of the work having reached an eight edition in 1872 is, therefore, a conclusive proof of its completeness as a system and a text-book." Still, Mill, the author concluded, "with all his errors and paradoxes, . . . will be long remembered as a thinker and reasoner who has largely contributed to the intellectual progress of the age." Hayward's estimate of Mill's accomplishments, being part of a stinging—to say the least—*Times* obituary, had caused great annoyance among Mill's admirers and friends. However, it is indicative of Mill's status in the late nineteenth century that Hayward's claim regarding the "completeness as a system and a text-book" of the *System of Logic*—a very contentious claim to make by 1873—was never challenged; rather it was deemed insufficient to balance the charges of dryness, error and paradox.[8]

It is quite difficult, if it is even possible at all, to estimate Mill's contribution "to the intellectual progress of the age"; more so with regard to isolating the impact of one specific work by a prolific writer such as Mill—Mill's "methods" being of no help here. Nevertheless an attempt must be made at such an assessment, focusing on some aspects of the reception of Mill's *Logic*—however imperfect and incomplete that attempt may be.

I.

The story of Mill's early study of logic found in his *Autobiography* (1873a) is well known[9]—though perhaps not as well known as his story of his learning ancient Greek and of first reading Plato at the ages of three and seven respectively.[10] In his critical biography of Mill, Alexander Bain (1818–1903) found Mill's early training in logic, commencing at twelve with Aristotle's *Organon*, "the one thing, in . . . [Bain's] judgment, where Mill was most markedly in advance of his years." Comparing Mill with his contemporaries, Bain claimed that he had "never known a similar case of precocity." Mill had not only "read treatises on the Formal Logic, as well as Hobbes's *Computatio sive Logica,* but . . . he was able to chop Logic with his father in regard to the foundations and demonstrations of Geometry."[11] In contrast, Bain was not quite as impressed with regard to Mill's attainments in Greek, noting that Mill's early reading "could be nothing but an exercise in the Greek language." The two stories however interconnect. And Mill made it clear how:

> The Socratic method, of which the Platonic dialogues are the chief example, is unsurpassed as a discipline for correcting the errors, and clearing up the confusions incident to the *intellectus sibi permissus*, the understanding which has made up all its bundles of associations under the guidance of popular phraseology.[12]

Mill's "strong relish for accurate classification," acquired by school logic and Plato's dialogues, was another sense in which his early education was a "course of Benthamism." Most importantly, the application of the Benthamite standard of the "greatest happiness" to law, ethics and politics (to which Mill was referring when he argued that his early education had been a "course of Benthamism") came a few years later than that of studying the

> close, searching *elenchus* by which the man of vague generalities, is constrained either to express his meaning to himself in definite terms, or to confess that he does not know what he is talking about; the perpetual

testing of all general statements by particular instances; the siege in form which is laid to the meaning of large abstract terms, by fixing upon some still larger class-name which includes that and more, and dividing down to the thing sought—marking out its limits and definition by a series of accurately drawn distinctions between it and each of the cognate objects which are successively parted off from it[.][13]

According to Mill, dissecting bad arguments and identifying fallacies was the "first intellectual operation in which . . . [he] arrived at any proficiency."[14] As this is not the place to pursue the link between Mill's Socratic and logical studies in any depth,[15] suffice it to say that his proficiency in logic did come in handy in the "polemics of the day." Bain was right in claiming that Jeremy Bentham (1748–1832) and James Mill (1773–1836) were at "war against vague, ambiguous, flimsy, unanalyzed words and phrases . . . in the wide domains of Politics and Ethics."[16] And this was a battle in which the younger Mill joined, with "Socratic dialectics" as the weapon of choice.[17] As we shall see later on, Mill's *Logic* was intended as a blow both to intuitionist ethico-political views as well as their metaphysical underpinnings.

In Bain's "estimate of Mill's genius," Mill "was first of all a Logician, and next a social philosopher or Politician."[18] But Mill was not the one without being the other. William Leonard Courtney (1850–1928) seemed thus to have been closer to the truth in his own biography of Mill:

> James Mill wished to educate his son to carry out his own work, to make a thinker after his own likeness, and especially to save his pupil from some of what he deemed the wasteful and unnecessary parts of his own development. The son, therefore, need not go through the same steps as the father, but commence almost at the very point which the older thinker had attained. He must begin by being at once a radical politician, a free-thinker, and a logician.[19]

At the height of the parliamentary reform debate, John Stuart Mill came to test the strengths of his early education—logical, economical, ethical and political—in the press, in journals, at clubs and societies; reason, the domain of logic, rather than feeling was employed in the assessment of educational, social, legal and political practices. In praise of the intellectual aspect of his early training, Mill, later in life, was "persuaded that nothing, in modern education, tends so much, when properly used, to form exact thinkers, who attach a precise meaning to words and propositions, and are not imposed on by vague, loose, or ambiguous terms" than "school logic." However, this did not mean that school logic itself was passively received: the young Utilitarians—branded "the Brangles" by Harriet Grote (1792–1878)—took up the study of syllogistic logic as a group in the mid-1820s, aiming to master it as well as to improve it.[20] Around this time—and due to his "Brangles" meetings—Mill began putting his ideas for a book on logic on paper.[21]

Yet it was not the abovementioned aspect of the young utilitarians' logical studies that formed part of their general perception. At the time, all that Mill, and his friends, waving high the banner of utilitarianism, "thought of was to alter people's opinions; to make them believe according to evidence, and know what was their real interest" ("evidence" being an operative word in the Benthamic dictionary[22]). Their "youthful fanaticism" and "sectarian spirit" thus led to the emergence of the caricature of a "Benthamite", i.e., "a dry, hard logical machine."[23] As Frederick Denison Maurice (1805–1872), whose insight that "all differences of opinion when analysed, [are] differences of method" guided Mill in the composition of the *Logic*,[24] noted in 1835: "The most University-hating priest-hating sect in England has taken Logic under its patronage; and scholastic pedantries, which would have furnished playwrights in the last age with excellent jokes against College Fellows, are now oftentimes the youthful Utilitarian's best passport to reputation." He immediately added: "The end which the Benthamites propose to themselves, is the detection of fallacies in the writings or speeches of Whigs, Tories, and, above all of Churchmen."[25] The error of these "dictators," Maurice argued, was setting logic up "as an ἐμπειρία [i.e., a skill or a routine] for the accomplishment of a specific purpose, instead of studying it as a branch of humanity," convincing only those who "had implicitly adopted all their opinions beforehand."[26]

In his *Autobiography*, Mill admitted that Maurice's view of the Benthamites was roughly an accurate description of himself during that period of his life.[27] But he soon underwent a great change in his opinions, following the well-known crisis in his "mental history." Reflected in his writings at the turn of the decade, this change led Mill to seek the company of Maurice and John Sterling (1806–1844) as well as Thomas Carlyle (1795–1881)—individuals not only free from the "narrowness" of Mill's circle up to the late 1820s but also highly critical of the utilitarian sect. For this reason, while the younger Mill was engaged in writing the *Logic*, James Mill's old associates viewed the younger Mill's "enlargement-of-the-utilitarian-creed" project with skepticism; Graham Wallas reported in his biography of Francis Place (1771–1854), "the radical tailor of Charing Cross," that Place thought that the younger Mill by 1838 had "made great progress in becoming a German metaphysical mystic"; Harriet Grote herself had called John Stuart Mill in a letter to Place a "wayward intellectual deity."[28]

However, particularly in his correspondence with Sterling and Carlyle, John Stuart Mill, as he made progress with the *Logic*, increasingly identified his "vocation" to be that of a "Scientist," rather than that of the "Artist."[29] He was less "wayward" than his radical friends supposed; still, the *Logic* seemed to offer an opportunity to be treated as a thinker in his own right. Writing to Carlyle in 1837, Mill noted his hope that he did not "overrate the value of anything I can do of that kind [that is, a treatise on logic] but it so happens that this, whatever be its value, is the only thing which I am sure I can do & do not believe can be so well done by anybody else whom I know of."[30] Importantly, he considered it to be part of his "task on earth" to say the things he had in mind on logic.[31]

Mill had already given a glimpse of what a writer on logic should attempt to do almost a decade earlier when asked to review George Bentham's (1800–1884) *An Outline of a New System of Logic* (1827); that is, "not only *be* superior, but *prove* himself to be superior, in knowledge of the subject, to the author[s] whom he criticizes." The readers, according to Mill, should see that the author differs from others on logic "because he knows more" than they do.[32] Having convinced himself that he had something original to say, by 1832 he had already made considerable progress in writing the *Logic*. But he was soon led to a halt "on the threshold of Induction." In 1837, William Whewell's (1794–1866) books on the history and philosophy of inductive sciences gave Mill the push he needed, like Dugald Stewart's (1753–1828) five years earlier—Auguste Comte's (1798–1857) *Cours de Philosophie Positive* (1830–1842) provided much help too (especially with Book VI).[33] In August 1837, he was "so immersed in Logic and . . . [was] getting on so triumphantly with it that . . . [he] loathe[d] the idea of leaving off to write articles" for the *London and Westminster Review*.[34] The *Logic* was advancing rapidly, as Mill was untying all the "hard knots" that he found along the way.[35] In December 1841, following complete rewriting—which provided the opportunity to incorporate reflection on Comte's and Whewell's new books—Mill's *magnum opus* was ready for the press. According to Sterling, who had written an introduction for Mill to a prospective publisher, the *Logic* was the product of "labour of many years of a singularly subtle, patient, and comprehensive mind. It will be our chief speculative monument of this age."[36]

Right at the outset, Mill explained that his book was a product of "practical eclecticism";[37] he did not aim "to supersede, but to embody and systematize, the best ideas" on the subject. In laying no claim to originality other than this synthesis, he did acknowledge however that what he had attempted was no small feat:[38]

> To cement together the detached fragments of a subject, never yet treated as a whole; to harmonize the true portions of discordant theories, by supplying the links of thought necessary to connect them, and by disentangling them from the errors with which they are always more or less interwoven; must necessarily require a considerable amount of original speculation.[39]

On one hand, in the early draft of his *Autobiography*, Mill confessed that "eclecticism," "looking out for the truth which is generally to be found in errors when they are anything more than mere paralogisms, or logical blunders," was part of his process of breaking through the narrowness of his former education. On the other hand, Mill informed the readers of his autobiography that his expectations were limited to "keeping the tradition unbroken of what . . . [he] thought a better philosophy," having to combat "the opposite school of metaphysics, the ontological and 'innate principles' school."[40] In the past, too much stress had been given to the first, giving rise to the caricature of Mill "as a good-natured but slack-minded eclectic," as Alan Ryan put it.[41] In the last half-century or so, too much stress on the second has given rise to the caricature of Mill as a "systematizer," one who obsessively, and ingeniously, attempted to follow wherever it led him what he "thought a better philosophy," even when it led him to absurdities. Scholars have thus pointed out a tension with regard to Mill's *Logic*. Did Mill want "to do justice to the opinions of philosophers outside his own tradition," as William Kneale and Martha Kneale noted?[42] Or were the "goals, method, and characteristic style of Mill's philosophy . . . to a great extent intelligible in terms of his dislike of . . . intuitionism"?[43]

In his *Autobiography*, Mill claimed that "the *System of Logic* supplies what was much wanted, a text-book of the opposite doctrine [to the "German, or *à priori* view of human knowledge, and of the knowing faculties"]—that which derives all knowledge from experience, and all moral and intellectual qualities principally from the direction given to the associations." There was much value, according to Mill, in the "analysis of logical processes" and in "possible canons of evidence," i.e., in what they could do "towards guiding or rectifying the operations of the understanding,"—a value of logic that Mill had come to appreciate in walks with his father while he was still growing up.[44] More than three decades later, Mill provided an insight, both as to the rationale behind writing the *Logic* and writing it the way he did, which deserves to be quoted at length:

> The notion that truths external to the mind may be known by intuition or consciousness, independently of observation and experience, is, I am persuaded, in these times, the great intellectual support of false doctrines and bad institutions. By the aid of this theory, every inveterate belief and every intense feeling, of which the origin is not remembered, is enabled to dispense with the obligation of justifying itself by reason, and is erected into its own all-sufficient voucher and justification. There never was such an instrument devised for consecrating all deep seated prejudices. And the chief strength of this false philosophy in morals, politics, and religion, lies in the appeal which it is accustomed to make to the evidence of mathematics and of the cognate branches of physical science. To expel it from these, is to drive it from its stronghold: and because this had never been effectually done, the intuitive school . . . had in appearance, and as far as published writings were concerned, on the whole the best of the argument. In attempting to clear up the real nature of the evidence of mathematical and physical truths, the *System of Logic* met the intuition philosophers on ground on which they had previously been deemed unassailable; and gave its own explanation, from experience and association, of that peculiar character of what are called necessary truths, which is adduced as proof that their evidence

must come from a deeper source than experience. Whether this has been done effectually, is still *sub judice*; and even then, to deprive a mode of thought so strongly rooted in human prejudices and partialities, of its mere speculative support, goes but a very little way towards overcoming it; but though only a step, it is a quite indispensable one; for since, after all, prejudice can only be successfully combated by philosophy, no way can really be made against it permanently until it has been shewn not to have philosophy on its side.[45]

However, Mill wrote of his polemical intentions in composing the *Logic* approximately a decade after the *Logic*'s original publication. The following is from his introduction to the *Logic*: "I can conscientiously affirm, that no one proposition laid down in this work has been adopted for the sake of establishing, or with any reference to its fitness for being employed in establishing, preconceived opinions in any department of knowledge or of inquiry on which the speculative world is still undecided."[46] How could Mill, in just a decade—while revising the *Logic* for a new edition—make these conflicting claims?[47]

II.

Mill was not unaware that his book would be at odds with what was , as he claimed, the dominant philosophical school of the day. But to the best of his ability, he told Sterling, he tried to "keep clear" of the debate regarding "the perception of the highest Realities by direct intuition."[48] Writing to Carlyle, Mill had argued that logic was not the art of "knowing things" but "of knowing whether you know them or not";[49] discovering "truth" did not fall within the domain of logic, but deciding whether what one has found out was indeed "truth."[50] As Mill argued, his book

> professes to be a logic of *experience* only, & to throw no further light upon the existence of truths not experimental, than is thrown by shewing to what extent reasoning from experience will carry us. Above all mine is a logic of the indicative mood alone:—the logic of the imperative, in which the major premiss says not *is* but *ought*—I do not meddle with.[51]

Restricting logic "to the laws of the investigation of truth by means of extrinsic evidence whether ratiocinative or inductive," as Mill attempted to do, would still contradict some parts "of the supersensual philosophy"—though only subordinate, not fundamental, parts.[52] Logic offered a way of testing experience—finding that "outward standard, the conformity of an opinion to which constitutes its truth."[53] Mill argued that he had not developed any final thoughts on the "great matters" of the time[54]—he even admitted that may have had "something to learn on this subject from the German philosophers."[55] Mill did seem to seriously take under consideration Sterling's advice on reading a few German books on logic, contemplating postponing his plans for revising the *Logic*.[56]

In his epistolary discussions with Sterling, Mill noted that understanding each other on the definition, and domain, of logic required "a good deal of explanation."[57] Maurice, as we saw, protested to viewing logic as merely a skill; his underlying assumption seemed to be that logic combined with metaphysics would provide access to higher "truths." Mill took up the question of the scope of logic in the *Logic*'s Introduction. First, Mill considered whether logic was the science and art of reasoning. But defining logic as the analysis of what takes place when one reasons as well as the rules, based on that analysis, for reasoning correctly (to reason, in this sense, as Mill immediately added, "is simply to infer any assertion, from assertions already admitted"—including both deductive and inductive processes), Mill answered, was too limiting.[58] Second, Mill wondered whether logic was "the science which treats of the operations of the human understanding in the pursuit of truth." Some such operations included naming, classification, definition but also conception, perception, memory and belief. But this definition, according to Mill, included too much. The province of logic was distinct from that of "metaphysics" (i.e., trying to determine "what part of the furniture of the mind belongs to it originally, and what part is constructed out of materials furnished to it from without"). Mill did not consider the distinction between what the mind "receives from and what it gives to, the crude materials of its experience" as essential to the study of logic:[59]

> The province of logic must be restricted to that portion of our knowledge which consists of inferences from truths previously known; whether those antecedent data be general propositions, or particular observations and perceptions. Logic is not the science of Belief, but the science of Proof, or Evidence. In so far as belief professes to be founded on proof, the office of logic is to supply a test for ascertaining whether or not the belief is well grounded.

According to Mill, logic was nothing short than the master science, "the science of science itself"; though it does not observe, invent or discover, logic judges whether conclusions follow from data; logic illustrates the conditions under which facts may prove other facts: "Logic, then is the science of the operations of the understanding which are subservient to the estimation of evidence: both the process itself of advancing from known truths to unknown, and all other intellectual operations in so far auxiliary to this." Mill's aim was thus to define "a set of rules or canons for testing the sufficiency of any given evidence to prove any given proposition."[60]

Mill's *Logic* consisted of six books. Book I dealt with names and propositions. In this Mill followed tradition, in commencing a book on logic with a discussion of terms; he argued that correct usage of language (i.e., the "signification and purposes of words") eliminates an important source of poor reasoning.[61] At the same time, however, with the discussion of types of names (general or singular; concrete or abstract; connotative or non-connotative; relative or absolute; univocal or equivocal), Mill included a discussion of types of "nameable things" (feelings, or states of consciousness; minds; bodies; relations).[62] What was important to logic with regard to the subject and the predicate of a proposition, Mill argued, was not the relation of two ideas but of the two phenomena that the ideas express—true propositions depended on what was denoted by the subject possessing the attributes connoted by the predicate.[63] In Book II, Mill began discussing the two kinds of reasoning involving such propositions: induction and ratiocination, or reasoning from particulars to generals (i.e., "inferring a proposition from propositions *less* general than itself") and reasoning from generals to particulars (i.e., "inferring a proposition from propositions *equally* or *more* general").[64] In his treatment of the *dictum de omni et nullo*, and the axiom that Mill favored in its place—"whatever possesses any mark possesses that which it is a mark of"—Mill laid the groundwork for his own theory of induction, against the background of the traditional relation between deduction and induction.[65] As William Hamilton (1788–1856) argued in 1833:

> The Deductive and Inductive processes are elements of logic equally essential. Each requires the other. The former is only possible through the latter; and the latter is only valuable as realizing the possibility of the former. As our knowledge commences with the apprehension of singulars, every universal whole is consequently only a knowledge at second-hand. Deductive reasoning is thus not an original and independent process. The universal major proposition, out of which it developes the conclusion, is itself necessarily the conclusion of a foregone Induction, and, mediately, or immediately, an inference—a collection, from individual objects of perception, and consciousness. Logic, therefore, as a definite and self-sufficient science, must equally vindicate the formal purity of the synthetic illation, by which it ascends to its wholes, as the analytic illation by which it re-descends to their parts.[66]

However, according to Mill, only induction involves "real" inference, that is, inference from known truths to unknown, since ratiocination cannot prove anything other than what is contained in the premises. Distinguishing between the registering part and the inferring part of reasoning, Mill argued that only the major premise of a syllogism can be thought as a product of inference, but in reality, even that was merely an "intermediate halting-place for the mind, interposed by an artifice of language between the real premises and the conclusion":

> All reference is from particulars to particulars: General propositions are merely registers of such inferences already made, and short formulae for making more: The major premise of a syllogism, consequently, is

a formula of this description: and the conclusion is not an inference drawn *from* the formula, but an inference drawn *according to* the formula: the real logical antecedent, or premise, being the particular facts from which the individual instances from which the general proposition was collected by induction.[67]

The syllogism thus, Mill argued, involved a *petitio principii*, but there was value in the rules of the syllogism, i.e., as a "system of securities for the correctness" of the reasoning process—going from the "real" (inductive) premises to the conclusion.[68]

Mill went as far as to argue that even mathematical reasoning followed the same process.[69] According to Mill, mathematical truths were not necessary, at least in the sense usually assigned to the term "necessary." Mill argued that a person failing to conceive the opposite of a truth does not make that truth necessary—it is merely an instance of the psychological law of indissoluble or inseparable association. To this effect, whatever necessity is affirmed of arithmetic or the conclusions of geometry consists merely in that they follow correctly or legitimately from previous assumptions, whose certainty is not to be questioned. Thus the "peculiar certainty attributed" to such "truths" is an "illusion": all first principles are generalizations from experience, and as such are dependent on evidence and observation, since no science can be "conversant with non-entities."[70] The propositions of arithmetic and geometry are not "verbal" but "real" as they are grounded on experience.[71] These mathematical sciences followed the usual route of demonstrative or deductive sciences, i.e., reasoning from hypotheses: "tracing the consequences of certain assumptions; leaving for separate consideration whether the assumptions are true or not, and if not exactly true whether they are a sufficiently near approximation to the truth." The hypothetical element in the "Science of Number," Mill explained, was that "all the numbers are numbers of the same or of equal units," i.e., that $1 = 1$.[72]

The first two books aimed at establishing Mill's view that logic was both ratiocinative and inductive; that all inference and all proof (and all discovery of not-evident truths, but Mill did not expand on this in Books I and II) comprises of inductions and interpretation of inductions. However, this brought Mill to an important question that Books III and IV aimed at answering: under what conditions can an induction be legitimate? This was the main question of logic, according to Mill—one that had been entirely ignored.[73] It was a question that led Mill to attempt a "reduction of the inductive process to strict rules and to a scientific test, such as the Syllogism is for ratiocination."[74] Mill thus attempted to provide those great desiderata in logic, identified by James Mill almost three decades prior to the publication of his son's *Logic*: "an accurate map of the inductive process" and "a complete system of rules, as complete, for example, as those which Aristotle provided for the business of syllogistic reasoning," aiming to direct "the inquirer in the great business of interpreting nature, and adding to the stock of human instruments and powers."[75] This was what the younger Mill attempted to do; and for some he did it better than other things he tried to do in *Logic*.[76]

Mill defined induction as the operation of discovering and proving general propositions; it is a process of inference, proceeding from the known to the unknown, that is, "the process by which we conclude that what is true of certain individuals of a class is true of the whole class, or that what is true at certain times will be true in similar circumstances at all times." If the whole class is already known, then there would be no induction involved, but merely a "short-hand registration of facts known," that is a "Colligation of Facts," in Mill's use of William Whewell's term. In this way, according to Mill, induction, in a scientific study, does not simply describe facts, but explains or predicts them. Drawing a correct inference from facts leads to one correct explanation (and prediction), whereas a number of descriptions may be true of a collection of facts—induction includes colligation, not vice versa.[77] Induction had a dual function—inference as well as investigation.[78]

As generalizing from experience involves explanation and prediction, there is a central assumption, Mill argues, in every induction: "that there are such things in nature as parallel cases; that what happens once, will, under a sufficient degree of similarity of circumstances, happen again, and not only again, but as often as the same circumstances recur," i.e., that the course of nature is uniform. This axiom is not a self-evident truth; it is itself an induction, a (not so obvious) generalization founded on prior generalizations. However, by being the ultimate major premise of all inductions, when put into the form of a syllogism, it is itself not proved nor does it contribute to proving the conclusion, but forms a necessary condition of the conclusion being proved.[79] The process of reaching that ultimate major premise was not unlike every other process of scientific induction. There is an "unprompted tendency of the mind . . . to generalize its experience, provided this points all in one direction; provided no other experience of a conflicting character comes unsought." In a way, the uniformities existing among phenomena that people experience "force themselves upon involuntary recognition."[80] Philosophers and scientists investigate those phenomena, revealing the limits of these spontaneous generalizations or showing that their truth is contingent on other previously unobserved circumstances.[81]

According to Mill, scientific induction gives accuracy and precision to the process of determining certain and universal inductions, beyond "the loose and uncertain mode of induction *per enumerationem simplicem*,"[82] allowing further enquiry into causes and effects. The law of universal causation seemed to follow, or evolve, from the uniformity of nature.[83] Mill summarized the practice of experimental scientists in four methods (and five canons)—that are now known as "Mill's methods"—the method of agreement, the method of difference (and the joint method of agreement and difference), the method of residues and the method of concomitant variations.[84] Mill's underlying idea was that phenomena that regularly appear or occur together are more likely to be causally connected; these methods assisted in the identification of causal relations, replacing—or rather, improving—the "unscientific" inductive reasoning by simple enumeration with a stricter process.[85] However, there were limits to what these experimental methods could do, especially when dealing with complex phenomena. For this reason, Mill re-introduced in his discussion a three-fold Deductive Method (induction, ratiocination, verification): reasoning from a general law to a particular case by identifying which result would fulfill the law ascertained by direct induction and then verifying it by specific experience.[86] If a hypothesis is used to fill in some blanks in the process of understanding a phenomenon, however perfectly it does, the absence of a better hypothesis does not amount to a proof of the one employed. Hypotheses can only be considered plausible conjectures in the process of making sense of chaos, i.e., by decomposing it "into single facts,"[87] at least until they meet the criteria Mill established.[88]

Books III and IV, in which induction, and what Mill called subsidiary operations to it (i.e., naming, conception, abstraction, observation, etc.), took the center stage, do much to show why Mill claimed that his *Logic* was a "logic of *experience* only." As he noted, "we need experience to inform us, in what degree, and in what cases, or sorts of cases, experience is to be relied on."[89] Mill seemed to be taking at face value his father's distinction, noted in the last pages of the elder Mill's *Analysis of the Phenomena of the Human Mind* (1829), between the "theoretical" and "practical" part of the "doctrine of the human mind." According to the elder Mill, the latter contained "the Practical Rules for conducting the mind in its search after Truth."[90] This seems to throw some light on why the younger Mill considered himself justified in claiming, almost fifteen years after his father's attempt to undermine the "intuition school,"[91] that logic "is common ground on which the partisans of Hartley and Reid, of Locke and of Kant, may meet and join hands."[92] Repeating time and again that logic was the science of proof and of evidence, "the entire theory of the ascertainment of reasoned or inferred truth,"[93] Mill held it to be irrelevant to the debates on the "reality of Noumena, or Things in themselves." This allowed him to claim even in 1865 that "every essential doctrine of . . . [the *Logic*] could stand equally well with" either "metaphysical" school.[94] But if he was right in 1843 in claiming that his *Logic* was "neutral," it was only because he failed in estimating just how far his opponents' "metaphysics" blended with their logic.[95] By 1854, when Mill was working on the first draft of his *Autobiography*, he had come to see that the *Logic* took its "place as the standard philosophical representative in English (unhappily now the only one) of the anti-innate principle & anti-natural-theology doctrines."[96]

Mill thought that he had put the fundamental "theoretical" issues that divided the partisans of the two schools aside by viewing the problem of the definition of logic to be simply a matter of choice between the narrow and the broad definitions of logic. The narrow definition viewed logic as formal logic, the logic of consistency; the broad definition had to do with what Mill called the logic of truth. In the fourth edition, more than a decade after the *Logic*'s publication, and following the first reviews of his work, he added a footnote in the Introduction acknowledging that he was working with a different definition of logic than that used by William Hamilton and his students, i.e., logic as "the Science of the Formal Laws of Thought." From Mill's perspective, this definition, to be accurate, required limiting "thought" to "reasoning," while "laws of thought" should refer to "immediate" rather than "ultimate" laws. On the other hand, this definition, Mill added, should be expanded to include "*all* the processes which the mind goes through when it proves a proposition, or judges correctly of proof."[97] Mill's point, as he clarified in later editions, was that he was not simply trying to construct a system of the logic "of consistency," but that "of truth":

> The Logic of Consistency is a necessary auxiliary to the logic of truth, not only because what is inconsistent with itself or with other truths cannot be true, but also because truth can only be successfully pursued by drawing inferences from experience, which, if warrantable at all, admit of being generalized, and, to test their warrantableness, require to be exhibited in a generalized form; after which the correctness of their application to particular cases is a question which specially concerns the Logic of Consistency.[98]

Hamilton and others had taken formal logic to be the whole of logic, but as Mill seemed to understand it, formal logic was a part, not the whole, i.e., an "instrument of the human intellect in the discovery of truth."[99] The logic of truth involved the distinction between "things proved and things not proved, between what is worthy and what is unworthy of belief."[100] Truths that a person comes to know intuitively, i.e., by direct consciousness—not by means of other truths—did not fall within the domain of logic, Mill argued. But to certain types of questions, when inference is involved (often people mistake truths inferred for self-evident truths, Mill added) and when the answer is supplied only by means of evidence, logic does provide the requisite tests for deciding whether a proposition is true or false.[101]

Thus, Mill seemed to occupy the middle ground on the "logic question,"[102] by trying to move beyond the "old scholastic-Aristotelian formal logic," while keeping logic and metaphysics as far from each other as possible. Still, in moving beyond scholastic logic, he was unwilling to follow his contemporaries who at the time were breaking new ground in formal logic by quantifying the predicate. Having acknowledged that the "Science of Number" was the "grand agent for transforming experimental into deductive sciences," Mill's criticism of Augustus De Morgan's (1806–1871), George Boole's (1815–1864) and William Stanley Jevons's (1835–1882) works on logic highlight just how much Mill's "broad" view of logic was still an offspring of his Benthamite background:

> [Jevons] is a man of some ability, but he seems to me to have a mania for encumbering questions with useless complications, and with a notation implying the existence of greater precision in the data than the questions admit of. His speculations on Logic, like those of Boole and De Morgan,

and some of those of Hamilton, are infected in an extraordinary degree with this vice. It is one preeminently at variance with the wants of the time, which demand that scientific deductions should be made as simple and as easily intelligible as they can be made without ceasing to be scientific.[103]

Logic was not meant only for a "school exercise." There was philosophical value in what these thinkers were doing, but Mill questioned if the results of their labors were "worth studying and mastering for any practical purpose":

> The practical use of technical forms of reasoning is to bar out fallacies: but the fallacies which require to be guarded against in ratiocination properly so called, arise from the incautious use of the common forms of language; and the logician must track the fallacy into that territory, instead of waiting for it on a territory of his own.[104]

Logic was not the science of science only; it was equally applicable to business and life: "if the principles and rules of inference are the same whether we infer general propositions or individual facts; it follows that a complete logic of the sciences would be also a complete logic of practical business and common life."[105] Mill, as John Skorupski has noted, tried "to bring pure philosophy into contact with life and thought."[106]

Logic, John Stuart Mill argued in his Rectorial Address at the University of St. Andrews in 1867, "is the great disperser of hazy and confused thinking; it clears up the fogs which hide from us our own ignorance, and make us believe that we understand a subject when we do not."[107] That "master vice of the understanding," James Mill scribbled down in his private notes half a century earlier, "mental partiality,"

> depraves the judgement, makes men bad reasoners, both for speculation, and for practice—Makes men bad husbands, bad fathers, bad judges, bad legislators, bad every thing. This is the very source of injustice.— Strength of mind consists in the vigilant habit of attending to evidence, and estimating accurately its force.[108]

For this reason, for the elder Mill, "[o]ne of the grand objects of education should be, to generate a constant and anxious concern about evidence; to accustom the mind to run immediately from the idea of the opinion to the idea of its evidence, and to feel dissatisfaction till it is known that the evidence has been all before the mind, and fairly weighted."[109] Similarly, the younger Mill argued that

> Logic compels us to throw our meaning into distinct propositions, and our reasonings into distinct steps. It makes us conscious of all the implied assumptions on which we are proceeding, and which, if not true, vitiate the entire process. It makes us aware what extent of doctrine we commit ourselves to by any course of reasoning, and obliges us to look the

implied premises in the face, and make up our minds whether we can stand to them.[110]

For the younger Mill, logic guards against "bad deduction," but also against "bad generalization, which is a still more universal error. If men easily err in arguing from one general proposition to another, still more easily do they go wrong in interpreting the observations made by themselves and others."[111] John Stuart Mill's preoccupation with the "practical purpose" of logic is most evident in the final two books of his *Logic*.

"The philosophy of reasoning," Mill wrote in Book V, "to be complete ought to comprise the theory of bad as well as of good reasoning." Mill's "Philosophy of Error" aimed in inculcating habits of proper examination of the opinions one comes to hold—in scientific matters, or in everyday matters—examining whether they are grounded on "real" or "apparent" evidence.[112] A fallacy is committed, Mill argued, when one has inferred some fact from some other fact that does not really prove it, unifying the two facts by admitting a general proposition that is nevertheless groundless. It may be groundless because the inference supporting it was erroneous (the error was committed in collecting, using or interpreting the facts) or because it was not based on extrinsic evidence at all—i.e., being grounded on "natural prejudices." Mill examined five classes of fallacies: fallacies of observation, generalization, ratiocination and confusion and *a priori* fallacies. In classifying these fallacies, Mill moved beyond the false opinions individuals happen to have to the way in which individuals come to have them.[113] Book VI of Mill's *Logic*, as it dealt with the "Logic of the Moral Sciences," has not escaped the attention of students of Mill's moral and political thought. It contains what Mill called the best chapter of the whole work, "Liberty and Necessity,"[114] a sketch of the "new science" of character formation, i.e., "Ethology," complementing his ideas on psychology and sociology, but also a plan of a "Doctrine of Ends," which has been used in revisionist interpretations of his utilitarian theory.[115] Book VI also examines the two dominant methods of examining moral and political matters, and rejects them for a third one that, according to Mill, combines what's best in them—the Deductive Method in its two versions, the direct and the inverse.[116] These two books, with the exception of the chapter on "Liberty and Necessity,"[117] were the least discussed parts in reviews of the *Logic*; and while, for the most part, Book VI dominates treatments of Mill's *Logic* today, the relation of Book V to other works has not had the fortune of a similar rediscovery.[118]

III.

Mill's *A System of Logic* was published in spring 1843, alas with limited expectations.[119] Making his worry known to his friends, he noted: "I don't suppose many people will read anything so scholastic, especially as I do not profess to upset the schools but to rebuild them—& unluckily everybody who cares about such subjects nowadays is of a different school from me."[120] However, his expectations were exceeded. Mill never did really understand "[h]ow the book came to have, for a work of the kind, so much success, and what sort of persons compose the bulk of those who have bought [it]"—he was reluctant to say "read it."[121]

The book, and its reviews, became part of a revival in the study of logic taking place in the second quarter of the nineteenth century in Britain. According to a contemporary, "Not a month passes which does not bring us new publications on Logic." Mill, Hamilton and Richard Whately (1787–1863) were acknowledged to be the "revivers" of logic in England.[122] "Such writers," another reviewer remarked, "as Whewell, Mill, Boole, Spencer, Bain . . . have . . . a large and growing audience." That Mill's book marched steadily from edition to edition, the reviewer added, was an "unmistakable fact" showing that there was "a solid demand for solid books on abstract subjects."[123]

Mill placed his hopes for immediate attention to the *Logic* "on the polemical propensities of Dr. Whewell," whom Mill expected to respond to his critical remarks soon after making their appearance.[124] Indeed, following the publication of Whewell's *Of Induction: With Especial Reference to Mr. J. Stuart Mill's System of Logic* (1849), the comparison between Mill and Whewell became a frequent theme in reviews; their controversy was recast as a *lutte corps à corps* between the "experience" and the "intuition" schools.[125] Richard Hold Hutton (1826–1897) was the first to make an extensive comparison in his joint review of Mill's and Whewell's accounts of induction.[126] Importantly, according to Hutton, Mill's

> writings appear to have quite subdued the not very independent spirit of English philosophy. The prolonged silence with which his book has been received by English critics seems to imply a surrender without terms; and in fact the qualities of Mr. Mill's mind are eminently calculated to impress and frighten our countrymen into silence, even when unconvinced.[127]

However, both Mill's and Hutton's estimates were mistaken. On the one hand, Mill did not need Whewell to bring his book into notice after all; as Bain noted:

> From the moment of publication, the omens were auspicious. Parker's trade-sale was beyond his anticipations, and the book was asked for by unexpected persons, and appeared in shop windows where he never thought to see it. Whately spoke handsomely of it; and desired his bookseller to get an additional copy for him, and expose it in the window.[128]

In just a year and a half, Mill expected that the book would be soon out of print, having gotten "into the hands of almost everybody who could be supposed to read such a book."[129] In 1849, Whewell himself acknowledged that Mill needed no help from him in getting notice: "Mr. Mill's work has had, for a work of its abstruse character, a circulation so extensive, and admirers so numerous and so fervent, that it needs no commendation of mine."[130] Almost immediately after the publication of Mill's *Logic*, some claimed that it had "obtained just celebrity."[131]

On the other hand, even though plans for prospective reviews in *Edinburgh Review* and *Quarterly Review*, the periodicals with the widest circulation, did not come into fruition,[132] in the 1840s, as in the 1850s and the 1860s, Mill's *Logic* was noticed regularly in periodicals and books, leaving no stone unturned (especially as regards the work's first three books).[133] Bain's remark that Mill's *Logic* had "been about the best attacked book of the time" was not wide off the mark.[134] By 1872, Mill saw the book through the press seven more times after its original publication, each time making revisions as well as replying to criticisms.[135]

The first notice of Mill's *A System of Logic,* came out in April 1843 in the *British Critic*; the author however was reluctant "to express a confident judgment on the details of Mr. Mill's work," not having sufficient time to study it. But despite Mill's "immoral and unchristian" views, which made their way into the *Logic*, the author noted, it was a work that combined "power, depth, originality, precision, and completeness of thought in a most unusual degree."[136] The reviewer, showing knowledge of Mill's earlier essays, promised to discuss the work in greater detail at a later issue; one did eventually appear in October 1843.

William George Ward's (1812–1882) "adverse criticism," Bain reported, "gave Mill very great satisfaction, all things considered."[137] However, even though quite long, Ward's review did not receive serious consideration from Mill, partly because Ward knowingly did not focus much on "matters of logical principle."[138] Ward had a specific point in mind to criticize: "if Mr Mill's principles be adopted as a full statement of the truth, the whole fabric of Christian Theology must totter and fall." Thus, Ward put particular emphasis on that view, and its various manifestations, which he thought to undermine "religious faith," i.e., that all knowledge derives from experience.[139] Before moving on to consider *a priori* moral knowledge, Ward focused on Mill's discussion of axioms of geometry—his sole object being "to vindicate against Mr. Mill the existence of à priori sources of knowledge." Ward charged Mill with serving "the necessities of a theory, which he is unwilling to relinquish," by failing to recognize that "the means by which we derive our *first idea* of line and angle" is but a trivial difference between his theory and the *a priori* school. Once one has acquired these ideas, Ward argued, Mill himself had admitted that

we are free from all further dependence on the senses; that by a mere mental process, we are able to arrive at an indefinite number of new truths; and that these truths will be absolutely certain, neither dependent for their trustworthiness on any proof of the uniformity of the laws of nature, nor liable to overthrow from the progress of experiment.[140]

Intuitions were divided by Ward into "sensible" and "à priori"; he seemed to follow established practice in considering mathematical axioms and notions such as time and space to be of the second kind.

When Ward did get around to discussing the "information derivable from our conscience or moral perception," he did not refer to Mill's *Logic*, but to Mill's earlier works, as this was a subject that Mill purposely avoided in *Logic*. Anticipating Mill's *Utilitarianism* (1861), having had Mill's essays on Adam Sedgwick (1835) and Bentham (1838) in mind, Ward argued that Mill was inconsistent with his principles: denying *a priori* moral knowledge, "by means of which all of us . . . introduce the balance of eternal and immutable morality, to test, value, and compare withal, as to their real essence, the appearances of this sensible world," while at the same time recognizing "man as a being capable of pursuing spiritual perfection as an end; of desiring, for its own sake, the conformity of his own character to his standard of excellence, without hope of good or fear of evil from other source than his own inward consciousness."[141] Ward argued that indeed "certain pleasures are more permanent, intense, satisfying, than certain others; that they disqualify us less for intellectual speculation, or sympathetic feeling, or the business of life; all this may doubtless be gathered from experience." However, he added, "when we apply such epithets as 'high,' 'noble,' 'elevating,' 'worthy of rational creatures,' and the like to those rather than these, we are using mere unmeaning sounds, deceiving ourselves by words without ideas, unless we have the faculty, which Mr. Mill denies us, of direct communion with the spiritual world."[142] As Bain noted, Ward's review "was not so much a review of the *Logic*, as of Mill altogether."[143]

In May 1843 a review of Mill's *Logic* appeared in *Westminster Review*, by Alexander Bain, who had used the sheets from the printers to prepare it. It "was even more laudatory than Mill liked," Bain admitted.[144] That Bain did not engage critically with Mill in 1843—he would do so in later works—was owed perhaps to the role he himself had in Mill's final revisions to the *Logic* just prior to its publication.[145] He began his review with a warning to readers: "[t]he name Logic does not and cannot convey to the reader any notion of the contents of Mr Mill's book, because they are such as no reader has seen under this or any other title."[146] Mill, Bain added, discussed everything that has to do with the discovery and proving of truth, except those parts that have been discussed in other books on logic—in the parts that Mill did seem to be treading on familiar ground, Mill "harmonized and summed up into positive results" the "best thoughts" of the "great thinkers" on the subject at hand.[147]

Bain attempted to give a respectful summary of Mill's *Logic* "without any attempt at a general estimate or balanced critique of its worth."[148] Unlike other reviews, Bain spent considerable time in illustrating the implications of Mill's treatment of names to his approach to logic. According to Bain, the most important part of Mill's discussion on names was the distinction between denotation and connotation; Mill's emphasis on the theory of connotation, Bain argued, allowed him to present a tenable and "clear philosophy of evidence."[149]

Mill's originality, however, according to Bain, was manifested primarily in his treatment of the syllogism and the discussion on the nature of inference. When there is sufficient evidence to warrant making an inference from particulars to particulars, as Bain summarized Mill's view, one may make a formula for drawing this inference—that formula is registered by a general proposition. However, applying the formula to some specific case is not an act of inference but an act of interpretation of the registered, that is, of the general proposition. This act of interpretation is very important and requires strict rules for its correct performance—i.e., the syllogism.[150]

According to Bain, Mill's view of induction was "a kind of revolution in the science of logic": proving truth amounted to establishing the validity of inductions.[151] The core of the inductive operation, Bain argued, was correctly determining the laws of nature and ascertaining the results flowing from them—i.e., establishing causation—by eliminating all extraneous conditions and circumstances, to find out unconditional—not only invariable—sequences of phenomena. Mill, according to Bain, provided a kind of a "manual of inductive art," for determining the effects of every cause, and the causes of all effects. Mill's experimental methods, "the theoretical statement of the shortest and surest road to experimental truth,"[152] Bain argued, challenged traditional views—Baconian and Newtonian.[153] In 1882, writing with almost a complete knowledge of Mill's works, and the *Logic*'s sources, Bain noted that the third book of Mill's *Logic*, on Induction, was "the best piece of work that he ever did."[154] In his own *Logic*, Bain noted that he had fully adopted Mill's views on deduction and induction.[155]

Like Bain, William Henry Smith (1808–1872), *Blackwood's Edinburgh Magazine*'s reviewer, focused on what he thought to be some of Mill's most original ideas. First, with regard to the syllogism, the Smith argued that Mill did the reverse of Whately. According to Whately, Smith reported, the traditional criticism that the syllogism involved a *petitio principii* amounted to claiming no reasoning could lead to new truth (since all reasoning could be thrown into syllogistic form). But Mill, Smith added, "has resolved the syllogism, and indeed all deductive reasoning whatever, ultimately into examples of induction," by illustrating how one "can acknowledge that the process of reason can be always exhibited in the form of a syllogism, and yet not be driven to the strange and perplexing conclusion that our reasoning can never conduct us to a new truth."[156] Second, by giving an inductive spin to the debate over whether the syllogism contains a *petitio principii*, Mill denied the existence of necessary truths—propositions the negations of which are not only false but also inconceivable. Smith seemed to side with Mill rather than Whewell, who was Mill's sparring partner on this matter (as in several others); one could distinguish between contingent and necessary truths, but this was not a distinction in things themselves—unlike Whewell's, Smith argued, Mill's discussion of the distinction was clear-headed.[157] Finally, the third aspect of Mill's *Logic* that Smith discussed was the law of causation—accepting Mill's claim that a complete discussion of the issue was beside the scope of the *Logic*. According to the reviewer, Mill had made a "happy addition" to the debate on causation: cause was not merely "invariable succession" but also "unconditional succession"; as the reviewer noted, the cause of a phenomenon is the "antecedent, or the concurrence of antecedents, upon which it is invariably and *unconditionally* consequent."[158] The reviewer praised Mill for boldness and precision on this issue; Smith once again cited long passages from Mill, without even the pretence of putting Mill's claims to the test.[159]

In 1844, beginning with Mill's definition of logic, the *Eclectic Review* critic argued that the traditional, narrow definition of logic viewed the "one-half of the mental processes in the investigation of truth . . . susceptible of the most rigid analysis, the other (and often more important) half . . . incapable of being reduced to any science at all." To this effect, the task of Mill's "system of inductive logic" was a difficult one: Mill had to refute the view of his predecessors—particularly Whately's—that, though the deductive and inductive processes are "intimately connected," the validity of inductive inferences are "an extra-logical process."[160] Passing over Book I, the reviewer focused on Mill's account of the syllogism. Objecting to Mill's claim that all inference is from particulars to particulars, the reviewer argued that Mill had attempted to simplify the reasoning process—claiming that the general premise in a syllogism is essentially a mnemonic device—for no reason. Not only does the conclusion suppose the truth of the general proposition, when we reason from a particular to a particular, but also we often do reason explicitly with reference to the general proposition. The reviewer also criticized Mill's claim that nothing can be proved by the syllogism, which was not known—or assumed to be known—beforehand (which leads to Mill's claim that the syllogism contains a *petitio principii*).[161] According to the reviewer, one may indeed argue that there is no process of inference from "All men are mortal" to the conclusion "Socrates is mortal;" however, not for the reasons Mill offered, but because the minor premise "Socrates is a man" is not a *"real* premise." "Socrates" is equivalent to "this man," and so "this man is a man" does not require independent proof. This makes the conclusion "this man is mortal" merely a verbal transformation of the major premise, by limiting its quantity. A *"real* syllogism", the reviewer argued, would be:

> Every citizen has a right to refuse an unjust impost
> Church-rates are unjust
> Therefore, we have a right to refuse church-rates.

The minor premise is not contained in the major premise, and the conclusion is not contained in either premise alone. And this is a real process of inference because no one can hold both of them as true and deny the conclusion, as "the thing to be proved, is not assumed in either premise."[162] Mill was aware of this review; he told Bain that the reviewer "differs from him on the Syllogism which he understands, and agrees with him on the rest of the book without seeming to understand it."[163]

By 1846 more critical reviews of Mill began to appear. The *British Quarterly Review* critic noted that Mill had "totally failed" in his "elaborate attempt to reduce to a consistent system the entire body of the laws of inference."[164] Mill's *Logic*, the reviewer added, was not destined to make him "the founder of a new era in the science of logic."[165] Once again a reviewer first took issue with Mill's definition of logic. The reviewer accused Mill of arbitrarily leaving out of his discussion of the auxiliary "intellectual operations" of understanding, operations such as memory, consciousness and perception, while leaving in naming, classification and definition. Mill's claim that the latter belonged to metaphysics was not convincing, according to the reviewer, since he had pointed to no "tangible principle . . . for determining where logic ends and metaphysics begin."[166] Mill would have been convincing in his choice, however, had he defined logic, not as the analysis of the laws of thought, but as the analysis of the products of thought. Failing to do so, according to the reviewer, Mill had fallen into the same error as some of his predecessors in including too much in the domain of logic, trying to make "it accomplish more than could . . . be expected from it."[167]

Although the reviewer had focused on a number of issues with regard to Mill's *Logic*—comments on Mill's takes on Aristotle's categories and on definition had touched on Mill's underlying "experience-school" metaphysics[168]—Mill responded primarily to the criticisms made on the suggested *petitio principii* of the syllogism.[169] In the third and fourth editions Mill justified his choice of focus on this particular part of the review by noting that he welcomed discussion on his "new" theory of the syllogism, "to ensure that nothing essential to the question escapes observation."[170] As Mill noted:

> The difference between the reviewer's theory and mine may be thus stated. Both admit that when we say, All men are mortal, we make an assertion reaching beyond the sphere of our knowledge of individual cases; and that when a new individual, Socrates, is brought within the field of our knowledge by means of the minor premise, we learn that we have already made an assertion respecting Socrates without knowing it: our own general formula being, to that extent, for the first time *interpreted* to us. But according to the reviewer's theory, the smaller assertion is proved by the larger: while I contend, that both assertions are proved together, by the same evidence, namely, the grounds of experience on which the general assertion was made, and by which it must be justified.[171]

The reviewer considered Mill's view "ingenious and plausible," nevertheless it was not "irrefragable," as Mill had claimed.[172] The *British Quarterly Review* critic raised the same issue as the *Eclectic Review* critic: as long as the premises in the syllogism are not verbal propositions, the syllogism does not involve a *petitio principii*.[173] Although the reviewer did not claim that Socrates' mortality is proved by the major premise that "all men are mortal," he did note that the evidence which was used to establish the major premise could be used to establish the particular case at hand—by means of the minor premise, one can know that the subject of the conclusion "can be brought within the scope of the major premiss."[174] Mill's examples, according to the reviewer, were "quasi-syllogisms" that assisted Mill in proving his point, i.e., that the syllogism was not a process of real inference, failing however to go the bottom of the issue.[175]

Mill's views on induction received similar negative treatment in the periodical press—especially following the publication of Whewell's pamphlet in 1849. In his comparison of Mill and Whewell, Hutton argued that Mill had given a "shadowy *basis* . . . for inductive science."[176] The reason was, Hutton argued, that Mill could not accept that there are causes incapable of being directly observed or deduced from data directly observed—as Mill's rejection of all *a priori* truth, for example, indicated.[177] Any theory that introduced any contrary notion, Hutton added, would give cause to Mill to protest "in his majestic, judicial way" against pointing out "as proof of a fact in external nature, any necessity which the human mind may be conceived to be under, of believing in it." However, Hutton added, Mill was inconsistent. Hutton argued that the possibility of scientific rules according to Mill rested on a propensity humans have to make "loose empirical connections" between observed facts, before putting them to scientific tests capable of establishing causal connections (with varying degree of certainty). But it was Mill's own theory, Hutton noted, that obliged "him to identify in their [i.e., the insufficient generalizations] ultimate foundation, the associative and the reasoning faculty."[178] The law of association was exactly such a "necessity of the human mind" in forming a particular belief, which Mill had denied as relevant in logic.[179] Mill's theory required putting "faith in the laws of our own mind . . . if we are to believe anything about future events at all, even of those of external nature" as much as any other theory.[180] Identifying the "Common-Sense" root of Mill's take of induction (e.g., Stewart and Brown),[181] another reviewer noted his own adherence to the traditional view of the relation of deduction and induction (summarized by Hamilton at the commencement of the revival of logical studies, as we saw), and criticized Mill for ignoring, once again, the obvious, i.e., that it is not enough to assert that individuals just perceive individual facts: "the perception of a fact is a process requiring as much explanation as the apprehension of a law." Vacant minds perceive nothing, the reviewer noted; "from the moment [a fact] is apprehended, it is modified by the mind, which forgets . . . some of the elements and retains the rest as generalised maxims."[182]

Even though reviewers generally agreed that, following the success of Mill's *Logic*, "neither young nor advanced students must be allowed to forget that we have now a Logic of Induction quite as important as the Logic of Deduction,"[183] critics also agreed that Mill's "metaphysical opinions" had misled him in developing a problematic system, one which left "the great problem of Induction" exactly where he had found it.[184]

As we saw, Mill considered his "logic of truth" to enjoy equal "metaphysical neutrality" to Hamilton's "logic of consistency." However, Mill's *Logic* failed to convince on this supposed neutrality. As a reviewer noted, "there is little or nothing in formal Logic, which of itself, tends to the prejudice or vindication of any theory, philosophical or religious"; but "in the hands of Mr. Mill, Logic is not the innocent thing he describes it."[185] Importantly, in parts of the *Logic*, Mill's reluctance to concede any ground to a "spiritual or purely mental element," for the sake of "unity to his entire theory," led him to "flagrant inconsistencies and contradictions at every turn,"[186] showing "in the uncertainty of his views the helplessness of pure empiricism."[187] Mill had given a considerable push to the study of logic—because of his inductive logic rather than his treatment of syllogistic logic—according to James McCosh (1811–1894), but his contribution "would have been of much more value had he left out the constant defences of his empirical metaphysics."[188]

According to a like-minded reviewer, Alexander Campbell Fraser (1819–1914), Hamilton's definition of logic as "the *rationale* of the conditions under which we must think about anything"—notions being "purified" of their connection with things—came into sharp contrast with Mill's definition of logic as "the *rationale* of the conditions for extracting real science from the things about which we may think."[189] Mill's logic was an example, according to Fraser, of a "Mixed or Material Logic"; in particular, it was an example of what Hamilton named "Modified Logic," that is a "mere mixture Logic and (Empirical) Psychology;" which, according to Hamilton, was a "scientific accident, ambiguously belonging either to Logic or to Psychology."[190] The difference in the definition of logic, another reviewer—a friendly critic this time—pointed out, was one of principle, not merely a disagreement on terms; but "[t]he differences," the critic went on, "between him and his critics have struck their roots deep into the soil of metaphysics." Mill's attempt to develop a system of logic solely on the foundation of experience was "the battle-field on which the contest between him and his opponents has been most warm."[191]

From the moment of the publication of Mill's *Logic*, reviewers had noted that those trained in "a different school of thinking, those who have adopted the metaphysics of the transcendental philosophy," would find much on which to disagree.[192] Perhaps, what was unexpected, as it was noted, was that "[e]ven some of those who have been Mr. Mill's stanch allies on other points have deserted him" in his attempt to build a system on the basis of experience.[193] For this reason, reviewers would not hesitate to place him the head of the "experience school."[194] In July 1872, a *Quarterly Review* of Mill's *Logic* did eventually appear, under the title of "Mr John Stuart Mill and his School," by John Rickards Mozley (1840–1931); Mozley had reviewed Mill's *Logic* in 1869 also.[195] Although what Mill wrote was "generally sound," Mozley noted in 1872, "unsound material" creeps into Mill's writings "when he thinks it necessary to prop up his spontaneous beliefs by artificial supports." Mill's major flaw, the reviewer added, was doing philosophy thinking that there are two philosophical schools, "one radically right, the other radically wrong." In an ironic twist, given Mill's critique of his utilitarian predecessors, the reviewer argued that Mill had exercised a "narrowing influence upon English philosophy," primarily by allowing his psychological prejudices to undermine the soundness of his philosophical system.[196]

IV.

In 1872, Mozley protested against Mill's dominance at the universities: "[w]e must lament that one of the most useful and distinguished of English Universities, the University of London, should have almost formally excluded from the examinations any other philosophy than that of Mr. Mill and Mr. Bain."[197] But not everyone agreed with Mozley. More than fifteen years earlier, a reviewer noted that Mill's *Logic* was "admirably qualified to be a learner's book." Although it was not elementary, the reviewer added, the *Logic* was simple and systematic, while being able to "[lure] the young curiosity onwards to the inner sanctuary." The reviewer regretted that Mill was not recognized by "The Schools," while being read by all students of philosophy.[198] However, according to Patrick Leary, the secret behind Mill's *Logic*'s success would eventually "lay in the growing university market." Mill himself seemed to think the same.[199]

Indeed, upon a visit to Oxford in 1863, following an invitation to her husband, George Grote, "the Historian of Greece," Harriet Grote was told that

> Grote and Mill may be said to have revived the study of the two master sciences—History and Mental Philosophy—among the Oxford undergraduates. A new current of ideas; new and original modes of interpreting the past; the light of fresh learning cast upon the peoples of antiquity: such are the impulses given by those two great teachers, that our youths are completely kindled to enthusiasm towards both at the present time.[200]

Harriet Grote's interlocutor was probably not exaggerating. On 8 July 1867 William Lambert Newman (1834–1923), fellow and lecturer of Balliol College Oxford, under examination by the select committee on the Oxford and Cambridge Universities Bill, claimed that the "progress of education" at Oxford depended "enormously on the books that are published on the different subjects"—two or three books had "made quite a revolution in the education of Oxford". In particular, Newman added, "Mr. Mill's books have done an enormous deal for the studies at Oxford."[201] Already by 1843, there were reports of the *Logic* being studied at Oxford.[202] Hippolyte Taine (1828–1893) captured the hold Mill had over the universities, by reporting a discussion taking place at Oxford on England's original thinkers.[203] Taine's interlocutor claimed that Mill—be the subject politics, economics or logic— was an original thinker. In his *Logic*, Taine's friend noted:

> [Mill] does not attitudinize majestically in the character of a reformer of science; he does not declare like your Germans, that his book is destined to inaugurate a new era for the human race. He proceeds step by step, slowly, and often creepingly, over a multitude of particular facts. He excels in giving precision to an idea; in disentangling a principle; in tracing it through a number of different facts; in refuting, in distinguishing, in reasoning.[204]

What Mill did, Taine's friend noted, was "to construct the best theories, and lay down the best practical rules." Still, the need to be able to follow Mill's views led in the 1860s to the publications of handbooks, attempting to simplify Mill's *Logic* for students.[205]

Three decades passed from the first to the last edition of Mill's *Logic*. Reviews of the last edition had the benefit of knowing the reception Mill's *Logic* had enjoyed—a reviewer argued that it was "the most important and most valuable work of this generation." Mill did what no one had managed to do, placing "a complete rationale of inference . . . before the world." The reviewer explicitly denied trying to exaggerate about the *Logic*'s influence. And if today we have trouble seeing why the success of Mill's *Logic* could not be accounted for by its "intrinsic excellencies," that was obvious to the reviewer back in December 1872:

> If the dreams of transcendentalism have been almost banished to the pulpit, if Oxford is forgetting its old ecclesiastical conservatism and a new body of Academical Radicals is making Torydom tremble, if medicine is become scientific, if the tide of unbelief in exceptions to causation has risen so high that the Mrs Partingtons of the Christian Evidence Society find it necessary to lay in a new stock of mops,[206]—the book before us has been the principal instrument, though not the only one, of the change.

The reviewer did not hesitate to note a similar influence of Mill in France, Germany and the Netherlands.[207] Others, just a month after Mill's death, claimed that should Mill's influence become "either weakened, warped, or forgotten," it would constitute a "national calamity."[208] Likewise, a reviewer of Mill's *Consideration of Representative Government* (1861) took a moment to say the following about "[t]he greatest of English thinkers":

> No living writer has exercised so great and profound an influence on his cotemporaries as John Stuart Mill. It is impossible to recal [sic] the

attitude and tendency of English speculation twenty years since, with all its velleities towards German ontology, without at once attributing the remarkable change it has undergone to the publication of Mr Mill's Logic.[209]

As David Masson noted, with a tinge of irony, in 1866, "[i]t is Mill that our young thinkers at the Universities, our young legislators in Parliament, our young critics in journals, and our young shepherds on the mountains, consult, and quote, and swear by."[210]

It was perhaps such unreserved admiration of Mill that led his works to being subjected to a thorough attack soon after he died—particularly by Jevons.[211] However, if we take Thomas Hill Green's (1836–1882) lectures on logic as an example of how Mill's *Logic* was treated at the universities, then the *Logic* had already been subjected to severe examination before Jevons took up the mantle of criticism in the periodical press.[212] As another reviewer noted, the success of *Logic* was due to Mill's boldness in attempting "to contradict the whole educated world in regard to subjects, all the facts pertaining to which are equally and fully before every attentive mind." It remained to be seen, the reviewer added, "whether it is the boldness of superior insight or of blind desperation."[213] By Mill's death in 1873, the "educated world" had not yet settled this question.

NOTES

1. J. S. Mill to M. Kyllmann, 30 May 1865, *CW*: XVI.1063n4. Mill was not too far off claiming that he was "getting the ear of England," believing that he had won that of America (for an example why, see Varouxakis, 2013: ch. 2), since, as Henry Sidgwick noted, "from 1860–1865 or thereabouts he ruled England in the region of thought as very few men ever did." See H. Sidgwick to C. H. Pearson, 10 May 1865 (quoted in Schultz, 2004: 141). All references to Mill's works are to the authoritative edition of *Collected Works of John Stuart Mill* (Mill, 1963–1991—cited as *CW*, followed by volume and page number), unless otherwise indicated. I am grateful to Stephen Schwartz and Elijah Millgram for providing insightful comments and suggestions which allowed me to clarify a number of points.
2. J. S. Mill to H. S. Chapman, 9 Mar. 1847, *CW*: XIII.708–09.
3. Hunter (1873: 68).
4. Levy (1873: 36).
5. To some extent, Mill was right—these were the two works most discussed when reviewers were taking stock of his achievements.
6. Little has changed since John Skorupski's comment in 1989 that "there is a desperate lack of up-to-date commentary" on Mill's *Logic* (Skorupski, 1989: xiii).
7. Levy (1873: 36). For a more detailed discussion of the publication of Mill's *Logic*, see Leary (1998); for a more detailed discussion on the circumstances of Mill's writing the *Logic*, see Kubitz (1932: ch. 1) and Robson (1974).
8. Hayward (1873:5). Abraham Hayward had reportedly also written, and published, a defamatory (now lost) letter on Mill. For responses to Hayward,

see Holyoake (1873) and Christie (1873); see also Conway (1873). For the circumstances surrounding Hayward's notices of Mill see, Mineka (1972). For a critical survey of notices of Mill's death, and Mill's posthumous fame, see Stack (2011).

9. For a brief retelling of this story, see *infra*, chapter two.

10. As Mill strikingly noted: "I have no remembrance of the time when I began to learn Greek. I have been told that it was when I was three years old. . . . I also read, in 1813, the first six dialogues (in the common arrangement) of Plato, from the *Euthyphron* to the *Theaetetus* inclusive: which last dialogue, I venture to think, would have been better omitted, as it was totally impossible I should understand it." See Mill (1873a, CW: I.9).

11. Bain (1882: 24–26).

12. See Mill (1873a, CW: I.25). A different connection, and commoner in the old debate between "moderns vs. ancients," between Greek (as well as Latin) and logic, was made in Mill's rectorial address to St. Andrews (Mill, 1867, CW: XXI.228–29). It is of interest to note, that in 1856, Mill, in his replying to a critic on the issue of causation, showcased a detailed knowledge of the history of philosophy, rather than a simple appreciation of various schools of thought in times past. See Mill (1843, CW: VII.363ff, contra Tulloch, 1855: 44ff).

13. See Mill (1873a, CW: I.25).

14. See Mill (1873a, CW: I.23).

15. For Mill's classical influences and the study of logic, see Rosen (2013b); on Mill's classical influences as regards Mill's political thought, see Urbinati (2002). For a broader perspective on Mill and the classics, see Devigne (2006). See further, Demetriou and Loizides (2013a), Loizides (2013).

16. Bain (1882: 26).

17. Mill (1873a, CW: I.24, 69; 1859, CW: XVIII.251). See further Rosen, 2013b.

18. Bain (1882: 117).

19. Courtney (1889: 35).

20. See Lady Eastlake (1880: 44–45). For Mill's account, see (1873a, CW: I.123).

21. Mill (1873a, CW: I.123, 167). The last book which the "Society of Students of Mental Philosophy" (for the name, see Ellis, 1888) studied was James Mill's *Analysis of the Phenomena of the Human Mind* (1829). But it is of much more historical interest to note that, according to Lady Eastlake (1880: 44–45), "the quantification of the predicate" and "the inconceivability of the opposites" were some of the subjects discussed at these meetings.

22. For an attempt to explore the connection between Mill's *Logic* and Bentham's *Rationale of Judicial Evidence* (Bentham, 1827), which Mill edited, see Kubitz (1932: 50ff).

23. Mill (1873a, CW: I.23, 25, 67, 69, 82, 111–13).

24. J. S. Mill to J. Sterling, 20 Oct. 1831, CW: XII.79. In his review of Mill's *Logic*, W. G. Ward compared Mill and Maurice to illustrate their differences as philosophers, highlighting Mill's clarity and consistency as a thinker (Ward, 1843b: 354–55).

25. This was an allusion to *Parliamentary History and Review*, a short-lived radical periodical (1826–1828), in which the "philosophical radicals"—James Mill, George Grote (1794–1871), John Stuart Mill, among others—accompanied reports of parliamentary debates with commentaries pointing out fallacies committed by speakers of the house. See, Mill (1873a, CW: I.121–23). See also Maurice's sketch of the elder Mill (1828), in which Maurice anticipated Thomas Babington Macaulay's (1800–1859) famous critique of utilitarian philosophy and politics (1829).

26. Maurice (1835: 60–61).

27. Mill (1873a, CW: I.111–13).

28. F. Place to T. Falconer, 2 Sept. 1838; H. Grote to F. Place, 16 Aug. 1837; in Wallas (1898: 91, 91n4).
29. For a brief discussion on Mill's "vocation," see Demetriou and Loizides (2013b: 1–7). See also Robson (1966).
30. J. S. Mill to T. Carlyle, 30 June 1837, *CW*: XII.340.
31. J. S. Mill to G. D'Eichthal, 10 Jan. 1842, *CW*: XIII.496.
32. J. S. Mill to J. Bowring, 10 Mar. 1828, *CW*: XII.23.
33. Reviewers viewed Comte's and Mill's works as "as mutual commentaries upon each other, or rather, we regard the one as a methodical exposition of principles evolved, and carried to their legitimate consequences by the other." See Jennings (1854: 437); also, Atwater (1856: 91).
34. J. S. Mill to J. Robertson, 6 Aug. 1837, *CW*: XII.345. At the time Mill was the "real" but not the "ostensible" editor of the *London and Westminster Review* (Mill, 1873a, *CW*: I.207).
35. At the turn of the decade, Mill was repeatedly informing his friends and associates that he was hard on writing the *Logic*. For some examples, see J. S. Mill to W. Molesworth, [18 Oct. 1838], *CW*: XIII.390; to R. B. Fox, 23 Dec. 1840, *CW*: XIII.455 and 6 May 1841, *CW*: XIII.474 and 24 July 1841, *CW*: XIII.481; to A. Fonqblanque, [17 June 1841], *CW*: XIII.478; to J. Robertson, 7 Sept. 1841, *CW*: XIII.485; to E. Chadwick, [21 Sept. 1841], *CW*: XIII.485; to S. Austin, 4 Oct. 1841, *CW*: XIII.485; to A. Comte, 8 Nov. 1841, *CW*: XIII.489 and 18 Dec. 1841, *CW*: XIII.491.
36. See J. Sterling to J. Symonds, 1 Jul. 1842, in Carlyle (1851: 298–99), and to J. Murray, 16 Dec. 1841, in Smiles (1891: 348). See also Leary (1998: 39n1, 40).
37. For Mill's use of the phrase, see J. S. Mill to G. D'Eichthal, 7 Nov. 1829, *CW*: XII.42.
38. According to Edith Simcox (1873: 300), "Mill's *Logic* has an authentic pedigree of three centuries to say the least, and it was natural that he should acknowledge so respectable an ancestry."
39. Mill (1843, *CW*: VII.cxi). The *Athenaeum* reviewer of Mill's *Logic* had not only praised him for having "a due appreciation of the merits of his predecessors," but also for producing "in this age of plagiarism, a work of original thought, deserving to take rank with the immortal works of Locke and Bacon" (Cooke Taylor, 1843: 1101–02). Years later, other reviewers would criticize him for his attempted synthesis of the work of his predecessors (e.g., Mozley, 1872: 117).
40. Mill (1873a, *CW*: I.231).
41. Ryan (1990: x).
42. Kneale and Kneale (1962: 372).
43. Ryan (1990: xxvi).
44. Mill (1873a, *CW*: I.21).
45. Mill (1873a, *CW*: I.233–35).
46. Mill (1843, *CW*: I.14–15). The final version of the unfinished *Autobiography* which was published in 1873 repeats the early draft almost *verbatim*.
47. Attempts have been made to resolve this contradiction; see McRae (1974: xxiv*ff*).
48. J. S. Mill to J. Sterling, 28 Sept. 1839, *CW*: XIII.406. Writing to H. Taine, on occasion of the latter's review of Mill's *Logic* (Taine, 1861), Mill noted:

> Quand j'ai écrit mon livre, j'étais à peu près seul de mon opinion; et bien que ma manière de voir ait trouvé un degré de sympathie auquel je ne m'attendais nullement, on compte encore en Angleterre vingt philosophes a priori et spiritualistes contre chaque partisan de la doctrine de l'expérience (J. S. Mill to H. Taine, 15 Mar. 1861, *CW*: XV.723).

49. A few years prior to this discussion, Mill identified knowing "what knowledge *was*, and how it was to be come at," as Socrates' as well as his own special skill. See, J. S. Mill to T. Carlyle, 5 Oct. 1833, CW: XII.181.

50. J. S. Mill to T. Carlyle, 8 Aug. 1837, CW: XII.347. This was one point that Mill's reviewers would later criticize. Thomas Kingsmill Abbott (1858: 102) argued that even though Mill had high hopes for induction, i.e., in providing a new method for physical science, his rejection of "every *a priori* element" in the inductive process led to the abandonment of "all intention of guiding practical discoverers." Bain similarly argued that Mill had seen that Proof was more important than Discovery," and he had indeed discussed methods of investigation as aids of discovery and means of proof, but he had "never explained the mutual bearings of the two" (Bain, 1882: 68). See also, Mozley (1869: 77).

51. J. S. Mill to J. Sterling, 4 Nov. 1839, CW: XIII.412.

52. J. S. Mill to J. Sterling, 28 Sept. 1839, CW: XIII.406. He did leave it open that what he thought "subordinate parts" may have been as important as what he identified to be the fundamental principles.

53. As Mill noted: "Evidence is not that which the mind does or must yield to, but that which it ought to yield to, namely, that, by yielding to which, its belief is kept conformable to fact" (Mill, 1843, CW: VII.564).

54. Responding to Sterling's question, Mill claimed that identifying laws that underpin all phenomena was one such matter (J. S. Mill to J. Sterling, 4 Nov. 1839, CW: XIII.411–12).

55. J. S. Mill to J. Sterling, 4 Nov. 1839, CW: XIII.412.

56. J. S. Mill to J. Sterling, 3 Dec. 1840, CW: XIII.450 and 5 Jan 1841, CW: XIII.461–62; see also, J. S. Mill to R. B. Fox, 12 Dec. 1841, CW: XIII.469 and 23 Dec. 1840, CW: XIII.455. He would have never considered consulting the Germans on logic twenty years before. In his "Traité de Logique" (1820–1821), Mill noted:

> Cette différence d'opinion [among the various schools of logic] provient le plus souvent de la manie de raisonner sur des sujets au delà du pouvoir borné de l'esprit humain. Laissons aux têtes Germaniques toutes ces obscurités, et rendons grâce à notre aimable legèreté qui nous empêche de nous enthousiasmer pour ce que nous ne pouvons pas comprendre. (CW: XXVI.147)

See also, J. S. Mill to A. Comte, 8 Nov. 1841, CW: XIII.489.

57. J. S. Mill to J. Sterling, 4 Nov. 1839, CW: XIII.412.

58. Mill (1843, CW: VII.3–4). Mill defended Whately's against Hamilton's strictures in *Hamilton* (1865, CW: IX.348ff).

59. Mill (1843, CW: VII.6–9, 54).

60. Mill (1843, CW: VII.11–12). As Bain noted, Mill's *Logic* "methodized with a completeness previously unknown" inductive logic (Bain, 1870: I.254).

61. Mill (1843, CW: VII.19–20).

62. Mill (1843, CW: VII.19–20). For a criticism on this discussion, see Mozley (1872: 90–92).

63. Mill (1843, CW: VII.89, 97, 157–58). Mill acknowledged using the terms "denote" and "connote" somewhat idiosyncratically in comparison with standard practice (see *ibid.*, 20–40, 40n-41n). Connotation was to be taken under consideration in Mill's "peculiar theory of reasoning" (Blakey, 1851: 464). On Mill's theory of names, see *infra*, chapter one.

64. Mill (1843, CW: VII.162).

65. See further, Ryan (1990: 21ff), Scarre (1989: 26ff), Skorupski (1989: 103ff).

66. Hamilton (1833: 227). Cf. Mill (1828, *CW*: XI.11–14).
67. Mill (1843, *CW*: VII.193). See also, *ibid.*, 199–200. On Mill's views on ratiocination and induction, and their sources, see *infra*, chapter two.
68. Mill (1843, *CW*: VII.199–200). For a brief summary of the various confusions inherent in Mill's account see, Kneale and Kneale (1962: 376–77).
69. On Mill's philosophy of mathematics, see *infra*, chapter three. Typically, Mill's account of mathematics was treated as an exemplary case of having to go at great lengths "to base arithmetic upon the crude empiricism of sense-impressions" (Sigwart, 1895: II.35n1). See also the more famous treatment of Mill, Frege (1960: §7–10, §12, §23–25).
70. Mill (1843, *CW*: VII.225).
71. Mill (1843, *CW*: VII.225ff, 253ff).
72. Mill (1843, *CW*: VII.224–25, 227, 236–37, 257–59). Interestingly, James Mill had also suggested that mathematical truths are hypothetical, without however explaining what he meant (see, J. Mill, 1815: 192–93). John Stuart Mill's discussion on "necessary truths" was one of the most debated parts of the *Logic*—a discussion in which Mill's consistency was tested; see, e.g., Bosanquet (1911: II.226ff), Spencer (1853: 521–6), Ward (1871). The first and subsequent editions of Mill's *Hamilton* attempted to respond to such criticisms; for a list of reviews to which Mill did try to respond in *Hamilton*, see Mill (1865, *CW*: IX.ciii–cv). Richard Fumerton argues that Mill did not essentially respond to his critics on the issue, missing their point—that it is impossible to "conceive of two straight lines enclosing a space because it is in the nature of straight lines that such a possibility is precluded," and not merely because we have limited imaginations (Donner and Fumerton, 2009: 162–63; for a similar criticism see Russell, 1956: 124–25). However, the "problem of induction," Mill argued, consisted in not knowing why a single instance is sufficient in some cases "for a complete induction while in others, myriads of concurring instances, without a single exception known or presumed, go such little way towards establishing an universal proposition" (Mill, 1843, *CW*: VII.314).
73. Mill (1843, *CW*: VII.283).
74. Mill (1873a, *CW*: I.217).
75. J. Mill (1815: 193). Although the comparison with Aristotle may surprise us some two hundred years later, it was not uncommon in the nineteenth century; for example, the reviewer of the younger Mill's *Logic* in the *Athenaeum* claimed that Mill "had [not] done as much for Inductive, as Aristotle for Deductive Logic" (Cooke Taylor 1843: 1102).
76. As Bertrand Russell noted in his "Lecture on a Master Mind" (1955), "[e]verything that Mill has to say in his *Logic* about matters other than inductive inference is perfunctory and conventional" (Russell, 1956: 123).
77. Mill (1843, *CW*: VII.284, 288, 294, 299–302). For the debate with William Whewell stirred up by Mill's definition of induction, see *infra*, chapter four.
78. See further, Kubitz (1932: 139ff).
79. Mill (1843, *CW*: VII.306–08).
80. Robert Blakey thus pointed out that a Humean theory of causation and a Hartleyan theory of association of ideas lie at the background of Mill's *Logic* (Blakey, 1851: 465).
81. Mill (1843, *CW*: VII.312, 318–19).
82. Mill (1843, *CW*: VII.567). Mill considered the demarcation of "scientific induction" an advance from previous practice (see Mill, 1873b, *CW*: XI.481–82). Bosanquet argued that "scientific induction" was a misnomer, "something of a contradiction in terms," since scientific analysis refers to "a precise determination and skilful resolution" of the content of observations, i.e., of instances, not the enumeration and of calculation of chances of instances (Bosanquet, 1911: II.118).

83. Mill (1843, *CW*: VII.567), Kubitz (1932: 138; 146ff).
84. For a brief summary of Mill's methods, see Donner and Fumerton (2009: 168–73).
85. Mill (1843, *CW*: VII. bk III, ch. 8).
86. See *infra*, Chapter 10, for a discussion of Mill's deductive method—especially as applied to political phenomena.
87. Mill (1843, *CW*: VII.379). See also, Ryan (1990: 50–52).
88. Mill (1843, *CW*: VII. bk III, chs. 11, 14). Kubitz (1932: 126) traces the sources of this particular argument in Mill to Dugald Stewart. For the implications of this spontaneous propensity of individuals as reasoning agents for Mill's views on theoretic and practical reason, see *infra*, chapter seven. Bosanquet argued that Mill failed to separate hypothesis from induction, in admitting that the *vera causa* may not be known to be present in cases of making an induction (Bosanquet, 1911: II.121n-22nl; 152–53).
89. Mill (1843, *CW*: VII.319). As Bain reported, Book IV "was made up of a number of subjects that he [Mill] did not know where to place" (Bain, 1882: 67).
90. These practical rules were to be spelled out in "the Book of Logic," according to James Mill. See, J. Mill, 1829: II.403. As the younger Mill noted, logic was not "the *theory* of reasoning but the *practice*" (J. S. Mill to T. Carlyle, 2 Aug. 1833, *CW*: XII.173).
91. Mill (1843, *CW*: VII.14).
92. Mill (1873a, *CW*: I.233).
93. Mill (1843, *CW*: VII.206).
94. Mill (1843, *CW*: VII.62n-63n). Contra Kubitz (1932: 54).
95. This was the main point of contention of W. G. Ward's reviews of Mill's *Logic*. See, e.g., Ward (1843b: 357, 410–15). See also, Atwater (1856: 92–93) and Mozley (1869: 80), who claimed that "logic and metaphysics are intersecting sciences."
96. J. S. Mill to H. Taylor Mill, 4 Feb. [1854], *CW*: XIV.149. See also, J. S. Mill to T. Gomperz, 19 Aug. 1854, *CW*: XIV.238–39.
97. Mill (1843, *CW*: VII.15n [original 1856 note]). Mill took up this discussion with more detail in his *Hamilton* (see Mill, 1865, *CW*: IX.352ff).
98. Mill (1843, *CW*: VII.208). Mill was aware that his definition of logic was different from that of Hamilton, already by 1833 (see J. S. Mill to T. Carlyle, 2 Aug. 1833, *CW*: XII.173).
99. Mill (1865, *CW*: IX.367, 371). See also, Mill (1873b, *CW*: XI.479).
100. Mill (1843, *CW*: VII.20).
101. Mill (1843, *CW*: VII.7–8, 20).
102. As Risto Vilkko (2009: 205) put it, in the first half of the nineteenth century, "the logic question sprung from a genuine doubt about the justification of the formal foundations of logic as the normative foundation of all scientific activity. On the one hand, most of the participants of the debate opposed Hegel's attempts to unite logic and metaphysics—on the other, reform was sought to overcome the old scholastic-Aristotelian formal logic."
103. J. S. Mill to J. E. Cairns, 5 Dec. 1871, *CW*: XVII.1862–63. Although it does not really go against the point Mill was making, symbolic logic had spread widely by the last quarter of the nineteenth century, which highlighted the public's interest in it (Peckhaus, 2009: 160. See further, Van Evra, 2000). For example, Bain's *Logic* contained "a full abstract of the novel and elaborate schemes of De Morgan and Boole" (Bain, 1870: iii). To this effect, some commentators argued that Mill's "neglect of quantitative determinations [was] the chief deficiency" in his *Logic* (Sigwart, 1895: II.346); still, some would see in Mill "an able and adventurous pioneer" in "[restoring] to logic its hold on living concrete thought" (Bosanquet, 1911: I.87).

104. Mill (1843, CW: VII.172). See also, Mill (1865, CW: IX.369–71).
105. Mill (1843, CW: VII.284).
106. Skorupski (1989: xi).
107. Mill (1867, CW: XXI.239). See further, *ibid.*, 238–40. See also Rosen (2013b).
108. J. Mill (2010: III.101r, 208).
109. J. Mill (1826: 14).
110. Mill (1867, CW: XXI.239).
111. Mill (1867, CW: XXI.240).
112. Mill (1843, CW: VII.735–36).
113. See further *infra*, chapter nine.
114. J. S. Mill to R. B. Fox, 14 Feb. 1843, CW: XIII.569. Interestingly, Mill told Herschel that the "most important" chapter of the *Logic* was on the "four Experimental Methods" (See J. S. Mill to F. W. Herschel, 1 May 1843, CW: XIII.583). For a discussion of Mill on free will, see *infra*, chapter six.
115. For Mill on the Art of Life, see *infra*, chapter eleven.
116. See further *infra*, chapter ten.
117. This chapter was the subject of a *Times* review for 10 April 1852. This particular review was the longest treatment of this chapter in a review in the periodical press. The author was quite unconvinced by Mill, charging him with confusion and fallacious reasoning. The chapter was problematic, the reviewer argued, not only because Mill failed to distinguish between desire and will (making Mill's distinction between fatalism and necessitarianism meaningless), but also because Mill avoided discussing moral responsibility ([Anon.], 1852a: 6). Mill's problematic treatment of man and society in most of Book VI, the reviewer argued, owed to Mill following Comte in ignoring the existence of God ([Anon.], 1852b).
118. For one of the rare discussions of Mill's Book V, see [Anon.] (1872b: 1281). See [Anon.] (1852b) and Mozley (1872: 100) for Book VI. Killick's (1870) and Stebbing's (1864) student handbooks on Mill's *Logic*, which did discuss the whole of Mill's *Logic*, merely offered a chapter by chapter summary. Bain's *Logic* seems to be the only book that follows Mill's *Logic* closely in discussing the logic of practice as well as fallacies (see Bain, 1870: bk V and VI).
119. Mill was very disappointed by John Murray's (1778–1843) delay in considering the manuscript and its eventual rejection, which caused the book to lose the 1842 publishing season. It was eventually published by John W. Parker (1792–1870). See Mill (1873a, CW: I.231). Patrick Leary argues that Mill's disappointment was due to Mill's extreme sensitivity to the timing of publication of his works, "believing that the key to a book or article's influence lay in its entering the field of public discourse at the precise moment that his intended audience would be most receptive" (Leary, 1998, 40–41). Leary is right to point out Mill's concern with good timing. However, Mill's refusing to allow for a cheap people's edition of the *Logic*, which Leary documents well (Leary, 1998: 50–51), suggests that the intended audience of the *Logic* were "a select few," even when Mill's expectations for the *Logic* were exceeded. Mill was more likely disappointed because of his excitement that the book was finally done. In private correspondence he was quite exuberant about what he had accomplished; in late May 1842, greatly relieved that he had finished his *Logic*, he told Caroline Fox (1819–1871), "My family have no idea how great a man I am" (see Fox, 1882: I.300; see also, Courtney, 1889: 77).
120. J. S. Mill to R. B. Fox, 6 May 1841, CW: XIII.474.
121. Mill (1873, CW: I.189–91, 215–17, 229–31). For a complete discussion for the development of the text of Mill's *A System of Logic*, see Robson (1974).

122. Jennings (1854: 421, 445). For a similar claim see also [Anon.] (1856: 736); Fraser (1860: 401–02). Bosanquet argued that "the reform of Logic *in this country* dates from the work of Stuart Mill," despite Mill's "philosophical short-comings" (Bosanquet, 1911: I.vii).
123. [Anon.] (1856: 735–36).
124. Mill (1873a, CW: I.231). In the 1847 edition of *Philosophy of the Inductive Sciences*, Whewell made a note of his intention to avoid commenting on Mill's *Logic*, postponing such a critique for a separate publication (Whewell, 1847: xii).
125. E.g., [Anon.] (1866a), Hutton (1850), Mozley (1869). Cf. Bowen (1849: 16).
126. Hutton (1850: 78–79). However, Hutton commented little on the debate between schools, even though he pointed it out. Following the publication of Mill's *Hamilton* in 1865, Hamilton replaced Whewell in the comparison between Mill and the *a priori* school; see, e.g., Masson (1866: 149ff, 256ff), Mozley (1869: 89ff); see also [Anon.] (1866b), Spencer (1865), Ward (1871; 1874; 1876). Interestingly, Hutton was perhaps the first who claimed that the controversy between Mill and Whewell was "one between two minds so little able to catch each other's point of view" (Hutton, 1850: 80. Bosanquet's *Logic* (1911) also worked extensively with the Whewell-Mill controversy). According to Mill, Hutton, a future correspondent of Mill, was an "intelligent reviewer" (Mill, 1843, CW: VII.331n), whose review was one of the few on which Mill spent time in addressing its points.
127. Hutton (1850: 110).
128. Bain (1882: 68–69). William Cooke Taylor (1800–1849)—to whom Whately was "patron and friend" (see Courtney, 1898: 478)—was the publisher's referee for Mill's book. Taylor's "so favorable an opinion, expressed in such complimentary terms" gave great satisfaction to Mill (understandably so, if Cooke Taylor's recommendation was anything like his review of Mill's *Logic* in the *Athenaeum*, soon after its publication in 1843). See J. S. Mill to J. W. Parker, 6 Apr. 1842, CW: XIII.514. See also, Bain (1882: 66).
129. J. S. Mill to H. S. Chapman, 8 Nov. 1844, CW: XIII.642.
130. Whewell (1849: 4–5).
131. Leechman (1845: 32). Boole and De Morgan, however, made only passing remarks to Mill's *Logic*, even though their works appeared a year after Mill's second edition (see, e.g., Boole, 1847: 2; De Morgan, 1847: 46).
132. See Robson (1974: lxxxi).
133. "Since its appearance (in 1843)," a reviewer noted in 1856, "the book has been the subject of innumerable reviews—fair and unfair, wise and foolish, learned and ignorant." [Anon.] (1856: 736). This was directly contradicted in another review a year later; making a note of "profound silence," the reviewer claimed that Mill "received . . . little [criticism]—we might almost say none. As a system it has neither been approved nor disproved; nor has any one venture to predict what rank it is destined to be assigned in the future history of philosophy" ([Anon.], 1857: 724). Both reviewers were exaggerating. For a book of its kind, Mill's *Logic* received many, not innumerable, reviews. For example, Whately's *Logic* (1826) was reviewed less than Mill's *Logic* in the periodical press, even though several editions appeared up to Whately's death.
134. Bain (1882: 67).
135. As Bain pointed out, Mill's alterations included toning down, or even effacing, some of his laudatory comments on Auguste Comte's work (Bain, 1882: 72–73).
136. Ward (1843a: 552). See also, Ward (1843b: 349, 353–54, 426–27). This was an estimate that all reviewers shared. For some early examples, see [Anon.]

(1844: 276, 280), [Anon.] (1846: 1, 37–38), Bain (1843: 456), Cooke Taylor (1843: 1102)Smith (1843: 415).

137. Bain, 1882: 69. In a letter to Ward several years later, Mill noted: "A candid adversary has as great a claim as a supporter, to one's best endeavours for making one's meaning clear to him, even if no change of opinion is likely to result. I never feel so sure of doing good as when I find that my writings have given matter for thought to those who differ from me" (J. S. Mill to W. G. Ward, 28 Nov. 1859, CW: XV.647). As Mill told the Fox sisters at the time, Ward's review was a "lofty panegyric," almost exhausting "language in admiration of me & my book, & then adds that notwithstanding I shall certainly go to ____" (J. S. Mill to C. Fox and A. M Fox, [23 Oct. 1843], CW: XIII.603). Mill also noticed Ward's references to him in his *Ideal of the Christian Church* (see J. S. Mill to A. Bain, [March 1845], CW: XIII.662; to A. Comte, 26 Apr. 1845, CW: XIII.664). For an example of what Mill considered "puff[ing] at every chapter," see Ward (1844: 33, 277). For Ward's interest in Mill, see W. Ward (1889: 18, 37, 46).

138. Ward (1843b: 355).

139. Ward (1843b: 355–56). Others protested that Mill, in his discussion of causation (and connected discussions, e.g., "Liberty and Necessity"), left no room for God (Jennings, 1854: 436; see also [Anon.], 1857; Tulloch, 1855: 22–39). Christian apologists, another reviewer noted, found "themselves under the necessity of combating its [the *Logic*'s] principles" (Atwater, 1856: 89).

140. Ward (1843b: 395–96).

141. Ward (1843b: 399–401). Ward was quoting from Mill's "Bentham" (1838, CW: X.95). Ward also took issue with Mill's notion of free will and its connection to Christian morality (see Ward, 1843b: 415ff). Ward had also criticized Mill's discussion of "necessary truth" following the publication of Mill's *Hamilton* (1865), to which criticisms Mill responded in subsequent editions of both the *Logic* and *Hamilton* (see, e.g., Mill, 1843, CW: VII.575n; 1865, CW: IX.165n).

142. Ward (1843b: 399). Ward had anticipated later reviews of Mill, who claimed that Mill's ethics display Mill "at his best, and at his worst" (Mozley, 1872: 101). For Mill on the different kinds of pleasures, see *infra*, chapter eight.

143. Bain (1882: 69).

144. Bain (1882: 69).

145. Although Mill and Bain were on the whole on the same "side" on many issues (both referring to the other's works frequently), they disagreed on a number of issues that came up in Mill's *Logic*. For example, Mill replied to Bain's comments on his views on definition (Mill, 1843, CW: VII.141n), on some of the aspects of Mill's treatment of the syllogism (VII.166n, 181n), on the compositions of causes (VII.377n), on experimental evidence in politics (VII.453n), on empirical laws (VII.589n), etc. Bain criticized Mill, either for looseness of expression or in substantive points, in almost all of his essays in his *Dissertations on Leading Philosophical Topics* (1903). As he wrote in his biography of Mill: "I have had myself full opportunities for expressing both agreements and dissents in regard to all the main points. Yet I could not pretend to say that criticism has been exhausted, or that imperfections and even inconsistencies may not even yet be pointed out" (Bain, 1882: 67–68). In *Autobiography*, Mill acknowledged that Bain had assisted him in writing the *Logic* by furnishing him with numerous examples; as Mill noted, he inserted these examples, as well as comments made by Bain in the *Logic* "nearly in [Bain's] own words." See Mill (1873a, CW: I.255). For the Mill-Bain relationship, see *infra*, chapter five.

146. Bain (1843: 414). In his biography of Mill, Bain was more forthcoming:

> It is long since I was struck with the seeming incompatibility between the definition of Logic in the Introduction—the Science of Proof or Evidence—and the double designation in the title—Principles of Evidence and the Methods of Scientific Investigation. Previous writers laid little stress on Proof, and Mill took the other extreme and made Proof everything. (Bain, 1882: 68)

According to Bain, Mill's view of logic amounted to the practical science of proof and a body of method assisting in the search after truth, but completely ignored logic as a theoretical abstract science. See Bain (1870: I.34).

147. Bain (1843: 419).
148. Bain (1843: 455).
149. Bain (1843: 420–21); cf. Blakey (1851: 466). Following a brief discussion of Mill's theory of names, Kneale and Kneale claim, as regards the influence of Mill's account, that "[a]fter Mill's book little was heard of the doctrine of real definition" (Kneale and Kneale, 1962: 374). However, Mill's account, more often than not, either went unnoticed or, when noticed, was criticized. For example, reviewers criticized that what Mill "does not venture definitely to assert, he does nevertheless tacitly assume"; Mill seemed to consider language to be the basis of reasoning, even though he explicitly claimed that language was only the instrument of reasoning (Mozley, 1872: 88–89; see also McCosh, 1866: 338–39). It took almost thirty years for a reviewer to attempt to get to the bottom of Mill's theory of names.
150. Bain (1843: 425–28). In his biography of Mill, Bain claimed that Mill's theory of the syllogism was not the whole solution to the problem—though it was more than a half solution (Bain, 1882: 145; cf. Spencer, 1855: 125–27. See further, Bain, 1903: 20–26). In his *Logic*, however, Bain had praised Mill on this exact point: "[t]he extrication from the puzzle [i.e., that the syllogism contains a *petitio principii*] is due to Mr. John Stuart Mill, and the consequences has been a total revolution in Logic" (Bain, 1870: I.208).
151. Bain (1843: 428).
152. As Ducheyne (2008) has argued, in subsequent editions of *Logic* Mill gradually qualified his views on the inductive results of his methods in establishing certainty as regards causation.
153. Bain (1843: 428–40).
154. Bain (1882: 146, 66). James McCosh (1866: 336) seemed to agree. In contrast, Mozley, with intimate knowledge of Mill's major books and essays, thought that Mill's *Considerations on Representative Government* (1861) was Mill's best work, whereas Mill's *Principles of Political Economy* (1848), the least successful in tracing the implications of its "ambitious theorems" (1872: 109, 111).
155. Bain (1870: I.iii).
156. Smith (1843: 416–21). Smith and Mill were early acquaintances (see Davis, 1964), but Mill did not respond to his review of *Logic*. Mill did respond however to a review of *Hamilton* by Smith (Mill, 1865, CW: IX.civ).
157. Smith (1843: 422–26). Bain also marked his agreement with Mill on this issue, but without critically examining either Mill's or Whewell's account (Bain, 1843: 429), but not all agreed; see, e.g. Spencer (1853: 522ff). Mill did reply to Spencer, but Spencer, as he claimed, was not "at all alarmed" (Mill, 1843, CW: VII.262ff; H. Spencer to W. G. Spencer, 26 Aug. 1856, in Duncan, 1908: 82).
158. Smith (1843: 426) quoting Mill (1843, CW: VII.340). Bosanquet would later criticize Mill for improper use of language with reference to causation; that

is, Mill's talk of causes as sums of conditions was not as appropriate as the phrase "totality of relations" (Bosanquet, 1911: I.251). Both the reviewer's and Bosanquet's remarks suggest that there was an ambiguity in the meaning of "unconditional," as Mill employed the term; for a discussion of four different meanings of the term, see Kubitz (1932: 160ff), who argued that "sum of conditions" and "necessity" conveyed part of its meaning, not the whole.

159. Smith (1843: 426–28). Mill's theory of causation, however, was a subject of attack for many years (see, e.g., Bowen, 1849: lecture 4; Mozley, 1872: 92ff; Ward, 1876). Interestingly, however, Smith did criticize Mill's discussion of hypotheses, but not for his views on the subject—which, according to the reviewer, were not quite as original as his other views—but for his "indulgence" of the "astronomical speculation of Laplace" (Smith, 1843: 428–30). However, Mill's view of hypothesis did differ from the received view, something that Bain had mentioned (Bain, 1843: 443–44).

160. [Anon.] (1844: 268–70).

161. [Anon.] (1844: 271).

162. [Anon.] (1844: 274–76).

163. Bain (1882: 80). As Books III to VI are merely summarized in the review, it is unclear what made Mill say that the reviewer did not understand him. The review ended approving of Mill's and Whately's treatments of the importance of evidence, arguing that their works provide "one of the best safe-guards, alike against German skepticism or mysticism, and Oxford popery" ([Anon.] (1844: 281). Earlier, however, the reviewer noted that Mill exhibited that his "metaphysical opinions" were of the "ultra-empirical school," which left the door open to "absolute Pyrrhonism, and so doing away with all reliance on logic" [Anon.] (1844: 280).

164. [Anon.] (1846: 1).

165. [Anon.] (1846: 2).

166. [Anon.] (1846: 2–4).

167. [Anon.] (1846: 5. Cf. Ward, 1843b: 356). Interestingly, Mill did make a reference to logic as the study of the products of thoughts in his *Hamilton* (Mill, 1865, *CW*: IX.361).

168. [Anon.] (1846: 6–8, 12–17). Kubitz (1932: 65) made a similar point.

169. See, Mill (1843, *CW*: VII.205n–07n). Mill did respond to an issue identified by the reviewer on definition (*ibid.*, 147n–48n) and his discussion of the syllogism addressed the reviewer's view of the *dictum de omni et nullo* (*ibid.*, 206n), but in focusing on the critic's account of the syllogism, Mill ignored the broader issue that the reviewer was pointing to as regards Mill's theoretical commitments, most evident in the reviewer's treatment of Mill's views on mathematics and necessary truths (see, [Anon.], 1846: 28ff). Moreover, the reviewer discussed Mill on induction; despite praising Mill's views on induction as clearer than those of Whately, the reviewer thought "that the *logic* of induction has yet to be written" (*ibid.*, pp. 33ff, 37; . see also, Hutton, 1850: 111).

170. Mill (1843, *CW*: VIII.1111). Interestingly, in the third and fourth editions Mill cited Whewell's approbation of his account of the syllogism when responding to the critic.

171. See Mill (1843, *CW*: VII.206n–07n).

172. [Anon.] (1846: 19; citing Mill, 1843, *CW*: VII.184). For the critic's summary, see [Anon.] (1846: 17–19).

173. [Anon.] (1846: 19–25).

174. [Anon.] (1846: 21–22). For a similar view of Mill, see Sigwart (1895: I.361).

175. [Anon.] (1846: 23). See also *ibid.*, 33. See further, Scarre (1989: chs 1 and 2).

176. Hutton (1850: 96); for a similar point see Mozley (1869: 88).

177. Hutton (1850: 80).
178. Hutton (1850: 87, 88). Abbott (1858: 105ff) also took issue with Mill basing his theory of induction on the mind's "natural tendency to generalise."
179. Hutton (1850: 91–92). See also, Blakey (1851: 470–71).
180. Hutton (1850: 93).
181. See also Simcox (1873: 299–300).
182. Mozley (1872: 92–94).
183. McCosh (1866: 328).
184. Abbott (1858: 122).
185. Jennnings (1854: 437). See also, Atwater (1856: 100), who argued that parts of Mill's *Logic* brought out his "obvious purpose" in reducing "all that is knowable to phenomena under the relations, succession, or co-existence, likeness or unlikeness," notwithstanding "all his protestations to the contrary."
186. Blakey (1851: 472).
187. Sigwart (1895: II.303).
188. McCosh (1892: v).
189. Fraser (1860: 402–03).
190. Fraser (1860: 407, 424, 426) quoting from Hamilton (1860: I.60–63); for a similar criticism, see McCosh (1866: 337–38). For Mill's comment on "Modified Logic," see Mill (1865, CW: IX.368). Fraser was trying to bring Hamilton's and Mill's approaches together as complementing parts, along with "the Cosmological and Ontological part of Logic" (Fraser, 1860: 403, 423ff). For a similar attempt, see [Anon.] (1866a) and Mozley (1869).
191. [Anon.] (1862: 257–58).
192. Smith (1843: 430). Still, the reviewer concluded, no one "can fail to recognize and admire in this author that acute, patient, enlarged, and persevering thought, which gives to him who possesses it the claim and right to the title of philosopher."
193. [Anon.] (1862: 258). The reviewer himself did not "abandon" Mill on this point.
194. Jennings (1854: 436). Writing to a friend soon after the publication of Mill's *Hamilton*, Hippolyte Taine noted that "[t]here is a new budding philosophy on England at present, with Stuart Mill, his father James Mill, Herbert Spencer and Bain" (H. Taine to E. de Suckau, 8 June 1865, in Taine, 1904: 266).
195. It was a review of "Mill altogether," more properly so than Ward's review three decades earlier. Two books by Bain also appeared on the head of the article. For the list of books reviewed, see Mozley (1872: 77). Similarly, [Anon.] (1872a, 1872b) placed Mill and Bain as the two main expounders of the "association psychology."
196. Mozley (1872: 81–82). Similarly, Mill's theory of causation and views on mathematical axioms, being grounded on Mill's psychological views, exhibited the same philosophical narrowness, which denied that "fact and law enter the mind inseparably and simultaneously" (*ibid.*, 94–100). For example, Mill's view of causation, according to the reviewer, exhibits a general symptom of his methodological commitment that the unknown has no place in science (*ibid.*, 91, 96ff). On the other hand, the reviewer tried to explain why Mill denied that propositions of mathematics are identical. The reviewer traced that denial in that Mill, and others like Mill, mistakenly grounded the abstractions of mathematics in the effort needed in making comparisons and the usefulness of a precise method of measurement in life (*ibid.*, 99–100). Mozley, in his previous review of Mill (in 1869), had tried to counter Mill's "narrowing" influence.
197. Mozley (1872: 116). Bain took credit for this in his *Autobiography* (Bain, 1904: 280).

198. [Anon.] (1856: 736).
199. Leary (1998: 45). See also, J. S. Mill to H. Taylor Mill, 29 Jan. [1854], *CW*: XIV.142.
200. H. Grote (1873: 268). According to Bain, George Grote considered Mill's *Logic* the best book in his library (Bain, 1882: 83). For Grote's brief comments on Mill's *Logic*, on occasion of a review of Mill's *Hamilton*, see Grote (1866: 285–86).
201. "It is impossible fully to estimate the enormous influence of these two books [i.e., Mill's *Logic* and *Political Economy*]." See, [Anon.] (1861: 92). Newman also included Grote's *History* in those influential books. See *Special Report from the Select Committee on the Oxford and Cambridge Universities Education Bill; together with the Proceedings of the Committee, Minutes of Evidence, and Appendix* (House of Commons, 31 July 1867: 82).
202. See Leary (1998: 45).
203. It is likely that this discussion took place in June 1860, during Taine's two-month stay in England (see Taine, 1904: 157).
204. Taine (1873: 8). For the French text, see Taine (1861: 46).
205. See Killick (1870) and Stebbing (1864). See also, J. S. Mill to W. Stebbing, 26 Mar. 1859, *CW*: XXXI.116.
206. For a discussion of the aims of the Christian Evidence Society, see Johnson (1981).
207. [Anon.] (1872a: 1203).
208. Simcox (1873: 298).
209. Masson (1866: 17). One can see a grain of truth in Masson's ironic comment, considering that, as Algernon Taylor (1830–1903)—Mill's stepson—recorded, a pleading of insanity at court was grounded, among other things, on that the defendant was "inclined to the teaching of John Stuart Mill" (Taylor, 1892: 69).
210. [Anon.] (1861: 91–92).
211. See Jevons (1877, 1878a, 1878b, 1879). See also, Ward (1874, 1876). Jevons considered Mill's influence as a thinker undeserved. He noted:

> [F]or my part, I will no longer consent to live silently under the incubus of bad logic and bad philosophy which Mill's Works have laid upon us. On almost every subject of social importance—religion, morals, political philosophy, political economy, metaphysics, logic—he has expressed unhesitating opinions, and his sayings are quoted by his admirers as if they were the oracles of a perfectly wise and logical mind. Nobody questions, or at least ought to question, the force of Mill's style, the persuasive power of his words, the candour of his discussions, and the perfect goodness of his motives. If to all his other great qualities had been happily added logical accurateness, his writings would indeed have been a source of light for generations to come. But in one way or another Mill's intellect was wrecked. The cause of injury may have been Mill's own life-long attempt to reconcile a false empirical philosophy with conflicting truth. But however it arose, Mill's mind was essentially illogical (Jevons, 1877: 169).

Mozley made a less general claim, i.e., that Mill's ethical system was illogical (1872: 101ff). But he seemed to be in agreement with Jevons: Mill "is, indeed, a kind of Procrustes, who takes the narrow and shrunken substance of other people's speculations, and tries by main force to expand them to the dimensions required by the age" (Mozley, 1872: 117).
212. See Green (1885: II.195–306).
213. Atwater (1856: 106).

REFERENCES

[Abbott, T.K.] (1858) "Logic of Induction—Mill," *North British Review* 28 (55): 101–22.

[Anon.] (1844) "Mill's System of Logic," *Eclectic Review* 16: 268–281.

———. (1846) "Mill's System of Logic," *British Quarterly Review* 4 (7): 1–38.

———. (1852a) "Mill's Logic of the Moral Sciences," *Times* 21086 (10 Apr.): 6.

———. (1852b) "Mill's Logic of the Moral Sciences," *Times* 21087 (12 Apr.): 8.

———. (1856) "Mill's Logic," *Saturday Review of Politics, Literature, Science and Art* 2 (59): 735–36.

———. (1857) "Mill's Logic," *Dublin University Magazine* 49 (294): 724–35.

———. (1861) "Mr Mill on Representative Government," *Westminster Review* 20 (1): 91–114.

———. (1862) "Mill's Logical Method," *London Review and Weekly Journal of Politics, Society, Literature and Arts* 5 (116; 20 Sept.): 257–59.

———. (1866a) "Mr. J. S. Mill and the Inductive Origin of First Principles," *Journal of Sacred Literature and Biblical Record* 9 (17): 1–35.

———. (1866b) *The Battle of the Two Philosophies; by an Inquirer* (London: Longmans, Green).

———. (1872a) "Mr Mill's System of Logic (First Notice)," *Examiner* 3384 (7 Dec.): 1203–04.

———. (1872b) "Mr Mill's System of Logic (Second Notice)," *The Examiner* 3387 (28 Dec.): 1280–81.

[Atwater, L. H.] (1856) "Mill's System of Logic," *Biblical Repertory and Princeton Review* 28 (1): 88–112.

[Bain, A.] (1843) "A System of Logic: By John Stuart Mill," *Westminster Review* 39 (2): 412–56.

———. (1870) *Logic*, 2 vols., 2nd ed. (London: Longmans, Green, Reader and Dryer 1873).

———. (1882) *John Stuart Mill: A Criticism with Personal Recollections* (London: Longmans, Green).

———. (1903) *Dissertations on Leading Philosophical Topics* (London: Longmans, Green).

———. (1904) *Autobiography* (London: Longmans, Green).

Bentham, G. (1827) *Outline of a New System of Logic, With a Critical Examination of Dr Whately's Elements of Logic* (London: Hunt and Clarke).

Bentham, J. (1827) *Rationale of Judicial Evidence, Specially Applied to English Practice, from the Manuscripts of Jeremy Bentham*, J. S. Mill (ed.), 5 vols. (London: Hunt and Clarke).

Blakey, R. (1851) *Historical Sketch of Logic, from the Earliest Times to the Present Day* (London: H. Baillière).

Boole, G. (1847) *The Mathematical Analysis of Logic; Being an Essay towards a Calculus of Deductive Reasoning* (Cambridge: Macmillan, Barclay & Macmillan).

Bosanquet, B. (1888) *Logic, or the Morphology of Knowledge*, 2 vols., 2nd ed. (Oxford: Oxford University Press, 1911).

Bowen, F. (1849) *Lowell Lectures on the Application of Metaphysical and Ethical Science to the Evidences of Religion* (Boston: Charles C. Little and James Brown).

Capaldi, N. (2004) *John Stuart Mill. A Biography* (Cambridge: Cambridge University Press).

Carlyle, T. (1851) *The Life of John Sterling* (London: Chapman and Hall).

Christie, W. D. (1873) *John Stuart Mill and Mr Abraham Hayward* (London: Henry S. King).

Comte, A. (1830-1842) *Cours de Philosophie Positive*, 6 vols. (Paris: Bachclier).

Conway, M. D. (1873) *In Memoriam: A Memorial Discourse in Honour of John Stuart Mill; with Hymns and Readings* (Finsbury: South Place Chapel, 25 May).

[Cooke Taylor, W.] (1843) "Reviews," *Athenaeum* 842 (16 Dec.): 1101–02.

Courtney, W. L. (1889) *Life of John Stuart Mill* (London: Walter Scott).

Courtney, W. P. (1898) "Taylor, William Cooke," in S. Lee (ed.) *The Dictionary of National Biography*, vol. 55 (London: Smith, Elder): 478–79.

Davis, K. W. (1964) "A Bibliography of the Writings of William Henry Smith," *Library* s5-XIX (1): 162–74.

De Morgan, A. (1847) *Formal Logic: Or, The Calculus of Inference, Necessary and Probable* (London: Taylor and Walton).

Demetriou, K. N.; Loizides, A., eds. (2013a) *John Stuart Mill: A British Socrates* (Basingstoke: Palgrave Macmillan).

Demetriou, K. N.; Loizides, A. (2013b) "Introduction," in K. N. Demetriou and A. Loizides (eds.) *John Stuart Mill: A British Socrates* (Basingstoke: Palgrave Macmillan): 1–16.

Devigne, R. (2006) *Reforming Liberalism; J. S. Mill's Use of Ancient, Religious, Liberal, and Romantic Moralities* (New Haven: Yale University Press).

Donner, W.; Fumerton, R. (2009) *Mill* (Malden, MA: Wiley-Blackwell).

Ducheyne, S. (2008) "J.S. Mill's Canons of Induction: From True Causes to Provisional Ones," *History and Philosophy of Logic* 29 (4): 361–76.

Duncan, D. (1908) *The Life and Letters of Herbert Spencer* (London: Methuen).

Ellis, E. E. (1888) *Memoir of William Ellis and an Account of his Conduct-Teaching* (London: Longmans, Green).

Fox, C. (1882) *Memories of Old Friends; Being Extracts from the Journals and Letters of Caroline Fox from 1835 to 1871*, H. N. Pym (ed.), 2 vols., 2nd ed. (London: Smith, Elder).

[Fraser, A. C.] (1860) "Province of Logic and Recent British Logicians," *North British Review* 33 (66): 401–27.

Frege, G. (1884) *The Foundations of Arithmetic*, J. L. Austin (trans.), 2nd ed. (New York: Harper and Brothers, 1960).

Green, T. H. (1885) *Works*, R. L. Nittleship (ed.), 3 vols. (London: Longmans, Greens)

Grote, G. (1866) "Review of John Stuart Mill on the Philosophy of Sir William Hamilton," in A. Bain (ed.) *The Minor Works of George Grote* (London: John Murray, 1873): 277–330.

Grote, H. (1873) *The Personal Life of George Grote*, 2nd ed. (London: John Murray).

[Hamilton, W.] (1833) "Recent Publications on Logical Science," *Edinburgh Review* 57 (115): 194–238.

———. (1860) *Lectures on Logic*, H. L. Mansel and J. Veitch (eds.), 2 vols. (Edinburgh and London: William Blackwood).

[Hayward, A.] (1873) "John Stuart Mill," *Times* (10 May): 5.

Holyoake, G. J. (1873) *John Stuart Mill: As Some of the Working Classes Knew Him* (London: Trübner).

Hunter, R. A. (1873) "His Position as a Philosopher," in H. R. Fox-Bourne (ed) *John Stuart Mill: Notices of his Life and Work; together with Two Papers Written by Him on the Land Question. Reprinted from the Examiner* (London: E. Dallow).

[Hutton, R. H.] (1850) "Mill and Whewell on the Logic of Induction," *Prospective Review* 6 (21): 77–111.

[Jennings, W.] (1854) "Tendencies of Modern Logic," *Dublin Review* 36 (72): 419–51.

Jevons, S. W. (1877) "John Stuart Mill's Philosophy Tested I," *Contemporary Review* 31 (Dec.): 167–82.

———. (1878a) "John Stuart Mill's Philosophy Tested II," *Contemporary Review* 31 (Jan.): 256–75.

———. (1878b) "John Stuart Mill's Philosophy Tested III," *Contemporary Review* 32 (Apr.): 88–99.

————. (1879) "John Stuart Mill's Philosophy Tested IV," *Contemporary Review* 36 (Nov.): 521–38.

Johnson, D. A. (1981) "Popular Apologetics in Late Victorian England: The Work of the Christian Evidence Society," *Journal of Religious History* 11 (4): 558–77.

Killick, A. H. (1870) *The Student's Handbook; Synoptical and Explanatory of Mr J.S. Mill's System of Logic* (London: Longmans, Green, Reader and Dyer).

Kneale W.; Kneale, M. (1962) *The Development of Logic* (Oxford: Clarendon Press).

Kubitz, O. A. (1932) *Development of John Stuart Mill's System of Logic* (Urbana: University of Illinois, *Illinois Studies in the Social Sciences* 18 (1–2)).

Lady Eastlake [Rigby, E.] (1880) *Mrs Grote: A Sketch*, 2nd ed. (London: John Murray).

Leary, P. (1998) "'Our Chief Speculative Monument of this Age': The Publishing of Mill's Logic," *Publishing History* 44: 39–57.

Leechman, J. (1836) *Logic: Designed as an Introduction to the Study of Reasoning*, 2nd ed. (Glasgow: James Maclehose, 1845).

Levy, J. H. (1873) "His Work in Philosophy," in H. R. Fox-Bourne (ed) *John Stuart Mill: Notices of his Life and Work; together with Two Papers Written by Him on the Land Question. Reprinted from the Examiner* (London: E. Dallow): 36–44.

Loizides, A. (2013) *John Stuart Mill's Platonic Heritage: Happiness through Character* (Lanham, MD: Lexington Books).

[Macaulay, T. B.] (1829) "Mill's *Essay on Government*: Utilitarian Logic and Politics," *Edinburgh Review* 49 (97): 159–89.

Masson, D. (1866) *Recent British Philosophy* (New York: D. Appleton).

[Maurice, F. D.] (1828) "Sketches of Contemporary Authors; No. XIII.—Mr. James Mill," *The Athenaeum; London Literary and Critical Journal* 34 (18 June): 527–29.

[————.] Rusticus (1835) *Subscription No Bondage* (Oxford: J. H. Parker).

McCosh, J. (1866) *An Examination of Mr J. S. Mill's Philosophy Being a Defence of the Fundamental Truth* (London: Macmillan).

————. (1870) *The Laws of Discursive Thought Being a Text-book of Formal Logic*, rev. ed. (New York: Charles Scribner's Sons, 1892).

McRae, R. F. (1974) "Introduction," in J. M. Robson (ed.), vols. VII and VIII of *Collected Works of John Stuart Mill*, (London/Toronto: Routledge and Kegan Paul/ University of Toronto Press): xxi–xlviii.

Mill, J. (1815) "Elements of the Philosophy of the Human Mind. By Dugald Stewart. Volume Second," *British Review and London Critical Journal* VI (Aug.): 170–200.

————. (1826) "Formation of Opinions," *Westminster Review* 6 (2): 1–23.

————. (1829) *Analysis of the Phenomena of the Human Mind*, ed. J. S. Mill, with notes by J. S. Mill, A. Bain, A. Findlater and G. Grote, 2 vols., 2nd rev. ed. (London: Longmans, Green, Reader and Dyer, 1878).

————. (2010) *Commonplace Books*, R. A. Fenn and K. Grint (eds.), 4 vols. (SCIH and London Library: www.intellectualhistory.net/mill).

Mill, J. S. (1820–1821) "Traité de Logique," in vol. XXVI (1988) of Mill (1963–1991): 145–90.

————. (1838) "Bentham," in vol. X (1969) of Mill (1963–1991): 77–115.

————. (1843) *A System of Logic, Ratiocinative and Inductive: Being a Connected View of the Principles of Evidence and the Methods of Scientific Investigation*, in vols. VII and VIII (1974) of Mill (1963–1991).

————. (1859) *On Liberty*, in vol. XVIII (1977) of Mill (1963–1991).

————. (1861) *Utilitarianism*, in vol. X (1969) of Mill (1963–1991).

————. (1865) *An Examination of Sir William Hamilton's Philosophy and of the Principal Philosophical Questions Discussed in His Writings*, in vol. IX (1979) of Mill (1963–1991).

————. (1873a) *Autobiography*, in vol. I (1981) of Mill (1963–1991).

————. (1873b) "Grote's Aristotle," in vol. XI (1978) of Mill (1963–1991): 473–510.

———. (1963–1991) *Collected Works of John Stuart Mill*, F.E.L. Priestly (gen. ed.), and subsequently J. M. Robson, 33 vols. (London/Toronto: Routledge and Kegan Paul/University of Toronto Press).

Mineka, F. E. (1972) "John Stuart Mill and Neo-Malthusianism, 1873," *Mill Newsletter* 8 (1): 3–10.

[Mozley, J. R.] (1869) "The Different Schools of Elementary Logic," *North British Review* 51 (101): 71–96.

———. (1872) "Mr John Stuart Mill and His School," *Quarterly Review* 133 (265): 77–118.

Peckhaus, V. (2009) "The Mathematical Origins of Nineteenth-Century Algebra of Logic," in L. Haaparanta (ed.) *The Development of Modern Logic* (Oxford: Oxford University Press): 159–95.

Robson, J. M. (1966) "Harriet Taylor and John Stuart Mill: Artist and Scientist," *Queen's Quarterly* 73 (2): 167–86.

———. (1974) "Textual Introduction," in F.J.M. Robson (ed.), vols. VII and VIII of *Collected Works of John Stuart Mill* (London/Toronto: Routledge and Kegan Paul/ University of Toronto Press): xlix-cviii.

Rosen, F. (2013a) *Mill* (Oxford: Oxford University Press).

———. (2013b) "The Philosophy of Error and Liberty of Thought: J. S. Mill on Logical Fallacies," in K. N. Demetriou and A. Loizides (eds.) *John Stuart Mill: A British Socrates* (Basingstoke: Palgrave Macmillan): 17–48.

Russell, B. (1956) *Portraits from Memory and Other Essays* (New York: Simon and Schuster).

Ryan, A. (1970) *The Philosophy of John Stuart Mill*, 2nd ed. (New Jersey: Humanities Press International, 1990).

Scarre, G. (1989) *Logic and Reality in the Philosophy of John Stuart Mill* (Dordrecht: Kluwer Academic Publishers).

Schultz, B. (2004) *Henry Sidgwick: Eye of the Universe, An Intellectual Biography* (Cambridge: Cambridge University Press).

Sigwart, C. (1889) *Logic*, H. Dendy (trans.), 2 vols., 2nd ed. (London: Swan Sonnenschein, 1895).

Simcox, E. J. (1873) "On the Influence of John Stuart Mill's Writings," *Contemporary Review* 22 (June): 297–317.

Skorupski, J. M. (1989) *John Stuart Mill* (London and New York: Routledge).

Smiles, S., ed. (1891) *A Publisher and his Friends; Memoir and Correspondence of John Murray with an Account of the Origin and Progress of the House 1768–1843*, T. Mackay (ed.) (London: Murray, 1911).

[Smith, W. H.] (1843) "Mill's Logic," *Blackwood's Edinburgh Magazine* 54 (336): 415–30.

Special Report from the Select Committee on the Oxford and Cambridge Universities Education Bill; together with the Proceedings of the Committee, Minutes of Evidence, and Appendix (House of Commons, 31 July 1867).

[Spencer, H.] (1853) "The Universal Postulate," *Westminster Review* 60 (118): 513–50.

———. (1855) *The Principles of Psychology* (London: Longman, Brown, Green, and Longmans).

———. (1865) "Mill versus Hamilton—The Test of Truth," in *Essays: Scientific, Political and Speculative, Vol. II*, (London and Edinburgh: Williams and Norgate, 1891): 188–218.

Stack, D. (2011) "The Death of John Stuart Mill," *Historical Journal* 54 (1): 167–90.

Stebbing, W. (1864) *Analysis of Mr Mill's System of Logic*, new ed. (London: Longmans, Green, 1888).

Taine, H. (1861) "Philosophie Anglaise Contemporaine—John Smart Mill et son Système de Logique," *Revue des Deux Mondes* 32 (1 Mar.): 44–82.

———. (1873) *English Positivism. A Study on John Stuart Mill*, T. D. Haye (trans.), 2nd ed. (London: Williams and Norgate).

[———.] (1904) *Life and Letters of H. Taine, 1853–1870*, R. L. Devonshire (trans.) (Westminster: Archibald Constable).

Taylor, A. (1892) *Memories of a Student, 1838–1888* (Chudleigh: H. A. Crook; privately printed).

Tulloch, J. (1855) *Theism: The Witness of Reason and Nature to an All-Wise and Beneficent Creator* (Edinburgh and London: William Blackwood and Sons).

Urbinati, N. (2002) *Mill on Democracy: From the Athenian Polis to Representative Government* (Chicago: University of Chicago Press).

Van Evra, J. (2000) "The Development of Logic as Reflected in the Fate of the Syllogism 1600–1900," *History and Philosophy of Logic* 21: 115–34.

Varouxakis, G. (2013) *Liberty Abroad: J. S. Mill on International Relations* (Cambridge: Cambridge University Press).

Vilkko, R. (2009) "The Logic Question during the First Half of the Nineteenth Century," in L. Haaparanta (ed.) *The Development of Modern Logic* (Oxford: Oxford University Press): 203–21.

Wallas, G. (1898) *The Life of Francis Place, 1771–1854*, rev. ed. (London: George Allen and Unwin, 1918).

Ward, W. (1889) *William George Ward and the Oxford Movement*, 2nd ed. (London: Macmillan, 1890).

[Ward, W. G.] (1843a) "Notices of Books," *British Critic, and Quarterly Theological Review* 33 (66): 538–53.

[———.] (1843b) "Mill's *Logic*," *British Critic, and Quarterly Theological Review* 34 (68): 349–427.

———. (1844) *The Ideal of a Christian Church* (London: James Toovey).

[———.] (1871) "Mr Mill's Denial of Necessary Truth," *Dublin Review* 27 (53): 285–318.

[———.] (1874) "Mr Mill's Denial of Freewill," *Dublin Review* 22 (44): 326–61.

[———.] (1876) "Mr Mill on Causation," *Dublin Review* 27 (53): 57–82.

Whately, R. (1826) *Elements of Logic; Comprising the Substance of the Article in the Encyclopaedia Metropolitana, with Additions* (London: Mawman).

Whewell, W. (1840) *The Philosophy of the Inductive Sciences Founded upon their History*, 2 vols., 2nd ed. (London: John W. Parker, 1847).

———. (1849) *Of Induction: With Especial Reference to Mr. J. Stuart Mill's System of Logic* (London: John W. Parker).

1   Mill on Names[1]

Stephen P. Schwartz

Bertrand Russell is dismissive of Mill's *A System of Logic* (1843), which he first read when he was eighteen. Although initially he greatly admired it, he came to think that "[e]verything that Mill has to say in his *Logic* about matters other than inductive inference is perfunctory and conventional."[2] Russell is especially scornful of Mill's treatment of names. "On the subject of names, with which modern logic has been much concerned, what he has to say is totally inadequate."[3] Russell is here referring to Mill on proper names, but he is only slightly less scornful of Mill's theory of Kind names.

Russell does not expound his objections to Mill's theory of proper names, but we can surmise them when we soon come to contrast Mill's theory with Russell's distinctly different view of proper names. Ironically the dominant contemporary opinion is that Mill is insightful about proper names and Russell's approach to ordinary proper names is clearly and demonstrably "totally inadequate." Saul Kripke, in his groundbreaking *Naming and Necessity* (1972), famously resurrected Mill's theory of proper names. The situation with general names, which we would now call general terms,[4] is less clear. A great deal of attention recently has been paid to natural kind terms, which Mill called Kind names, by Kripke, Hilary Putnam, and others. Although the Kripke-Putnam account of natural kind terms diverges from Mill's, much remains controversial. As it turns out, Russell's rejection of Mill on natural kinds is as out of step as his critique of Mill on proper names.

I.

Ordinary proper names such as "John Stuart Mill," "the United Nations" and "Alaska" present several puzzles for logicians and philosophers of language. Although my dictionary, *The American College Dictionary*, includes an entry for J. S. Mill (and one for his father James Mill) it does not give a definition in the usual sense: "Mill, John Stuart, 1806–73, British philosopher and economist." That's it. My dictionary does not use precisely these words for any other thinker, but I note that other dictionaries "define" "J. S. Mill,"

"Jeremy Bentham," "Adam Smith" and "John Maynard Keynes" each as "British philosopher and economist," differing only in dates.

It seems, however, that dictionaries ought not contain proper names. For one thing, which ones to include is arbitrary. A standard American dictionary will leave out obscure or obsolete words of English, but even an unabridged dictionary would have to leave out a vast number of proper names. Furthermore, names just do not seem to have definitions in anything like the usual sense. "Alaska" is a proper name of a place or a whole collection of places. We could give all sorts of facts about Alaska, such as that it is the northernmost state of the US, it is the forty-ninth state, admitted in 1959, and so on. Indeed my dictionary, which I have had since my school days, "defines" "Alaska" as a territory of the US. Did the meaning of "Alaska"—the name—change when Alaska was admitted to the Union? Did the meaning of "Pluto" change when Pluto was demoted from planethood? My dictionary also gives the population of Alaska. Surely the meaning of "Alaska," if it has one, does not include facts about population, otherwise the meaning would change every time a new Alaskan baby was born. But then why are these facts included in a dictionary that purports to give the meanings of words? My dictionary defines "dictionary" as a book giving the meanings of words in a language and other facts about them (e.g., pronunciation, part of speech, etc.). But then a dictionary of the English language, as my dictionary purports to be, ought not to contain proper names, because they are not part of the English language. Is "John Stuart Mill" a word (or words) of the English language? Is it not also used without alteration in French, German and Italian texts? My dictionary also contains entries for Bach, Beethoven and Kant. Proper names clearly "mean" and function differently from general terms like "tiger," "computer" or "grandmother," which clearly do belong in a dictionary.

These are puzzles about proper names, and a simple and clear way to solve them, and other more trenchant puzzles as Kripke claimed, is to deny that proper names have meanings or definitions at all (and thus do not belong in dictionaries). This is precisely the path that Mill takes in *A System of Logic*.

II.

Mill distinguishes between general names, which we will discuss in more detail later, and singular or individual names, which is our current topic. A general name, such as "tiger" or "grandmother" may correctly apply to many individuals, whereas a singular name, such as "J. S. Mill" or "the current president of the US," applies to at most one. Mill draws other distinctions, such as between concrete and abstract names, which are subsidiary for us here. He states that one of the most important distinctions is between connotative and non-connotative names. Mill insists that proper names are non-connotative.

Any term, general or singular, according to Mill, and the entire linguistic tradition since, may have either a denotation or a connotation or both. Standardly a general term would have both. The denotation of a term is the thing or things that the term refers to. A concrete general term such as "grandmother" denotes the individuals that are correctly called grandmothers. The connotation of the term "grandmother," on the other hand, includes the attributes (properties or qualities) that an individual must have to be correctly called a grandmother—being the mother of a parent. In technical contexts the connotation is often called the intension of the term, whereas the denotation is often called the extension of the term.[5] In non-technical contexts "connotation" has come to mean something different from the meaning that Mill gave it. "Connotation" has come to mean the notions or ideas loosely and culturally associated with a term. For Mill the connotation (i.e., intension) of a term is tightly connected to it. For a term that has a connotation, and all concrete general terms have connotations according to Mill, it is the meaning of the term and it is given by a good definition of it. The denotation depends on the connotation. If an item has the attributes in the connotation of a general term, then it is denoted by the term, otherwise not. This makes for a very neat theory. It explains all sorts of things about language. We can communicate using the term "grandmother" because we grasp the connotation of the word. When we assert a proposition we state that the subject has the attributes connoted by the predicate, and so on.

Mill's claim, then, is that proper names have no connotations. "Proper names are not connotative: they denote the individuals who are called by them; but they do not indicate or imply any attributes as belonging to those individuals."[6] As we have seen, this is initially plausible and has sometimes been called the conventional or naïve theory of proper names.[7] The most compelling point in its favor is that the name "John Stuart Mill" does not itself tell us anything about the bearer beyond some facts based on our general knowledge of the practices of naming: e.g., that Mill's father was also named Mill, that he was male and that most likely his parents or namers spoke English. But these are mere surmises. "John Stuart Mill" might be the name of a female Bengal tiger that was named by a Hindi-speaking maharaja. On the other hand, if I say "J. S. Mill was a philosopher," I have ascribed certain properties to him with the use of the concrete general term "philosopher"—those that are included in the connotation of "philosopher." This is why proper names do not belong in a dictionary but such words as "philosopher" do. Proper names have no definitions; they are non-connotative according to Mill.

We certainly have ideas or images connected to the proper names that we use and a proper name brings these ideas to mind, but the ideas are not definitional. General terms also invoke such ideas or images. I may think of cookies and milk and warm smiles when I think of a grandmother, but these are not part of the definition or intension of the term "grandmother," even for me. Likewise the images or ideas that I have when I think of J. S. Mill are not part of the connotation (definition, intension) of the name, nor are the facts mentioned in the dictionary entry under that name.

> When we impose a proper name . . . [w]e put a mark, not indeed upon the object itself, but if I may so speak, upon the idea of the object. A proper name is but an unmeaning mark which we connect in our minds with the idea of the object, in order that whenever the mark meets our eyes or occurs to our thoughts, we may think of that individual object.[8]

Of course, that individual object is the denotation of the name. The key phrase to note in this quote is "unmeaning mark." For Mill, names are unmeaning marks for objects named.[9]

Even when a proper name appears to be descriptive it is not, or at least the description is not part of a supposed connotation of the name. Mill notes that people are named "Johnson" whose fathers are not named "John." Mill also remarks that the name "Dartmouth" would still be the name of that town even if the River Dart changed its course. Such names as "the United Nations," "the Holy Roman Empire" and "the Democratic People's Republic of Korea" (which is the name of North Korea) merely tag independently of their descriptive meaning—that is the name of North Korea even though North Korea is not democratic and not a people's republic. These examples also illustrate that we cannot always tell a proper name by its surface form. A singular name such as "the father of J. S. Mill" does have both a connotation and denotation, according to Mill, and is not a proper name. To state "James Mill was the father of J. S. Mill" does convey information about James Mill and that information is conveyed by the phrase "the father of J. S. Mill."[10]

According to Mill, then, a singular name has a denotation of at most one, unlike a general name that potentially denotes several individuals. A proper name is a mere tag of an individual that it denotes, but has no connotation (i.e., no intension, no dictionary definition). It may invoke ideas and images, but these are not part of the connotation of the proper name. The name is unmeaning. This is a simple, clear theory that solves certain puzzles about names as I mentioned above. Unfortunately, it is faced with other severe puzzles. These other puzzles are what led Russell to deem Mill's theory of proper names to be "totally inadequate."

III.

We will consider two puzzles here. Either of these is sufficient to undermine confidence in Mill's theory of proper names. Until Kripke, most philosophers followed Russell and thought that these puzzles buried Mill's theory. As we will see this judgment was hasty.

Puzzle #1: Many names name individuals who are no longer with us. Socrates no longer exists nor does J. S. Mill. How then can a name be a mere tag of something that does not exist? Likewise, we have names for fictional characters such as Hamlet. How can a name name something non-existent? Mill states that giving a proper name is like putting a chalk mark on a house so that we can distinguish it from others. Although he does say, perhaps recognizing the puzzle under discussion, that we put the mark upon the idea or image. But we cannot put a mark upon Socrates or Hamlet. Others may have put a mark, his name, upon Socrates, but to continue the metaphor once the house is gone, so is the chalk mark upon it. Mill struggles with this issue. In discussing the chalk mark analogy Mill ends by writing that the proper name with its attendant ideas and images enables us ". . . to know that what we find asserted in a proposition of which it is the subject, is asserted of the individual thing with which we were previously acquainted."[11] Was I previously acquainted with Socrates? With Hamlet?[12]

Because of this issue, Russell held that we could only have genuine proper names for objects that we are immediately acquainted with.

> The names that we commonly use, like 'Socrates', are really abbreviations for descriptions; not only that, but what they describe are not particulars but complicated systems of classes or series. A name, in the narrow sense of a word whose meaning is a particular, can only be applied to a particular with which the speaker is acquainted, because you cannot name anything you are not acquainted with . . . We are not acquainted with Socrates, and therefore cannot name him.[13]

So Russell, contrary to Mill, held that the ideas and images that we associate with an ordinary proper name such as "Socrates" or "Hamlet" comprise a connotation, a meaning in the strict sense. Thus the name "Socrates" means in Mill's sense of connotation "the ancient philosopher who wrote nothing, but founded the discipline of philosophy, was the teacher of Plato" and so on. "Hamlet" would also have a descriptive definition. Viewed this way "Socrates" and "Hamlet" would have connotations but no denotations if the denotation is supposed to be an individual named—the exact opposite of Mill's theory. If we want a uniform theory, and of course we do, we cannot stop with names of the deceased and fictional characters, but must view all ordinary proper names as connotative, the connotation being just those ideas and images that Mill mentions. If the object named is still around and not fictional or deceased, then the name would also have a denotation.

One possible way for a Millian to escape having to postulate connotations for names as a result of this puzzle is to insist that Socrates and Hamlet do exist right now today and thus can be tagged. Although they do not exist concretely, they exist abstractly. They no longer have a place or concrete presence (Hamlet never did), but they persist eternally as abstract objects.[14] Such a postulation is, however, at odds with Mill's fundamentally down-to-earth scientific philosophy. He does allow that abstract singular names such as "whiteness" denote attributes, but these are physically realized. Mill in

A System of Logic rejects the notion that there are abstract, eternal, platonic mathematical and geometrical objects. Surely allowing proper names to be connotative is a much less jarring move for a scientifically minded philosopher than is populating a platonic heaven with vast hordes of abstract people, cats, dogs, places, institutions, etc. In any case, it would still be puzzling how we could be directly acquainted with such abstract eternal individuals.

Puzzle #2: This second puzzle was considered to be even more serious than the first. It was originally propounded by Frege in his essay "On Sense and Reference" (1892) and is often called Frege's Puzzle. Frege gives a very succinct and compelling argument that names must have connotations. Adding to the terminological confusion, Frege calls the connotation (i.e., intension) of a name its sense (*Sinn* in German), whereas he calls its denotation the reference (*Bedeutung*), thus the original title of his classical article "Über Sinn und Bedeutung."

At the very beginning of his essay Frege notes that "a = a" differs from "a = b" in cognitive content. Assuming that "a = b" is true it is not likely to be obviously true. Clearly one could believe "a = a" and not believe "a = b" even if both were true. This can poignantly occur when an individual has two different proper names. A famous example is:

1) Hesperus = Hesperus
2) Hesperus = Phosphorus

The first is trivial, but the second was an interesting discovery. Both "Hesperus" and "Phosphorus" are names of the same object—Venus. On Mill's theory, then, they have the same denotation, and since they have no connotations but are mere unmeaning tags, we find nothing to distinguish them except their lexical shape. Thus 1) would have the same cognitive content as 2). But it does not. Frege also argued that these sorts of problems infect other contexts such as propositional attitude statements about beliefs, desires, and doubts. Thus, again assuming that we want a uniform theory of proper names, Mill's theory would be deemed "totally inadequate" as Russell claimed. "It is obvious that with a sign (name, phrase or written character), besides the indicated object which we may call the reference, there is also connected what I would like to call the sense of the sign, which contains the manner of presentation."[15]

Nor can we appeal to the ideas and images that according to Mill are loosely associated with a name to solve Frege's Puzzle. They might help explain the difference in the cognitive significance of 1) versus 2), but the differences go deeper. 1) is *a priori*, whereas 2) is *a posteriori*. This can only be based on a difference in meaning between 1) and 2), which in turn must be a difference in meaning between the two names. Which in turn entails that they each have a meaning, i.e., they have a connotation in Mill's sense.

As mentioned above, this is the approach Russell takes with ordinary proper names. Each has a definition or connotation and many also have denotations that are complex constructed objects.

> The name "Romulus" is not really a name but a sort of truncated description. It stands for a person who did such-and-such things, who killed Remus, and founded Rome, and so on. It is short for that description; if you like, it is short for "the person who was called 'Romulus'".[16]

According to Russell, all the proper names of our common language are disguised descriptions.

> What are commonly called proper names—e.g. "Socrates"—can if I am right, be defined in terms of qualities and spatio-temporal relations, and this definition is an actual analysis [i.e. gives the meaning or connotation]. Most subject-predicate propositions, such as "Socrates is snub-nosed," assert that a certain quality, named by the predicate, is one of a bundle of qualities named by the subject.[17]

From the time of Frege until the Kripke Revolution all prominent philosophers of language assumed some version of the description theory of the connotations of proper names and rejected Mill's account, though there were differences in detail. Wittgenstein and others moved toward a cluster theory, which John Searle characterizes as follows:

> [S]uppose we ask, "Why do we have proper names at all?" Obviously to refer to individuals. "Yes, but descriptions could do that for us." But only at the cost of specifying identity conditions every time reference is made: suppose we agree to drop "Aristotle" and use, say, "the teacher of Alexander", then it is a necessary truth that the man referred to is Alexander's teacher—but it is a contingent fact that Aristotle ever went into pedagogy (though I am suggesting that it is a necessary fact that Aristotle has the logical sum, inclusive disjunction, of properties commonly attributed to him).[18]

The reason it is a necessary fact, according to the cluster theory, is that the connotation in Mill's sense of the name "Aristotle" is a cluster—a disjunction—of attributes, rather than a conjunction. This reflects the fact that we may discover that Aristotle did not have some of the attributes usually attributed to him.

The description theory of proper names solves the puzzles that Mill's purely denotative theory of proper names stumbles over. It tells us how we can refer to historical figures that no longer exist and how we can talk about fictional characters. It solves Frege's puzzle about co-denotative proper names. It fits proper names in with the rest of language that contains general terms that have descriptive definitions. As Kripke puts it succinctly: "Frege and Russell, then, appear to give the natural account of how reference is determined [by proper names]; Mill appears to give none."[19]

IV.

The only problem with the Frege-Russell description theory of proper names, as Kripke demonstrated, is that it is wrong. Mill was closer to the truth about proper names. Typically, ordinary proper names are non-descriptive.

The key arguments against the description theory are due to Kripke.[20] I will only briefly summarize them here.[21] One of the key arguments is a modal argument; the other is an epistemological argument.

Mill might not have approved of the modal argument since it smacks of hoary metaphysics, but we are going to field it anyway. There is a possible world in which Aristotle did nothing that is usually attributed to him, contrary to Searle's claim. "It would seem that it's a contingent fact that Aristotle ever did *any* of the things commonly attributed to him today, *any* of these great achievements that we so much admire."[22] Aristotle might have died as a child in a plague that swept his home town. I am not talking about somebody else. I am talking about Aristotle, that very man. This entails that Searle is wrong, and so is Russell. For example, surely Julius Caesar might have been named something else by his parents or whoever named him. This demonstrates that none of the features, ideas, images that we commonly associate with a proper name are part of a connotation of the name, otherwise these counterfactual situations would be impossible, just as it is impossible for someone to be a grandmother in some possible world but not be the mother of a parent. If the name "Julius Caesar" means "the man uniquely named 'Julius Caesar'" as Russell claims, then it is necessarily true that Julius Caesar is named that. But it's not. So Russell is wrong. Nor is it necessarily true that Caesar crossed the Rubicon or did any of the things usually attributed to him.

The second argument is epistemological. If Frege, Russell and Searle are correct, then the descriptions, ideas, images associated with a name are part of its Millian connotation. This entails that such sentences as "Aristotle was the teacher of Plato" and "Aristotle was the teacher of Plato or the author of the *Nicomachean Ethics* . . . or was the teacher of Alexander the Great" are *a priori* and analytic. But they are not. Clearly, Russell was sensitive to this problem which is why he defines "Julius Caesar" as the man named "Julius Caesar." That does seem to be *a priori* and analytic. But it is not despite appearances. It might not even be true. Maybe the historians got it all mixed up and his name was actually something else. In general we can conceive of discovering that any of the descriptions, ideas, images associated with an individual are not true of him. People are concerned to discover if Shakespeare really did write all those plays and sonnets. If "the author of all those plays and sonnets" is part of the meaning of the name "William Shakespeare," then they are wasting their time (I think they are anyway), because it is true by definition that Shakespeare was the author of those plays. But clearly it is not. We could discover that Gödel did not discover the incompleteness of arithmetic, but that someone else did and that Gödel was a huge fraud. (I am *not* saying that this is likely or that I expect this.) This demonstrates that none of these facts are parts of the definitions of the names. Indeed typically ordinary proper names have no connotations, i.e., no intensions, no meanings, no definitions, no Fregean senses.

Mill was right about proper names, and Russell's theory is patently false and "totally inadequate." Why did Russell *et al.* stick to it with such persistence and not notice such evident failings? Because of the eminence of Frege and his puzzle. This was not stupid. Why was Kripke able, so easily really, to overturn the description theory of names? Because Kripke elaborates the non-connotative theory of proper names and argues for it in more detail than did Mill.

Kripke suggests possible solutions to some of the puzzles we discussed. **Puzzle #1:** Kripke sketches a causal- or historical-chain theory of the reference of proper names. A child is given the name "Socrates" by his parents (say). Then the name is handed on generation after generation in a continuous chain in which current users intend to use the name the same way as those they got it from. This requires a practice or institution of using names and of handing them on and maintaining reference. Kripke's discussion of this is worth quoting at length because it contains a lot of wisdom about proper names that Mill would approve of.

> A speaker . . . who has heard about, say Richard Feynman, in the market place or elsewhere, may be referring to Richard Feynman even though he can't remember from whom he first heard of Feynman or from whom he ever heard of Feynman. He knows that Feynman was a famous physicist. A certain passage of communication reaching ultimately to the man himself does reach the speaker. He then is referring to Feynman even though he can't identify him uniquely . . . [B]ut, instead, a chain of communication going back to Feynman himself has been established, by virtue of his membership in a community which passed the name on from link to link, not by a ceremony that he makes in private in his study: "By 'Feynman' I shall mean the man who did such and such and such and such."[23]

Kripke's theory also solves other subsidiary puzzles. Many individuals have been named "Socrates." How does a particular use of that name refer to one of those individuals and not another? Mill would mention the differing ideas and images. A Russellian would ruefully shake his head despondent over the vagueness and ambiguity infecting ordinary language. More fruitful is to note that the difference rests on the difference between the causal chain linking my use of "Socrates" in philosophy discussions with that great man and, e.g., the causal chain linking my use of "Socrates" when talking about my friend's cat. Contexts and intentions determine which causal chain is in play. It is curious to note that the cat's name "Socrates" is also causally linked in a roundabout way to Socrates, but it is the wrong sort of link, so it is not a name of Socrates (the ancient Greek, not the cat). Obviously, a lot is still left to be sorted out, which is why Kripke refused to call his theory a theory, but only a sketch or a picture of how names get their reference.[24]

Puzzle #2—Frege's Puzzle: Alas, this continues to be of concern for Mill's theory of proper names. Kripke claimed that typically proper names are rigid designators. Roughly, a rigid designator refers to the same individual when talking about other possible worlds as it does in the actual world. Nobody else is Aristotle in any other possible world, according to Kripke. Likewise nothing else but Venus is Hesperus or Phosphorus. According, then, to this view both

1) Hesperus = Hesperus
2) Hesperus = Phosphorus

are necessarily true—true in every possible world in which Venus exists. 1) is *a priori* but 2) is *a posteriori*. Thus 2) is necessary but *a posteriori*. This goes some way to clarifying the issues involved in Frege's Puzzle, and we will shortly see that necessary *a posteriori* propositions play a key role in the semantics of natural kind terms. But it looks like we need some sort of Fregean sense to explain the difference between 1) and 2). Surely, however, it cannot be anything like Russell's proposals if we are to have a uniform theory of proper names.[25] Furthermore Frege's Puzzle is not unique to Mill's theory. Recent work indicates Frege's Puzzle infects many theories of content, including Frege's own.[26]

V.

In the mid-1970s Kripke and Putnam pioneered the theory that natural kind terms such as "gold," "tiger" and "water," as well as more technical scientific kind terms, are semantically like proper names. Their view is that natural kind terms are to be thought of as non-connotative rigid designator proper names of natural kinds. In this they diverge from Mill for whom all concrete general names are connotative, although Mill does distinguish between Kind names and other concrete general terms in other ways. Again, Kripke is worth quoting at length:

> According to the view I advocate, then, terms for natural kinds are much closer to proper names than is ordinarily supposed . . . It is interesting to compare my views to those of Mill . . . He says of 'singular' names that they are connotative if they are definite descriptions but non-connotative if they are proper names. On the other hand, Mill says that *all* 'general' names are connotative; such a predicate as 'human being' is defined as the conjunction of certain properties which give necessary and sufficient conditions for humanity—rationality,

animality, and certain physical features. The modern logical tradition, as represented by Frege and Russell, seems to hold that Mill was wrong about singular names, but right about general names. More recent philosophy has followed suit . . . My own view, on the other hand, regards Mill as more-or-less right about "singular names," but wrong about "general" names . . . Certainly "cow" and "tiger" are *not* short for the conjunction of properties a dictionary would take to define them, as Mill thought.[27]

Kripke is being unfair to Mill here in that Mill's theory of natural kind terms is subtler and closer to Kripke's than we would gather from this passage. Also Russell did not approve of Mill's treatment of natural kind terms, because he felt that Mill took insufficient account of Darwin's theory of evolution.[28] Russell also misses the subtlety of Mill's ideas.

Mill distinguishes Kinds from other named sorts in that the members of a Kind share an unlimited number of attributes, many of which we are unlikely ever to fathom.

But if we contemplate any one of the classes so formed, such as the class animal or plant, or the class sulphur or phosphorus, or the class white or red, and consider in what particulars the individuals included in the class differ from those which do not come within it, we find a very remarkable diversity in this respect between some classes and others. There are some classes, the things contained in which differ from other things only in certain particulars which may be numbered, while others differ in more than can be numbered, more even than we need ever expect to know. Some classes have little or nothing in common to characterize them by, except precisely what is connoted by the name: white things, for example, are not distinguished by any common properties except whiteness; or if they are, it is only by such as are in some way dependent on, or connected with, whiteness. But a hundred generations have not exhausted the common properties of animals or of plants, of sulphur or of phosphorus; nor do we suppose them to be exhaustible, but proceed to new observations and experiments, in the full confidence of discovering new properties which were by no means implied in those we previously knew. While, if any one were to propose for investigation the common properties of all things which are of the same color, the same shape, or the same specific gravity, the absurdity would be palpable.[29]

The inexhaustible classes are, as Mill calls them, real Kinds or as we would now say natural kinds.

Mill is quite clear that Kind names are connotative and in places sounds like Kripke's caricature. "Of the innumerable properties, known and unknown, that are common to the class man, a portion only, and of course a very small portion, are connoted by its name."[30] And what are these salient properties connoted by "man"? "The word man, for instance, exclusively of what it connotes in common with animal, also connotes rationality, and at least some approximation to that external form, which we all know, but which, as we have no name for it considered in itself, we are content to call the human."[31] But Mill is sensitive to the fact that Kind terms acquire other, often more technical, connotations than "the conjunction of properties a dictionary would take to define them."

> Suppose, however, that being naturalists, we, for the purposes of our particular study, cut out of the genus animal the same species man, but with an intention that the distinction between man and all other species of animal should be, not rationality, but the possession of "four incisors in each jaw, tusks solitary, and erect posture." It is evident that the word man, when used by us as naturalists, no longer connotes rationality, but connotes the three other properties specified; for that which we have expressly in view when we impose a name, assuredly forms part of the meaning of that name . . . [B]ut the connotation may be special—not involved in the signification of the term as ordinarily used, but given to it when employed as a term of art or science.[32]

Astonishingly, and apparently unacknowledged by Kripke and others, Mill states concisely a view that is in the vicinity of the Kripke-Putnam theory of natural kind terms only to reject it.

> A word which carries on its face that it belongs to a nomenclature,[33] seems at first sight to differ from other concrete general names in this— that its meaning does not reside in its connotation, in the attributes implied in it, but in its denotation, that is, in the particular group of things which it is appointed to designate; and can not, therefore, be unfolded by means of a definition, but must be made known in another way. Mr. Whewell seems to incline to this opinion which, however, appears to me erroneous.[34]

Unfortunately Mill does not argue in any detail for his opinion in this matter. He does offer an alternative to Whewell's position.

> Words belonging to a nomenclature differ, I conceive, from other words mainly in this, that besides the ordinary connotation, they have a peculiar one of their own: besides connoting certain attributes, they also connote that those attributes are distinctive of a Kind. The term "peroxide of iron," for example, belonging by its form to the systematic nomenclature of chemistry, bears on its face that it is the name of a peculiar Kind of substance. It moreover connotes, like the name of any other class, some portion of the properties common to the class.[35]

Mill's suggestion, then, is that being a Kind is added to the connotation of Kind names. This is a reasonable alternative, but does not provide an answer to Kripke's powerful arguments that natural kind terms, at least many typical ones, are non-connotative. Kripke's arguments, if sound, demonstrate in opposition to Mill's view, that at least many common natural kind terms have no descriptive connotations and thus are like proper names.

Kripke's arguments that natural kind terms do not have descriptive connotations parallel his arguments about proper names. Again we can distinguish both a modal argument and an epistemological one. Again, I can only briefly summarize these arguments here.[36]

The epistemological argument is trickier than with proper names as we will shortly see. We can imagine discovering that, e.g., gold is not an element, not a metal, not yellow, not atomic number 79. We can imagine discovering that tigers are not animals. The claim that "all tigers are animals" is not refutable by a supposed individual tiger that is not an animal whereas all the rest are, but we could discover that our whole theory of tigers is mistaken and that none of the tigers are animals. Putnam states that we can imagine discovering that cats are robots sent from Mars to spy on us. We can imagine discovering that our chemical and physical theories are all wrong and that gold is not an element, and so on. Since we can imagine discovering these things, such statements as "All tigers are animals" or "Gold is an element" are not analytic and thus being an animal is not part of the meaning of "tiger" nor is being an element part of the meaning of "gold." These represent very well established empirical facts about tigers and gold. Presumably the same sort of considerations would eliminate any of the standard features of our natural kinds from being parts of definitions of the terms that name the kinds. Contrast this with, e.g., "grandmother." We could not imagine discovering that grandmothers are not the mothers of parents—that our whole theory of grandmothers is mistaken.[37]

The reason that the epistemological argument is tricky is that the modal argument seems to contradict it, but actually does not. According to Kripke, and this seems correct, nothing could be gold that was not atomic number 79, no substance could be water that was not H_2O, nothing could be a tiger that did not share the genetic code of tigers or some other similar underlying biological trait. Even if in some other possible world there is a substance that has all the marks and features that we associate with gold, it would not be gold unless it was atomic number 79; likewise another substance that mimicked all the properties of water that we observe would not be water unless it was H_2O. These other substances would be fool's gold or ersatz water. Putnam has us imagine Twin Earth, which is just like earth except that the lakes and rivers of Twin Earth are filled with XYZ instead of H_2O. XYZ exactly mimics all the superficial properties of water—it is potable, clear, freezes, etc.—but chemically it is not water. The inhabitants refer to their XYZ as "water." But it isn't.[38] These considerations indicate that none of the superficial observable characteristics are part of the definition of a natural kind term such as "gold," "water" or "tiger," otherwise any other substance that had those characteristics in any other possible world would be correctly called by the Kind name. But it isn't, so the characteristics are not part of the definitions of the terms. Indeed no characteristics are part of the definitions and they thus seem not to have Millian connotations. Nor is, e.g., being H_2O the new modern definition of "water." The epistemological argument shows that "Water is H_2O" is not analytic. Nor does it seem that others who are unaware of the chemical nature of water mean something other by "water" than does the scientist. Fundamental to the Kripke-Putnam view of natural kind terms is that they do not change meaning on the basis of new scientific discoveries. The Kripke-Putnam theory is that "All tigers are animals," "Gold is atomic number number79," and "Water is H_2O" are necessarily true. But also that they represent well-grounded empirical discoveries. Thus these are further examples of statements that are necessary but *a posteriori.*

The apparent conflict between the epistemological and the modal arguments is evident. How could we discover that, e.g., water is not H_2O when water is necessarily H_2O? The answer is that we could not. The claims most carefully stated are "If water is in fact H_2O, then it is necessarily H_2O," "If tigers are in fact animals, then nothing that was not an animal, no matter how closely it otherwise resembled our tigers, would be a tiger" and so on. The epistemological argument rests on the idea that it is consistent with our epistemic situation that we can imagine that the antecedents are false. This would not be the case if the claims were analytic. Contrary to Mill, Kripke denies that new discoveries involve change of meaning.

> Note that on the present view, scientific discoveries of species essence do not constitute a "change of meaning"; the possibility of such discoveries was part of the original enterprise. We need not even assume that the biologist's denial that whales are fish shows his "concept of fishhood" to be different from that of the layman; he simply corrects the layman, discovering that "whales are mammals, not fish" is a necessary truth. Neither "whales are mammals" *nor* "whales are fish" was supposed to be *a priori* or analytic in any case.[39]

In a remarkable anticipation of Kripke, Mill via a passage from Whewell discusses the example of whales:

> Whales are or are not fish according to the purpose for which we are considering them. "If we are speaking of the internal structure and physiology of the animal, we must not call them fish; for in these respects they deviate widely from fishes; they have warm blood, and produce and suckle their young as land quadrupeds do. But this would not prevent our speaking of the whale-fishery, and calling such animals fish on all occasions connected with this employment; for the relations thus arising depend upon the animal's living in the water, and being

caught in a manner similar to other fishes. A plea that human laws which mention fish do not apply to whales, would be rejected at once by an intelligent judge."[40]

I must side with Kripke on this. I cannot understand or believe that whales are fish in any literal sense. Nevertheless several philosophers have argued that Kripke and Putnam have exaggerated the non-connotivity of natural kind terms and argued for positions in some ways closer to Mill's, often without mentioning him except in passing. They point out that many of our natural kind terms have shifting and various meanings depending on context. The term "cedar," just to give one example, refers to a wide variety of trees but also in other contexts to wood that comes from many different types of trees in different parts of the world.[41] Mill's view that Kind names can have differing connotations when used by laypeople and scientists and that new discoveries are then included in an evolved connotation for technical purposes is a live option. Kripke's and Putnam's arguments that natural kind terms are non-connotative may gain plausibility from the very restricted set of examples they employ.

Finally Kripke's claim that natural kind terms are rigid designators has been questioned.[42] It is not clear what a natural kind term like "tiger" is to rigidly designate. (And Mill is not always entirely clear on what the denotation of a general term is.) With a rigid proper name the designation that stays the same from world to world is the individual named. The designation of a general term is usually taken to be its extension, but the extension of "tiger" changes from world to world. Some tigers that exist in the actual world fail to exist in other possible worlds and some tigers in those worlds do not exist in the actual world. But suppose we say that a natural kind term designates or denotes the kind or species. Thus the term "tiger" would denote not tigers but the kind or species *tiger*. Mill at one point embraces this view. "What is imperative, therefore, is not that the name [of a Kind] shall denote one particular collection of objects, but that it shall denote a Kind, and a lowest Kind. The form of the name declares that happen what will, it is to denote an *infima species*."[43] This seems like a natural proposal (although it is not without its difficulties).[44] However, if the Kind name denotes the Kind, then it also seems natural to treat the Kind name as just that—a proper name of the Kind. Much earlier in *A System of Logic* Mill suggests this at the same time as insisting "All concrete general names are connotative." He goes on immediately to state: "The word *man*, for example, denotes Peter, Jane, John, and an indefinite number of other individuals, of whom taken as a class, it is the name. But it is applied to them, because they possess, and to signify that they possess, certain attributes."[45] This seems sensible and in the vicinity of the Kripke-Putnam theory of natural kind terms. The difference is that for Mill the attributes are part of the connotation of the term whereas for Kripke and Putnam they are associated with it only empirically, just as being a philosopher is an empirical fact about J. S. Mill and not part of the connotation of his name.

VI.

"Everything that Mill has to say in his *Logic* about matters other than inductive inference is perfunctory and conventional."[46] Well I suppose Mill's philosophy of proper names may in some respects be considered perfunctory and conventional. But its correctness makes up for a lot of that. On the other hand his treatment of natural kinds and Kind names is anything but perfunctory, although it may be considered conventional, but only because so much of it seems so sensible. And Mill might not object to the charge of being conventional. The first sentences of the preface to *A System of Logic* make this clear.

> This book makes no pretence of giving the world a new theory of our intellectual operations. Its claim to attention, if it possess any, is grounded on the fact that it is an attempt not to supersede, but to embody and systematize, the best ideas which have been either promulgated on its subject by speculative writers, or conformed to by accurate thinkers in the scientific inquiries.[47]

We know what Russell's notion of philosophy is: "The point of philosophy is to start with something so simple as not to seem worth stating, and to end with something so paradoxical that no one will believe it."[48] No wonder Russell was unhappy with Mill's *A System of Logic*! Mill missed the whole point of philosophy! Mill's *Logic* is anything but paradoxical and incredible.[49]

Mill's theory of proper names is a valuable contribution to the philosophy of language, and anticipates and helps support the best contemporary work on proper names. His treatment of Kind names is profound and detailed; and anticipates, helps guide and supports challenges to the foremost contemporary theories of the semantics of natural kind terms—the theories of Kripke and Putnam.

NOTES

1. I would like to thank Mark Balaguer for helpful comments on an early draft of this essay.
2. Russell (1951: 123).
3. Russell (1951: 123).
4. Today we use "term" in the way that Mill used "name," and reserve "name" for proper names. Thus we would today not speak of general names, but rather general terms. I will mostly follow this practice, although in deference to Mill will at times write of general names. "General name" means the same as "general term." (Mill does in places use "term" instead of "name.").
5. Besides extension, the denotation of a term is sometimes called its reference. The connotation these days is also called the term's sense, or just its meaning. Mill sometimes uses "extension" in its contemporary sense.

6. Mill (1843, CW: VII.33). All references to Mill are to his *A System of Logic* (1843), in the version of the authoritative edition of *Collected Works of John Stuart Mill* (Mill, 1963–1991—cited as *CW*, followed by volume and page number), unless otherwise indicated.

7. In a brief passage in *An Examination of Sir William Hamilton's Philosophy* Mill attributes the non-connotative view of proper names to Thomas Reid, but also notes that other philosophers have treated proper names as connotative general terms (Mill, 1865, CW: IX.322–23).

8. Mill (1843, CW: VII.35).

9. Mill's theory is thus different from what is called the Millian theory of proper names in contemporary philosophy of language. The Millian theory is the view that the meaning of a proper name is its bearer.

10. Since Russell's classical article "On Denoting" (1905) such terms have been called definite descriptions. Russell diverges from Mill in arguing that definite descriptions do not have any meanings in isolation. They are what Russell calls incomplete terms.

11. Mill (1843, CW: VII.35).

12. Another similar puzzle may afflict Mill's theory. This is the puzzle of negative existential claims. How, on Mill's account, do I deny that something exists? E.g., "Romulus did not exist" seems to be devoid of meaning if true because the non-connotative name has nothing to tag.

13. Russell (1971: 201).

14. Recently a leading metaphysician, Timothy Williamson, has in fact argued for just such a position. See Williamson 2002.

15. Frege (1892: 25).

16. Russell (1971: 243). Russell is given to stating odd things about names. "Every person has a number of characteristics that are peculiar to him; Caesar, for example, had the name 'Julius Caesar'" (Russell, 1948: 301). First of all, it is very unlikely that Julius Caesar is the only person ever named that. And how likely is it that Romulus, even if there was such a person, was called "Romulus"?

17. Russell (1948: 84).

18. Searle (1958: 160).

19. Kripke (1972: 28).

20. See Kripke (1972).

21. See Schwartz (1977; 1979) for more detailed expositions.

22. Kripke (1972: 75).

23. Kripke (1972: 91–92).

24. Names of fictional characters would require more complicated explanations. The causal chains would start not with a "baptism" but with a storyteller or folk custom, as with the name "Santa Claus."

25. Several philosophers have attempted to deal with Frege's Puzzle by attributing non-descriptive connotations to proper names. For a thorough discussion of all the intricacies and a promising proposal see Devitt (*forthcoming*).

26. See Salmon (1986).

27. Kripke (1972: 127–28).

28. See Russell (1951: 126).

29. Mill (1843, CW: VII.122).

30. Mill (1843, CW: VII.127).

31. Mill (1843, CW: VII.128).

32. Mill (1843, CW: VII.129).

33. For Mill a nomenclature is the collection of all the names of the Kinds in any branch of knowledge.

34. Mill (1843, CW: VIII.705).

35. Mill (1843, *CW*: VIII.705).
36. See Schwartz (1979) for more detailed explanations.
37. Although Putnam does suggest that even terms like "grandmother" can acquire something like a natural kind semantics.
38. See Putnam (1975) where Putnam introduced the Twin Earth thought experiment.
39. Kripke (1972: 138).
40. Mill (1843, *CW*: VIII.716; quoting Whewell (1858: 286–87)).
41. For lengthy and stimulating discussion of these sorts of objections to the Kripke-Putnam theory of natural kind terms see Dupré (1981) and LaPorte (1996). Dupré says that Kripke's claim that whales are not fish is debatable.
42. See Schwartz (2002) and Soames (2002).
43. Mill (1843, *CW*: VIII.706). Mill is concerned that Kinds so defined be *infimae species*. His remarks in this regard are obscure and were ridiculed by Russell. In current discussions of natural kinds the term "*infima species*" rarely if ever occurs.
44. See articles by Schwartz and Soames cited above (n41).
45. Mill (1843, *CW*: VII.31).
46. Russell (1951:123).
47. Mill (1843, *CW*: VII.cxi).
48. Russell (1971:193).
49. I have the highest regard for Bertrand Russell and his philosophical and logical contributions, and I do not think he meant his statement about the point of philosophy quite seriously—it was given in response to difficult questions about his logical atomism. I do think his negative judgement about Mill's *Logic* is unduly harsh and not fully considered.

REFERENCES

Devitt, M. (*forthcoming*) "Should Proper Names Still Seem so Problematic?" (http://web.gc.cuny.edu/philosophy/faculty/devitt/Still%20Problematic2.pdf).
Dupré, J.(1981) "Natural Kinds and Biological Taxa," *Philosophical Review* 90 (1): 66–90.
Frege, G. (1892) "Über Sinn und Bedeutung," *Zeitschrift für Philosophie und philosophische Kritik* 100: 25–50.
Kripke, S. (1972) *Naming and Necessity* (Cambridge, MA: Harvard University Press).
LaPorte, J. (1996) "Chemical Kind Term Reference and the Discovery of Essence," *Noûs* 30: 112–32.
Mill, J. S. (1843) *A System of Logic, Ratiocinative and Inductive: Being a Connected View of the Principles of Evidence and the Methods of Scientific Investigation*, in vols. VII and VIII (1974) of Mill (1963–1991).
———. (1865) *An Examination of Sir William Hamilton's Philosophy and of the Principal Philosophical Questions Discussed in his Writings* in vol. IX (1979) of Mill (1963–1991).
———. (1963–1991) *Collected Works of John Stuart Mill*, F.E.L. Priestly (gen. ed.), and subsequently J. M. Robson, 33 vols. (London/Toronto: Routledge and Kegan Paul/ University of Toronto Press).
Putnam, H. (1975) "The Meaning of 'Meaning'," in K. Gunderson (ed.) *Language, Mind, and Knowledge* (Minneapolis: University of Minnesota Press): 131–93.
Russell, B. (1924) "Logical Atomism," reprinted in A. J. Ayer (ed.) *Logical Positivism* (New York: The Free Press, 1959): 31–50.

———. (1948) *Human Knowledge: Its Scope and Limits* (New York: Simon and Schuster).

———. (1951) *Portraits from Memory and Other Essays* (New York: Simon and Schuster).

———. (1971) "The Philosophy of Logical Atomism," in R. C. Marsh (ed.) *Logic and Knowledge: Essays 1901—1950* (New York: Capricorn Books): 175–281 (Originally delivered as lectures in 1918).

Salmon, N. (1986) *Frege's Puzzle* (Cambridge, MA: MIT Press).

Schwartz, S. P. (1977) "Introduction," in S.P. Schwartz (ed.), *Naming, Necessity, and Natural Kinds* (Ithaca: Cornell University Press): 13–41.

———. (1979) "Natural Kind Terms," *Cognition*, 7: 301–15.

———. (2002) "Kinds, General Terms, and Rigidity," *Philosophical Studies* 109: 265–77.

Searle, J. R. (1958) "Proper Names," reprinted in C. E. Caton (ed.) *Philosophy and Ordinary Language* (Urbana, IL: University of Illinois Press, 1963): 154–61.

Soames, S. (2002) *Beyond Rigidity* (New York: Oxford University Press).

Whewell, W. (1858) *Novum Organon Renovatum; Being the Second Part of the Philosophy of the Inductive Sciences* (London: John W. Parker and Sons).

Williamson, T. (2002) "Necessary Existents," in A. O'Hear (ed.) *Logic, Thought and Language* (Cambridge: Cambridge University Press): 233–51.

2 The Sources of Mill's Views of Ratiocination and Induction

Steffen Ducheyne and John P. McCaskey[*]

INTRODUCTION

By 1800, at least in the British Isles, logic in the old Scholastic sense was, as a scholarly discipline, nearly dead. Only at Oxford was it still a meaningful part of the curriculum but even there scholarship was slight and examinations were cursory.[1] Edward Copleston thought the decline had gone far enough when there was a move just after 1809 to replace Henry Aldrich's already skeletal thirty-seven-page *Artis Logicae Compendium* (Aldrich, 1691) with Henry Kett's new *Logic Made Easy* (Kett, 1809). Copleston and a few others complained not only about the shallowness of studies in traditional logic but also about the wholesale replacement of that topic with Baconian and Lockean epistemologies.[2] Copleston and his collaborators, especially his student Richard Whately, successfully revived a scholarly interest in logic in the early nineteenth century.[3] John Stuart Mill's *A System of Logic, Ratiocinative and Inductive* (1843) was, as we will see, a part of the sweeping revival.

Copleston and colleagues had to address two major challenges. One was an assault on the syllogism. In the seventeenth century, most notably in Francis Bacon's *Novum Organum* (1620),[4] there were criticisms that syllogistic logic was about words and not things and therefore hollow and corrupt. In the late eighteenth century there was increasing criticism that the syllogism committed the fallacy of *petitio principii*. The *petitio principii* charge states that the syllogism is fallacious because knowledge of the major "contains" or "presupposes" that of the conclusion.[5] Opponents also complained that the syllogism cannot lead to new knowledge.

The second challenge was that the widely admired Baconian induction simply did not fit into the slot allocated for induction in the Scholastic topology. In that topology, induction was, with the enthymeme and example, a minor sort of propositional inference, to be dealt with in a few sentences that showed how the inference was made valid by conversion to a first-figure syllogism. But Baconian induction was not as much a kind of propositional inference as a logic for identifying causal definitions and classifying thereby.

A few logicians of the late nineteenth century tried to argue that Baconian induction and Aristotelian logic could be reconciled,[6] but to successfully do so would have required driving a wedge between a true Aristotelianism and Aristotle as the Scholastics understood him. The attempted reconciliation did not get far and mainstream English-language epistemology, as that of Thomas Reid and Dugald Stewart,[7] remained committed to Baconian induction as against Scholastic.

Richard Whately's *Elements of Logic*, published first in 1823 as two volumes in the *Encyclopaedia Metropolitana* then as a standalone volume in 1826, addressed both of these challenges and more. The book went through fourteen editions. In the 1844 edition, Whately felt justified in taking credit for "[t]he *revival* of a study which had for a long time been regarded as an obsolete absurdity."[8] He said—probably without exaggeration—that the revival he attempted must have looked like trying to restore a fossil to life but that now the book was used in every one of the colleges in the US.[9] In 1860 Auguste De Morgan said Whately deserved to be called the "restorer of logical study in England."[10] In his *Autobiography*, Mill reports having studied several works on logic.[11] Only Whately's was less than a hundred years old. Mill wrote a fifteen-thousand-word review of Whately's "excellent treatise" in the *Westminster Review* in 1828.[12]

In *A System of Logic* Mill provided an empiricist explication of two types of reasoning, "popularly said":[13] the syllogism (or ratiocination), which is treated in Book II, and induction, which is dealt with in Book III. In the early 1830s Mill began composing an early tract on logic that would evolve into *A System of Logic*. Although the exact dates of this early manuscript remain tentative, three phases of its composition can be distinguished.[14] In the first phase (ca. 1830–1832), Mill drafted what became in the first edition the general introduction, Book I, Chapters i–vi (on names and propositions), and Book II, Chapters i–iii (on reasoning and the syllogism). In the second stage (ca. 1834), he rewrote and expanded what became Book I, Chapter vi (on verbal propositions), composed what became Book I, Chapters vii and viii (on classification and definition) and composed material that resulted in Book III, Chapters ii and iii (on induction). The difficulties that Mill experienced when dealing with induction brought him to a halt, which he says lasted until 1837.[15] In the third stage (ca. 1837), he composed what became Book II, Chapters iv–vi (on trains of reasoning and necessary truths). By 1838 he completed the first draft of Book III and by 1840 he finished the entire draft. From 1841 to 1843 he worked on the press-copy manuscript, in which he reworked the early version, considerably expanded Book III (on induction) and composed Books IV (on operations subsidiary to induction), V (on fallacies) and VI (on the logic of the moral sciences).[16]

In what follows, we will discuss the sources on which Mill drew when formulating his views on ratiocination and induction proper and analyze their significance for his ideas on these matters.

I. RATIOCINATION

Two works were of vital importance for the development of Mill's views on the syllogism: Richard Whately's *Elements of Logic* (1826) and the second volume of Dugald Stewart's *Elements of the Philosophy of the Human Mind* (1814). Mill, as will be shown, was not a slavish follower of their work. Instead, he subjected their work to critical examination and in the course of doing so he arrived at an idiosyncratic account of the syllogism that challenged more than two thousand years of orthodoxy regarding logic.

In his early twenties Mill was a member of what Ethel E. Ellis dubbed the "Society of Students of Mental Philosophy." It met twice a week at George Grote's house in London between 1825 until early 1828 and then again in 1829.[17] Its members were particularly interested in logic and at their meetings they discussed books on the subject.[18] It was in this context that the group dealt with Richard Whately's *Elements*, in which one "will find stated with philosophical precision, and explained with remarkable perspicuity, the whole of the common doctrine of the syllogism," as Mill later stated in *A System of Logic*.[19] Whately's work was the only contemporary textbook that Mill and his friends discussed—all other textbooks that they discussed were predominantly scholastic and dated back to the seventeenth century. In early 1828, Mill's review of Whately's *Elements* appeared in the *Westminster Review*.[20] Whately's *Elements* was *the* source on which Mill based his study of the syllogism.[21] At least two particular features of Whately's *Elements* were important for the development of Mill's views on deductive reasoning. First, Mill endorsed Whately's line of thought according to which the syllogism—or, as the latter referred to it, the "Grammar of Reasoning"—provides "a test to try the validity of any argument" because it is "the form to which *all* correct reasoning may be ultimately reduced."[22] Second, Mill scrutinized and ultimately rejected Whately's claim that one could neutralize the charge that the syllogism, insofar as it is considered a process to establish new truths, involves a *petitio principii*.[23]

Although several opponents of Aristotelian logic had accused the syllogism of committing the logical fallacy of *petitio principii*, most of them were not crystal clear on what the fallacy actually involved.[24] George Campbell seems to have been the first to clearly formulate the *petitio principii* charge.[25] In his *Philosophy of Rhetoric* (1776) he argued that the syllogism is epistemologically wanting because it assumes "in the proof the very opinion or principle proposed to be proved."[26] The *petitio principii* charge states, in other words, that the syllogism is fallacious because knowledge of the major "presupposes" that of the conclusion.[27] According to proponents of the inductive philosophy, the syllogism begs the question because, in the order of knowing, the major is epistemologically posterior to its conclusion. In other words, their criticism of the syllogism was tied up with their view on how knowledge is acquired. In their view, knowledge is acquired from particular facts to general principles and not the other way round. A different charge that frequently accompanied the *petitio principii* charge complained that, since the syllogism only renders explicit what is contained in its general principle, it cannot lead to new knowledge. Although both charges are distinct, they were frequently confounded by defenders and opponents of the syllogism alike.

In his characterization of the *petitio principii* charge, Whately was blending the *petitio principii* charge and the charge that the syllogism cannot lead to new knowledge. To nullify the *petitio principii* charge against the syllogism Whately distinguished between physical and logical discoveries. Physical discoveries refer to the establishment of matters of fact, which "were, before they were discovered, *absolutely* unknown, being not implied by anything we previously knew."[28] Logical discoveries, by contrast, refer to the mere deducing and unfolding of "the assertions wrapt up, as it were, and implied in those with which we set out, and to bring a person to perceive and acknowledge the full force of that which he has admitted; to contemplate it in various points of view; to admit in one shape what he has already admitted in another, and to give up and disallow whatever is inconsistent with it."[29] With the above distinction at hand, Whately argued that syllogistic reasoning establishes logical discoveries only and that the criticism that syllogism involves a *petitio principii* insofar as it is considered as a reasoning process that establishes new truths rests on the mistaken assumption that the aim of syllogistic reasoning is to establish physical discoveries.[30] In his review on Whately's rebuttal of the *petitio principii* charge, Mill commented, "he refutes this imputation most triumphantly, and his ideas on the entire subject are philosophical and just."[31] Mill observed that, although Whately did not fully explain how "mankind may correctly apprehend and fully assent to a general proposition, yet remain for ages ignorant of myriads of truths which are embodied in it," he was correct in claiming that ratiocination establishes unforeseen (logical) truths. "Of this fact the whole science of mathematics is a perpetual proof," he added.[32] When he composed his review of Whately's *Elements*, Mill still believed that ratiocination consists in reasoning from premises.[33]

Although the exact details are lacking, a couple of years later Mill began to doubt whether the syllogism leads to new (logical) truths and whether it is a form of reasoning from premises.[34] When he began to commit his views on logic to paper in the early 1830s, he began to perceive a difficulty in Whately's treatment of the syllogism, and it was in Dugald Stewart's writings that he, according to his own testimony, found a clue as to how to resolve it:

> As to the fact there could be no doubt; as little could it be doubted, that all reasoning was resolvable into syllogisms and that in every syllogism the conclusion is actually contained and implied in the premises. How being so contained and implied, it could be new truth, and how the theorems of geometry . . . could be all contained in them, was a difficulty which no one, I thought, had sufficiently felt, and which at all events no one had

succeeded in clearing up. The attempts at explanation by Whately and others seemed rather explainings away; and though they might give a temporary satisfaction, always left a mist still hanging over the subject. At last, when reading for the second or third time the chapters on Reasoning in the second volume of Dugald Stewart, interrogating myself on every point and following out the various topics of thought which the book suggested, I came to an idea of his about the use of axioms in ratiocination, which . . . seemed to me to be not only true of axioms but of all general propositions whatever, and to lead to the true solution of my perplexity. From this germ grew the theory of the syllogism propounded in the second book of the Logic: which I immediately made safe by writing it out.[35]

Mill now became convinced that "in every syllogism, *considered as an argument to prove the conclusion,* there is a *petitio principii.*"[36] Syllogistic arguments in his view beg the question because the conclusion is required in the proof of the major premise.[37] His argumentation ran as follows:

When we say,
All men are mortal,
Socrates is a man,
therefore
Socrates is mortal;

> it is unanswerably urged by the adversaries of the syllogistic theory, that the proposition, Socrates is mortal, is presupposed in the more general assumption, All men are mortal: that we cannot be assured of the mortality of all men, unless we are already certain of the mortality of every individual man: that if it be still doubtful whether Socrates, or any other individual we choose to name, be mortal or not, the same degree of uncertainty must hang over the assertion, All men are mortal: *that the general principle, instead of being given as evidence of the particular case, cannot itself be taken for true without exception, until every shadow of doubt which could affect any case comprised with it, is dispelled by evidence* aliundè; *and then what remains for the syllogism to prove? That, in short, no reasoning from generals to particulars can, as such, prove anything: since from a general principle we cannot infer any particulars, but those which the principle itself assumes as known.*[38]

Note that Mill's rendering of the *petitio principii* charge against the syllogism is based on the interconnected presuppositions that the major premise is but "an aggregate of particular truths,"[39] that the relation between a premise-set and its conclusion is essentially that which holds between a major premise and its instances,[40] and that, accordingly, the truth of a major premise requires the truth of all its instances. It is only under these (debatable) assumptions that the *petitio principii* charge emerges.

Having set up the problem, Mill criticized Whately, as follows:

> When you admitted the major premise, you asserted the conclusion; but, says Archbishop Whately, you asserted it by implication merely: this, however, can here only mean that you asserted it unconsciously; that you did not know you were asserting it; but, if so, the difficulty revives in this shape—Ought you not to have known? *Were you warranted in asserting the general proposition without having satisfied yourself of the truth of everything which it fairly includes?*[41]

Mill became equally convinced that the only way to steer out of the *petitio principii* problem was to make a quite idiosyncratic move: *to deny that the syllogism involves inference.*[42] As he pointed out in *An Examination of William Hamilton's Philosophy* (1865):

> Nor is its refutation [of the *petitio principii* charge], I conceive, possible, on any theory but that which considers the Syllogism not as a process of Inference, but as the mere interpretation of the record of a previous process; the major premise as simply a formula for making particular inferences; and the conclusions of ratiocination as not inferences from the formula, but inferences drawn according to the formula.[43]

Inference properly conceived of involves "a progress from the known to the unknown: a means of coming to a knowledge of something which we did not know before"[44] and, as we will see, only induction fills that bill.

If syllogistic arguments do not involve inference, then what is their function? The chapters on mathematical axioms and deductive reasoning in the second volume of Dugald Stewart's *Elements of the Philosophy of the Human Mind* (1814), which Mill's father, James Mill, reviewed,[45] served as an important source of inspiration for Mill's treatment of the function of the syllogism.[46]

In the second volume of his *Elements*, Stewart launched a rather vague criticism of the status of mathematical axioms as principles of reasoning. Traditionally, mathematical axioms are seen as the founding premises *from which* a myriad of mathematical truths *are deduced*. Taking a clue from Locke's denial that general maxims are useful in the establishment of knowledge,[47] Stewart observed that "it cannot with any propriety be said, that the axioms are the foundation on which the science rests; or the *first principles from which* its more recondite *truths are deduced*."[48] The true principles of reasoning in mathematics are the definitions: "the principles of mathematical science are, *not* the axioms but the *definitions*; . . . From what principle are the various properties of the circle derived, but from the definition of a circle? From what principle the properties of the parabola or ellipse, but from the definitions of these curves? A similar observation may be extended to all the other theorems which the mathematician demonstrates: . . ."[49]

Instead, Stewart argued that "although they [i.e., mathematical axioms] are not the principles of our reasoning, either in arithmetic or in geometry, *their truth is supposed or implied in all our reasonings in both; and, if it were called in question, our further progress would be impossible.*"[50] Moreover, Stewart urged that the "idea that all demonstrative science must rest ultimately on axioms, has been borrowed, with many other erroneous maxims, from the logic of Aristotle."[51]

That Stewart served as a source of inspiration can be seen from the content of *A System of Logic*, Book II, Chapter iii, in which Mill addressed the functions of the syllogism. There Mill pointed out that:

> It is justly remarked by Dugald Stewart, that though the reasonings in mathematics depend entirely on the axioms, it is by no means necessary to our seeing the conclusiveness of the proof, that the axioms should be expressly adverted to . . . This remark of Stewart, consistently followed out, *goes to the root, as I conceive, of the philosophy of ratiocination*; and it is to be regretted that he himself stopt short at a much more limited application of it. He saw that *the general propositions on which a reasoning is said to depend, may, in certain cases, be altogether omitted, without impairing its probative force.* But he imagined this to be a peculiarity belonging to axioms; and argued from it, that axioms are not the foundations or first principles of geometry, from which all the other truths of the science are synthetically deduced . . . but are *merely necessary assumptions, self-evident indeed, and the denial of which would annihilate all demonstration, but from which, as premises, nothing can be demonstrated* . . . [H]e contended that axioms are in their nature barren of consequences, and that the really fruitful truths, the real first principles of geometry, are the definitions . . . Yet all that he had asserted respecting the function to which the axioms are confined in the demonstrations of geometry, holds equally true of the definitions.[52]

According to Mill, Stewart's analysis of the role of mathematical axioms in mathematical demonstration applies to all major premises in syllogistic argumentation. Correspondingly, he argued that the proposition "the Duke of Wellington is mortal" is "not an inference drawn *from* the formula ['all men are mortal'], but an inference drawn *according to* the formula: the real logical antecedent, or premise, being the particular facts from which the general proposition was collected by induction."[53] This quotation reveals an important feature of Mill's views on logic: namely, he believed that *logical antecedents* ought to correspond to *evidential antecedents* that are grounded in particular facts.[54] In Mill's view, the general major premise "all men are mortal" does not have probative force in itself, it serves as an *aide mémoire* only: "The proposition, All men are mortal . . . shows that we have had experience from which we thought it followed that the attributes connoted by the term man, are a mark of mortality. But when we conclude that the

Duke of Wellington is mortal, we do not infer this from the memorandum, but from the former experience. All that we infer from the memorandum is our own previous belief . . . concerning the inferences which that former experience would warrant."[55] The real inference, Mill contends, is finished once we have established the inductive generalization "all men are mortal"; the descent from the major to "the Duke of Wellington is mortal" is "not a process of inference, but a process of interpretation."[56] The proper form of the major premise, according to Mill, is therefore the following:

> In the argument, then, which proves that Socrates is mortal, one indispensable part of the premises will be as follows: "My father, and my father's father, A, B, C, and an indefinite number of other persons, were mortal;" which is only an expression in different words of the observed fact that they have died. This is the major premise divested of the *petitio principii*, and *cut down to as much as is really known by direct evidence*.[57]

Although the syllogism is not a process of inference, it is not entirely useless, for it "furnishes a test of the validity of reasonings, by supplying forms of expression into which all reasonings may be translated if valid, and which, if they are invalid, will detect the hidden flaw."[58] In view of his analysis of the syllogism, Mill concluded that all inference is "from particulars to particulars,"[59] and that "all processes of thought in which the ultimate premises are particulars, whether we conclude from particulars to a general formulae, or from particulars to other particulars according to that formula, are equally Induction."[60]

II.   INDUCTION

The philosophical background important to Mill's theory of induction has two major components: Richard Whately's introduction of the uniformity principle into inductive inference and the loss of the idea of formal cause.

Surprisingly, David Hume (1711–1776) is of little importance here. Hume was not associated with induction in his own day, in Whately's or in Mill's. The association was not made until the 1920s.[61] In the early nineteenth century, the philosopher considered most important for induction was still Francis Bacon. Even those writers criticizing Bacon or his inductive method acknowledged his pervasive influence. Richard Whately was one such critic.[62]

Whately's project was to reverse the trends wrought by Bacon, John Locke and especially their followers. But to do so, Whately could not simply return to Scholasticism, at least not regarding induction. He made a proposal that has been so successfully revolutionary, we now take it for granted. To understand it and then Mill's framework, we need to have a sense of the Scholastic and then Baconian conceptions of induction.[63]

In Scholastic logic, induction is a kind of propositional inference made good by complete enumeration (actual or presumed). The inference is valid because the induction can be converted into a syllogism. A common example was "This, that and the other magnet attract iron; therefore all magnets attract iron." It was claimed that this could be rendered—and would gain inferential force by being rendered—as a syllogism, which is done by supplying the missing (minor) premise "all magnets are this, that and the other." If the list was not fully enumerated but could be treated as if it were, "et cetera" could be added to both premises.

Renaissance humanists reading Aristotle's *Topics*, Cicero's works and other ancient texts discovered another conception of induction, one that justified universal statements not by converting an argument into a syllogism but by identifying the essential features that make something the kind of thing it is, that is, by identifying the "formal cause" or "form" of something. Because of associations with Socrates' search for universal definitions, this kind of induction was in the ancient world and then again in the Renaissance called "Socratic induction." Francis Bacon's project was to codify and systematize Socratic induction.[64]

In the seventeenth century, the Baconian/Socratic conception of induction supplanted the Scholastic, and adherents of the new conception were typically also the thinkers losing interest in syllogistic logic. That logic seemed to them concerned only with words in debates and not with things in the world. Bacon said the first distemper of learning is "when men study words and not matter."[65] The Royal Society, inspired by Bacon's writings, adopted *nullius in verba* as its motto. Philosophers' attention turned from formal logic to how the human mind processes sense experience, how it forms universal concepts, how it judges and what the relation is between judgments, concepts and experiences, and objects and attributes in reality. The major epistemological works were no longer commentaries on Aristotelian logic but works on "human understanding" or "intellectual powers." By the early nineteenth century, the stock way to describe this change was that "mental philosophy" had replaced "formal logic."

Whately's project was to revive formal logic. But since Baconian induction had become so widely considered the foundation of successful experimental science, Whately could not simply return to a cursory treatment of induction. He also recognized the shortcomings of the Scholastic conception. He adopted the Scholastic framework, but made an important change.[66]

What we nowadays would call an induction justified by complete enumeration was called by Scholastics "an enthymeme in Barbara with the minor premise suppressed." That is, it is a syllogism such as this:

(major) Father, Son and Holy Ghost are eternal.
(minor) [God is Father, Son and Holy Ghost.]
(concl.) Therefore, God is eternal.

Whately claimed this was the wrong way to understand induction. Induction is not, he said, an enthymeme (or syllogism) with the *minor* premise suppressed, "as Aldrich represents it,"[67] but a syllogism with the *major* premise suppressed. Of course, it was not just Aldrich who thought this.[68] Whately was overturning the whole history of induction.[69]

Whately was also reversing a fundamental principle of logic. Normally, the minor term is the subject of the conclusion and the major term is the predicate. And subject and predicate are meant ontologically, not grammatically. Whether one says, "tyrannies are short-lived," "being short-lived is a property of tyrannies," or "the property of short-lived belongs to tyrannies," the content of the proposition does not change and if this is the conclusion of a syllogism, the minor term is "tyrannies" and the major term is "short-lived." But for Whately, as for Copleston, and as against the Baconians, logic is just a grammar. It is not about things in the world. It is about how we put words together. So which is subject and which is predicate, that is, which is the minor term and which is the major term, is determined by the form of the sentence. So Whately can then form the inductive syllogism he wants, an enthymeme in Barbara with the major premise suppressed:

(major) [A property of the examined tyrannies is a property of all tyrannies.]
(minor) <u>The property of being short-lived is a property of the examined tyrannies.</u>
(concl.) Therefore, the property of being short-lived is a property of all tyrannies.
(concl.) That is, all tyrannies are short-lived.

This is the introduction of the uniformity principle into induction theory.

To serious students of logic, the import of Whately's new syllogism was readily apparent. William Hamilton called Whately's move destructive, "palpably suicidal."[70] An anonymous reviewer of Whately's *Elements of Logic*, writing in the *Westminster Review* in early 1828, had the opposite view. He applauded the good effect Whately's book was already having on the study of logic at Oxford and in England generally. The reviewer said not only that Whately's new view of induction was "original" and "extremely important" but also that this "one remark [about major and minor] would have sufficed to correct the erroneous notion the ancients had of induction, and to which Lord Bacon justly ascribes the gross errors they committed in the investigation of nature. They in fact mistook altogether the inductive syllogism, completing it by the addition of a *minor*, instead of a *major*."[71] The reviewer was suggesting that the whole Baconian era could have been avoided had someone identified the Scholastic error before Bacon advanced his alternative. The reviewer was twenty-one-year-old John Stuart Mill.

Mill began work on *A System of Logic* soon afterward. And he made good progress on Book I (on name and propositions) and Book II (on ratiocination), drawing heavily on his readings of Aldrich and other authors in the Scholastic tradition. For Book III (on induction) he wrote a few pages, "Of Induction in General," "Of the Various Grounds of Induction" and "Of the Uniformity in the Course of Nature." Whately's new syllogism was central.

> Archbishop Whately remarks, that every Induction is an imperfect Syllogism, with the major premiss omitted. The remark is just . . . [T]he principle which we are now considering, that of the uniformity of the course of nature, will come forth as the invariable major premiss, immediately or remotely of all inductive argumentations.[72]

But Mill then hit an impasse, "stopped and brought to a halt on the threshold of induction."[73] His last words in the draft were these:

> Why is a single instance in one case sufficient for a complete Induction, while in another myriads of concurring instances without a single exception known or presumed, goes so slight a way towards establishing a general proposition? Whoever can solve this question, knows more of the Philosophy of Logic, than the wisest of the ancients, and has solved the great problem of Induction.[74]

Mill said he could go no further without a "comprehensive and . . . accurate view of the whole circle of physical science."[75] In 1837, he found what he needed in William Whewell's *History of the Inductive Sciences*, published early that year. He then reread *A Preliminary Discourse on the Study of Natural Philosophy* by Whewell's friend John F. W. Herschel, and by autumn of 1837 Mill had "substantially completed" his theory of induction.[76] Whewell published his own theory of induction in *The Philosophy of the Inductive Sciences* in 1840, and Mill was delighted to have found an antagonist.[77]

Mill's project was to further Whately's anti-Baconian revival of formal logic. Whewell's was to advance Bacon's system of experimental induction by updating it.[78] The two Victorians disagreed on much about induction—even on whether its use was good or bad for society—but they agreed that, as used in the two centuries after Bacon, an induction was validated by identification of a cause. But Mill had a much different conception of cause than Bacon had.

Up until Bacon's time, Aristotle's four causes—material, efficient, final and formal—were the canonical reference point for discussions of cause. Bacon said it is the formal cause that one must find to validate an induction. What Bacon meant by formal cause or form is what any Aristotelian of his day meant: A form is what makes something the kind of thing it is. He scolded those Aristotelians who thought this was some ineffable essence hidden within a substance. For Bacon, a form is ultimately just the arrangements and motions of (sometimes imperceptibly small) components. It can be discovered by carefully using an experimental and iterative method: begin with a varied inventory of observed instances, related absences and related variations; then explore similarities and differences to find first a genus and then a differentia. Bacon noted that this exploration often proceeded haphazardly, but that it need not. He identified twenty-seven kinds of comparisons, "prerogatives," that were particularly helpful. A researcher, he said, should vary conditions—we would say "design experiments"—so as to make these prerogative comparisons possible.

When Bacon uses his method to discover the formal cause of heat, he concludes that heat is a particular kind of motion of small particles. He then makes the extraordinarily universal claim, that if in any body whatsoever you can arouse this particular kind of motion, you will certainly generate heat, not because this motion will generate heat or the heat will generate the motion, but because this kind of motion *is* heat and heat *is* this kind of motion.

The notion of experimentation and of seeking causes to justify inductive inference survived, but the notion of formal cause did not. Bacon and others in seventeenth century had, in effect, shown that formal cause could be reduced to combinations of the other types, that is, to matter (the material cause) interacting (the efficient cause) with other matter, possibly for some purpose (the final cause). After Newton's grand synthesis, simplification of the causal taxonomy accelerated. By Mill's day, debates about cause had been reduced to whether material objects literally move the objects they interact with or it is consciousness—a person's in the case of bodily actions or God's in the case of the natural world—that effects the motion. Efficient cause came to mean the action of a consciousness, ultimately God's, and a physical cause to mean the action we perceive. Mill took his answer to this question from Thomas Brown.[79] Brown rejected a separate efficient cause operating in nature; what is going on in the mind of God is wholly inaccessible to us and whether it is involved or not in physical motion is irrelevant. Mill concurs, "The causes I concern myself with are not efficient, but *physical* causes."[80] Mill accepted that "The notion of Cause . . . [is] the root of the whole theory of Induction,"[81] but, following Brown, by the cause of something Mill meant (and meant only) the antecedent that invariably and unconditionally precedes it. "The only notion of a cause which the theory of induction requires is . . . that invariability of succession . . . found by observation to obtain between every fact in nature and some other fact which has preceded it."[82] Mill's concept of cause is purely temporal.

When discussing induction, Bacon generally paired "cause" with "nature," not with "effect." Given some nature, he wanted to know its cause. Mill, on the other hand, writes, "Inductive inquiry . . . [has] for its object to ascertain what causes are connected with what effects."[83] Bacon had three tables and twenty-seven prerogatives. Herschel had simplified these down to a multistage process with ten rules and a few ancillary supports.[84] Mill reduced all this to just four rules, his Methods of Experimental Inquiry.[85] Mill does not say these were the methods researchers *should* use, rather that they were the ones researchers *did* use.

Mill says the first two, the Method of Agreement and the Method of Difference, are the "simplest and most obvious." The third, probably following Herschel, "has been aptly named the Method of Residues."[86] Mill's fourth, what "may be termed the Method of Concomitant Variation," highlights why Mill does not say researchers *should* use these four methods. This fourth method says that when two phenomena vary together, one is the cause of the other or the two have one mutual cause. Mill knew this was of limited use. It runs counter to the very principle that mere correlation does not establish causality. None of these conventional methods, Mill says, can be used when an effect could have multiple causes and an effect could be "mixed and confounded with any other co-existent effect."[87] He called these two limiting conditions "Plurality of Causes" and "Intermixture of Effects." And because of the pervasiveness of these two conditions, advanced science requires some method other than induction.

Henceforth induction theory would face two challenges. The first is whether the uniformity principle could be justified. Mill returned to the question late in Book III and elaborated on his proposal that this is one universal principle that can in fact be established by simple enumeration. The second challenge is that inductive inference could no longer rely on the ampliation earlier presumed inherent in abstraction and concept-formation. To know for sure whether all cardinals are red, all water boils at 100°C and all magnets attract iron we need to know what makes a cardinal a cardinal, water water and a magnet a magnet. But once formal cause was abandoned, such questions got disconnected from induction theory. So induction got disconnected from "mental philosophy" and made into a kind of mathematical inference. Since the late nineteenth century, the core issue for induction theory has been to determine the chances that the suppressed major is true in some individual case, i.e., determine the probability that what is true of a sample is true of all.

III. CONCLUSION

The sources that Mill consulted served as working tools that helped him develop a series of original ideas that reformed the study of logic. Mill's *A System of Logic* was in many ways a revolutionary work. His overarching philosophical goal was to show that "[t]he doctrine that truths external to the mind may be known by intuition or consciousness, independently of observation and experiment" is misguided.[88] For Mill, *all* meaningful statements—including mathematical ones[89]—ultimately derive from experience of particular facts. His empiricism had clear repercussions on his treatment of inference.[90] Inference in his view always proceeds from particulars to particulars.

In accordance with his conception of inference, Mill argued that the conclusion of a syllogism is not *inferred* from the major premise. Instead, it is inferred from the particulars of which the major provides a memorandum. Despite his denial that the syllogism involves inference, he nevertheless maintained that it provides a very useful tool to test the validity of arguments. In other words, on the one hand, we see Mill defending the usefulness of the syllogism, even relying on it when he shows how induction depends on a uniformity principle. Yet, on the other hand, we see him denying its longstanding inferential significance.

What was furthermore revolutionary about Mill's *magnum opus* was that it attempted to provide the conditions under which real inferences, i.e., inductive arguments, are valid. By contrast, Whately claimed that the discovery of universal statements, which serve as the basis for syllogistic arguments, is simply "out of the province of Logic."[91] "The business of Inductive Logic," Mill commented, "is to provide rules and models (such as the Syllogism and its rules are for ratiocination) to which if inductive arguments conform, those arguments are conclusive, and not otherwise."[92] Whereas in the early editions of *A System of Logic* Mill was quite optimistic that his Canons of Induction would furnish the required rules on the basis of which indisputable inductive conclusions could be established, in its later editions he emphasized that the Canons only establish provisional conclusions and that they provide guidance only in very simple cases, in which Plurality of Causes and Intermixture of Effects are absent.[93]

Mill had come to a dead-end with ratiocination and induction. If the syllogism is understood as a kind of inference, he decided, the criticism that it commits the fallacy of *petitio principii* is valid. He concluded that the syllogism is simply not a kind of inference; it is rather a process of interpreting existing knowledge. It cannot provide new knowledge. Induction, on the other hand, is a kind of inference and could produce new knowledge, but, in the induction Mill got from Whately, a valid induction requires a uniformity principle that itself relies on induction. Even if this difficulty can be assuaged, Mill's four methods of inductive inquiry are effective only when there is no plurality of causes or intermixture of effects. For the most important advances in human knowledge, Mill concluded, we must look elsewhere. He proposes that "the main source of the knowledge we possess or can acquire respecting the conditions, and laws of recurrence, of the more complex phenomena,"[94] the method that has been responsible for the human mind's "most conspicuous triumphs in the investigation of nature,"[95] is what Mill calls the Deductive Method: develop an hypothesis using simplistic induction, deduce its implications using syllogistic reasoning and verify or reject the hypothesis by comparison to experimental results.[96] Mill was sure this would be the dominant method in the future.

When Charles Darwin published the *Origin of Species* in 1859, he appealed on its frontispiece to the principles of Francis Bacon and he hoped most for the approbation of Mill's nemesis, the neo-Baconian William Whewell.[97] But Thomas Huxley, the man who would become "Darwin's Bulldog," had been extolling Mill's Deductive Method as early as 1854[98] and in 1860 was saying Darwin's method was "rigorously in accordance with the canons of scientific logic," with the proper "process of scientific investigation," with the process described in "Mr. Mill's admirable chapter 'On the Deductive Method.'"[99] In 1889, John Stuart Mill's biographer, W. L. Courtney, said this method is sometimes called the "hypothetico-deductive method."[100] And that is how we know it today.

NOTES

* This chapter is collaborative work and no significance attaches to the alphabetical order of the authors' names. Section 2 was written by Steffen Ducheyne. He is indebted to John P. McCaskey for stimulating comments. Section 3 was written by John P. McCaskey. He thanks Steffen Ducheyne and Laura J. Snyder for helpful comments. Both authors are indebted to Antis Loizides for useful feedback.

1. Jongsma (1982: 121–23, 259–61).
2. Jongsma (1982: 268–311).
3. See McKerrow (1987).
4. Bacon (1857–1874: I.214–15).
5. Jongsma (1982: 33–38).
6. Jongsma (1982: 217–18, 256).
7. E.g., Reid (1785: 369); Stewart (1829: II.229–63).
8. Whately (1844: xi).
9. Whately (1844: xii).
10. De Morgan (1860: 341).
11. Mill (1873, CW: I.125). All references to Mill are to the authoritative edition of *Collected Works of John Stuart Mill* (Mill, 1963–1991—cited as CW, followed by volume and page number), unless otherwise indicated.
12. See Mill (1828).
13. Mill (1843, CW: VII.162).
14. See Robson (1974: lv–lxv [esp. lviii–lxi], xcviii–xcix).
15. Mill (1873, CW: I.109).
16. Mill (1843, CW: VII.lxii).
17. See, Mill (1873, CW: I.125); Ellis (1888). See also Robson and Stillinger (1981: xii).
18. Other books on the syllogism that the society discussed included Philippe Du Trieu's *Manuductio ad Logicam* (1618), Thomas Hobbes' *Computatio sive Logica*, i.e., the first part of *De Corpore* (London: s.n.,1655), and Henry Aldrich's *Artis Logicae Compendium* (Oxford: E Theatro Sheldoniano, 1691). See Mill (1873, CW: I.125). According to his own testimony, Mill read Aristotle's *Prior Analytics* and *Posterior Analytics* at the age of twelve (*ibid.*, 21). In the following two years he personally read Samuel Smith's *Aditus ad Logicam* (London: W. Stansby, 1613), Edward Brerewood's *Elementa Logicae* (London: [W. Stansby] apud Ioannem Billium, 1614), Robert Sanderson's *Logicae Artis Compendium* (London: Excudebat Iosephus Barnesius, 1615), Franco Petri Burgersdijk's *Institutionum Logicarum Libri Duo* (1637), Hobbes' *Computatio sive Logica* and Du Trieu's *Manuductio ad Logicam* (see Appendix B, "Mill's Early Reading," in CW: I.567–68, 572).
19. Mill (1843, CW: VII.166).
20. See Mill (1828).

21. Kubitz (1932: 25ff). *A System of Logic* contains some fifty references to Whately's *Elements* (see Appendix K, in *CW*: VIII.1233–35). For in-depth studies of Mill's views on syllogistic reasoning, see Ryan (1970: ch. 2); Scarre (1989: ch. 4); and, Skorupski (1989: chs. 1–3). For general background on nineteenth century logic, see Heis (2012).
22. Whately (1831: 12); also Mill (1828, *CW*: XI.9–11).
23. Whately (1831: 255ff).
24. Jongsma (1982: 32).
25. Jongsma (1982: 149, 154).
26. Campbell (1776: I.174).
27. Jongsma (1982: 33–38).
28. Whately (1831: 240).
29. Whately (1831: 237).
30. Whately (1831: 251–52, 256–57). There is a complication, however: earlier in his *Elements* Whately had argued that what counts as a *petitio principii* depends merely on one's state of knowledge (Whately, 1831: 160–61; Jongsma, 1982: 389–93).
31. Mill (1828, *CW*: XI.33).
32. Mill (1828, *CW*: XI.34).
33. Mill (1828, *CW*: XI.16).
34. It is not very surprising then that Mill exempted his review of Whately's *Elements* from the papers collected in his *Dissertations and Discussions* (Mill, 1859; see also Kubitz, 1932: 33; Sparshott, 1978: vii).
35. Mill (1873, *CW*: I.189–90).
36. Mill (1843, *CW*: VII.184 [italics added]).
37. When characterizing the *petitio principii* charge Mill followed Whately, who had defined it as the logical fallacy "in which *the Premise* either appears manifestly to be the same as the Conclusion, or *is actually proved from the Conclusion* or, is such as would naturally and properly so be proved" (Whately, 1831: 199 [italics added]; cf. Mill, 1843, *CW*: VIII.820).
38. Mill (1843, *CW*: VII.184 [italics added]).
39. Mill (1843, *CW*: VII.186).
40. Kneale and Kneale (1962: 376); Jongsma (1982: 36–38); Scarre (1984: 23–24 and 1989: 22, 39, 63–64).
41. Mill (1843, *CW*: VII.185 [italics added]).
42. Scarre (1989: 65–79).
43. Mill (1865, *CW*: IX.416).
44. Mill (1843, *CW*: VII.183).
45. In his review James Mill did not discuss Stewart's views on deduction. He pointed out, however, that Stewart failed to give "what is yet so great a desideratum in logic, [namely] a complete system of rules, as complete, for example, as those which Aristotle provided for the business of syllogistic reasoning" (Mill, 1815: 193).
46. Anschutz (1953: 135–36, 149–150); Kubitz (1932: 121–25).
47. Locke (1689, III.iv, §11, 601–02).
48. Stewart (1829: II.21 [italics added]).
49. Stewart (1829: II.27, cf. II.107, 112, 127, 142).
50. Stewart (1829: II.28–29 [italics added]).
51. Stewart (1829: II.185).
52. Mill (1843, *CW*: VII.190–91 [italics added]).
53. Mill (1843, *CW*: VII.193).
54. This may be seen further from Mill's attempt to replace the *dictum de omni et nullo* by an evidentialist principle based on "marks" (Mill, 1843, *CW*: VII.180; Scarre, 1989: 32–37). In his seminal study Kubitz claimed that the

legalistic approach epitomized in Jeremy Bentham's *Rationale of Judicial Evidence*, which Mill edited in his early twenties (Bentham, 1827; Capaldi, 2004: 51–52), "may . . . be taken as one of the first circumstances to influence the development of Mill's logical doctrines" (Kubitz, 1932: 23, cf. 49–53). Mill referred twice to the *Rationale* in *A System of Logic* (1843, CW: VII.598, 627) and in his autobiography he asserted that Bentham's theory of evidence, which he considered as "one of the most important of his subjects," was "thoroughly imprinted" upon him (1873, CW: I.119; Mill's notes on the *Rationale* are in CW: XXXI.5–92). Taken as a statement regarding the details of Mill's logical doctrines, Kubitz' claim remains highly unconvincing. If Kubitz' claim is construed more broadly, i.e., as implying that Bentham's writings on judicial evidence influenced Mill's views on the priority of evidence in logic and reasoning, then it is fairly plausible as John M. Robson has pointed out (Robson, 1989: xv–xvi). It seems that Mill took over Bentham's expression "the probative force (of evidence)" (J. Bentham, 1827: I.58; Mill, 1843, CW: VII.183, 191, 256; see also Mill, 1827, CW: XXXI.13, 25, 38, 88).

55. Mill (1843, CW: VII.194–95).
56. Mill (1843, CW: VII.194).
57. Mill (1843, CW: VII.210 [italics added]).
58. Mill (1865, CW: IX.390); cf. Mill (1843, CW: VII.198).
59. Mill (1843, CW: VII.193, 88–190).
60. Mill (1843, CW: VII.203). In an early draft of *A System of Logic* Mill was more explicit on the implications of the view that all reasoning is from particulars to particulars: "We have now shown, that the distinction between Induction & Reasoning [i.e., Ratiocination], as commonly understood, has no real foundation. There are not two modes of arriving at truth, one proceeding upwards from particulars to generals, another downwards from generals to particulars" (see Appendix A, CW: VIII.1074).
61. Keynes (1921: 272).
62. Also of only secondary importance here is Auguste Comte. In the *Autobiography*, Mill says, "My theory of induction was substantially completed before I knew of Comte's book [*Cours de Philosophie Positive*]," though he does add, "Nevertheless, I gained much from Comte, with which to enrich my chapters in the subsequent rewriting [April to December, 1841]: and his book was of essential service to me in some of the parts which still remained to be thought out" (Mill, 1873, CW: I.217).
63. For a fuller treatment, see McCaskey (2006).
64. For a fuller treatment, see McCaskey (2013).
65. Bacon (1857–1874: III.284).
66. He got this from his teacher and colleague Edward Copleston (1776–1849), as also the conviction that logic is a grammar, about words and not things. See Copleston (1809).
67. Whately (1826: 209).
68. Once the forthcoming debate got underway, Whately realized his oversight. In the fifth edition of *Elements of Logic*, in 1834, the discussion, now moved from the footnote to the main body and expanded to several pages, referred not to Aldrich but to "most logical writers."
69. Even Baconians, though they did not typically use the description, could make the old Scholastic one serviceable enough. They, as Aristotle had in *Prior Analytics* II 23, used identification of essence, rather than complete enumeration, to justify the suppressed minor. See McCaskey (2007).
70. Hamilton (1833: 231).
71. Mill (1828, CW: XI.33).
72. See Appendix A, "Early Draft of *A System of Logic*," CW: VIII.1106.

73. Mill (1873, CW: I.215).
74. See Appendix A, CW: VIII.1110.
75. Mill (1873, CW: I.215).
76. Mill (1873, CW: I.217).
77. Mill (1873, CW: I.231).
78. For Whewell and his debate with Mill, see Snyder (2012), literature cited there, and Snyder (2006). The debate is also addressed in *infra*, chapter four, "Mill's and Whewell's Competing Visions of Logic."
79. In the preface to the first and second editions, Mill writes, "[A] previous familiarity with the earlier portion of Dr. Brown's *Lectures* or with his treatise on Cause and Effect, would, though not indispensable, be advantageous" (1843, CW: VII.cxiv). He mentions Brown several times elsewhere.
80. Mill (1843, CW: VII.326).
81. Mill (1843, CW: VII.326).
82. Mill (1843, CW: VII.326–27).
83. Mill (1843, CW: VII.384).
84. Herschel (1831: pt. 2, ch. 6).
85. See Ducheyne (2008).
86. Whewell had used the term a few years earlier. But when Whewell later criticizes Mill's four methods, he does not take credit for this one. Mill's use probably derives more directly from John F. W. Herschel's discussion of "residual phenomena." Whewell says all four come from among Bacon's twenty-seven prerogatives.
87. Mill (1843, CW: VII.434).
88. Mill (1873, CW: I.232, cf. 134)
89. For Mill's views on mathematical knowledge, see *infra*, chapter 3, "Mill and the Philosophy of Mathematics."
90. For the extremes to which he took empiricism, see Snyder (2006, 106ff).
91. Whately (1831: 230). In a letter to John Bowring in 1828, Mill criticized George Bentham's *Outline of a New Logic* (1827), which contains a critical examination of Whately's *Elements*. According to Mill, Bentham produced "nothing but minute criticism" (J.S. Mill to J. Bowring, 10 Mar. 1828, CW: XII.23). Nevertheless, as the years progressed, Mill came to share Bentham's opinion that the search for "inductive rules" is "a portion of the study of Logic" (G. Bentham, 1827: 18, 172–74).
92. Mill (1843, CW: VII.430).
93. Ducheyne (2008: 362–63).
94. Mill (1843, CW: VII.454).
95. Mill (1843, CW: VII.462).
96. Mill (1843, CW: VII.454–63, "Of the Deductive Method").
97. Snyder (2006: 185–202).
98. Huxley (1854: 86n1).
99. Huxley (1860: 293).
100. Courtney (1889: 80).

REFERENCES

Aldrich, H. (1691) *Artis Logicae Compendium* (Oxford: E Theatro Sheldoniano).
Anschutz, R. P. (1953) *The Philosophy of J. S. Mill*, reprint (Oxford: Clarendon Press, 1963).
Bacon, F. (1857–1874) *The Works of Francis Bacon*, J. Spedding, R. L. Ellis, D. D. Heath (eds.), 14 vols. (Boston: Houghton, Mifflin).

Bentham, G. (1827) *Outline of a New System of Logic* (London: Hunt and Clarke).

Bentham, J. (1827) *The Rationale of Judicial Evidence*, J. S. Mill (ed.), 5 vols. (London: Hunt and Clarke).

Campbell, G. (1776) *The Philosophy of Rhetoric*, 2 vols. (London: W. Strahan, T. Cadell and W. Creech).

Capaldi, N. (2004) *John Stuart Mill: A Biography* (Cambridge: Cambridge University Press).

Copleston, E. (1809) *The Examiner Examined; or, Logic Vindicated* (Oxford: printed for the author).

Courtney, W. L. (1889) *Life of John Stuart Mill* (London: Walter Scott).

De Morgan, A. (1860) "Logic," in Charles Knight (ed.), *The English Cyclopædia, A New Dictionary of Universal Knowledge, Arts and Sciences*, vol. 5 (London: Bradbury and Evans): 340–54.

Ducheyne, S. (2008) "J. S. Mill's Canons of Induction: From True Causes to Provisional Ones," *History and Philosophy of Logic* 29 (4): 361–76.

Ellis, E. E. (1888) *Memoir of William Ellis and an Account of his Conduct-Teaching* (London: Longmans, Green).

[Hamilton, W.] (1833) "Recent Publications on Logical Science," *Edinburgh Review* 57 (115): 194–238.

Heis, J. (2012) "Attempts to Rethink Logic," in A. W. Wood and S. S. Hahn (eds.), *The Cambridge History of Philosophy in the Nineteenth Century (1790–1870)* (Cambridge: Cambridge University Press): 95–132.

Herschel, J. (1831) *A Discourse on the Study of Natural Philosophy* (London: Longman).

Huxley, T. H. (1854) "On the Educational Value of the Natural History Sciences", in *Lay Sermons, Addresses, and Reviews* (London: Macmillan, 1870): 72–93.

———. (1860) "The Origin of Species", in *Lay Sermons, Addresses, and Reviews* (London: Macmillan, 1870): 255–98.

Jongsma, C. (1982) *Richard Whately and the Revival of Syllogistic Logic in Great Britain in the Early Nineteenth Century* (University of Toronto, PhD dissertation).

Kett, H. (1809) *Logic Made Easy, or, A Short View of the Aristotelic System of Reasoning, and Its Application to Literature, Science, and the General Improvement of the Minde; Designed Chiefly for the Students of the University of Oxford* (Oxford: Oxford University Press).

Keynes, J. M. (1921) *A Treatise on Probability* (London: Macmillan).

Kneale, W.; Kneale, M. (1962) *The Development of Logic*, reprint (Oxford: Clarendon Press, 1984).

Kubitz, A. O. (1932) *Development of John Stuart Mill's System of Logic* (Urbana: University of Illinois).

Locke, J. (1689) *An Essay Concerning Human Understanding*, Peter H. Nidditch (ed.), reprint (Oxford: Clarendon Press, 1975).

McCaskey, J. P. (2006) *Regula Socratis: The Rediscovery of Ancient Induction in Early Modern England* (Stanford University, PhD dissertation).

———. (2007) "Freeing Aristotelian Epagôgê from *Prior Analytics* II 23," *Apeiron* 40 (4): 345–74.

———. (2013) "Induction in the Socratic Tradition," in Paolo Biondi and Louis Groarke (eds.), *From Socrates to Pragmatism: New/Old Perspectives on Induction* (Frankfurt: Ontos Verlag).

McKerrow, R. E. (1987) "Richard Whately and the Revival of Logic in Nineteenth-Century England," *Rhetorica* 5 (2): 163–85.

Mill, J. (1815) "Elements of the Philosophy of the Human Mind. By Dugald Stewart, Esq. F.R.S. Edinburgh; Honorary Member of the Imperial Academy of Sciences at St. Petersburgh; Member of the Royal Academy of Berlin, and of the American Philosophical Society, Held at Philadelphia; Formerly Professor of Moral

Philosophy in the University of Edinburgh. Volume Second," *British Review and London Critical Journal* VI (Aug.): 170–200.

Mill, J. S. (1827) "Editorial Comments to Jeremy Bentham's *Rationale of Judicial Evidence*," in vol. XXXI (1989) of Mill (1963–1991).

———. (1828) "Whately's *Elements of Logic*," in vol. XI (1978) of Mill (1963–1991): 3–35.

———. (1843) *A System of Logic: Ratiocinative and Inductive* in vols. VII and VIII of Mill (1963–1991).

———. (1859) *Dissertations and Discussions: Political, Philosophical and Historical*, 2 vols. (London: John W. Parker).

———. (1865) *An Examination of Sir William Hamilton's Philosophy and of the Principal Philosophical Questions Discussed in his Writings*, in vol. IX (1979) of Mill (1963–1991).

———. (1873) *Autobiography*, in vol. I (1981) of Mill (1963–1991).

———. (1963–1991) *Collected Works of John Stuart Mill*, F.E.L. Priestly (gen. ed.), and subsequently J. M. Robson, 33 vols. (London/Toronto: Routledge and Kegan Paul/University of Toronto Press).

Reid, T. (1785) *Essay on the Intellectual Powers of Man*, reprint (Cambridge: John Bartlett, 1852).

Robson, J. M. (1974) "Textual Introduction", in J. M. Robson (ed.), vols. VII and VIII of *Collected Works of John Stuart Mill* (London/Toronto: Routledge and Kegan Paul/ University of Toronto Press): xlix-cviii.

———. (1989) "Introduction," in (ed.), vol. XXXI of *Collected Works of John Stuart Mill* (London/Toronto: Routledge and Kegan Paul/ University of Toronto Press): vii–l.

Robson, J. M.; Stillinger, J. (1981) "Introduction," in (ed.), vol. I of *Collected Works of John Stuart Mill* (London/Toronto: Routledge and Kegan Paul/ University of Toronto Press): vii-liv.

Ryan, A. (1970) *The Philosophy of John Stuart Mill* (London: Macmillan).

Scarre, G. (1984) "Proof and Implication in Mill's Philosophy of Logic," *History and Philosophy of Logic* 5 (1): 19–37.

———. (1989) *Logic and Reality in the Philosophy of John Stuart Mill* (Dordrecht: Kluwer).

Skorupski, J. (1989) *John Stuart Mill* (London: Routledge).

Snyder, J. (2006) *Reforming Philosophy: A Victorian Debate on Science and Society* (Chicago: University of Chicago Press).

———. (2012) "William Whewell," *The Stanford Encyclopedia of Philosophy*, E. N. Zalta (ed.), Winter 2012 Edition (http://plato.stanford.edu/archives/win2012/entries/whewell/).

Sparshott, F. E. (1978) "Introduction," in (ed.), vol. XI of *Collected Works of John Stuart Mill* (London/Toronto: Routledge and Kegan Paul/ University of Toronto Press): vii–lxxvi.

Stewart, D. (1792–1827) *Elements of the Philosophy of the Human Mind*, 3 vols., reprinted in *The Works of Dugald Stewart*, 7 vols. (Cambridge: Hilliard and Brown, 1829).

Whately, R. (1826) *Elements of Logic* (London: Mawman).

———. (1831) Elements of Logic, 4th ed., revised (London: Fellowes).

———. (1844) Elements of Logic, 8th ed. (London: Fellowes).Whewell, W. (1837) *History of the Inductive Sciences, from the Earliest to the Present Times*, 3 vols. (London/Cambridge: John W. Parker/J. and J. J. Deighton).

———. (1840) *The Philosophy of the Inductive Sciences, Founded upon their History*, 2 vols. (London/Cambridge: John W. Parker/J. and J. J. Deighton).

3 Mill and the Philosophy of Mathematics
Physicalism and Fictionalism

Mark Balaguer

I will do three things in this chapter. First, in section 1, I will provide a brief description of Mill's philosophy of mathematics. Then in section 2, I will explain why Mill's view can't account for contemporary mathematics or even the mathematics of his own day. Finally, in section 3, I will explain what Mill *should have* said about mathematics, given his background philosophical commitments.

Before starting, I should say that the section 1 presentation of Mill's view will be fairly brief. I'm not going to try to bring out all of the different features of his view. My aim is to present just the central core of his view. This will be enough to set up the arguments in section 2 for the claim that Mill's view isn't right.

I. MILL'S PHILOSOPHY OF MATHEMATICS

In order to understand Mill's philosophy of mathematics, you first have to understand what motivates him to say what he says. What motivates him are his background commitments to a thoroughgoing empiricist epistemology and a naturalistic worldview, i.e., a physicalistic, anti-platonist worldview. These background views *seem* to be incompatible with the discipline of mathematics. For (a) mathematics doesn't seem to be an empirical science—it seems to be an *a priori* science—and (b) it doesn't seem to be giving us theories of the physical world; rather, it seems to be giving us theories of platonistic mathematical structures like the natural-number sequence. So mathematics is a problem case for Mill. He needs to give an account of mathematics to show that it isn't a counterexample to his overall philosophical view.

In what follows, I will mostly be concerned with Mill's view of arithmetic, but I want to start by saying a few words about his view of geometry. To this end, let's consider a simple geometrical sentence that Mill discusses:

(R) All of the radii of a circle are equal in length.

What kinds of objects is this sentence *about*? Well, obviously, it's about circles and radii. But what kinds of objects are they? One natural response to this question is that circles and radii are *platonic* objects, or abstract objects—i.e., non-physical, non-mental, non-spatiotemporal objects. But given Mill's background philosophical commitments, it seems that he can't say this. So what he says instead is that ordinary geometrical sentences like (R) are about *physical* things—e.g., real circles drawn on a page with pen and ink. Now, since no physical circle is a *perfect* circle—or put differently, since no physical object satisfies the mathematical *definition* of a circle—Mill is forced to say that ordinary geometrical sentences like (R) are *not strictly speaking true*. In fact, the point here isn't simply that (R) isn't true of *all* circles; according to Mill, the sentence (R) ". . . is not exactly true of any circle [i.e., any real, physical circle]; it is only *nearly* true[.]"[1]

As long as we read (R) as being about physical circles, as opposed to platonistic circles, this point is entirely obvious. If I draw a circle on a page, and if I then proceed to draw several radii of that circle, then no matter how careful I am, it simply won't be true that all the radii I draw will be *exactly* equal in length; they will only be *nearly* equal in length. So on Mill's view, sentences like (R) are strictly speaking *false*.

It is important to note, however, that Mill does think that a certain sort of necessity attaches to geometrical sentences like (R). In particular, he thinks that they follow of necessity from the definitions and axioms of geometry. Here is Mill assenting to this view:

> When, therefore, it is affirmed that the conclusions of geometry are necessary truths, the necessity consists in reality only in this, that they correctly follow from the suppositions from which they are deduced.[2]

Mill is here denying that the theorems of geometry are necessary truths about real objects; there may be some necessary truths in the vicinity of geometry, but they aren't the theorems themselves, as ordinarily stated; they're *conditionals*—e.g., sentences like the following:

> (R#) If the axioms of geometry are true, and if there are objects answering to the definitions of geometry (e.g., if there are objects that really satisfy the precise definition of a perfect circle), then speaking of these perfect circles, we can say that (R) is strictly and literally true—i.e., we can say that all of the radii of a (perfect) circle are (exactly) equal in length.

On Mill's view, sentences like (R#) are not just true, but necessarily true. But this is perfectly consistent with a physicalistic, empiricist worldview; for (R) is *analytic*; its antecedent analytically entails its consequent.

Let me move on now to Mill's view of arithmetic. And, again, let me begin by looking at what Mill says about a simple arithmetical sentence. Here's one that he discusses:

(A) 2 + 1 = 3.

Prima facie, this sentence seems to be a claim about three numbers—namely, 1, 2 and 3—but, once again, this face-value reading seems to be off limits to Mill, given his background philosophical commitments. For, *prima facie*, it seems that if there are any such things as numbers, then they're abstract objects; and it seems that Mill can't allow that sentences like (A) are about abstract objects. Thus, to avoid claiming that (A) is literally about *numbers*, Mill takes it to be a general claim about all objects—or more precisely, all *collections* of objects, or *piles* of objects, or some such thing.[3] Mill puts the point as follows:

> All numbers must be numbers of something; there are no such things as numbers in the abstract. *Ten* must mean ten bodies, or ten sounds, or ten beatings of the pulse. But though numbers must be numbers of something, they may be numbers of anything. Propositions, therefore, concerning numbers have the remarkable peculiarity that they are propositions concerning all things whatever, all objects, all existences of every kind known to our experience.[4]

If we take the sentence (A) as our example, then we can read Mill as saying (roughly—more on this below) that (A) is equivalent to the following sentence:

> (A-M) For any two (disjoint, i.e., non-overlapping) piles of objects x and y, if there are two objects in x and if there's one object in y, then the pile that's made up of x and y together has three objects in it.

For instance, to use an example that Mill likes to use, the sentence (A) tells us, among other things, that if we push two pebbles together with one pebble, we will have three pebbles.

This gives Mill the desired result that arithmetical sentences like (A) are about ordinary physical objects, or piles of objects, rather than numbers. And it also gives him a way of claiming that sentences like (A) are *empirical*; for on Mill's view, these sentences are universal generalizations about piles of physical objects, and we come to know that these sentences are true by *induction*—in particular, from the many experiences that we have with ordinary piles of physical objects from early childhood on. Mill assents to this view in a number of places. For instance, after saying that the real fact behind (A) is that any three-membered pile of objects can be rearranged into a two-membered pile and a singleton pile, he says:

> The Science of Number is thus no exception to the conclusion previously arrived at that the processes even of deductive sciences are altogether inductive and that their first principles are generalizations from experience.[5]

So Mill's view of arithmetic is similar to his view of geometry in that he takes both branches of mathematics to be concerned with *physical* objects, and in both cases, he thinks that our knowledge is ultimately based in *empirical* knowledge of the relevant physical objects.

But does Mill think that the claims of arithmetic are strictly speaking false, in the way that those of geometry are? It depends. If we take a sentence like (A) and we apply it to things like *weight*—i.e., if we use it to calculate the weight of a pile of one-pound weights—then (A) will be only approximately true. For no physical object that goes by the name "one-pound weight" will actually weigh exactly one pound. So if we push one of these things together with two of them and infer that the whole pile weighs three pounds, this will be only approximately true. But as long as we're talking about just the *number* of things in a pile, as opposed to something like their weight, then arithmetical claims can be exactly true, according to Mill. For instance, if I have (exactly) two pebbles in my left hand and (exactly) one pebble in my right hand, then (assuming I have only two hands) I have *exactly* three pebbles in my hands.

Given this stance of Mill's, I think we have to conclude that it's not quite right to say that according to Mill, (A) is equivalent to (A-M). On his reading, (A) is even more general than (A-M); it entails (in a way that (A-M) doesn't) that two pounds and one pound make three pounds. This consequence of (A) isn't strictly speaking true, but it's still a consequence of that sentence, on Mill's view. In any event, in what follows, I will ignore this complication and write as if Mill takes (A) to be equivalent to (A-M). This will simplify the discussion, and no harm will come from simplifying in this way. In particular, none of the objections that I raise against Mill's view relies in any important way on this simplification.

There is a lot more that could be said about Mill's philosophy of mathematics; the remarks I've made here give only a brief introduction to his view. But these remarks are enough to see how Mill thinks that someone with his background philosophical views (i.e., someone who is committed to a naturalistic, anti-platonistic ontology and an empiricist epistemology) can account for mathematics. And as we'll presently see, the brief remarks I've provided here are also already enough to bring out the fact that Mill's view of mathematics is untenable.

II. PROBLEMS WITH MILL'S VIEW

Let me start by talking about Mill's view of arithmetic. The above remarks already make clear that Mill is committed to a certain view of the semantics of the language of arithmetic. In particular, he is committed to the idea that the sentences of arithmetic are about physical objects. I think this theory is clearly false. To see why, consider the following sentence, which was proved by Euclid:

(B) There are infinitely many prime numbers.

I'm not aware of Mill discussing sentences like this anywhere, but he seems to be committed to taking such sentences to be about physical objects, or piles of physical objects, or some such thing. After all, we presumably want to endorse a uniform semantics for all of arithmetic. So if sentences like (A) are to be read as being about physical objects, then we're going to have to read sentences like (B) in this way as well. But the problem is that there doesn't seem to be any plausible way to take (B) to be about physical objects. To see why, imagine a mathematics professor teaching Euclid's proof of sentence (B) to a classroom full of students, and imagine a student (say, Beatrice) raising her hand with the following objection:

> There couldn't be infinitely many prime numbers because my physics professor told me that there are only finitely many physical objects in the whole universe.

It seems reasonable to think that Beatrice just *doesn't understand*; she doesn't understand what Euclid's proof is supposed to show. For in the context of Euclid's proof, it doesn't *matter* how many physical objects there are. Even if it's true that there are only finitely many physical objects in the universe, this is simply *not* a good reason to reject Euclid's proof. And the only reasonable conclusion we can draw from this, I think, is that Euclid's theorem—i.e., sentence (B)—should not be interpreted as being about physical objects. It has to be read as being about something else; for if it *were* about physical objects, then Beatrice's worry would *not* be misguided. Thus, since Beatrice's worry *is* misguided—since it involves a failure to understand what Euclid's theorem is *about*—we have to conclude that Euclid's theorem is not about physical objects.

This problem with Mill's view is made more vivid if we switch to set theory. Now, you might think it's unfair to ask whether Mill's view can handle the claims of set theory, since set theory wasn't developed until long after Mill developed his view; but I disagree with this. First of all, the last edition of *A System of Logic* didn't appear until 1872. But the main point I want to make here is that I don't think the chronology matters. Set theory is an important branch of mathematics, so I think it's important to see whether the general Millian approach to mathematics can handle the development of this new theory. So let's consider the following theorem of set theory, which was proven by Cantor in 1870:

> (C) There are infinitely many transfinite cardinals that keep getting bigger and bigger without end.

Once again, it's hard to see how we can interpret this sentence as being about physical objects. Imagine a professor proving this theorem in class, and imagine a student (say, Big Red) complaining that this so-called "theorem" couldn't really be true because there aren't enough physical objects in the whole universe to make it true. It seems clear that what we ought to say about Big Red is that he *doesn't understand*; in particular, he doesn't understand what (C) *says*. For in the context of Cantor's theorem, the question of how many physical objects there are in the universe is entirely irrelevant. And given this, we have no choice but to infer that Cantor's theorem is simply not about physical objects.

A second problem with Mill's view is that it's out of touch with the actual methodology of actual working mathematicians. Mill's theory implies that the right methodology for determining whether sentences like (B) and (C) are true would involve an empirical investigation into the number of physical objects in the universe. But this means that it implies that the proofs of Euclid and Cantor are not just mistaken but completely wrongheaded in their methodology. If Mill were right, then Euclid and Cantor should have used empirical methods. But, of course, this is crazy. There's nothing wrong with the methodology of mathematical proof; the problem here is that Mill's view is simply false.

Very quickly, here's a third argument against Mill's view: when we apply his physicalistic approach to set theory, we get the conclusion that expressions that are supposed to refer to sets should be interpreted as referring to piles of physical objects. But this can't be right, because corresponding to every pile of physical objects—indeed, to every individual physical object—there are infinitely many sets. Corresponding to a ball, for instance, is the set containing the ball, the set containing its molecules, the set containing its atoms, and so on. Moreover, in addition to the set containing, say, the atoms, there's also the set containing that set, the set containing that set and so on to infinity. Clearly, these sets are not supposed to be purely physical objects, because (a) they are all supposed to be numerically distinct from one another, and (b) they all share the same physical base (i.e., the same pile of matter and the same spatiotemporal location). Thus, if these sets exist at all, then there must be something non-physical about them, over and above the physical base that they all share—i.e., the physical matter that makes up the ball. So sets cannot be purely physical objects. Or to put the point in semantic terms, the singular terms of set theory are not supposed to refer to purely physical objects. And the problem is that it's hard to see how we can accommodate this result without completely abandoning the Millian approach to mathematics.

I think there's something very telling about the inability of the Millian philosophy of mathematics to provide a plausible account of set theory. For insofar as Mill takes arithmetic to be about *piles* of objects, it seems to me that if his view can't provide a tenable account of the mathematical theory of *sets* of objects, then there's something seriously wrong with his view.

Finally, let's turn to geometry. Mill's view of the semantics of the language of geometry is counterintuitive in the extreme. It just seems hard to believe that when we do geometry, we're talking about real (i.e., imperfect) squares and circles and so on, and that when we assert the theorems of geometry, we're asserting strictly false near-truths about physical objects. This just flies directly in the face of our semantic intuitions about what we're talking about when we do geometry. The much more natural line to take here, on the semantics of the language of geometry, is that we're talking about perfect squares and circles, regardless of whether they exist.

But rather than just relying on an appeal to our semantic intuitions, let me offer a quick argument against Mill's view of geometry. His view seems to be completely incompatible with our response to the development of non-Euclidean geometries. If Mill were right, then geometry would be an empirical science about actual physical space, and the question of whether we ought to adopt Euclidean geometry or some non-Euclidean geometry would be a difficult empirical question for physicists. But whereas there may well be a difficult empirical question here about the structure of physical space, that's a question for *applied* mathematics. It's got nothing at all to do with *pure* mathematics. As far as pure mathematics is concerned, all there is to say is that Euclidean geometry is a good theory of Euclidean geometrical spaces, and Lobachevskian geometry is a good theory of Lobachevskian geometrical spaces, and so on. This is how the mathematical community has in fact responded to the discovery of non-Euclidean geometries. And this is the *right* response. And the reason it's the right response is that insofar as a geometrical theory is a pure mathematical theory, it simply isn't about anything physical. It isn't about real physical circles, as Mill contended, and it isn't about actual physical space.

III.   WHAT MILL SHOULD HAVE SAID ABOUT MATHEMATICS

I think there's another view that Mill could have endorsed in connection with mathematics that would have been consistent with both (a) his background philosophical commitments (i.e., naturalism, anti-platonism, empiricism, etc.) and (b) the actual facts about mathematical practice. To get at the view I've got in mind, let's start by making sure that we satisfy constraint (b)—i.e., by making sure we come up with a view that's consistent with actual mathematical practice. And let's begin here by trying to come up with the right semantic theory for ordinary mathematical discourse.

III.i.   What's the Right Semantic Theory for the Language of Mathematics?

Mill took ordinary mathematical sentences to be about physical objects, and I have argued here that this view is untenable. My argument focused on sentences like (B) and (C)—i.e., on sentences about infinities—but given that we want a uniform semantics for the language of arithmetic, the argument applies equally to simple sentences like (A), i.e., to sentences like "2 + 1 = 3." So let's start by trying to figure out what we should say about sentences like this. Or to simplify things even more, let's switch to a simple sentence of the form "*Fa*"—i.e., to a sentence like

(D) 3 is prime.

Prima facie, this sentence seems to be of the form "*Fa*." In other words, it seems to have the same logical form as sentences like "Mars is round." Just as the latter sentence says that a certain object (namely, Mars) has a certain property (namely, roundness), so too (D) seems to say that a certain object (namely, the number 3) has a certain property (namely, primeness).

Mill presumably thinks that if we accepted this view, then as empiricists and naturalistic anti-platonists, we would be led immediately into trouble. And so he rejects the face-value reading of arithmetical sentences. Again, he interprets (A) not as a claim about the numbers 1, 2 and 3, but as a universal generalization about all objects, or piles of objects. This, as we've seen, was a mistake. But I think there's a prior mistake already inherent in the decision to reject the face-value reading of sentences like (A)–(D). To appreciate this, let's forget about mathematics for a minute and just think about how we ought to proceed when we're doing empirical semantics, i.e., when we're interpreting the speech of ordinary humans. In this connection, it seems to me that the following principle is extremely plausible:

> *Face-value-ism*: When we interpret people's speech, the default setting is always to take them to be speaking literally, or at face value. To motivate a non-face-value interpretation of a given sentence, we have to motivate the claim that the speaker or speakers in question have positive intentions to be saying something other than what the sentence says literally, i.e., something other than what the sentence says when read at face value.

When I say that the speakers in question have to have *positive* intentions to be saying something non-literal, I don't mean that they have to have *conscious* intentions to be saying something non-literal; all I mean is that there has to be something about their overall psychology that makes it the case that they mean to be saying something other than what the sentence says at face value. When this point is appreciated, Face-value-ism becomes something close to a truism. Suppose that when sentence S is read at face value, it says that P, and suppose further that when people utter S, they don't have *any* intention, conscious or unconscious, to be saying anything other than P; then it's hard to see how we could plausibly maintain that when people utter S, they're actually saying something other than P. Let me illustrate this with an example. To this end, consider the following two sentences:

(M1) Mars is round.
(M2) The average mother has 2.4 children.

Read at face value, both of these sentences seem to say that a certain object has a certain property. (M1) seems to say that the object Mars has the property of roundness, and (M2) seems to say that a different object (namely, the average mother) has the property of having 2.4 children. But, of course, this isn't really what (M2) says. Or at any rate, this isn't how typical utterances of sentences like (M2) should be interpreted; if someone actually uttered (M2), it would almost certainly be the case that what the person was actually saying was that *on average, mothers have 2.4 children.* So in connection with sentences like (M2), it's plausible to endorse a non-face-value interpretation. But this is *only* because we have good empirical reasons to think that when people utter sentences like (M2), they intend to be speaking non-literally, and they *don't* intend to be interpreted at face value, i.e., as speaking of weird objects like *the average mother.*

But the situation with respect to (M1) is entirely different. When people say things like this, they usually don't have any intention to be saying anything non-literal. Now, of course, we could construct a case in which someone used an utterance of (M1) to say just about anything—e.g., that the microfilm is hidden in the foie gras. But (a) this would be true only if the speaker in question had an intention to be saying something non-literal, and (b) in connection with *ordinary* utterances of sentences like (M1), where the speaker doesn't have any such intention, there is no plausible way to treat these utterances as saying something non-literal.

If Face-value-ism is right, then we need to ask the following question: when ordinary mathematicians and ordinary folk utter ordinary mathematical sentences like (A)–(D), do they have any intention to be speaking non-literally? The answer to this question is, I think, obvious; in ordinary cases, when people utter ordinary mathematical sentences, they do *not* have any intention to be speaking non-literally. Only someone who was worried about the philosophical implications of our mathematical utterances—someone like Mill—would ever have such an intention. And so it seems to me that we have strong reasons to think that ordinary utterances of mathematical sentences like (A)–(D) should be read at face value. Thus, if we focus on (D)—i.e., on the sentence "3 is prime"—it should be read as making a claim about the number 3; in particular, it should be read as saying that that object has the property of primeness.

Now, you might think that accepting this conclusion is incompatible with Mill's background philosophical commitments—i.e., with the adoption of a naturalistic, anti-platonistic metaphysics and an empiricist epistemology. But let's keep an open mind about this, and let's keep pursing the current line of thought.

If we endorse a face-value interpretation of the sentence "3 is prime," then the next question we need to ask is what the singular term "3" is supposed to refer to (or equivalently, what the sentence "3 is prime" is supposed to be about). There are three possible answers to this question:

Semantic physicalism: Numerals like "3" are supposed to refer to physical objects, and so ordinary arithmetical sentences like "3 is prime" are best interpreted as straightforward claims about physical objects.

Semantic psychologism: Numerals like "3" are supposed to refer to mental objects, presumably ideas in our heads, and so ordinary arithmetical sentences like "3 is prime" are best interpreted as straightforward claims about mental objects, i.e., things that exist in actual human heads.

Semantic platonism: Numerals like "3" are supposed to refer to abstract objects—i.e., non-physical, non-mental, non-spatiotemporal objects—and so ordinary arithmetical sentences like "3 is prime" are best interpreted as straightforward claims about abstract objects.

There are several problems with semantic physicalism. First, given that we're reading "3" as a singular term, i.e., a term that's supposed to denote a unique object, if we take it to refer to a physical object, then it's hard to see *which* physical object it could be referring to. It's not as if we're going to unearth the number 3 on an excavation in South Dakota. The problem here is that there is no specific physical object that could plausibly be taken as being the referent of the numeral 3. If we're going to endorse a physicalistic philosophy of arithmetic, the only reasonable way to proceed is the Millian way—i.e., to abandon the face-value interpretation of "3 is prime" and to read it as a general claim about all three-membered piles of physical objects. In addition to this, semantic physicalism has all the problems that Mill's view has. For instance, it seems that if semantic physicalism were true—if numerals were supposed to refer to ordinary physical objects—then it would be reasonable to worry that there aren't enough objects in the entire universe to serve as referents for all of the various numerals (or to make sentences like "There are infinitely many prime numbers" true). Thus, since this is in fact *not* a reasonable worry about arithmetic, it seems that semantic physicalism is false.

Similar arguments can be run against semantic psychologism. For starters, it seems clear that if this view were right, then it would be reasonable to worry that there aren't enough mental objects in the universe to make our mathematical sentences and theories true. To appreciate this, imagine that after being taught Euclid's proof (or Cantor's proof), Big Red raised his hand and said this:

There couldn't be infinitely many prime numbers (or infinitely many transfinite cardinals) because my psychology professor told me that there are only finitely many ideas in each human head, and my astronomy professor told me there are no aliens with thoughts, and so there are only finitely many mental objects in the whole universe.

Once again, it seems reasonable to conclude from this little speech that Big Red *doesn't understand*. In the context of Euclid's and Cantor's proofs, it doesn't *matter* how many mental objects there are in the universe. Even if it's true that there are only finitely many mental objects in the universe, this is simply not a good reason to reject the two proofs. And the only reasonable conclusion we can draw from this, I think, is that the two theorems—i.e., the sentences that say that there are infinitely many primes and infinitely many transfinite cardinals—should not be interpreted as being about actual mental objects that exist in our heads.

It's important to note that the worry here is not that humans can't *conceive* of an infinite set. The worry has to do with the number of actual mental objects (i.e., distinct number-ideas, or set-ideas) that are *actually residing* in human heads. Semantic psychologism implies that in order for standard arithmetical theories like Peano Arithmetic (PA) to be true, there has to be an infinite number of actual mental objects. Why? Because PA implies that there are infinitely many numbers; it implies that there is such a thing as the number 1, and there is such a thing as the number 2, and 2 is not identical to 1, and so on. Thus, if semantic psychologism were right, then the truth of PA would depend on there actually existing infinitely many distinct number-ideas in human heads. But, in fact, the truth of PA clearly *doesn't* depend on this; if you're worried that PA might be false because there aren't enough actual ideas to go around, then that just shows that you don't understand what PA *says*. And so the conclusion we should draw here is that semantic psychologism is false.

A second problem with semantic psychologism is that it implies that our mathematical theories are empirical theories and that the right methodology for determining whether there are, say, infinitely many primes would involve an empirical investigation into the number of actual number-ideas that exist in the universe. In other words, semantic psychologism implies that Euclid's proof is not just mistaken but completely wrongheaded in its methodology. If semantic psychologism were true, then Euclid should have used empirical methods. But, of course, this is crazy. There's nothing wrong with the method of mathematical proof; the problem here is that semantic psychologism is false.

You might complain that these arguments are directed at a silly or trivial version of semantic psychologism that no one would ever endorse. Well, I agree with that. The view is crazy. (As Frege says, "Weird and wonderful . . . are the results of taking seriously the suggestion that number is an idea."⁶) But the problem is that there's no way to get rid of the craziness, or the silliness, without altering the view in a way that makes it the case that it's no longer a psychologistic view at all. Suppose, for instance, that someone said something like this:

> The psychologistic view isn't that mathematics is about *actual* ideas that really exist inside of human heads. We can take the view to be that mathematical sentences are about what it's *possible* to do in our heads. For instance, to say that there are infinitely many prime numbers is not

to say that there really exists an actual infinity of prime-number ideas inside of human heads; it's to say that it's possible to construct infinitely many prime numbers in our heads.

There are a few problems with this view. In the present context, the main problem is that the view described here isn't a version of semantic psychologism at all, and so it's no defense against the above objections. Semantic psychologism is the view that mathematical sentences are about mental objects. The above view rejects this, and so it's not a version of semantic psychologism. Rather, it's a version of non-literalism, or non-Face-value-ism; in particular, on this view, "3 is prime" doesn't say that a certain object (namely, 3) is prime; rather, it says something about what it's possible for humans to do. But as an empirical hypothesis about what ordinary people actually mean when they utter sentences like "3 is prime," this is extremely implausible; there's simply no *evidence* that people really mean to say things like this when they utter sentences like "3 is prime." (Again, the only people who ever mean things like this by mathematical claims are people who are worried about philosophy.)

In any event, if we stick with semantic psychologism, the view is completely implausible for the reasons given above. And if this is right, then the only option we're left with is semantic platonism. Now, you might object here that just as there are reasons to resist semantic physicalism and semantic psychologism, so too there are reasons to resist semantic platonism. For you might think it's implausible that ordinary people intend to be speaking of abstract objects when they say things like "3 is prime." But semantic platonists don't need to say that people have such intentions, and indeed, they *shouldn't* say this. What they should say is that (a) people are best interpreted as speaking literally when they say things like "3 is prime," and so these sentences have to be taken as being about objects (in particular, numbers); and (b) our semantic intentions are straightforwardly incompatible with semantic physicalism and semantic psychologism, and so there's no way to interpret us as talking about physical or mental objects when we say things like "3 is prime" (this is what the above arguments show); and (c) there's nothing in our intentions that's incompatible with semantic platonism; and so (d) even if people don't have a positive intention to be referring to abstract objects when they say things like "3 is prime," the best interpretation of these utterances has it that they *are* about abstract objects—or at any rate that they're *supposed* to be about abstract objects, or that they *purport* to be about abstract objects, or some such thing.

So if all of the arguments in this section are correct, then semantic platonism is the best semantic theory of ordinary mathematical discourse. And it's worth noting that the argument I've given for this claim is entirely *empirical*. It's based on considerations about what actual people (mathematicians and ordinary folk) are really saying when they utter sentences like "3 is prime." In a nutshell, the idea is that (a) we should interpret people as speaking literally when they engage in talk of numbers, and (b) there's no plausible way of taking them to be talking about physical or mental objects. It's hard to see how Mill could plausibly deny either of these claims. And so it seems to me that we have good reasons to endorse semantic platonism.

(In response to my claim that the argument I've constructed here is empirical, you might ask what the relevant empirical *data* are. The answer is that the data I'm using here are the intuitions of ordinary speakers—e.g., the intuition that facts about how many physical objects there are in the universe are completely irrelevant to the truth values of ordinary mathematical claims about how many prime numbers and transfinite cardinals there are. Now, I haven't actually performed an "X-phi" study to verify that people really do have this intuition; but I think it's pretty obvious that anyone who understood the relevant sentences (i.e., sentences like "There are infinitely many prime numbers" and "There are infinitely many transfinite cardinals") would have this intuition. Maybe I'm wrong about this, but if I'm right, then I think we have good empirical reason to reject the idea that these sentences should be interpreted as being about physical objects.)

III.ii. Fictionalism

It might seem that semantic platonism is incompatible with Mill's background philosophical commitments. Indeed, it seems likely to me that something like this thought is why Mill jumped ship at the start and denied that arithmetical sentences like "3 is prime" should be read at face value. For insofar as Mill wants to endorse a physicalistic ontology, he can't very well countenance the existence of non-physical abstract objects. But I have not argued here for the existence of abstract objects. All I've argued for is a *semantic* conclusion. What I've argued, in a nutshell, is that our mathematical sentences and theories are *supposed* to be about abstract objects—or that we should read them as *purporting* to be about abstract objects, or some such thing. But it doesn't follow from this that there *are* abstract objects. To help bring this point out, let's switch to a different case. Consider the following semantic theory:

> *Semantic theism*: The word "God" (in ordinary English) is supposed to refer to an intelligent creator of the universe—i.e., it should be interpreted as *purporting* to refer to such a creature.

It seems to me that this theory is obviously true. But, of course, it doesn't follow from this that *theism* is true, i.e., that there really is a God who created the universe. And the same thing is true in the case of mathematics. From the mere fact that we use the numeral "3" in a way that makes it the case that it's supposed to refer to an abstract object (namely, the number 3), it doesn't follow that there really is such a thing as the number 3.

But whatever we say about theism and semantic theism, it might seem that in the case of mathematics, there is an easy argument from semantic platonism to platonism. In particular, it might seem that we can argue in the following way:

(i)   Semantic platonism is true—i.e., ordinary mathematical sentences like "3 is prime" are straightforward claims about abstract objects (or more precisely, they're *supposed* to be about abstract objects). Therefore,
(ii) Mathematical sentences like "3 is prime" could be true only if platonism were true—i.e., only if abstract objects really existed. But
(iii) Mathematical sentences like "3 is prime" *are* true. Therefore,
(iv) Platonism is true (where platonism is just the view that there exist abstract objects and our mathematical theories are descriptions of these objects).

Prima facie, this argument seems very compelling. I've already argued for premise (i). Moreover, (ii) seems to follow immediately from (i). To appreciate this point, think of the sentence "Mars is red"; this sentence couldn't be true unless Mars existed. And likewise, given (i), "3 is prime" couldn't be true unless an abstract object existed; in particular, it couldn't be true unless the number 3 existed. So it seems that (ii) is true. Moreover, (iii) seems entirely obvious, and when we put (ii) and (iii) together, they entail platonism. So it seems that semantic platonism leads directly to platonism.

But there's a way out of this argument. We can reject premise (iii) and endorse mathematical fictionalism. This view can be defined as follows:

Mathematical fictionalism: (a) semantic platonism is true—i.e., ordinary mathematical sentences like "3 is prime" are supposed to be about abstract objects (or they *purport* to be about abstract objects, or some such thing); but (b) there are no such things as abstract objects; and so (c) ordinary mathematical sentences like "3 is prime" are not true.[7]

Fictionalism doesn't just give us a way of responding to the above argument for platonism. It is also, I think, capable of giving Mill everything he wants in a philosophy of mathematics. But to appreciate this point, we first need to develop the view in a bit more detail. There are a number of objections that you might raise against fictionalism, but the most obvious one is probably the following:

Since fictionalism entails that sentences like "3 is prime" are untrue, it seems to give us no account of the difference between "3 is prime" and, say, "3 is even." It seems beyond doubt that there's some important sense in which "3 is prime" is *right*, or *correct*, or some such thing, whereas "3 is even" is *not* correct. This seems to be an objective fact that we can't simply ignore, and so fictionalists need to say what the correctness of sentences like "3 is prime" consists in.

Hartry Field (1989) responded to this worry by claiming that the sense in which "3 is prime" is correct and "3 is even" is incorrect is roughly equivalent to the sense in which "Alice entered Wonderland by falling down a rabbit hole" is correct and "Alice entered Wonderland by falling down a man hole" is incorrect. More specifically, on Field's view, the so-called correctness of "3 is prime" consists in the fact that it's *true in the story of mathematics*, or *part of* the story of mathematics.

This, I think, is a good start, but fictionalists need to say more. In particular, they need to say what the story of mathematics consists in. According to Field (1998), the story of mathematics consists (roughly) in the various axiom systems that are accepted in the various branches of mathematics, and so on his view, the relevant sort of mathematical correctness—what we might call "fictionalistic mathematical correctness"—comes down (roughly) to following from accepted axioms. But I have argued elsewhere (2009) that this view can't be right and that fictionalists should instead endorse the view that the story of mathematics consists in the claim that platonism is true, i.e., the claim that there really do exist abstract objects of the kinds that our mathematical theories purport to be about. On this view, we can say that a mathematical sentence S is *fictionalistically correct* if and only if it would have been true if platonism had been true; or what is perhaps simpler, we can say that S is fictionalistically correct if and only if the following sentence is strictly and literally true:

(S#) Necessarily, if platonism is true (i.e., if there exist abstract objects of the kinds that our mathematical theories purport to be about), then S is true.

If we endorse this view, then all the mathematical sentences that we ordinarily think of as true (e.g., "3 is prime") will be fictionalistically correct, and all the mathematical sentences that we ordinarily think of false (e.g., "3 is even") will *not* be fictionalistically correct. And given this, fictionalists can say that what really matters in mathematics is fictionalistic correctness, not literal truth. (I think it can also be argued that fictionalistic correctness is what matters in the applications of mathematics, i.e., in the use that empirical scientists make of mathematics; I can't argue this point here, but see my (1998).)

There's a lot more that could be said in defense of mathematical fictionalism, but I think I've said enough to motivate the claim that this view fits perfectly with Mill's overall philosophical view. First, it is clearly a naturalistic, physicalistic view; i.e., it doesn't commit to the existence of any metaphysically occult objects. Second, fictionalism is perfectly compatible with a thoroughgoing empiricism. The only sentences in the neighborhood of mathematics that are literally (and non-vacuously[8]) true, on this view, are sentences of the form (S#), e.g., sentences like "Necessarily, if platonism is true (i.e., if there exist abstract objects of the kinds that we have in mind when we do mathematics), then 3 is prime." But sentences like this are *analytic*; their antecedents analytically entail their consequents, and so knowledge of these sentences should be compatible with empiricism. Indeed, Mill is already committed to the idea that we can have knowledge of such sentences. This came out in our discussion of Mill's view of geometry; in particular, it is very clear in the following passage from Mill:

> When, therefore, it is affirmed that the conclusions of geometry are necessary truths, the necessity consists in reality only in this, that they correctly follow from the suppositions from which they are deduced.[9]

Given this stance of Mill's, I think he ought to allow that sentences of the form (S#) are true and that we can have knowledge of these sentences by simply working out the consequences of the existence of things like the natural-number sequence. In other words, I think Mill ought to see the fictionalist line here as a plausible alternative to his own view.

(Mill might want to resist fictionalism because he might think that platonism is *impossible*, and given this, he might say that *every* mathematical sentence comes out as fictionalistically correct. I think this response is misguided, but I can't get into this here. It's worth noting, however, that this stance isn't forced on us by the other background philosophical views that I've been assuming in this chapter; i.e., it's not forced on us by endorsing views like naturalism, anti-platonism, empiricism and so on.)

Now, of course, if we endorse fictionalism, then we'll have to say that ordinary mathematical sentences like "3 is prime" are strictly speaking false (or at least untrue), and you might think that this is a cost. To this, I have two things to say. First, it's hard to see why *Mill* would consider it a cost. We've already seen that he was perfectly comfortable with the idea that certain kinds of mathematical claims that we ordinarily think of as obviously true are, in fact, *false*. Once again, this emerged in our discussion of Mill's philosophy of geometry. The claim that all of the radii of a circle are exactly equal in length is, according to Mill, strictly speaking false. On Mill's view, there are no such things as perfect circles; the only circles that really exist are imperfect physical circles; but in connection with these imperfect circles, it's simply not true that all of their radii are all exactly equal in length. So, again, Mill was already committed to the idea that certain mathematical sentences that seem obviously true are actually false. And given this, it's hard to see why he would balk at the claim that "3 is prime" is false—i.e., at the claim that whereas "3 is prime" is obviously "right" in some sense of the term (in particular, whereas it's fictionalistically correct), it isn't strictly speaking true.

The second point I want to make in response to the above worry is just this: I think it can be argued that there actually isn't any substantive cost to claiming that ordinary mathematical sentences like "3 is prime" are strictly and literally false. For I think it can be argued that what really matters in mathematics is fictionalistic correctness, not literal truth, and I think it can also be argued that fictionalistic correctness gives us everything we might have rationally wanted out of mathematical truth. I obviously can't argue for these sweeping claims here, but see my (1998) and (2009).

In any event, if I'm right about this, then there aren't any costs to Mill for endorsing mathematical fictionalism. But there is a huge gain. For unlike Mill's own view, fictionalism dovetails with the actual facts about mathematical practice. It doesn't have any of the odd consequences that Mill's view does. In particular, fictionalism doesn't entail the cogency of the weird worries described above about the proofs of Euclid and Cantor. If fictionalism is the right philosophy of mathematics, then when the above-described students object to the proofs of Euclid and Cantor on the grounds that there aren't enough physical objects in the universe to make their theorems true, we can respond in the way that we intuitively *want* to respond, i.e., by saying something like this:

> What are you talking about? The theorems of Euclid and Cantor aren't about physical objects. They're about mathematical objects. Or at any rate, they *purport* to be about mathematical objects; in particular, they purport to be about numbers and sets.

And if someone responded to this by pointing out that there are no such things as mathematical objects like numbers and sets, then we could respond by saying this: "So what? All that shows is that the theorems of Euclid and Cantor aren't literally *true*. But that doesn't matter. They're still *good* in the sense that matters in mathematics because they're fictionalistically correct. In other words, they're true in the story of mathematics. Or to put the point still another way, the theorems of Euclid and Cantor are good, or fictionalistically correct, because the following claim is strictly and literally true: necessarily, if there are abstract objects of the kinds that platonists have in mind (i.e., the kinds that our mathematical theories purport to be about), then there are infinitely many prime numbers, and there are infinitely many transfinite cardinals that keep getting bigger and bigger without end.

In short, then, my conclusion is that Mill should have endorsed mathematical fictionalism. If he had done this, he could have hung onto views like naturalism, anti-platonism, empiricism and so on while providing a much more satisfying and plausible theory of mathematics.

NOTES

1. Mill (1843, CW: VII.226). Emphasis added. All references to Mill's works are to the authoritative edition of *Collected Works of John Stuart Mill* (Mill, 1963–1991—cited as CW, followed by volume and page number), unless otherwise indicated.
2. Mill (1843, CW: VII.227).

3. Mill uses the term "collections", but it's pretty clear that he's *not* thinking of *sets*; or at any rate, he's not thinking of sets in the way that we think of them today; in particular, he's not thinking of collections as abstract objects. He's thinking about purely physical collections. I will talk of these as *piles* to make their physicality clear, but of course I do not mean to suggest by this that the objects have to be piled on top of each other. Thus, e.g., on my lingo, the Eifel Tower and the Empire State Building form a perfectly good "pile."
4. Mill (1843, CW: VII.254–55).
5. Mill (1843, CW: VII.254–55).
6. Frege (1884: section 27).
7. This view was first introduced by Field (1980), and it has been further developed by myself (1998), Rosen (2001), Yablo (2002) and Leng (2010).
8. According to fictionalists, lots of universal mathematical sentences are vacuously true. E.g., "All even numbers are divisible by 2" is true for the simple reason that there *are* no numbers; i.e., it's true for the same reason that "All unicorns are purple" is true. But this is completely unimportant and uninteresting. After all, "All even numbers are *purple*" comes out true on this view as well.
9. Mill (1843, CW: VII.227).

REFERENCES

Balaguer, M. (1998) *Platonism and Anti-Platonism in Mathematics* (Oxford: Oxford University Press).
———. (2009) "Fictionalism, Theft, and the Story of Mathematics," *Philosophia Mathematica* 17: 131–62.
Field, H. (1980) *Science without Numbers* (Princeton, NJ: Princeton University Press).
———. (1989) *Realism, Mathematics, and Modality* (New York: Basil Blackwell).
———. (1998) "Mathematical Objectivity and Mathematical Objects," in C. MacDonald and S. Laurence (eds.) *Contemporary Readings in the Foundations of Metaphysics* (Oxford: Basil Blackwell): 387–403.
Frege, G. (1884) *The Foundations of Arithmetic*, J. L. Austin (trans.) (Oxford: Basil Blackwell, 1953).
Leng, M. (2010) *Mathematics and Reality* (Oxford: Oxford University Press).
Mill, J. S. (1843) *A System of Logic, Ratiocinative and Inductive: Being a Connected View of the Principles of Evidence and the Methods of Scientific Investigation*, in vols. VII and VIII (1974) of Mill (1963–1991).
———. (1963–1991) *Collected Works of John Stuart Mill*, F.E.L. Priestly (gen. ed.), and subsequently J. M. Robson, 33 vols. (London/Toronto: Routledge and Kegan Paul/University of Toronto Press).
Rosen, G. (2001) "Nominalism, Naturalism, Epistemic Relativism," *Noûs* 35 (Issue Supplement s15, J. Tomberlin (ed.) *Philosophical Perspectives 15: Metaphysics*): 69–91.
Yablo, S. (2002) "Go Figure: A Path through Fictionalism," *Midwest Studies in Philosophy* 25: 72–102.

4   Mill's and Whewell's Competing Visions of Logic[1]

Elijah Millgram

While John Stuart Mill was, he tells us, revising his draft of the *System of Logic*:

> Dr. Whewell's *Philosophy of the Inductive Sciences* made its appearance; a circumstance fortunate for me, as it gave me what I greatly desired, a full treatment of the subject by an antagonist, and enabled me to present my ideas with greater clearness and emphasis as well as fuller and more varied development, in defending them against definite objections, and confronting them distinctly with an opposite theory.
>
> . . . What hopes I had of exciting any immediate attention, were mainly grounded on the polemical propensities of Dr. Whewell; who, I thought, from observation of his conduct in other cases, would probably do something to bring the book into notice, by replying, and that promptly, to the attack on his opinions.[2]

William Whewell did take Mill's objections seriously, and did reply, in his *Of Induction*; he subsequently revised his *Philosophy of the Inductive Sciences* and reissued it as three differently titled volumes; when he did so, one of these, the *Philosophy of Discovery*, contained a chapter rebutting Mill's objections.[3]

Because both Whewell and Mill ended up prominent figures in the intellectual world of their day, the back and forth was noticed. As the "Mill-Whewell debate" is remembered today, it was a disagreement between two philosophers of science about both scientific method and the correct analysis of induction. John Stuart Mill, we are told, thought that the scientific method was built around what we now call "induction"—one observes, say, that a number of crows are black and infers that the next one will also be black—although Mill fortified that basic inference pattern with the "Four Methods" that are even at the present time taught in critical thinking classes, as well as with a number of further methods, specific to particular types of sciences, that are less widely known. Whewell, for his part, is thought of as perhaps anticipating views we associate today with Philip Kitcher, on which scientists adopt theories that unify results across theoretical domains, or perhaps as advancing an ancestor of abduction and inference to the best explanation.[4]

If the Mill-Whewell debate really had this shape and content, it would be of no more than historical interest. The positions that are attributed to the opponents are familiar, and we do not need archaic Victorian-era formulations to assess their merits. And in general, while a great deal of energy is expended by historians of philosophy over whether the label for a well-understood contemporary position sticks to a dead philosopher—for instance, on whether Hume was an internalist or Aristotle a metaphysical realist—if the dead figure's view really was the well-understood position, we do not need him. Dead philosophers are worth figuring out when their views are unfamiliar; it is especially in those cases that we are likely to learn something from them.

But both the issues at stake in the disagreement between Mill and Whewell, and the positions they took, have been erroneously located in philosophy of science, or so I will suggest here. Much of the common ground between the two of them was indeed the insistence that we must look to the history of science to determine what it is to reason correctly about matters of fact. But in the psychologistic way of thinking that was taken for granted until Frege and Husserl, the study of what it is to reason correctly is logic.[5] So the dispute is properly characterized as belonging to philosophy of logic, and both the positions and the arguments will be surprising to most turn-of-the-millennium philosophers.

I will first recap Mill's view of induction, sketch the main elements of Whewell's view and remark on a few parallels between the positions. Then I will turn to the protagonists' respective modes of argumentation. Mill was committed to arguing for his inductivism inductively; Whewell was analogously committed to giving an argument for his notion of induction that conformed to his views about what it was, and I will describe how he attempted to do that. I will turn to the question of why it is that, almost always, Whewell and Mill strike readers as talking past one another. I will argue that this is a misconception, and explain how it was that each of them did their best to provide argumentation that the other party to the dispute would be forced to accept on his own terms.

I.

Mill's views in logic and the philosophy of science are in one way a little like his moral and political opinions: it is too easy on first or even second reading to assimilate them to what are mainstream notions today, and so fail to notice his more startling claims. Both to preempt this, and to prepare the way for comparison with Whewell, I'm going to take a slightly unusual route into Mill's inductivism. The so-called New Riddle of Induction, it turns out, was not all that new—although in the middle of the last century

Nelson Goodman managed to convey its force more vividly than perhaps ever before. Mill was quite aware that induction doesn't treat all predicates alike, and his understanding of the problem was more nuanced than Goodman's. It is not just that some predicates (like "green") are treated as legitimately mediating conclusions drawn on the basis of empirical evidence, and others (like "grue") are not: we treat the predicates we do take to be legitimate very differently from one another. (If the New Riddle is new to you, I've put a recap in this footnote.[6])

> When a chemist announces the existence and properties of a newly-discovered substance, if we confide in his accuracy, we feel assured that the conclusions he has arrived at will hold universally, though the induction be founded but on a single instance. We do not withhold our assent, waiting for a repetition of the experiment . . . Now mark another case, and contrast it with this. Not all the instances which have been observed since the beginning of the world, in support of the general proposition that all crows are black, would be deemed a sufficient presumption of the truth of the proposition, to outweigh the testimony of one unexceptionable witness who should affirm that in some region of the earth not fully explored, he had caught and examined a crow, and had found it to be grey.[7]

We correctly induce more confidently on some predicates than on others. At the limit, we (correctly!) refuse to proceed with inductive inferences driven by certain predicates. The puzzle then is: what makes similarities better and worse bases for induction? And Mill tells us, "Whoever can answer this question knows more of the philosophy of logic than the wisest of the ancients, and has solved the problem of induction."[8]

Mill's solution to the problem is very much in the spirit of Goodman's later attempt on it: some types of induction have a better track record than others.[9] We start out our collective history with the simplest, crudest inductions-by-enumeration: we have observed a great many crows and found them all to be black; we conclude that the next one will be black as well. Over the course of time, we experiment with more careful and complicated variations on the technique, and, again over time, we come to see (and this is itself an inductive inference) which work best, and which work in which domains. Mill's various Methods—the famous Four Methods, and the further Methods that, over the course of the *System of Logic* he spells out and argues are suitable for different sorts of science—are metainductively warranted *refinements* of those initial and so very crude inductions.[10] His treatment is only partial, but is ambitious enough to make him, following on that "knows more . . . than the wisest of the ancients," no doubt inadvertently immodest.

Two of these refinements deserve special notice. First, Mill holds that all inductive inference proceeds from particulars to particulars: I observe a great many black crows and properly speaking infer not the general claim that all crows are black, but that various particular crows that I have yet to observe will prove to be black. The general claim, Mill argues, is not part of any inference, but rather a mnemonic device: a reminder of the evidence I have seen, and a way of encoding it that allows me to keep track of which conclusions about particulars that evidence warrants. Since it is not part of any inference, a syllogism constructed using such a general claim as a major premise cannot count as inference, and as deductive inference was in Mill's day understood to be captured by syllogisms, Mill was arguing that there is no such thing as deductive inference at all: what appears to us to be syllogistic deduction is in fact a refinement (albeit an important one) of *inductive* technique; not argument, but a way of monitoring and controlling the progress of our inductive arguments. In Mill's view, *all* inference about matters of fact is inductive.[11]

Second, the more mature sciences can be systematized so thoroughly that results in the science can be derived from a small set of axioms. Like a syllogism's major premise, the axioms are compressed encodings of the evidence base for the science; even the axioms of apparently *a priori* sciences such as arithmetic and geometry are, Mill claims, merely encodings of observational evidence and the warrant it provides. When Mill calls a science "Deductive," we must not be confused; systematized sciences, including "Deductive" sciences, are further and dramatic refinements—once again, warranted by our experience with them over the history of inquiry—of our inductive reasoning.

If logic is, as Mill and his contemporaries understood it, the study of inference, and if there is no deduction as we understand it, but only inductive inference, then a theory of induction *is* a full-featured theory of logic—and that conclusion is borne out in the title, *A System of Logic*, which Mill chose for his *magnum opus*. Mill understood himself to be, first and foremost, a philosopher of logic.

II.

Whewell tells us that

> *Induction* is a term applied to describe the *process* of a true Colligation of Facts by means of an exact and appropriate Conception.
>
> An Induction is not the mere *sum* of the Facts which are colligated. The Facts are not only brought together, but seen in a new point of view. A new mental Element is *superinduced* . . . once this is effectually done, the novelty of the conception is overlooked, and the conception is considered as part of the fact.[12]

Whewell's central concept, "Colligation," is not one of our words, so I will walk through the central elements of Whewell's view in a slightly anachronizing vocabulary. (As I introduce Whewell's own vocabulary, I will mark it by reproducing his capitalization, but only on the initial use: the modern reader's patience with the orthography of the time is quickly exhausted.) At any given stage in the development of science, we will find ourselves with a repertoire of Ideas, in terms of which our observations are couched; we will also find ourselves with a collection of Facts. For instance, we observe logs (thus deploying ideas such as that of a physical object); we notice that when you divide a log in two parts, each part is hard to lift, but not as hard to lift as the both of them together; we notice that when you burn a log, the ashes are easier to lift than the log was; we introduce devices such as scales to systematize such observations, and over the course of time perhaps collect a great many of them.[13]

At the ensuing stage (the Epoch of the emerging science), an especially insightful scientist might introduce a new idea, *Weight*. It has proved possible, remarkably often, to spell out the content of an idea formally or semiformally: in the development of geometry, the novel idea is that of Space, whose content is unpacked by Euclid's axiomatization; analogously, the content of the idea of weight will be given by statements like: any physical object has a weight, weights can be treated arithmetically, weight is conserved. This process of spelling out the content of an idea is the move to a *Conception*. (As someone might say when making this move: we all have an intuitive idea of weight, but now let me explain my conception of it.[14]) At this point a new science—perhaps called "Barology"[15]—will crystallize around the idea. In this science, the conception of weight will allow one to derive the many and varied lower-level facts about scales, lifting logs and so on.[16]

The test for correctness of an idea is Consilience, that is, the ability to draw together phenomena and theoretical treatments that had seemed qualitatively different enough to belong to distinct subject matters. In another much-discussed illustration, Newton's theory of universal gravitation drew together the heliocentric theory of Copernicus, the fact that the "Satellites of Jupiter and Saturn revolve according to Kepler's Laws," the tides being "produced by attraction of Moon and Sun on Sea," the "Fall of heavy bodies" and much else.[17] Whewell is quite confident that a theoretical advance whose organizing idea makes possible the consilience of a wide range of different classes of fact will not need to be walked back, and he believes his confidence to be supported by the history of science in its entirety.[18] Although consilience has been the focus of discussion of Whewell's philosophy of science over the last century, it is important to remember that, for him, it is invoked to spell out—to provide a conception of—the idea he took to be central, namely, colligation. If we focus so exclusively on a secondary or subsidiary concept that we lose track of the idea it is there to elucidate, we will fail to understand what Whewell thought he was doing.[19]

The novel idea, if successfully introduced and spelled out, will induce something like an aspect shift: as the idea is clarified, it gradually becomes obvious that the weight of the smoke *must* be the weight of the logs minus the weight of the ashes.[20] "We do not see [Ideas], we see *through them*."[21] The hard-won empirical facts, in this case, about which physical objects tip the scales which way, about how hard it feels to lift them and so on turn out, in retrospect, to have a large *necessary* and *a priori* component, in this case, the arithmetic manipulability of the values we use the scales to assign:[22] "in the progress of that exact speculative knowledge which we call Science, Facts which were at a previous period merely Observed Facts, come to be known as Necessary Truths".[23] The aspect shift induced by colligation (in this case, of the lower-level facts by the idea of weight) makes what was formerly an exotic Theory, advanced in order to accommodate evidence, into a fact in its own turn, which can now be drawn upon in the search for the next scientific advance.

Whewell more than acknowledged his debt to Kant, and we should see colligation as an historicized adaptation of the Kantian notion of synthesis—not quite as we are taught it today, but as it was received in the nineteenth century—to the philosophy of science.[24] Like Kantian cognitions, which are synthesized into larger cognitions via the addition of a further conceptual element provided by the cognizer, facts are colligated, through the addition of a further idea, into larger facts. (Conversely, just as, in Kant, anything we are aware of is *already* a product of synthesis, *every* fact is Janus-faced—it contains subordinate facts colligated by an appropriate idea—all the way down.) The history of science is the history of progressive colligations; unlike Kantian syntheses, the last two-and-a-half thousand years of these are recorded episodes in our collective intellectual history, and they are *achievements*, each one turning on the introduction of an idea whose content is deeply novel relative to the facts it assimilates; like Kantian syntheses, colligations, or more narrowly, the ideas introduced in the course of colligations, are the source of emergent necessity and aprioricity.

How is that last supposed to be possible? Whewell was quite scholarly about ancient philosophy, and his writings contain Aristotelian moments as well, one of which can serve as a partial explanation. Facts, Whewell suggests, are to ideas as matter is to form.[25] Now, when you eat your bread, tomatoes and olive oil, Aristotle thinks, they become specifically human flesh, and when your form relaxes its grip in death, your flesh becomes mere meat: in living beings, matter is dependent on form. Analogously, in colligation, when facts are brought within the ambit of an idea, it metabolizes them. Once the idea of an ellipse is introduced by Kepler, you can no longer see the raw astronomical data as was: you see the points, willy nilly, *as points on an ellipse*. In our toy example of a moment ago, when a log is hard to pick up, you take yourself to be *registering its weight*. More primitively, your sensations are experienced through the lens of the ideas of space, time, substance and so on: so you are no longer able to experience your visual qualia as unlocated, as not yet within a temporal order, as free-floating sense-data rather than, say, the colors of objects. The aspect shift induced by a successful colligation "lead[s] us to regard the views we reject as not only false, but inconceivable."[26]

The Mill-Whewell debate is often read as a disagreement over what induction is—that is, over what the word means—and thus as merely terminological.[27] I am in the course of suggesting that it is a great deal more interesting than that, but to sidestep the distraction, let's use "induction" for what Mill means by it (just because it is pretty much our own usage), and "colligation" for the intellectual activity that Whewell describes.

Perhaps because "reasoning" was at the time so closely tied to deductive inference, Whewell does not begin by announcing himself as a philosopher of logic.[28] But that is evidently what he is: he is explaining how inference is correctly conducted on the most challenging and most admired playing field, that of novel and dramatically successful scientific theorizing, which makes him a logician by Mill's lights. Whewell reserves the term "Logic" for "a system which teaches us so to arrange our reasonings that their truth or falsehood shall be evident in their form," and once he has explained what he takes induction to be, he goes on to treat of the "Logic of Induction," understood as analogous to the "Logic of Deduction," i.e., the syllogistic.[29] So he is a logician by his own lights as well.[30]

III.

It is quite normal, when reading Mill's and Whewell's responses to one another, to have the sense that they are too far apart to be having a successful conversation. Both to see what is producing that effect, and to help us see past it, let's do a little compare and contrast.

Both Mill and Whewell are committed to allowing science to ground their views about logic. In Mill's case, the reason is clear: all inference about matters of fact is inductive, and so if logic is a science, the arguments it appeals to must be inductions from, especially, past cases of successful inference about matters of fact—and what better showcase of past successes could there be than science? (If logic is an "art," Mill thinks, that is, a collection of practical dicta, those dicta must be underwritten by a corresponding science.) We will presently explain why Whewell thought he had to appeal to the history and practice of science, but for the moment it is quite clear that he did: while working on *The Philosophy of the Inductive Sciences*, he was simultaneously paying his dues by writing up his three-volume *History of the Inductive Sciences*, which he described as "a survey of the present state of knowledge, in order to learn from it the best method of philosophizing, and the right view of philosophy," and of which he insisted that "it [wa]s essential in order to give anything like consistency to [his] views of the method of philosophising."[31]

Neither Whewell nor Mill exhibit much philosophical interest in the workings of deduction. As I have already mentioned, Mill argues that there is no such thing as deductive (properly so-called) inference, and accordingly contents himself with a standard review of the forms of the syllogism.[32]

Whewell thinks that, often enough, the content of an idea is spelled out deductively, and allows the deductive reconstruction of the facts it colligates, but he does not seem to think that deductive logic needs its own treatment within the frame of his discussion, which is confined by stipulation to the inductive sciences.[33] I am not entirely sure that this is a principled decision: because settled sciences *become* necessary, the necessity and aprioricity of deductive logic do not distinguish it from other sciences which Whewell takes to be within the scope of his treatment (and indeed, geometry and arithmetic are both presented as colligations of empirical observations, having to do with land surveying and counting respectively, by the ideas of space and number). I would very much have liked to see Whewell's colligationist analysis of deduction.

However, deduction is in the background as a model; both Mill and Whewell aspire to present their logic as formally as possible, which in historical context meant, as closely resembling traditional presentations of the syllogistic as they could manage. In Mill, this aspiration accounts for the way he lays out his Four Methods, making them appear much more mechanically applicable than they in fact are. In Whewell, the analogous presentation is found in his "Inductive Tables" of colligations. (These appear in his books as folded inserts, and are well worth a close look.) In these "Tabular arrangements,"[34] we see facts at one stage of a science collected together above the theory produced by colligating them, which is in turn collected together, along with others belonging to the same stage, above the theory produced by colligating *them*.[35] Whewell thinks of the Inductive Brackets that mark these collections as logical notation, and says of the graphical presentation that although a table of colligations can be as difficult to work out as a syllogistic presentation of a deductive train of thought, once produced, "it supplies the means of ascertaining the truth of our *inductive* inferences, so far as the *form* in which our reasoning may be stated can afford such a criterion,"[36] and is "the Criterion of Inductive Truth, in the same sense in which Syllogistic Demonstration is the Criterion of Necessary Truth."[37]

Beyond this point, the disagreements commence. Whewell thinks that the heart of scientific inference is the invention of the colligating idea; it is overstating his view only slightly to say that once the right idea has been hit upon, the remaining intellectual activity is just mopping up. Mill holds that the content of any claim can be reduced to sense-impressions; thus there can be no irreducible, genuinely novel ideas of the sort that Whewell takes to induce colligations.[38] Mill allows that inductions may require newly invented concepts or descriptions, of the tamer sort which he allows, but insists that generating them is an operation "subsidiary" to the reasoning proper.[39] Mill holds that because colligations *collect* already available facts, they are mere summaries or compendia of them, and so not inference at all. He famously compares colligating one's data to filling in a map on the basis of a sea voyage; when, staring at the completed map, you suddenly realize that you have sailed around an island, notwithstanding the novel concept, you have not actually inferred a new conclusion at all, but merely recapitulated what you already knew.[40]

Whewell takes the task of philosophy of science to include accounting for the *necessity* of scientific truths. Mill was a loyal empiricist, who understood Hume to have shown that necessity takes what we today would call a noncognitivist analysis; that something is necessary is never a *fact*, but at most, an observer's feeling.[41] He had in addition been impressed by Auguste Comte's doctrine of the three stages of a science: "Speculation he conceives to have . . . three successive stages; in the first of which it tends to explain the phenomena by supernatural agencies, in the second by metaphysical abstractions, and in the third or final state confines itself to ascertaining their laws of succession and similitude."[42] But the metaphysical abstractions, such as necessities or forces, are just the supernatural agents with their dramatic personalities effaced, and consequently Mill regarded the alleged necessities for which Whewell was trying to account as superstitious atavisms—"this character of necessity," he tells us, "is an illusion"—and he dismissed them as side-effects of habituation.[43]

When we look over the list of disagreements, we will not be surprised at the impression that their readers have often had, that the parties to the debate were unable to engage one another philosophically. I can testify to the disconnect myself: I read Mill before I discovered Whewell, and came away from the *System* understanding colligations to be something like lists; so little of the Kantian picture in the background was conveyed, that when I did get around to reading Whewell, it was natural to assume that Mill must not have understood him. Moreover, an argument can only persuade one's opponent if he accepts its premises; Mill and Whewell don't share enough common ground for the disagreement to be productive—or so it seems.

IV.

In fact, the disagreement goes deeper even than that. Mill and Whewell differ not only on background views to which their arguments might appeal, but on what would *count as an argument*. And this is on display especially in Whewell's most mature presentation of his own position.

Whereas there are no doubt various inference patterns at work in the sciences, the important results are arrived at by colligation. To establish this would be an important result in the philosophy of science; philosophy of science is itself a scientific endeavor; we should attempt to arrive at the result by colligation. To do so, Whewell first must identify ranges of facts that are candidates for colligation, and then select the "appropriate" idea[44]—the one that will effectively colligate them. Colligations are effective when they exhibit consilience—a consilience involves "an hypothesis which, assumed in order to explain one class of phenomena, has been found also to account exactly for another"[45]—so the relevant ranges of facts must be drawn from what before the colligation seem to be different subject matters. The history of science—construed broadly, to include not just the usual suspects, but such varied sciences as botany, crystallography and "those Sciences which contemplate the universe, the earth, and its inhabitants, with reference to their historical changes and the causes of those changes"[46]—provides a good deal of the required variation; observations by empiricist and Kantian philosophers provide others. (For instance, that on the one hand, science is responsible throughout to empirical observation, but, on the other, that the deepest of its results have the look and feel of necessary truth—a pair of claims that look to amount to an antinomy.) Remarkably, the appropriate idea proves to be colligation itself, and it is to be spelled out, that is, converted into a conception, via the very discussion we have so tersely recapitulated.

Once the conception of the idea of colligation is on hand, if the colligation deploying that conception is successful, it will induce an aspect shift. If the history did indeed corroborate the colligationist account, it will have documented episodes in the development of science that proceeded in accord with Whewell's template; the empirical historical data will have been, as far as the investigators who collected it were concerned, contingent. However, when the aspect shift kicks in, it will become clear in retrospect that progress in science *must* happen via colligation; the historical episodes will be inevitably redescribed in the vocabulary of the conception, and the appearance of a contingent and merely empirical historical record will be permanently lost.[47]

Briefly, on Whewell's view, colligation is inference, and so an argument-by-colligation is being used first to establish that colligations are legitimate arguments, and second, that when the science is taking a major step forward, colligation is the mode of inference. Recall once again that Mill understands all inference about matters of fact (where the laws of logic are included under this heading) to be inductive—as *he* understands induction; it follows that colligation cannot be inference. Whewell and Mill cannot so much as agree on what a legitimate form of argument is; how can we expect them to have a useful exchange of any kind?

V.

Although each of them devoted the preponderance of their respective discussions to arguments that would count as properly reasoned by their respective lights, both Mill and Whewell took time out to assemble arguments that conformed to the *other's* canons of argumentation.

Once again, Mill took logic to be an inductive science, and the successes of past science were to be the basis for the metainduction that would show logic to be inductive. Whewell agreed that the history of science was to be the touchstone, and he had devoted himself to it so thoroughly that when someone said of him that "science is his forte and omniscience ... his foible," the tag line stuck.[48] So Whewell was in a position to object that Mill's views were not borne out by the track record, a complaint that Mill should have been unable to shrug off.

Mill's Four Methods were supposed to be a refinement of crude inductions-by-enumeration, and their warrant had to be that inductions so conducted had been the stuff of successful science. Whewell asked rhetorically: "Who will tell us which of the methods of inquiry those historically real and successful inquiries exemplify? Who will carry these formulae through the history of the sciences, as they have really grown up; and show us that these four methods have been operative in their formation?"[49] After framing the objection that *he* takes to be the decisive one—that when you apply Mill's Method of Agreement, say, and observe that As are always followed by *as*, your having the concepts "A" and "*a*" in the first place has been left entirely unexplained—Whewell is going on to argue that even in retrospect, that is, even after we are already equipped with the relevant concepts, we cannot see Mill's Methods at work in the history of science.[50] And Whewell had likewise dryly preempted Millian invocations of social science, on the grounds that in its current state we cannot plausibly take it to be part of the record of scientific success.[51]

Mill dismissed consilience, inference to the best explanation and the importance of making surprising predictions.[52] But Whewell could point back to his having documented one after another scientific revolution that had turned on all of these: most extensively, the Newtonian synthesis, with the wave theory of light as a close runner-up.[53] Where Mill regarded the effort of arriving at concepts in whose terms successful inductions are formulated as not part of the reasoning proper, Whewell drew the lesson from his history of mechanics that "the discoverer [has] to struggle, not for intermediate steps of reasoning between remote notions . . . but for a clear possession of ideas which [are] near each other, and which he [is un]able to bring into contact, because he [does] not yet [have] a sufficiently firm grasp of them"—that is, that attaining control of the concepts is where the intellectual work is done.[54]

And where Mill followed Comte in treating necessity as a superstition, and consequently in dismissing Whewell's attempts to account for the emergence of necessities in science, Whewell replied that "Comte's . . . distinction of the three stages of sciences, the theological, the metaphysical and the positive, is not at all supported by the facts of scientific history. Real discoveries always involve what he calls *metaphysics*."[55] Briefly, Whewell's complaint was that Mill did not live up to his official views.

Whewell, for his part, was committed to the claim that once the facts had been assembled and placed side by side with the idea that colligates them, the colligation could be seen to be necessary, in something like the way that the conclusion of a valid argument could be seen to be inescapable.[56] (Whewell insisted, however, that it might take some time, practice, public discussion, and intelligence to appreciate the force of the considerations supporting the colligation.) Colligation was being presented as the idea that colligated the facts Whewell had assembled in his survey of the history of science. So Mill made a point of talking through selected episodes in that history without bringing to bear the idea of colligation, and visibly without finding deployment of the idea to be inevitable or compelled.[57]

Where Whewell took it that what needed to be explained in the history of science was the emergence of one after another necessary truth, Mill insisted that the only phenomenon in question was merely psychological rather than logical: that once a theory becomes entrenched, alternatives to it become, as a matter of psychological fact, inconceivable. And the empiricist doctrine of the association of ideas fully accounts for that sort of inconceivability; after a while, you are simply so used to thinking about things one way that you can't think about them any other way.[58]

Whewell took it that the key step in a scientific advance is the introduction of a novel idea whose content is cashed out as a structure of general claims (in the paradigmatic case, Euclidean geometry, as definitions and axioms). Mill insisted, to the contrary, that whereas inductions in the sciences typically are cast as having general conclusions, in principle the general claim is an optional step: the real inference proceeds from particulars to particulars, and the syllogistic monitoring can be skipped.[59] When it is, the concepts deployed in the induction must be those that can be directly applied to the particulars, and cannot have built into them the sort of content that Whewell insisted on in his colligating ideas. And in any case, Mill noted, concepts are being added to one's raw perceptions *whenever* one describes what one sees, and no one ever called most of *that* "induction."[60]

Mill is making a point of not getting Whewell's point, because in Whewell's intellectual world, that should itself count as an argument against the colligating idea (in this case, the idea of colligation at the center of Whewell's logical theory).[61] Mill's uncharacteristic posture of obtuseness is his ingenious shot at providing an argument whose force his opponent will have to allow.

VI.

It is not my purpose here to try to resolve the disagreement I have been describing; I am in any case not sure that there is a point, a century and a half after the event, in declaring one or the other of the parties the winner. But I think that their exchange can serve both as a model of philosophical conduct and as a cautionary reminder.

The Mill-Whewell debate was a dramatic illustration of challenges posed by philosophy of logic, and of what it can look like to try to meet them. Views in logic are views about what counts as an argument. A thoughtful philosopher of logic—and both Mill and Whewell were that—will realize that the arguments one advances for one's logical views ought to conform to the strictures those views imply. But then a philosopher with opposing views is unlikely to see them as arguments at all, and to think that the question at issue has been violently begged. On the other hand, if you try to satisfy your opponent, and the arguments you give fail to conform to your own views about what a successful argument is, why should you count them as support at all?

Both Mill and Whewell faced up to the problem by providing two distinct types of argument for their logical views. Each developed arguments that by their own lights were satisfactory (inductivist arguments, in Mill's case; colligationist arguments, in Whewell's). But each also produced arguments tailored to their opponent's views about argumentation (complaints about Mill's inductive of the history, in Whewell's case; a performance meant to show that Whewell's colligating idea was not demanded by his data, in Mill's). It is perhaps not the most principled solution; as it so happened, each of the parties thought that his twin modes of argumentation both delivered the same conclusion, but what is one to say when that sort of convergence proves unavailable? Nevertheless, it behooves philosophers today to be alert to the problem to which Mill and Whewell were responding, and—if no better way of solving it comes to mind—at least to do what they did: produce arguments both for oneself and for one's opponent, and if necessary, formally very different arguments.

NOTES

1. I'm grateful to Mariam Thalos for comments on an earlier draft, to Anya Plutynski for discussion, to the participants in Whewell reading groups at the University of Utah and the University of Arizona, and to the Arizona Freedom Center for support.
2. Mill (1873, CW: I.231/A 7:3–4). All references to Mill's works are to the authoritative edition of *Collected Works of John Stuart Mill* (Mill, 1963–1991—cited as CW, followed by volume and page number), unless otherwise indicated; the *Autobiography* and the *System of Logic* will be given additional slashed cites, with a chapter:paragraph and book:chapter:section, respectively. A biographer of the period endorses Mill's expectations: "Dr Whewell was always unwisely prompt in noticing the criticisms of reviewers" (Todhunter, 1876: I.72).
3. Whewell (1849); Whewell (1847); Whewell (1860: ch. 22). Whewell (1860: 338–40, 349f, 470f) directly responds to arguments in the *System of Logic*.
4. For the Four Methods, see Mill (1843, CW: VII.388–406/III:viii), and for this sort of appropriation of Mill, Skyrms (1975: 89ff). For such a consilience-oriented view, see Kitcher (1981); for instances of this way of reading Whewell, see Forster (1988), Thagard (1977b: 15, 17). The resemblance to abduction is not simply coincidence; as Fisch (1991: 12, 106f, 109f, 131) reminds us, Charles Sanders Peirce read and approved of (but did not sufficiently credit) Whewell.
5. For Mill's psychologistic rendering of the subject matter of logic, see Mill (1843, CW: VII.4–12/Introduction:4–7); at *ibid.*, VII.202/II:iii:7, he calls induction "that great mental operation," at *ibid.*, VII.206/II:iii:9, describes logic as "the entire theory of the ascertainment of reasoned or inferred truth" and at *ibid.*, VIII.735/V:i:2, he describes his subject matter as "the philosophy of reasoning."

6. Suppose you aren't bothered by David Hume's Problem of Induction: you are willing to allow that the future resembles the past. Goodman (1979) noticed that we haven't made sense of inductive inference until we have a way of saying *which way* it's reasonable to expect the future to resemble the past, and I'll borrow his very famous illustration. Consider a simple induction-by-enumeration:

    1. The grass was green this morning.
    2. The grass was green yesterday morning.
    3. The grass was green in the morning the day before yesterday.
    4. The course of nature is uniform. (I.e., we're not going to be detained by Hume's objections.)
    5. So, tomorrow morning, the grass will be green.

This seems to be more or less in order, leaving to one side worries about whether I'm going to remember to water the lawn. But now, let's define a new color predicate:

    x is *grue* iff *x* is observed today or earlier, and is green, or *x* is observed tomorrow or later, and is blue.

That puts us in a position to assemble another simple induction-by-enumeration:

    1. The grass was grue this morning.
    2. The grass was grue yesterday morning.
    3. The grass was grue in the morning the day before yesterday.
    4. The course of nature is uniform.
    5. So, tomorrow morning, the grass will be grue.
    6. If the grass is grue tomorrow morning, it will be blue (by definition of "grue").
    7. Tomorrow morning, the grass will be blue.

Obviously, our first induction, if not all that strong, was anyway sane, while the second, very similar-looking induction was crazy, and clearly, not both of them can predict the color of the grass tomorrow. Goodman's problem is to say why.

    Since Scarre (2002), it has been the received wisdom that early nineteenth-century philosophers were unaware of Hume's skepticism about induction, and thus Mill could not have been responding to it. Whewell's works remind us that this is very unlikely: gestures at Humean skepticism are frequent, and terse enough to presuppose a widely shared understanding of what it amounted to (e.g., Whewell, 1847: I.75; 1860: 222, 333; or 1857: I.193, where Algezeli's "deni[al of] the possibility of a known connexion between cause and effect" is called "a prelude . . . to the celebrated argumentation of Hume"). And we know that Mill read Whewell closely. For a reconstruction of Mill's solution to Hume's problem of induction, see Millgram (2009).

7. Mill (1843, *CW*: VII.314/III:iii:3); Holland *et al.* (1986: 241–43) documents that as a matter of psychological fact people do discriminate as Mill says. Mill gives an explanation of the contrast at hand at *op cit.*, VII.585f/III:xxii:7.

8. Mill (1843, *CW*: VII.314/III:iii:3).

9. Mill (1843, *CW*: VII.318–19/III:iv:2). Goodman claimed that the predicates that we correctly allow to drive inductions are better "entrenched." However, he was never able to spell out satisfactorily what counted as entrenchment; see Zabludowski (1994) and its sequels.

10. See Mill (1843, *CW*: VII.188/II:iii:3; VII.567f/III:xxi:2), where Mill concludes "that induction per *enumerationem simplicem* . . . is in reality the

only kind of induction possible; since the more elaborate process depends for its validity on a law, itself obtained in that inartificial mode"; and compare the remarks made in early editions of the *Logic*, to the effect that "all that is requisite to support the Canons of Induction is, that the generalization which gives the Law of Universal Causation should be a stronger and better induction" (*ibid.*, VII.572n/III:xxi:4). At *ibid.*, VIII.833/VI:i:1 we are told that "we should never have known by what process truth is to be ascertained, if we had not previously ascertained many truths . . . In scientific investigation . . . the way of obtaining the end is seen as it were instinctively by superior minds in some comparatively simple case, and is then, by judicious generalization, adapted to the variety of complex cases." At *ibid.*, VII.312/III:iii:2, Mill describes induction by enumeration as "the induction of the ancients," and he attributes the shortcomings in previous theories of induction to "want of sufficient acquaintance with the processes by which science has actually succeeded in establishing general truths." That is, to arrive at "practical rules, which might be for induction itself what the rules of the syllogism are for the interpretation of induction," more attention needs to be paid to the track record (*ibid.*, VII.283/III:i:1).

11. Mill (1843, *CW*: VII.183/III:i:1; VII.159/II:i.2). One can give top-down deductions about what to do, as when a judge applies a law, but even here Mill regards this as interpretation rather than inference proper (*ibid.*, VII.193f/II:iii:4; cf. *ibid.*, VIII.944/IV:xii:2).

12. Whewell (1858: 70f), italics deleted.

13. I am piecing together a Whewell-like example—as opposed to one of Whewell's own—in order to avoid both an over-discussed but atypical case, Kepler's Laws, and some of Whewell's well-worked-out but overly lengthy illustrations. Components of the example I am assembling can be found at Whewell (1860: Appendix K), (1857: I.71–72) and Forster (2011: sec. 5).

14. I'm grateful to Richard Healey for this way of putting it; Whewell (1857: II.117) gives a different illustration of how the content of an idea can be unpacked, in this case, that of Universal Gravitation.

15. Mill's English rendering of Auguste Comte's preferred name for it (Mill, 1865, *CW*: X.283).

16. Buchdahl (1991) takes this to allow him to classify Whewell as a "deductivist" about scientific justification, but this is a mistake evidently arising from exclusive attention to Whewell's treatments of the physical sciences, in which (as Whewell says of the theory of machine construction) "the determination of the results and conditions of any combination of materials and movements becomes really a mathematical deduction from known principles" (1857: II.440). Perhaps this is understandable; Whewell had after all authored the *Mechanical Euclid*. However, when discussing the life sciences and mineralogy (that is, sciences in which natural kinds are picked out by similarity), Whewell points out that their definitions needn't be extensionally correct: because there are, say, plants that fail to satisfy the correct botanical definition of "rose," but are roses nonetheless (1858: 175). In a passage that Mill takes the trouble to quote at length, after reminding us that "in the family of the rose-tree, we are told that the *ovules* are *very rarely* erect, the *stigmata usually* simple," Whewell continues, "particulars which are included in a class, though they transgress the definition of it . . . are so contrary to many of the received opinions respecting the use of definitions, and the nature of scientific propositions, that they will probably appear to many persons highly illogical and unphilosophical. But a disposition to such a judgment arises in a great measure from this, that the mathematical and mathematico-physical sciences have, in a great degree, determined men's views of the general nature

and form of scientific truth" (Mill, 1843, CW: VIII.717f/IV:vii:4). When "the type [of the Rose family] must be connected by affinities with most of the others of its group . . . near the center of the crowd, and not one of the stragglers," among the facts colligated by the idea, rose, some will not follow deductively from one's worked out conception. Thus not every such unpacking takes the form of an axiomatization. (Mill, for his part, complains that this way of doing things "is inconsistent with Dr. Whewell's own statement of the fundamental principle of classification, namely, that 'general assertions shall be possible'" (*ibid.*, VIII.721/IV:vii:4).)

17. From the "Inductive Table of Astronomy" in Whewell (1847: II. facing 118); see further discussion of Whewell's Tables, below.

18. Oddly, since he describes nature's horror of a vacuum as such a consilience, since rejected (Whewell, 1857: II.51). His confidence is both less and more naive than it seems. On the one hand, once we have come to organize an array of facts via the newly adopted idea, when we encounter an apparent exception to the generalizations the idea seems to warrant, instead of treating it as a counterexample, we will insist that there must be a "disturbing cause." (E.g., when we encounter an apparent violation of Kepler's Laws, "in the case of Uranus, a new planet" (Whewell, 1860: 453).) That is, Whewell has very much the reasons for confidence in the stability of a consilience-driven induction that Kuhn had for the stability of his paradigms. On the other hand, although the ideas that sciences crystallize around demand the utmost in inventiveness and intellectual acuity, and may take arbitrarily long to enter the scientific vocabulary, we are preequipped to come up with just *these* ideas (as we will shortly see, in something like the way that, for Kant, we already come with just *these* categories of the understanding), and God has arranged the world so that just these ideas will allow us to understand, albeit only ever partially, its real structure: "the human mind can and does put forth, out of its natural stores, duly unfolded, certain Ideas as the bases of scientific truths: These Ideas are universally and constantly verified in the universe: And the reason of this is, that they agree with the Ideas of the Divine Mind according to which the universe is constituted and sustained" (Whewell, 1860: 374).

19. Colligation, importantly, is not restricted to the sciences; Snyder (2011: 255), following Todhunter (1876: I.44), recaps an example from architecture; compare Whewell (1857: I.261–63).

20. Whewell (1860: 344, 472f); remarkably, given the date, this has the sound of pre-Lavoisier chemistry. But Whewell has this much right: these sorts of conservation laws seem obvious in retrospect but not in prospect. Aristotle thought that when you dissolve a drop of wine in a bucket of water, the wine is just *gone*; we think that it *can't* be gone (*De Generatione et Corruptione* 328a25ff; cf. 322a10f, 33f; however, Ariane Shemmer has objected that this is not so far removed from our current ways of thinking; after all, when you put a little bit of hot water into a lot of cold water, the hot water is not thought to persist, albeit diluted by the cold water—rather, it *turns* cold).

21. Whewell (1847: I.40).

22. Whewell (1860: 330).

23. Whewell (1860: 302).

24. For instance, Whewell allows himself the hyperbole of describing parts of *The Philosophy of the Inductive Sciences* as "almost literal translations of chapters in the *Kritik der Reinen Vernunft*" (1860: 335, *sic*); Todhunter (1876: I.345) mentions Whewell's reading notes on the first *Critique*. Fisch (1991) tells the plausible and fascinating story of how Whewell arrived at the Kantian view, not in the first place by reading Kant, but by wrestling with the problems of authoring mathematics and physics textbooks.

When a view is described as an historically-oriented idealism, it is natural to ask whether the guiding light was perhaps not Kant but Hegel. This is unlikely: Whewell did not think much of Hegel at all (1860: Appendix H; Todhunter, 1876: I.207).

25. Whewell (1858: 72).

26. Whewell (1858: 32f).

27. E.g., "it would have been more convenient if each of the writers had invented a word for himself, and used it in his own sense, instead of disputing as to the proper application of a word involving so much controversy" (Todhunter, 1876: I.231). Whewell himself considers whether the disagreement "is a question merely of words," and replies that "such questions of definition are never questions of definition merely" (1860: 243). Mill agrees: "it is impossible to name [objects] properly except in proportion as we are already acquainted with their nature and properties" (1843, CW: VII.176/II:ii:3); "to determine . . . what should be, the meaning of a name . . . requires for its solution that we should enter, and sometimes enter very deeply, into the properties . . . of the things named" (*ibid.*, VII.150/I:viii:7; cf. *ibid.*, VIII.672/IV:iv:4).

28. Rather than contest the connection, as Mill does, Whewell at one point agrees that "Induction *is* inconclusive *as reasoning*. It is not reasoning . . . an inductive truth . . . is not *demonstrated*" (1860: 454); and he agrees as well that "there is no formula for the discovery of inductive truth" (1860: 456).

29. Whewell (1858: 105f and Book II, ch. 6, *passim*).

30. He once wrote to De Morgan: "I do not wonder at your denying these devices [my *Inductive Tables*] a place in Logic; and you will think me heretical and profane, if I say, *so much the worse for Logic*" (Todhunter, 1876: II.417, letter of 18 Jan. 1859); I was directed to this passage by Fisch (1991: 199n16).

31. Todhunter (1876: II.193, 248), letters to Herschel and to Jones, 4 Dec. 1836 and 6 Oct. 1834, respectively; I was alerted to these quotations by Fisch (1991: 111, 139). See esp. at Whewell (1857: I:viii) his insistence that his history is "a basis for the Philosophy of Science. It seemed to me that our study of the modes of discovering truth ought to be based upon a survey of the truths which have been discovered," and compare his concluding sentence at Whewell (1857: I.338).

32. Mill (1843, CW: VII.164ff/II:ii); remarkably, Whewell even seems willing to endorse Mill's "doctrine, that the force of the syllogism consists in an inductive assertion, with an interpretation added to it" (Whewell 1860: 289, emphasis deleted).

33. Whewell (1857: I.15).

34. Whewell (1858: 115).

35. The terms "theory" and "fact" turn out to be relational: "as the same person is a father and a son[,] Propositions are Facts and Theories, according as they stand above or below the Inductive Brackets of our Tables" (Whewell, 1858: 116).

36. Whewell (1858: 106).

37. Whewell (1858: 115).

38. Mill (1843, CW: VII.106f/I:v:7; VII.296/III:ii:4; cf. *ibid.*, VII.485/III:xiv:2).

39. Mill (1843, CW: VIII.647/IV:iv:4).

40. Mill (1843, CW: VII.292/III:ii:3).

41. He reclaims the word "necessary" for an acceptably low-key use at Mill (1843, CW: VII.339/III:v:6).

42. Mill (1843, CW: VIII.928/VI:x:8, see Mill, 1865, CW: X.267–79).

43. Mill (1843, CW: VII.224/II:v:1), and cf. the manuscript remarks at *ibid.*, VII.571/III:xxi:3.

118

44. Whewell (1857: I.64).
45. Whewell (1857: II.429).
46. Whewell (1857: II.229).
47. Fisch (1991: 22, 112, 165, 186n64, 193n12) notices that Whewell is going meta—that his argument for colligationist inference is itself a colligation of the history of science—and in general Fisch's treatment is highly recommended. However, he takes Whewell's primary colligating concept to be "antithetical knowledge," which seems to me a (rare) misstep on his part.

   When one misses the intended form of Whewell's argument, one ends up puzzled by what he takes the connections between the parts of his view to be. For instance, Laudan (1971: 378) complains that Whewell does not "offer any valid argument to support his claim" that consilience entails truth: that "the great characteristic of a true theory [is] . . . that the hypotheses, which were assumed in order to account for one class of facts, are found to explain another class of a different nature" (Whewell, 1857: II.436); that "such coincidences, or *consiliences* . . . are the test of truth (Whewell, 1857: II.429; cf. 370). Snyder (2006: 183f), takes the argument to be inductive—as Mill and as we ourselves understand the notion—which would be a methodological *faux pas* on Whewell's part. But allow that necessity does entail truth, for roughly Kantian reasons: because one synthesizes one's theoretical reconstruction of the world in accord with the idea. The colligation of the history of science by the idea of colligation, as rendered into a conception via the notion of consilience, is to show that scientific advances are driven by consilience, that they consist in colligations of the facts by an idea and that these colligations induce novel necessities. Since necessities entail truths, consiliences will entail truths; and as the demonstration was itself by colligation of the history of science, we will see the claim borne out in the history of science—in Whewell's view, inevitably.

   We can now see that the deductivist reading of Whewell (note 16, above) must be mistaken for a second reason: the case of most interest to Whewell himself cannot be rendered deductively. Whewell's own spelling out of colligation is nothing like an axiomatization, and of course it does not entail the reconstructed episodes of the history of science in anything like the way that Euclid's axioms entail geometrical theorems.
48. Todhunter (1876: I.410).
49. Whewell (1860: 264).
50. In the *Logic*, Mill of course had supplied examples of his Four Methods at work in science, especially at Mill (1843, *CW*: VII.407–433/III:ix). But he also felt that he didn't have nearly the command of the history that Whewell displayed, or anyhow made a point of saying so: "with [the present writer's] comparatively imperfect knowledge of the various physical sciences, the attempt would have been desperate unless the materials had been brought together, and had undergone a partial elaboration, by [Whewell and Herschel's] more competent hands" (*ibid.*, VII.284n/III:i:2). Whewell dismissed Mill's examples with this remark: "I confess that I have no expectation of any advantage to philosophy from discussions of this kind" (1860: 269).

   Mill's own reply to the putatively decisive objection—that it proves too much—can be found at Mill (1843, *CW*: VII.431/III:ix:6).
51. Whewell (1847: I.vii, 7f) and (1860: 269).
52. Mill (1843, *CW*: VII.495/III:xiv:4; VII.500/III:xiv:6; the subsequent pages make it clear that these remarks are directed to Whewell); and here is Mill's belittling take on Kepler's abduction: "boldly guessing that the path [of Mars] was an ellipse, and finding afterwards, on examination, that the observations were in harmony with the hypothesis" (*ibid.*, VIII.646/IV:i:3). And Whewell complained that "Mr. Mill . . . has borrowed the term . . . *Consilience*, but

has applied it in a different manner" (1860: 274)—perhaps having in mind Mill's appeal to "the accordance of . . . *à priori* reasoning and specific experience," at Mill (1843, *CW*: VIII.874/VI:v:6). (For an example of this sort of accordance, called "consilience" by Mill, see *ibid.*, VIII.920/VI:x:5.)

I remarked earlier on Mill's "Deductive" method, and it is perhaps in the use he makes of it in his program for social science that his rejection of abduction is most prominently on display. Mill insists on methodological individualism (1843, *CW*: VIII.879/VI:vii:1), and requires that the axioms of a deductive construction of social science be supplied by an independent and foundational science, psychology (*ibid.*, VIII.870/VI:v:5). The motivation is evidently that the laws of association (*ibid.*, VIII.852ff/VI:iv:3) can be directly established using the Four Methods, thus obviating the need for an abductive inference to axioms of sociology and accompanying concepts not immediately discernible in sense experience.

53. Whewell (1857: II.310).
54. Whewell (1857: II.38).
55. Whewell (1860: 275n19); Mill's rejoinder, which does not properly represent Whewell's objection, can be found at Mill (1843, *CW*: VIII.929n/VI:x:8).
56. Whewell (1847: II.79ff).
57. E.g., Mill (1843, *CW*: VII.464–483/III:xii–xiii); or see Mill's discussion of Aristotle's allegedly failed colligation of the facts of motion around the idea of natural motion (*ibid.*, VIII.657f/IV:ii:4). Mill pointedly substitutes the empiricist notion of abstraction for Whewell's colligations (as in the title to Book IV, ch. 2 of the *System*); here are a couple of characteristic remarks: "Dr. Whewell's . . . Colligation of Facts by means of appropriate Conceptions, is but the ordinary process of finding by a comparison of phenomena, in what consists their agreement or resemblance" (*ibid.*, VIII.648/IV:i:4); "hypotheses, or, as Dr. Whewell prefers to say . . . Conceptions" (*ibid.*, VIII.647/IV:i:4; cf. VIII.701/IV:vi:3).

One of these episodes was Kepler's discovery of his Laws, and now would be an appropriate time to explain why I have been sidestepping this case, which has served as an anchor for much of the subsequent discussion. Mill complains that since it was already known that the planets returned to their previous positions, and since all those positions had already been observed, Kepler was merely redescribing already available information, and that no new prediction was being made. Since the application of the idea, ellipse, had been adduced as a colligation (of facts about the positions of Mars), Mill is taking Whewell to be committed to colligations involving no prediction, and this, Mill thinks, cannot be what science is about (although he allows that such redescriptions can be "an advance" (1843, *CW*: VII.292–97, 303, 317/ III:ii:3–4, III:ii:5, III:iv:1)).

This is evidently unfair; Kepler's colligation is, by Whewell's lights, very unusual in this respect, and normally much of the warrant of a colligation comes from specifically *surprising* predictions being borne out. Whewell observed that "most scientific thinkers . . . have allowed the coincidence of results predicted by theory with fact afterwards observed, to produce the strongest effects upon their conviction; and that all the best-established theories have obtained their permanent place in general acceptance in virtue of such coincidences, more than of any other evidence" (1860: 273; see also 1847: II.62–65). For instance, "the great Newtonian Induction of Universal Gravitation," Whewell observes, "pointed out an interminable vista of new facts, too minute or too complex for observation alone to disentangle, but capable of being detected when theory had pointed out their laws, and of being used as criteria or confirmations of the truth of the doctrine" (1857: II.136). Or again compare Whewell (1857: III.27), where he remarks that "in order to give [a theory] full confirmation, it was to be considered whether any other facts, not immediately assumed in the foundation of the theory, were explained by it; a circumstance which, as we have seen, gave the final stamp of truth to the theories of astronomy and optics."

When Mill insists that "Dr. Whewell's theory of the logic of science . . . pass[es] over altogether the question of proof" (1843, *CW*: VII.304/III:ii:5), Mill is ignoring Whewell's explication of consilience, which he had explicitly presented as the mode of proof appropriate to colligation. Kepler's colligation is unusual in that respect also: it fails to produce consilience of facts from what were formerly regarded as disparate subject matters. (All of Kepler's data were after all observed positions of a single planet.) It is perhaps worth emphasizing that consilience was felt even at the time to be the central element of the Whewellian justification for a colligation; that much is clear from Thagard (1977a), reporting on Darwin.

58. Mill (1843, *CW*: VII.361/III:v:11; VII.242/II:v:6).
59. Thus, the point of the note at Mill (1843, *CW*: VII.287/III:ii:2) is that inductive inference is not confined to scientists, and that if nonscientists draw "direct inferences," we can conclude that "the intermediate stage of a general proposition" is dispensable, and thus the additional concepts alleged to be involved in that stage are unneeded as well. Compare his insistence that "if reasoning be from particulars to particulars, and if it consist in recognising one fact as a mark of another, nothing is required to render reasoning possible, except senses and association: senses to perceive that two facts are conjoined; association, as the law by which one of those two facts raises up the idea of the other" (*ibid.*, VIII.664/IV:iii:2).

As Snyder (2006: 106), observes, Mill thought he needed to show that there was no added value provided by the mind to experience, and so he argued that Kepler's colligating concept would be available in principle in the experience of a properly positioned observer: if Mars left a trail of glowing foam behind it, someone floating in space opposite and suitably distant could see that its orbit was elliptical. Snyder describes the move as "this strange argument of Mill's" (2006:105), but if we keep in mind that his objective was to resist Whewell's views of colligation, it should not seem strange at all.

60. Mill (1843, *CW*: VIII.645/IV:i:3); since Whewell insists that colligation goes all the way down, Mill's point is question begging if it is meant as a rebuttal of Whewell's claim, but entirely in order if what he wants to show is that you needn't see the phenomena Whewell's way.
61. Of course, Mill allowed himself "quite content to use Dr. Whewell's *term* Colligation" (1843, *CW*: VII.305/III:ii:5, my emphasis)—refusing, however, to let it mean what Whewell had wanted it to.

Snyder (2006: 173, 182) notices that Mill "did not directly address the issue of consilience," and if that were all there were to it, it would have been a grave oversight, and his use of Kepler would have been (for reasons covered in note 57) patently unfair. But Mill was handling it in what was the dialectically most effective way possible: namely, by doing without it entirely.

REFERENCES

Buchdahl, G. (1991) "Deductivist versus Inductivist Approaches in the Philosophy of Science as Illustrated by some Controversies between Whewell and Mill," in Fisch, M. and Schaffer, S. (eds.) *William Whewell: A Composite Portrait* (Oxford: Oxford University Press): 311–44.

Fisch, M. (1991) *William Whewell: Philosopher of Science* (Oxford: Oxford University Press).

Forster, M. (1988) "Unification, Explanation, and the Composition of Causes in Newtonian Mechanics," *Studies in History and Philosophy of Science* 19: 55–101.

———. (2011) "The Debate between Whewell and Mill on the Nature of Scientific Induction," in Gabbay, D., Hartmann, S. and Woods, J. (eds.) *Handbook of the History of Logic*, vol. 10 (Amsterdam: Elsevier): 93–116.

Goodman, N. (1954) *Fact, Fiction and Forecast*, 3rd ed. (Indianapolis: Hackett, 1979).

Holland, J., Holyoak, K., Nisbet, R., and Thagard, P. (1986) *Induction: Processes of Inference, Learning, and Discovery* (Cambridge, MA: MIT Press).

Kitcher, P. (1981) "Explanatory Unification," *Philosophy of Science* 48 (4): 507–31.

Laudan, L. (1971) "William Whewell on the Consilience of Inductions," *Monist* 55 (3): 368–91.

Mill, J. S. (1843) *A System of Logic, Ratiocinative and Inductive: Being a Connected View of the Principles of Evidence and the Methods of Scientific Investigation*, in vols. VII and VIII (1974) of Mill (1963–1991).

———. (1865) *Auguste Comte and Positivism*, in vol. X (1969) of Mill (1963–1991).

———. (1873) *Autobiography*, in vol. I (1981) of Mill (1963–1991).

———. (1963–1991) *Collected Works of John Stuart Mill*, F.E.L. Priestly (gen. ed.), and subsequently J. M. Robson, 33 vols. (London/Toronto: Routledge and Kegan Paul/University of Toronto Press).

Millgram, E. (2009) "John Stuart Mill, Determinism, and the Problem of Induction," *Australasian Journal of Philosophy* 87 (2): 181–97.

Scarre, G. (2002) "Was Mill Really Concerned with Hume's Problem of Induction?," in Sanchez-Valencia, V. (ed) *The General Philosophy of John Stuart Mill* (Aldershot: Ashgate): 31–48.

Skyrms, B. (1966) *Choice and Chance*, 2nd ed. (Belmont: Wadsworth, 1975).

Snyder, L. (2006) *Reforming Philosophy* (Chicago: University of Chicago Press).

———. (2011) *The Philosophical Breakfast Club* (New York: Random House).

Thagard, P. (1977a) "Darwin and Whewell," *Studies in the History and Philosophy of Science* 8 (4): 353–56.

———. (1977b) *Explanation and Scientific Inference* (University of Toronto, PhD Dissertation).

Todhunter, I. (1876) *William Whewell, Master of Trinity College, Cambridge*, 2 vols. (Cambridge: Cambridge University Press).

Whewell, W. (1840) *The Philosophy of the Inductive Sciences*, 2 vols., 2nd ed. (London: John W. Parker, 1847).

———. (1849) *Of Induction, With Especial Reference to Mr. J. Stuart Mill's System of Logic* (London: John W. Parker).

———. (1837) *History of the Inductive Sciences*, 3 vols., 3rd ed. (London: John W. Parker and Son, 1857).

———. (1858) *Novum Organon Renovatum* (London: John W. Parker and Son).

———. (1860) *On the Philosophy of Discovery* (London: John W. Parker and Son).

Zabludowski, A. (1994) "Concerning a Fiction about How Facts Are Forecast," in Stalker, D. (ed.) *Grue! The New Riddle of Induction* (Chicago: Open Court): 57–77.

5 A Double Helix
Mill and Bain on Logic, Psychology and Ethology

Frederick Rosen

In my recent book on John Stuart Mill I have devoted considerable attention to the continuing importance and relevance of his ideas on the logic
of the social sciences and, particularly, psychology and ethology (the science of character).[1] These aspects of Mill's philosophy have been neglected
partly because of the widespread, though mistaken, belief (originally suggested by Alexander Bain) that Mill abandoned ethology,[2] when he merely
abandoned a major treatise on the subject. There has also been a failure
to consider Mill's unique personal relationship with Bain, which bore fruit
precisely in the fields of logic, psychology and ethology. In this chapter I suggest that the relationship between the two philosophers might be usefully
depicted in terms of a double helix with the life and work of each spiraling
and linking with that of the other. It might be thought that Bain's and Mill's
writings on these topics were the productions of the two distinct people or
that one writer was the disciple of the other. The image of the double helix
is meant to suggest that despite inequality in age and experience, and differences in temperament, Mill and Bain produced one substantial body of
work in these fields.

I. LOGIC

In his *Autobiography* (1873) Mill first mentioned Bain in the context of
acknowledging his indebtedness to Harriet Taylor Mill for assistance with
various works. In contrast with the *Principles of Political Economy* (1848)
he noted that the *Logic* "owed little to her except in the minuter matters of
composition, in which . . . my writings . . . have benefited by her accurate
and clear-sighted criticism."[3] To this statement he added the following
footnote:

> The only person from whom I received any direct assistance in the prep-
> aration of the *System of Logic* was Mr. Bain, since so justly celebrated
> for his philosophical writings. He went carefully through the manu-
> script before it was sent to press, and enriched it with a great number of

additional examples and illustrations from science; many of which, as well as some detached remarks of his own in confirmation of my logical views, I inserted nearly in his own words.[4]

Mill then continued in his note to contrast his relationship with Bain to that of Comte, whom he had earlier praised. Unlike the case with Bain, Mill's obligations to Comte were "only to his writings" and presumably not to the man. The only person (besides Harriet Mill) of similar intellectual stature and personal proximity to Mill might have been George Grote, but Grote may have lacked the philosophical ability of Bain and Bain's unique capacity to carry forth Mill's intellectual projects. In the note, quoted above, one might weigh Mill's comment that Bain's remarks "confirmed" Mill's "logical views" and that Mill could insert them into the *Logic* "nearly in his own [i.e. Bain's] words."

The double helix began with the *Logic*. Bain (then just twenty-three years old) and Mill (twelve years his senior) had begun a correspondence in September 1841 encouraged by their mutual friend, John Robertson, and met in London in April 1842.[5] In a letter to Macvey Napier, editor of the *Edinburgh Review*, written in February 1842, prior to their meeting, Mill described Bain as "almost a youth," but he clearly thought highly of his abilities. He then added: "As for Bain, I can completely understand *him*, because I have been, long ago, very much the same sort of person, except that I had not half his real originality."[6] Although one might disregard some of the exaggeration in the letter, as it was what now might be considered a letter of reference, it remains a remarkable early piece of evidence for the relationship that was to develop.

In July 1842 Mill asked Bain to revise the manuscript of the *Logic*. Bain remained in London to work on this task, returning to his native Aberdeen in September, where he continued to work with several assistants. In his textual introduction to the new edition of the *Logic*, Robson has brought together the evidence to assess Bain's considerable contribution.[7] As for the revisions to Book VI, there is no indication of any direct involvement by Bain in changes to the material on psychology or ethology. Nevertheless, Book VI was "the last and most heavily revised" in the *Logic*, largely due to the influence of Comte, the last volume of whose *Cours de Philosophie Positive* appeared in 1842,[8] and dealt directly with themes that appeared in Book VI.[9] Bain, Mill and Comte also formed an intellectual threesome at this time, with some consequences for the future of positivism. In August 1843 Mill wrote to Comte that "we have made a conquest of the first order for our common philosophy, that of young Bain." "This is a true thinker," Mill continued, after acknowledging his help with the *Logic*. A year later in October 1844 Mill was even stronger in his admiration of Bain and his appreciation of his importance to the joint positivist legacy Mill and Comte hoped to leave. "I see only Bain," he wrote to Comte, "in whom, if I died tomorrow, I would be certain of leaving a successor." Later in the same letter he reflected on positivism in England: "In the younger generation, among those of my knowledge, I see in Bain the basis of a mind of the first rank, with his excellent intellectual habits. We can boast, you and I, that we have decided his direction. If he lives, and happily he has a strong constitution, he will do great things and will worthily support the cause of positivism among us."[10]

Bain's involvement with Mill's *Logic* continued for the rest of Mill's life. Not only did he assist Mill at numerous points, clarifying arguments and suggesting examples, but he also wrote an extensive, forty-page review (only two appeared) of the work for the *Westminster Review* that Mill, himself, somewhat unusually, criticized in draft prior to publication.[11] Following the publication of the seventh edition of the *Logic* in 1868, Robson notes a letter to Cliff Leslie in February 1869 that paid tribute to Bain's work: "The physical illustrations in my Logic were all reviewed & many of them suggested by Bain, who has a very extensive & accurate knowledge of physical science. He has promised me to revise them thoroughly for the next edition, & to put them sufficiently in harmony with the progress of science, which I am quite aware that they have fallen behind."[12] By the time Mill prepared the eighth edition (published in 1872, a year before his death), Bain's own *Logic* had been published,[13] and in the preface to his own work, Mill paid tribute to it:

> The additions and corrections in the present (eighth) edition, which are not very considerable, are chiefly such as have been suggested by Professor Bain's *Logic*, a book of great merit and value. Mr. Bain's view of the science is essentially the same with that taken in the present treatise, the differences of opinion being few and unimportant compared with the agreements; and he has not only enriched the exposition by many applications and illustrative details, but has appended to it a minute and very valuable discussion of the logical principles specially applicable to each of the sciences; a task for which the encyclopedical character of his knowledge peculiarly qualified him. I have in several instances made use of his exposition to improve my own, by adopting, and occasionally by controverting matter contained in his treatise.[14]

Not only had "Mr. Bain" become "Professor Bain" (with Mill's unswerving support), now, nearly thirty years later, Mill was using Bain's *Logic* to improve his own. But let us return to the 1840s. When Bain was spending summer vacations in London, according to Packe, they met twice a week at India House to walk back to Mill's mother's house in Kensington (where Mill was living).[15] For Packe, Bain thought of Mill as "his hero,"[16] though one might wonder if Bain's involvement with Mill can appropriately be described as hero-worship on the one side or with Bain depicted as a protégé on the other. The two very quickly developed a different sort of relationship with each enriching the work of the other.

II. PSYCHOLOGY AND ETHOLOGY

The spiral of the double helix continues to be evident when one examines Bain's extensive writing on psychology. Mill seems involved at every turn. Bain's two-volume work, published separately as *The Senses and the Intellect* (1855) and *The Emotions and the Will* (1859), bears the imprint of Mill's assistance. According to Bain, Mill revised the manuscript for *The Emotions and the Will* "minutely and, jotted a great many suggestions."[17] He recommended the first volume to Parker, the publisher, and together with Grote, offered a guarantee against loss of £100 for the second. He additionally promoted the success of the work by writing a major review, entitled "Bain's Psychology," published in the *Edinburgh Review* in 1859.[18] In this work Mill not only praised Bain's achievements, suggesting its superiority to Herbert Spencer's recently published *Principles of Psychology* (1855).[19] He also used the occasion to return to and restate themes from the *Logic* concerning German and English philosophy, the *a priori* and the *a posteriori* and related topics before placing Bain's achievement in the associationist tradition of Hobbes, Locke, Hartley and James Mill.[20] He additionally stressed the importance of the Scottish connection by referring explicitly to Hume, Dugald Stewart, Thomas Brown, James Mill, Sir William Hamilton and Bain himself as important Scottish writers in this field. He concluded by referring to Bain's work as "a remarkable book; which, once known and read by those who are competent judges of it, is sure to take its place in the very first rank of the order of philosophical speculation . . ."[21]

Nevertheless, Mill did not simply follow, agree with and publicize Bain's achievements. Once the importance of Bain's work is appreciated, Mill's own considerable achievement in associationist psychology becomes more significant as part of his overall philosophy. Besides his various chapters in the *Logic* and the essay, "Bain's Psychology," one of Mill's last major works was his participation (with Bain and Grote) in the production of the second edition of his father's *Analysis of the Phenomena of the Human Mind* (1869). Mill's contribution included several hundred pages of notes and extensive comments on James Mill's work as well as a useful preface to the new edition.[22] Thus, it would be a mistake to see Bain as simply a successor to both James and J. S. Mill. His relationship with the younger Mill was extraordinary with each developing intellectually from the other. Their mutual interaction—like a double helix, circling around each other in a spiral—made major contributions to philosophy and psychology in the nineteenth century.

Bain's writings, with Mill's assistance, were also important in the development of psychology itself as a separate science in the nineteenth century. According to Young, Bain "did more than any other single figure to free psychology from its philosophic context and make it a natural science in its own right."[23] In addition, Bain played an important role in the development of philosophical psychology not only in Victorian Britain, but also elsewhere, and his importance, for example, was acknowledged in the development of Pragmatism.[24]

It remains to establish the significance of these psychological writings for the new science of ethology, advocated by Mill in the *Logic*.[25] In none of Bain's works on psychology (e.g., *The Senses and the Intellect* and *The Emotions and the Will*) are there any references to character or ethology. In *The Emotions and the Will* Bain wrote on ethics,[26] moral habits[27] and belief,[28] but not on character.[29]

Nevertheless, Bain did not ignore character, and just after the publication of *The Emotions and the Will* in 1859 (when Mill was publishing *On Liberty* and writing *Utilitarianism*) he began a series of essays on phrenology, which, again with Mill's involvement, were published in *Fraser's Magazine* in 1860 and 1861, followed by a book, *On the Study of Character Including an Estimate of Phrenology* (1861).[30] In a letter to Bain in October 1859 Mill was encouraging: ". . . both on its own account & from the nature of the topics which it raises, [the book] is one of the most important things you could do."[31] When it was published, Mill wrote to Grote: "I quite agree in your high estimate of Bain's new book."[32]

"It would be extremely useful to know why Bain wrote *On the Study of Character* . . ." writes Young in his book, which contains the most elaborate and serious study of Bain's thought.[33] In part, he answers his own rhetorical question. He notes that Bain's approach "follows almost exactly the programme laid down by Mill" in the *Logic*.[34] He also points out how Bain's attempts "to show that the phrenological faculties are not the ultimate determinants of character and that a true science of character can be deduced from the laws of association, the pleasure-pain principle, and his own primitive mental elements."[35] Both of these points are substantially true, to which one might add a third, that the theme of phrenology was unfinished business for both Bain and Mill, left over from the encounter with Comte. Bain dealt with phrenology here, and Mill did not ignore the topic in his *Auguste Comte and Positivism* (1865), published four years later.[36]

In *On the Study of Character* Bain briefly noted the continuing significance of Mill's conception of ethology:

> Mr. John Stuart Mill, in his *System of Logic*, has indicated as a field of important inquiry the subject called by him Ethology, or the laws that govern the formation of character, individual and national. This supposes that the analysis and classification of characters are already made, and has for its object to determine the effects of *circumstances* in bringing about the varieties actually occurring. Ethology is the *science* which corresponds to the *art* of Education, in the widest sense of the term, including the formation of national or collective character, as well as individual. Such a science cannot be said to exist at the present time; so that the Educator's art is an exclusively empirical one.[37]

But why did Bain tackle phrenology, as opposed to simply writing on ethology? By 1861 the writings of the phrenologists (e.g., Franz Joseph Gall

(1758–1828), Johann Caspar Spurzheim (1776–1832) and George Combe (1788–1858)), though still very popular,[38] had already received considerable criticism, so that Bain's highly detailed exposition of the weaknesses of the system might have appeared then (as now) to be somewhat unnecessary. But Bain's agenda in this book was not only closely related to that of Mill but was also more complex than a straight-forward study of phrenology would require. For Bain argued that whereas phrenology apparently was meant to be established as a science of mind, showing for the first time the influence of the brain on mental life, it had failed precisely as a science of mind. Furthermore, if it had any standing, it would have had to be as a science of character or ethology.[39] As he put it:

> The affirmation to be proved is that phrenology, as hitherto exhibited, is at best but a *science of character*, and NOT a *science of mind*, as pretended; and that even as a science of character it is essentially dependent upon the degree of improvement realized by the science of mind *independently* cultivated.[40]

Thus, Bain reasserted in a new context Mill's important distinction, made in the *Logic*, between psychology and ethology,[41] though, like Mill, he also insisted that ethology was dependent, as a science, on psychology. Phrenologists had believed that they could ignore the philosophical psychology that had been established since Locke and whose main expositor in the nineteenth century, besides James Mill, was, in fact, Bain himself! In other words, they believed that they could derive principles of human character from various cranial protuberances and ignore associationist psychology. Yet Bain insisted that a science of mind had to develop independently of a science of character, and, hence, phrenology was no substitute for psychology. As he wrote:

> It will then be seen that the special method of phrenology—the reference to the development of the cranium—cannot dispense with the other method, and has in part failed from the very attempt to dispense with it. One may fully concede the propriety of constructing a system, or science of the elements and laws of CHARACTER, while denying that this should swamp the science of MIND as treated by the recognized methods. We go farther, and declare that the subject of the estimation of character will be dependent for its advance in a great measure on the progress made in the other directions.[42]

III.   BAIN'S ACCOUNT OF ETHOLOGY

As we have seen, Mill not only paid tribute to the importance of Bain's *Logic* in the final edition of his own *System of Logic*, but he also stated unequivocally that he and Bain differed little in their approach to the subject. Thus, if there was to be progress with regard to ethology, we would expect to find it in Bain's *Logic*, and one indeed finds there the fullest discussion of ethology after Mill's *System of Logic*.[43] He approached the theme of a science of character as a subheading under the logic of character. "The Science of Character," he wrote, "has reference to the *proportionate development* of the sensibilities and powers in different individuals. It presupposes the Science of Mind."[44] He explained this assertion as follows:

> The basis of any Science of Character must, therefore, be the ultimate analysis of Mind. There should be ascertained, as far as possible, the native and irresolvable Feelings, and the attributes of Volition and of Thought. If a mind were like a mineral, the statement of the degrees of these various fundamental attributes would be the account of a character. But the mind is a thing of indefinite growth, adaptation, acquisition; its first cast is greatly altered before the end; and, as what we usually desiderate is the character of a full-grown man or woman, we must provide an account of the acquired, as well as the native powers.[45]

Bain quickly dealt with phrenology by regarding it as a science of character. But its attempts to relate character to particular locations in the brain via the shape of the head were regarded as irrelevant to the development of such a science.[46] His approach to ethology was to list the main circumstances that determined character. Such an approach seemed to follow Mill's own understanding of ethology, as sketched out in a letter to Comte nearly thirty years earlier when he wrote: "I have called Ethology, the theory of the influence of diverse external circumstances, either individual or social, on the formation of character, moral and intellectual."[47] Bain's list, however, provided the fullest exposition of these circumstances, and enables us to grasp more fully just how he and Mill conceived the scope and extent of this new science.

The first of the "leading circumstances" was:

> The *physique* of the individual viewed from its purely physical side; the comparative strength or weakness of the different physical organs. A whole series of consequences to the character follow from the purely physical endowments. Great muscular strength gives a certain direction to the activities and pursuits, whatever be the proper mental tendencies.[48]

The second dealt with nourishment, health and the environment: "The physical *treatment* of the system in all that regards nourishment and the adjuncts of health . . . Climate, town or country life, poverty or affluence, indulgence or temperance, are obvious elements of this computation."[49]

For the third circumstance he turned to "natural *surroundings* as they affect the mind—the activities, feelings, or intelligence." Here, he referred to differences between "mountaineers" and "tenants of the plains," "seafaring nations and those in the interior of continents, between rural and urban populations." He then continued: "Not much precision has as yet been gained in the expression of those differences. But, if studied by the double method of induction and deduction, they may yield important laws."[50]

The fourth circumstance included "modes of industry" or "habitual occupation," where "the effects of occupation or profession have been a subject of frequent observation . . . The soldier, the sailor, the tiller of the ground, the trader, the priest, have each the stamp of their calling."[51] For the fifth circumstance he turned to the "Surrounding Society," which "moulds the individual as to feelings, and as to modes of thinking, in ways too numerous to exhaust, but yet capable of being stated with remarkable precision . . . The religious, ethical and political opinions of each person are, in the great mass of cases, the exact reflex of what prevails in the society about him."[52] The sixth circumstance was concerned with education:

> The express Education given by the schoolmaster should be added to the moulding influence of general society. This element admits of being clearly stated. A people sent regularly to school like the Scotch, or the Germans, acquires a distinct superiority of intellectual and moral character. Under this head, attention must be paid to the educational influence of Institutions; as, for example, an established church.[53]

The next circumstance was liberty. Like Mill, Bain distinguished political liberty from self-government, but regarded both as instruments for moulding character.[54] Finally, he included social institutions, laws and customs as influencing character: "the tenure and descent of Property, the Marriage Laws, improved means of Communication are obvious instances."[55]

In this material Bain confined his discussion to individual character and the influence of the listed variety of circumstances in determining it. He also considered national character, which he called "Political Ethology," and which was distinct from, though related to, individual character. Bain devoted a good deal of attention to this science.[56] For example, he considered the role of "the energetic disposition itself" in the character of nations as follows:

> Now this shows itself, as high or as low, in whole nations, and is of importance as respects both the Form of Government and many other political arrangements. The inhabitants of temperate climates are superior in natural energy, irrespective of all modes of stimulation to the dwellers either in the tropics or in the arctic circles. The English and Anglo-American peoples are probably at the top of the scale.
>
> Now this attribute has numerous social bearings. It favours private industry and the accumulation of wealth, an effect leading to many other effects. It is both directly and indirectly hostile to monarchical rule, and is, therefore, the parent and the guardian of liberty.[57]

This discussion, of which only a small portion can be set out here, follows closely but develops considerably, for example, Mill's discussion of national character in the *Considerations on Representative Government* (1861).

It also confirms Mill's position that individual and national character are closely related and that ethology is the key to progress in social science.

When Mill read Bain's *Logic* in 1870, he could write to Bain of the two works on logic:

> . . . I am much struck with the combination of nearly perfect agreement in the *fond* of our opinions on every part of it with so much originality in the manner in which you have presented many of them. This, if it stood alone, would make the book very valuable for there is no more important service to any set of thoughts than to vary their expression, & to deduce them from one another in different ways. But in addition to this, by varying the modes of statement you have illuminated points & aspects of our common doctrine which the previous exposition had left more or less in the shade. And you have followed out some of the principles into consequences not previously drawn.
>
> I find little or nothing, relating properly to Logic, from which I dissent . . .[58]

After thirty years of prodigious joint work in logic and associationist psychology, it is striking that Mill could write that they were in "nearly perfect agreement" and could refer to "our common doctrine." In my opinion Bain's *Logic*, hitherto mostly ignored, is an excellent exposition of Mill's *Logic* and shows how numerous ideas of Mill could be developed and extended with great skill and originality. Despite the fact that Mill never explicitly commented on the material on character and ethology, it remains the fullest statement of Mill's work on ethology, and one important development of the double helix. It also provides ample evidence that Mill never rejected or abandoned the science of ethology, as developed in the *Logic*.[59]

IV. CONCLUSION

The idea of seeing Mill and Bain as a "double helix" may seem preposterous to many philosophers and intellectual historians today who prefer a more individual approach to their subjects. Alternatively, they prefer various collective schools, from utilitarianism to idealism or to Marxism. Prior to Mill, one might focus on Bentham, who was notorious for sharing the writing and publication of his work with a number of important figures from Etienne Dumont to both James and John Stuart Mill. But Bentham remained the source of the ideas and inspiration for their development, even though others may have done a good deal of the work in producing the actual texts. The relationship between Mill and Bain as a double helix proceeded almost from the outset, and from this double helix the development of modern social science was considerably enhanced.

NOTES

1. See Rosen (2013: 72–94); Mill (1843, CW: VIII.831–952, esp. 844–74). All references to John Stuart Mill's works are to the authoritative edition of *Collected Works of John Stuart Mill* (Mill, 1963–1991—cited as CW, followed by volume and page number), unless otherwise indicated.
2. See Bain (1882: 78–9, 84; 1904: 159, 164).
3. Mill (1873, CW: I.255).
4. Mill (1873, CW: I.255n).
5. Robson (1974: lxviii). J. S. Mill to A. Bain, Autumn 1841, CW: XIII.487, 487n.
6. J. S. Mill to M. Napier, 18 Feb. 1842, CW: XIII.499.
7. Robson (1974: lxviiiff).
8. See Comte (1830–1842).
9. See Mill (1873, CW: I.255n).
10. J. S. Mill to A. Comte, 30 Aug. 1843, CW: XIII.594 and 5 Oct 1844, CW: XIII.638. For an assessment of Mill's important relationship with Comte, see Rosen (2013: 97–128). As for the accuracy of his prediction regarding Bain flying the flag of positivism, see Bain (1904: 54, 145–46, 153–54, 156–59, 194, 202). Bain's attempt to delay the publication in French of the Mill-Comte correspondence is recorded in Vogeler (1976: 20). More generally, see Cashdollar (1989: 21), which begins with the relationships between Bain, Mill and Comte.
11. See Bain (1843: 412–56); Robson (1974: lxxxiin); Packe (1954: 272).
12. Robson (1974: lxxxviiin) quoting J. S. Mill to T. E. Cliffe Leslie, 8 Feb. 1869, CW: XVII.1558.
13. See Bain (1870).
14. Mill (1843, CW: VII.cxvii).
15. See Packe (1954: 291).
16. Packe (1954: 289).
17. Bain (1882: 102–3); see also Sparshott (1978: lviiin).
18. Mill (1859, CW: XI.339–73).
19. See Mill (1859, CW: XI.342n).
20. See Mill (1859, CW: XI.352).
21. See Mill (1859, CW: XI.372).
22. See Mill (1869, CW: XXXI.95–253).
23. Young (1990: 6).
24. See Young (1990: 133n) citing Wiener (1949: 19). See also Fisch (1954: 413–44); Dixon (2003: 150ff).
25. See Rosen (2013: 72–94).
26. Bain (1859: 286ff).
27. Bain (1859: 500ff).
28. Bain (1859: 568ff).
29. Nor did Bain write on character in later works, such as Bain (1868; 1873). In the former of these, *Mental and Moral Science*, he referred to Mill under such topics as theories of the material world (1868: 212–14), a history of the free-will controversy (1868: 426–28), ethical systems, i.e., utilitarianism (1868: 702–14), and necessary truths (1868: appendix, 69–72), but without considering character or ethology.
30. See Bain (1904: 259–60); J. S. Mill to A. Bain, 15 Oct. 1859, CW: XV. 640n–1n; Bain (1861).
31. J. S. Mill to A. Bain, 15 Oct. 1859, CW: XV.640–1.

132   *Frederick Rosen*

32. J. S. Mill to G. Grote, 10 Jan. 1862, CW: XV.764.
33. Young (1990: 122–23).
34. Young (1990: 124).
35. Young (1990: 124).
36. Mill (1865, CW: X.297, 360).
37. Bain (1861: 13).
38. See Van Wyhe (2004).
39. See Bain (1861: 16, 24).
40. See Bain (1861: 29).
41. Mill (1843, CW: VIII.849–74).
42. Bain (1861: 30). Bain also turned to Mill's principles of induction as the logi-
    cal method that might be used to assess a so-called science like phrenology.
    He wrote: "The inductive logic of John Stuart Mill has made the principles
    of experimental proof accessible to every student; and if we but look at his
    chapter on 'Co-existences independent of causation' (*Logic*, Book iii, Chap. 22
    [Mill, 1843, CW: VII.578–90]) we shall find a clear account of the exact
    logical position of the phrenological affirmations. He points out that such
    propositions demand uniformity without a break, in order to establish them
    in their generality. There must not be one single real exception, otherwise
    the rule is as completely void as if there were not one instance in its favour.
    Consequently, every instance that seems to contradict the general affirmation
    must be met and shown to be only an apparent exception. But has this been
    done with any one of the phrenological organs?" (Bain 1861: 59–60).
43. Young misses the significance of Bain's *Logic*, and in the 1990 preface he
    provides a clue as to why he does so: "I privileged the category of biology
    as relatively unproblematic and, in spite of my own views on the history of
    ideas, I tended to denigrate philosophy as passé" (Young 1990: ix).
44. Bain (1870: II.286).
45. Bain (1870: II.287).
46. Bain (1870: II.287).
47. J. S. Mill to A. Comte, 30 Oct. 1843, CW: XIII.604.
48. Bain (1870: II.289).
49. Bain (1870: II.289).
50. Bain (1870: II.289).
51. Bain (1870: II.289).
52. Bain (1870: II.290).
53. Bain (1870: II.290).
54. Bain (1870: II.290).
55. Bain (1870: II.290).
56. See Bain (1870: II.317ff).
57. See Bain (1870: II.328).
58. J. S. Mill to A. Bain, 17 May 1870, CW: XVII.1718.
59. See Rosen (2013: 85–86); Ball (2000; 2010).

REFERENCES

Bain, A. (1843) [A Review of Mill's *System of Logic*] *Westminster Review* 39 (2):
    412–56.
———. (1855) *The Senses and the Intellect* (London: John W. Parker & Son).
———. (1859) *The Emotions and the Will* (London: John W. Parker & Son).
———. (1861) *On the Study of Character Including an Estimate of Phrenology*
    (London: Parker, Son, and Bourn).

———. (1868) *Mental and Moral Science. A Compendium of Psychology and Ethics* (London: Longmans, Green).

———. (1870) *Logic*, 2 vols. (London: Longmans, Green, Reader, and Dyer).

———. (1873) *Mind and Body: The Theories of their Relation* (London: Henry S. King and Co.).

———. (1882) *John Stuart Mill, a Criticism: With Personal Recollections* (London: Longmans, Green and Co.).

———. (1904) *Autobiography* (London: Longmans, Green and Co.).

Ball, T. (2000) "The Formation of Character: Mill's 'Ethology' Reconsidered," *Polity* 33 (1): 25–48.

———. (2010) "Competing Theories of Character Formation: James vs. John Stuart Mill," in G. Varouxakis, P. Kelly (eds.) *John Stuart Mill: Thought and Influence* (London and New York: Routledge): 35–56.

Cashdollar, C. D. (1989) *The Transformation of Theology, 1830–1980, Positivism and Protestant Thought in Britain and America* (Princeton: Princeton University Press).

Comte, A. (1830–1842) *Cours de Philosophie Positive*, 6 vols. (Paris: Bachelier).

Dixon, T. (2003) *From Passions to Emotions: The Creation of a Secular Psychological Category* (Cambridge: Cambridge University Press).

Fisch, M. (1954) "Alexander Bain and the Genealogy of Pragmatism," *Journal of the History of Ideas* 15: 413–44.

Mill, J. (1829) *Analysis of the Phenomena of the Human Mind*, ed. J. S. Mill, with notes by J. S. Mill, A. Bain, A. Findlater and G. Grote, 2 vols., 2nd rev. ed. (London: Longmans, Green, Reader, and Dyer, 1878).

Mill, J. S. (1843) *A System of Logic, Ratiocinative and Inductive: Being a Connected View of the Principles of Evidence and the Methods of Scientific Investigation*, in vols. VII and VIII (1974) of Mill (1963–1991).

———. (1859) "Bain's Psychology," in vol. XI (1978) of Mill (1963–1991): 339–73.

———. (1865) *Auguste Comte and Positivism*, in vol. X (1969) of Mill (1963–1991).

———. (1869) "James Mill's *Analysis of the Phenomena of the Human Mind*," in vol. XXXI (1989) of Mill (1963–1991): 95–253.

———. (1873) *Autobiography*, in vol. I (1981) of Mill (1963–1991).

———. (1963–1991) *Collected Works of John Stuart Mill*, F.E.L. Priestly (gen. ed.), and subsequently J. M. Robson, 33 vols. (London/Toronto: Routledge and Kegan Paul/University of Toronto Press).

Packe, M. St. John (1954) *The Life of John Stuart Mill* (London: Secker & Warburg).

Robson, J. M. (1974) "Textual Introduction," in J. M. Robson (ed.), vols. VII and VIII of *Collected Works of John Stuart Mill* (London/Toronto: Routledge and Kegan Paul/ University of Toronto Press): xlix–cviii.

Rosen, F. (2013) *Mill* (Oxford: Oxford University Press).

Sparshott, F. E. (1978) "Introduction," in J. M. Robson (ed.), vol. XI of *Collected Works of John Stuart Mill* (London/Toronto: Routledge and Kegan Paul/ University of Toronto Press): vii–lxxvi.

Spencer, H. (1855) *The Principles of Psychology* (London: Longman, Brown, Green, and Longmans).

Van Wyhe, J. (2004) *Phrenology and the Origins of Victorian Scientific Naturalism* (Aldershot: Ashgate).

Vogeler, M. (1976) "Comte and Mill: The Early Publishing History of their Correspondence," *Mill Newsletter* 11: 17–22.

Wiener, P. (1949) *Evolution and the Founders of Pragmatism* (Cambridge, MA: Harvard University Press).

Young, R. (1970) *Mind, Brain and Adaptation in the Nineteenth Century, Cerebral Localization and its Biological Context from Gall to Ferrier*, 2nd ed. (New York and Oxford: Oxford University Press, 1990).

6 In Defense of Mill's Theory of Free Will

Bernard Berofsky

I. HUME AND MILL ON THE FREEDOM OF THE WILL

The views of John Stuart Mill on the freedom of the will are very similar to those of David Hume. As empiricists, they both endorsed the status of the principle that all events have causes as both *a posteriori* and true, and agreed as well that acts of will are not exempt. Such acts are causes and effects in the same sense as any events. Experience tells us that every event has a cause and this doctrine implies that volitions are similarly caused by our desires, habits, aversions and dispositions, and those factors are themselves the effects of education and other early influences.[1] The will is neither uncaused nor self-caused. Moreover, our inner awareness of our willing does not provide us with special *a priori* knowledge of its causal powers.

In light of subsequent developments, Mill's confidence in determinism or necessitarianism appears overblown. There is, of course, the success of quantum mechanics as well as the use of stochastic theories in various disciplines, such as chemistry, sociology, economics and climatology. The failure of scientific psychology to produce more than a few accepted, deterministic laws in that discipline is another discouraging sign.

Although this is not the occasion for a full discussion of the prospects of determinism, one rebuttal often made by determinists is that psychology should not be judged by its failure to produce strict deterministic laws. After all, all other sciences, even physics, permit *ceteris paribus* laws. So the bar should not be made unfairly high in psychology. John Earman and John Roberts (2004) reject this defense for all the social sciences and argue that the latter's subject matter is just too complicated even for *ceteris paribus* laws. In the case of these sciences, causal and statistical explanations without even tacit reference to laws can suffice. But they do concede in the end that "'*ceteris paribus* laws' might . . . be elements of embryonic theories. As such, they are not ready to be confirmed or disconfirmed . . . in their current stage of development."[2]

It is rarely noted that the rejection of determinism, whether warranted by these developments or not, does not convert "the free will question" into a moot one. For the falsity of determinism as a general metaphysical theory about the world as a whole can coincide with the truth of some or several deterministic theories. And the latter might include theories relevant to the free will issue. For example, my decision might fall under some law of decision theory and I can surely then worry about the extent of my having made that decision freely. This "new" problem can be sufficiently genuine and worrisome even in an indeterministic world, that is, a world in which some sorts of events are not governed by deterministic laws. The point is that free will worries arise if there are deterministic laws that govern some sorts of (important?) acts of will.

We have yet to ponder specifically the nature of free will. Mill (1865) says something about this matter in response to Sir William Hamilton. He says that consciousness cannot give us direct knowledge of freedom, for the latter is an ability and consciousness provides direct knowledge of episodes rather than knowledge of what we are able to do. To be sure, there is a common feeling of free will; but whatever this feeling is, it cannot establish the metaphysical theory of free will as self-determination. It is true that—through the imagination, not reason—we retain the idea of a strong tie (between cause and effect) that can actually conflict with that feeling of freedom. But this idea of a tie or intimate link is anyway erroneous. As Hume had said, there is no special tie *anywhere* between cause and effect including the will and its effects.

There is also agreement with Hume that the knowledge of free will as an ability is conditional in character. As Mill puts it, the so-called feeling of (moral) freedom is just the knowledge that one can alter one's will if one wishes and one needs (past) experience to obtain knowledge of this sort of fact. It is true that we sometimes report having acted against our strongest desire, say to sin, suggesting a contracausal expression of our free will. But, according to Mill, we are rather reporting that our conscience, as our desire to do right, prevailed in this case as the truly stronger desire and we have once again instantiated rather than transcended the law of causation. There is never the awareness of the ability to will in opposition to the strongest desire.[3]

As Hume observed in a famous footnote,[4] we often feel that we can do either of two (or several) contrary acts. In Hume's terms, we have a *seeming* experience of the liberty of indifference. We feel a certain "looseness and indifference" that would permit the will to move either way, unburdened by a determining cause guiding us in a single direction.

The introduction of a conditional expression for the sort of liberty we *actually* possess (as opposed to the aforementioned *illusion* of the liberty of indifference) may be based on the prevalence of the conditional form of expression often used to express this feeling: I can do A if I wish (choose) and I can do B if I wish (choose). But as J. L. Austin (1961) famously argued, these grammatical conditionals most likely express nonconditional facts, for, if they were genuine conditionals, they would not imply, as they do, "I can do A (simpliciter)" and "I can do B (simpliciter)." So it is not so easy to annul the sense of a categorical sort of freedom.

Indeed, more modern efforts to analyze free will as an ability or power, expressible as a conditional, have confronted enormous difficulties.[5] Libertarians and anti-empiricists have raised questions about the status of the antecedent of the alleged conditional, desire or choice. Consider persons who would act differently had they wanted to, but did not want to. In itself, this may not be problematic—after all, the counterfactual "If they had wanted to do otherwise, they would have done otherwise" may still be true of them. But critics are fond of noting that there are often freedom-undermining explanations of the origins of the absence of desire or choice. If I do not want to do A because I was coerced or manipulated or if I was given a drug (either against my will or at least without my concurrence) that made it impossible for me to want to do A, I am surely not acting of my own free will when I choose B over A. When Mill defends the conditional nature of our freedom by noting that we are able to alter our wills or our character by our own actions, he also concedes the Owenite response that we must then consider whether or not we desire to alter our will. In addition, many critics of the empiricist/compatibilist tradition of Hume and Mill have observed that a reapplication of the conditional analysis to the antecedent (I want A, I choose A) of the conditional (for example, I would have chosen A, had X been the case) leads to an unsatisfactory infinite regress.

Moreover, empiricists or compatibilists have often not taken seriously enough the difficulties in distinguishing coercion, compulsion or manipulation from more normal cases of causation; but as long as such differences exist, a believer in free will, like Mill, can at least ward off wholesale rejections of free will, ones that regard free will as utterly negated in all cases by the very fact that the will is not exempt from the law of causation. If my will is caused, at least it does not follow that it is coerced; to choose from desire is not automatically to choose under compulsion or coercion.

On the other hand, if the feeling of freedom is not to be understood as expressible as a conditional, if that dimension of the Hume-Mill approach to freedom fails, then the compatibilist is left with an unanswered question as to the nature of the freedom that is not automatically nullified by governance by law. If I choose B, what is the nature of the ability or power to have chosen A?

In terms of the *positive* case of the incompatibilist that freedom is nullified by law governance, there are two convictions shared by Hume and Mill that are relevant here. I have shifted in this discussion from cause to law and that shift would be regarded by both of them as perfectly reasonable since causation itself is inherently lawlike. That is, the presence of a causal relation between token events e_1 and e_2 obtains in virtue of a general connection between event types (of which e_1 and e_2 are tokens) linked by law. The second conviction is the more important in terms of a response to the incompatibilist. It is the view that the sense in which laws are necessary is one that is compatible with the freedom of the will. The will can be both causally necessitated and free.

For Mill, necessitarianism or the doctrine of necessity at least acknowledges that the will falls under the same natural order as other events. The tendency to infer from this doctrine that we are unfree or that we possess a degraded natural state is based on confused associations with the concept of necessity. We illicitly move from necessity to the idea of a stronger tie, one that leads us erroneously to think that our willed actions are done under compulsion or irresistibility.[6]

What does legitimately follow from the fact that our wills cause our actions? First of all, we cannot literally say that the will causally necessitates action because an act of will is never causally sufficient for action. There are always other necessary conditions of action, such as at least a functioning neuromusculature. But the will is a part of a set of conditions that collectively causally necessitate action. Now, as a generalist, Mill (and Hume) would cite as crucial the fact of uniformity. To know the complete cause of any event is to know that the reappearance of those causal factors will in fact be followed by another instance of that sort of effect. The presence of a law is essentially the objective regularity obtaining between pairs of events. If an act of will W_1 in circumstances C_1 leads me to perform action A_1 and I am again facing the same sort of circumstances as C_1, then a willing similar to W_1 will lead to an action similar to A_1. This is all the law of causation tells us, according to Mill. We might also put the same point by saying that the action will take place unless it is interfered with, meaning that, should the total cause vary from before, if either the circumstances or the will changes, then, of course, the sort of action that follows may well be of a type different from the type of which A_1 is a token.

If a law is only a statement of uniformity or regularity, there is apparently no way in which an incompatibilist can argue that law "governance" confers impotence or inability on agents subsumed by the law. Just as one cannot infer an ought from an is, one cannot similarly infer a must—understood as stronger than mere uniformity, suggesting compulsion or irresistibility— from an is. Causal necessitation cuts across cases of genuine unfreedom (coercion, compulsion, manipulation, impotence) and cases of freedom (doing what I want to do or doing what I deem the right thing to be).

This conclusion, Mill observes, should not appear that strange to religious metaphysicians who believe in the freedom of the will. For divine foreknowledge entails that our acts are necessary anyway since, if God knows beforehand how we will act, then we must act as we do.

Mill's view appears to conflict with the well-known and widely accepted Consequence Argument, which claims that free will is incompatible with determinism. This argument depends, not on the assumption that necessity connotes compulsion or irresistibility, but rather on the prima facie acceptable assumption that no one can violate or alter a law of nature. Although there are different versions of the argument, the fundamental idea is roughly that, since no one can alter the laws of nature or the past, and since propositions reporting all actual human actions and decisions follow logically from determinism plus a conjunction of the laws of nature and the facts about the past, then no one can alter any actions or decisions he does in fact perform. But the power to decide or act differently from the way we do decide or act *is* free will. So universal governance by law, according to proponents of the Consequence Argument, does pose a genuine threat to free will. I will defend Mill by challenging this conclusion. But to do so, we must look more closely at Mill's defense of the regularity interpretation of laws.

Has Mill made a significant advance over Hume on the questions associated with freedom of the will? We know that he has in terms of the way in which he elaborated on the regularity approach to laws. I will first explain this elaboration, which is well known. I will then argue that elements of his thinking on the matter contain the seeds of a solution both to the problems associated with his elaboration as well as to the modifications made by twentieth century followers of his approach, Frank Ramsey (1928), R. B. Braithwaite (1957), David Lewis (1981, 1994), and Ernest Nagel (1961), to name several prominent ones. That is, within Mill's own writings about laws, one will find solutions to the problems that have continued to plague the improved versions of his doctrine offered by his successors. Mill's approach provides us with the basis for a solid solution to the free will problem. A significant corollary of this defense of Mill, as I have said, is the failure of the Consequence Argument, an argument I concede to be a valid (but unsound) one.

II.   MILL'S DEFENSE OF THE REGULARITY THEORY

The most famous problem confronting the doctrine that laws are empirical generalizations that state the uniform association of properties—the regularity theory of laws—is simply the existence of numerous true generalizations that are evidently not laws. Some properties are associated or co-occur even though they are not lawfully or causally related. Mill was well aware of the existence of these "accidental generalizations" or, at least, generalizations that fall short of what he called "Laws of Nature" in the strict sense.[7] He offered his own, well known example: day follows night, but night does not cause day.

Now, in saying that day does not cause night, or that there is no *causal* law linking the two, Mill is not denying that there is an empirical law relating day to night. After all, the phenomenon is an effect of a common cause. In fact it depends on the contingent association of two phenomena, the rotation of the earth on its axis in proximity to a sufficiently luminous body, such as our sun. Like many empirical laws, the generalization is conditional on these circumstances, circumstances that will in fact someday change.

Notice by the way that Mill is implying that some laws are contingent on facts about the world that are not themselves laws. Obvious examples are biological laws that depend upon the contingent facts of evolutionary history. Mill says that derivative laws "mostly depend on those ultimate laws and an ultimate fact, namely, the mode of co-existence of some of the component elements of the universe."[8] Moreover, this second element is "a collocation of causes . . . and . . . cannot itself be reduced to any law."[9] Many philosophers of science reject the idea of contingent laws, although it has been defended by Roberts (2010) and myself (2012).

These collocations do not exhibit any rule or uniformity. The most important one is the distribution of "the primeval natural agents through the universe."[10] We would think of these as the initial conditions, factors that, under the most sweeping sort of determinism, constitute a kind of exception to the deterministic doctrine. They are the raw materials on which the laws of the universe work, the ultimate surd that explains how the laws operate on everything else but themselves. Different possible universes begin in different ways and with different materials; there is no nondivine explanation of this fact.

The conditional character of the noncausal relation between day and night explains why we do not view the relation as necessary. Necessity connotes unconditionality or invariability and that fails in this case. We know that the relation is conditional through experience, of course, either the distant future experience of the sun's demise, based itself on current empirical knowledge, or present experience. For the latter, Mill says that we are justified "on experimental grounds in concluding that, if the sun were always above the horizon, there would be day, though there had been no night".[11] Although it is a fact that this relation will someday break down, this sort of case does not address those examples of de facto universality often invoked by necessitarians against the regularity theory. It is an easy matter to construct de facto true accidental generalizations and it behooves a regularity theorist to provide an explanation of their nonnomic status, a matter to which we shall return.

Mill, in fact, presents a variety of interesting distinctions among empirical generalizations; but since this chapter is not primarily concerned with his view of the nature of scientific laws, I will restrict myself to those facets of his view that bear on his version of the regularity theory that, itself, bears ultimately on the free will issue.

The aspect of Mill's view of laws that has been adopted by subsequent thinkers bent on improving the regularity theory of laws is the interconnection of derivative and ultimate laws. If we initially look to the level closest to the empirical, we find uniformities to which we give the title "empirical laws" whether or not we are in a position to provide a deeper explanation, whether or not we can deduce these empirical laws from more fundamental ones that would explain them. We know from the overriding law of causation that these empirical laws are derivative laws, whether or not we are now in a position to derive them from the ultimate laws of causation. Their status remains in limbo until they can be inserted into the system of the world through further empirical investigation. Lower-level generalizations are better established when deduced from higher-order generalizations that are better established. Indeed, when merely empirical generalizations present as confirmed only by direct empirical evidence, they are ripe for refutation by the slightest counterexample. But when they are certified by derivation from more ultimate laws and are seen as indirectly confirmed by said derivations, their entrenchment is more securely established.

Although we speak here of deduction, it is important to recall that derivative laws sometimes depend not just on ultimate laws, but also on ultimate facts of coexistence that are not themselves laws. Collocations cannot be reduced to laws, derivative or otherwise.

In examining the developments of Mill's doctrines, we should also note the importance he placed on simplicity. True Laws of Nature "designate the uniformities when reduced to their most simple expression."[12]

III. SUBSEQUENT DEVELOPMENTS: HUMEAN SUPERVENIENCE WITHOUT THE BEST SYSTEM ANALYSIS

Mill's ideas were presented in stricter form by Frank Ramsey in 1928 when he invoked both deductive systematization and simplicity and famously claimed that laws (universals of law) are the "consequences of those (general) propositions which we should take as axioms if we knew everything and organized it as simply as possible in a deductive system."[13] This idea evolved through the twentieth century and is now most closely associated with the version offered by David Lewis, according to which laws are those generalizations that belong to the best overall theory of the world, that is, one that achieves the most strength (informational content) with the least sacrifice of simplicity. If there is one such system, it is the Best. Hence, this theory of laws is known as the Best Systems Analysis (BSA).

It is easy to see that many de facto true generalizations we would not count as laws are eliminated by BSA. It is true that all the people on Elm Street bleed when stuck with a pin. But that generalization will not find its way into the Best System, for there is a more comprehensive generalization that accounts for the bleeding of all the people on Elm Street as well as many others, whereas the reference to Elm Street is a useless complexity.

Yet BSA and, indirectly, Mill's legacy, have been roundly criticized. A common locus of criticism is a corollary of BSA known as Humean Supervenience (HS). What is HS? The empiricist/regularity approach to laws is expressed by Mill in the following way: "From . . . separate threads of connection between parts of the great whole we term nature a general tissue of connection unavoidably weaves itself . . . These various uniformities . . . we call . . . Laws of Nature."[14] The world presents patterns and these are the basis of laws. The patterns determine the laws. In Lewis, this is HS. The laws summarize the facts. The alternative is the necessitarian or governance conception, according to which history unfolds in accordance with those patterns dictated by the laws history must adhere to. On this view, events must occur as they do because the law, as prior to history, determines such outcomes. For Mill, Lewis and other regularity theorists, on the other hand, the laws are determined by events. A consequence of HS is that there cannot be two distinct sets of laws for the same history. If the history of the world is known, the laws of that world automatically follow. Laws supervene on history.

HS has been a target for critics of the regularity approach. Without HS, BSA is indefensible.

The many critics of HS—D. M. Armstrong (1993, 1997), John Carroll (1994), Bas van Fraassen (1989), Mark Lange (2000), Michael Tooley (1977)—all invoke possible worlds whose extreme simplicity does not enable us to fix the laws of that world. Since a complete nonnomic description of the world does not dictate a nomic fact of the matter, we are able to speculate on various possibilities and can envisage that the world might be governed by any of a number of laws (or sets of laws). A world consisting of a single lone proton moving uniformly in a straight line might be governed by Newton's first law alone or by all the laws of Newtonian physics (vacuously satisfied save for the first law). There must be a nomic fact of the matter even if it is in principle unknowable. I have argued elsewhere that all these arguments either beg the question against HS by assuming that worlds that are identical nonnomically differ nomically (the point at issue) or they posit worlds that are too simple for the very distinction between laws and merely de facto true generalizations to gain purchase.

I believe that critics of HS regard John Carroll's case as the strongest and will, therefore, now try to show how Carroll actually begs the question against HS.[15] Carroll employs an argument that has come to be called the "Mirror Argument," designed to show that there can be two worlds that are identical nonnomically, but differ nomically. I will simplify the examples slightly for purposes of exposition.

Suppose a possible world U_1 with five X-particles and a Y-field, such that, whenever an X-particle enters the Y-field, it acquires spin up. It is, indeed, a law L that this is true for any X-particle entering a Y-field. Next to one of these particles, b, there is a mirror that is positioned such that it does not prevent the free movement of b into the Y-field. Call this position c.

Now suppose a second possible world U_2, identical to U_1, except that particle b acquires spin down when it enters the Y-field. Thus, in U_2, L is false and obviously not a law.

Add two other possible worlds, $U_1{}^*$ and $U_2{}^*$, in both of which the mirror is positioned so that b strikes and caroms off the mirror, thereby preventing b in each world from entering a Y-field. Call this position d. So in $U_1{}^*$, b is prevented from acquiring spin up by being prevented from entering the Y-field of that world, and in $U_2{}^*$, b is prevented from acquiring spin down by being prevented from entering the Y-field of that world.

It is crucial to note that U_1^* and U_2^* are identical nonnomically. Laws aside, the worlds are identical. Moreover, given that the description of the worlds is complete, there is no deeper structure that accounts for the difference between particle b in U_1^* (or U_1) and particle b in U_2^* (or U_2). B-particles in U_2^* worlds just happen to behave differently from b-particles in U_1^* worlds for no reason whatsoever.

Since U_1^* and U_2^* are nonnomically identical, HS dictates that they have the same laws. Carroll disputes this by appeal to SC*: If $\Diamond pP$ & $\Box p(P \supset Q)$, then if P were the case, Q would be the case. Since L is a law in U_1 and U_1^* differs from U_1 only in terms of the change of mirror position from c to d, a change that is physically possible, SC* dictates that L must also be a law in U_1^*. Had particle b had the opportunity to enter field Y in U_1^*, it would have had spin up. Now, in U_2, L is neither a law nor even true. The physically possible mirror change that yields U_2^* cannot convert L into a law in U_2^*. Thus, the truth of L, arising from b's failure to enter a Y field in U_2^* is vacuous and merely accidental. Since L is a law in U_1^*, but not a law in the nonnomically identical U_2^*, HS fails.

First of all, I believe that SC* is problematic. Here, Mill was right and many contemporary philosophers of science are wrong. Carroll and Lange, for example, reject contingent laws, laws that depend in part on contingent facts about the world. With respect to the existence and location of coal beds, Mill writes: "we cannot be assured that the original constitution of any other planet was such as to produce the different depositions in the same order as in our globe. The *derivative law* [emphasis mine] in this case depends not solely on laws, but on a collocation; and collocations cannot be reduced to any law."[16] Although Lange rejects contingent laws, he actually produces several excellent examples that depend on evolutionary accidents: "The change in stimulation necessary to excite a nerve cell is proportional to the initial value of the stimulation parameter."[17]

SC* aside, the argument fails anyway as it depends on our supposing for no reason that each starred world evolves from its original by a change in the mirror position. In this way, we derive the result that U_1^* must have the same laws as U_1 for the only *change* is a contingent one, namely, mirror position. If we look at U_1^* and U_2^* with unprejudiced eyes, however, we see (nonnomically) *identical worlds*. The opponent of HS must then *make the case* that they are nomically distinct. We ask the question of a world in which particle b is prevented from entering field Y, what it would have done. To be sure, we know that all the particles except particle b acquire spin up in the Y field. So what we have is a basic inductive exercise and it might look reasonable to suppose that particle b would behave the way other particles do. After all, there is no difference between particle b and the other particles. Under that supposition, U_1, not U_2, would be closer to U^* ($_1$ or $_2$). But then since L is a law in U_1, it would have to be a law in both U_1^* and U_2^*. So nonnomically identical worlds are nomically identical and HS is saved.

Even if we reject the conservative extension of the postulate that reason seems to dictate and insist on an agnostic posture, there is no reason to believe that the closest world to U_2* is U_2 rather than U_1, for we cannot say that particle b would have acquired spin down in the Y field. We would then have to remain agnostic about L as well in U_2* and cannot, therefore, conclude that U_1* and U_2*differ nomically. HS is again preserved.

What about the simple argument that, since L is not a law in U_2, Carroll's principle would dictate that, from the perspective of U_2, supposing a change in mirror position from c to d cannot make L a law. If we then conclude that U_2* must be closest to U_2 rather than U_1, we have no nonquestion-begging way to prevent the conclusion that U_1* is similarly closest to U_2 rather than U_1 since it looks the same as U_2*.[18] Again, same facts, same laws. HS survives.

The other assumption made by these critics of HS, to wit, that any world, no matter how simple, is law-governed, requires justification. A generalization G earns its lawhood in part when it displays invariance under a variety of actual variations and, by dint of its membership in a system of generalizations, inherits the confirmation of other generalizations in the system that covers data not directly in the set of confirming instances of G. The worlds contemplated by the advocates of governance are too simple for the concept of invariance to gain a foothold. Hence, instead of presenting us with worlds that are governed by unknowable laws—since all the data are compatible with several competing possible laws and even an omniscient scientist would not be able to determine the laws—they rather present us with worlds to which the concept of a law does not apply.

> Consider the example 'All white cats with blue eyes are deaf.' Suppose it were strictly true. It might still be a pure accident. Or it might be a law as, in fact, it was discovered to be (at least a statistical law), but only when it was discovered that the gene for whiteness can affect the way the cat's ears can develop. But the world needs some complexity in order to develop this explanation. One cannot advance structural explanations without structure. Similarly, 'All nauseous insects have vivid coloration' is not an accidental generalization because we can explain it in evolutionary terms; protective coloration offers a survival advantage. We cannot get a handle on the issues we need to address in order to categorize a generalization as a law in these absurdly simple worlds.[19]

Although BSA survives the challenge to HS, other problems abound. Obviously, we need an account of simplicity in order to apply this criterion in a serious way. More deeply, as Earman has said,[20] we really have no scale that would permit judgments as to whether or not the addition of information compensates for the loss of simplicity. There is a lot of hand waving here by defenders of BSA. Thus, regularity theorists may retain HS, but should attempt to capture the appeal to systematization inherent in the Mill-Ramsey-Lewis approach in a different way.

IV.   LAWS AND ACCIDENTAL GENERALIZATIONS

Philosophers often characterize the difference between laws and nonlaws in terms of the fact that only the former sustain their corresponding counterfactual conditionals. It is a law that all dry matches ignite when struck. It is not a law, but true nonetheless, that all people sitting on this park bench are Italians (G_a). This dry stick is not a match. But if it were, it would ignite when struck. O'Malley is not Italian. It is not, however, the case that he would be Italian if he were to sit on this park bench. There are problems in characterizing laws in terms of this criterion. But a regularity theorist is committed to view the differences in the way laws sustain counterfactuals as a derivative fact, grounded in actual examples that constitute evidence for the causal relations that in turn make certain counterfactuals true.

One of the barriers to the substantiation of this grand claim is the complexity of the class of nonlaws. There are many members of this class that cannot properly be labeled "accidental generalizations" as they are not accidental at all. Mill was well aware of the variety within this class. For example, he makes an important distinction between complex derivative laws of causation and propositions I would call nonnomic explanatory generalizations or, in the language of James Woodward and Christopher Hitchcock (2003), invariant generalizations. The latter are generalizations, for example, "Watering plants helps them to grow," that are pretty robust and hold within a sufficiently wide range of relevant cases to be invoked in explanations. They fail to be laws, not because of the absence of some mysterious nomic property, necessity, but simply because they are too limited or vague to be so counted. The fact that Mill counts them as laws of a sort is less important than what he says about them. "The inferiority of evidence . . . [of derivative causal laws] is trifling compared with that which is inherent in uniformities not known to be laws of causation at all . . . [W]e cannot tell on how many collocations, as well as laws, their truth may be dependent; . . . [they are] unfit to be relied on beyond the limit of time, space, and circumstance, in which the observations have been made."[21] It may be that Mill, as a determinist, is including both what I have called "nonnomic explanatory generalizations" and generalizations that might properly be called "accidental," such as "All the men in this room are wearing green shirts" or "All the screws in Smith's car are rusty." Even the latter two differ, although neither is an explanatory generalization. There might be an explanation of the second generalization in terms of the lengthy exposure to oxygen of all the screws in Smith's car, but the first might be a pure coincidence that can only be thought to have some sort of explanation in principle by a determinist. But whatever classification we prefer, the status of many generalizations we might prefer not to call laws can be established without our having to look beyond the actual evidence in the world.

Some philosophers have relied heavily on restrictions on the sorts of terms that may appear in laws. The familiar demand on laws that they only contain "purely qualitative" terms as opposed to ineliminable references to particular individuals or particular times and places has been invoked to explain the distinctive nature of laws. We will not pursue this approach since it is anyway insufficient—there will be accidental generalizations that pass this test—and suffers from counterexamples anyway (Kepler's Laws being the most famous example).

We still need a criterion to distinguish laws from nonlaws, especially since generalizations like "All the pillowcases in my bedroom are red" along with an infinite number of similar general truths will not be eliminated given the rejection of the criterion described in the preceding paragraph. For a regularity theorist, a successful criterion is prohibited from invoking nomic necessity or cognate concepts in distinguishing (causal and noncausal) laws from 1) other explanatory generalizations, 2) generalizations linking the effects of a common cause (characterized by some as derivative laws) and 3) accidentally true generalizations.

We have already dealt with (1). A regularity theorist does not believe that there is a difference in principle between laws and other explanatory generalizations. The latter fail to be laws because they do not work in a variety of extreme cases (true to a certain extent of laws), are too imprecise or vague and require numerous background conditions. Explanatory generalizations or invariant generalizations do not become laws by the acquisition of a modal property that a generalization either possesses or lacks in toto. (2), as I said, may be regarded as derivative laws. But their deficiencies are illuminating. If Tom and Mary always eat together and both get food poisoning one evening, this occasion is an instance of the nonaccidentally true generalization that whenever Tom gets food poisoning, so does Mary. But we know that Tom's condition does not cause Mary's (there is no direct causal law linking the two) because there is an intervention that would cause food poisoning in Tom only. We know this through our general knowledge that the guilty pathogenic bacteria can be introduced into Tom's body and not Mary's. This knowledge is grounded on principles of induction taught to all philosophers of science in the last century-and-one-half by John Stuart Mill!

I mention this example for another reason. What about the cases in which we have not made or even cannot make the relevant intervention? In order to address this problem, let us turn finally to accidental generalizations proper. Suppose "Everyone who sits on this park bench is Italian" (G_a) is true. (It might be true because the neighborhood is Italian or it might be a pure coincidence.) We might intervene and induce a Croatian to sit on the bench. But what if we don't? So it remains eternally de facto true. BSA would have us look at the effects of adding this generalization to our knowledge and it may well be possible to rule it out on the basis of a principle inherent in BSA—Benefit-Free Complexity. (We can explain why anyone [whether or not he sits on the bench] is Italian—genetic facts—without invoking facts about the bench.) That is, if a generalization provides no explanatory benefit and adds complexity to our system, it is eliminated. We might indeed attempt to extract this useful principle without adopting BSA as a whole.[22]

The failure of BSA rests, as we know, on the failure to construct a measure that would permit us to determine whether the information addition of a generalization is sufficient to compensate for the increase in complexity created by its addition. Perhaps, instead of looking at the proper mesh within a system of laws, we should look at the potential damage of adding generalizations to an existent system. Many generalizations are accidental because accepting them as lawful or explanatory would conflict with a vast network of *non*correlations that have actual instances. To use the bench example again, if we were to think of G_a as a law, we would have a conflict between that supposition and the knowledge that people move all their lives without changing their race or ethnicity. We would have to explain why benches in other locations are occupied by persons of varying origin. If G_a were a genuine law, such explanations would be forthcoming. To be sure, this account is in need of extensive elaboration; but I believe that it leads us in the right direction.

V. MILL'S CONTRIBUTION

This core idea is suggested by Mill. "What has really put an end to these insufficient inductions is their inconsistency with the stronger inductions subsequently obtained by scientific inquiry."[23] Mill was referring here primarily to superstitions, such as astrology, but the point applies equally to accidental generalizations. I propose to develop Mill's insight into an explanation of the distinction between laws and accidental generalizations that a regularity theorist can live with.

These inconsistencies can be codified by principles affirming a *non*nomic connection between factors. I think it is more natural to invoke such principles to explain why a generalization is *not* a law rather than principles, like BSA, that positively determine that some generalization *is* a law. Although both BSA and the approach taken here share the core idea that lawhood has something to do with systemic connections with the rest of our knowledge, our approach emphasizes exclusion whereas BSA emphasizes inclusion. Although I cannot produce a full account of the position taken here, some details can be fleshed out.[24]

A generalization that purports to be a law supposes a causal or nomic connection, in the simplest case, between the properties expressed by the predicates in the generalization rather than the extensions of those predicates. "All copper conducts electricity" is, therefore, not ruled out from the class of laws because copper is red and not all red things (e.g., clay) conduct electricity. So the relevant properties in our target accidental generalization G_a are "Sitting on this park bench" and "Being of Italian descent." The failure of a nomic (causal) connection between those properties rests on the massive failure of a nomic connection between other determinates of the determinables "Being at a specific location" (or "Being on a bench") and "Being of some natural origin," which are, respectively, determinables of these determinate properties. There is instead massive causal independence as we find people from a vast variety of national origins occupying other benches. G_a is not an invariant generalization either because, to quote Woodward, it is not "stable or robust in the sense that it would continue to hold under a relevant class of changes."[25] It may be true that, whenever I toss the coin, it comes up heads (H), but H is not a law of nature because it "conflicts" with highly well-confirmed generalizations about the variability of tosses of coins and similar objects. This discrepancy requires us to view the generalization as a contingent generalization rather than a law.

Another way of making this point is to note that, were we to regard G_a as a law, we would have no way to explain the absence of any connection between benches and national origin in so many other cases.

Incidentally, we have stated another reason that the very existence of laws depends on a world with sufficient complexity, a world in which different sorts of generalizations have taken hold. In a world containing only fair coin tossing events, the fact that the first one hundred of them are heads tells me neither what is to come nor the nomic status of "All one hundred tosses are heads."

This principle, that generalizations proposed as laws cannot be deeply incoherent in the way I have tried to describe, must be more precisely rendered and embodied in a theory of laws that is required to show how and why laws are used for prediction, explanation and systematization. I have certainly not done that here; but I have suggested the direction I believe will lead to a solution to the question of the difference between laws and accidental generalizations that is congenial to the view of necessity espoused by Mill.

The insights embodied in Mill's account of laws are, I believe, quite striking. There are problem areas, for example, the possible inconsistency between Mill's determinism and his recognition of collocations, cosmic facts that do not apparently admit of explanations. Yet Mill saw that there are contingent laws and that there is a way of dealing with accidental generalizations, once one sees how deeply they can conflict with well-entrenched laws. These contributions alone help to keep alive the regularity theory of laws and its way of preserving freedom of the will.

Yet many thinkers have not found a deterministic universe congenial to freedom of the will and a principal basis for their outlook in recent decades is to be found in the Consequence Argument. Of the several versions in the literature, some are valid (see Michael Huemer 2000) and can be rejected by a Millian only if one of the premises is rejected. The idea that I could have done otherwise although my action is governed by law cannot be dismissed, as we have seen, by an appeal to a conditional analysis of "could have done otherwise." The two key premises of the Consequence Argument are that I cannot act contrary to the actual past and I cannot act contrary to the Laws of Nature. From those premises and determinism, the proponent of the argument may validly conclude that, for any action I perform, I could not have acted otherwise. It seems to me that a Millian, a defender of a regularity theory of laws, must reject the premise that I could not have acted contrary to the laws of nature. This rejection is controversial, to be sure. But a regularity theorist grounds this stance in the core rejection of a necessitarian interpretation of laws. I do concede that we lack the ability to violate most laws of nature. But it would be a mistake to argue that, since it is a conceptual truth that laws of nature are true, we cannot act contrary to any law of nature. It follows only that we do not in fact act contrary to any law of nature. To think otherwise is to fall under the sway of fatalism, a doctrine that, I believe, has been thoroughly discredited.

Moreover, this power is a categorical, not a hypothetical, power. This is not a view that Mill actually took and many find it strongly counterintuitive. But I believe (and have argued in 2012, ch. 12) that it is defensible and the best way for a regularity theorist to show that there is no inherent conflict between determinism and freedom of the will.

NOTES

1. See Mill's "On the Freedom of the Will" in *An Examination of Sir William Hamilton's Philosophy* (1865, CW: IX.ch. 26). His position is basically the same as the one he presents in the better known *A System of Logic* (1843, CW: VIII.Book 6, ch. 2). All references to Mill's works are to the authoritative edition of *Collected Works of John Stuart Mill* (Mill, 1963–1991—cited as CW, followed by volume and page number), unless otherwise indicated.
2. Earman and Roberts (2004: 241).
3. Mill (1865, CW: IX.448–54).
4. Hume (1748: 103).
5. See Berofsky (2011).
6. See Mill (1843, CW: VIII.837–38, 814).
7. Mill (1843, CW: VII.315).
8. Mill (1843, CW: VII.518).
9. Mill (1843, CW: VII.519).
10. Mill (1843, CW: VII.518).
11. Mill (1843, CW: VII.340).
12. Mill (1843, CW: VII.315).
13. Ramsey (1928: 150).
14. Mill (1843, CW: VII.315).
15. A more detailed presentation of the argument is found in Berofsky (2012: 195–99).
16. Mill (1843, CW: VII.519).
17. Lange (2000: 229).
18. A similar point is made by Helen Beebee (2004: 272).

19. See Berofsky (2012: 213).
20. Earman (1984: 198).
21. Mill (1843, *CW*: VII.524).
22. If we eliminate a generalization through the principle of Benefit-Free Complexity, it may re-emerge as a theorem of the Best System. For example, "All copper conducts electricity" is a law in spite of the fact that, since all metal conducts electricity, the lower-order generalization is in principle eliminable.
23. Mill (1843, *CW*: VII.321).
24. For details, see Berofsky (2012: 230–38).
25. Woodward (2000: 197).

REFERENCES

Armstrong, D. M. (1983) *What Is a Law of Nature?* (Cambridge: Cambridge University Press).

———. (1993) "The Identification Problem and the Inference Problem," *Philosophy and Phenomenological Research* 53: 421–22.

———. (1997) "Singular Causation and Laws of Nature," in J. Earman and J. Norton (eds.) *The Cosmos of Science* (Pittsburgh: University of Pittsburgh Press): 498–511.

Austin, J. L. (1961) "Ifs and Cans," in J. O. Urmson and G. Warnock (eds.) *Philosophical Papers* (Oxford: Clarendon Press): 153–80.

Beebee, H. (2004) "The Non-Governing Conception of Laws of Nature," in J. W. Carroll (ed.) *Readings on Laws of Nature* (Pittsburgh: Pittsburgh University Press): 250–79.

Berofsky, B. (2010) "Free Will and the Mind-Body Problem," *Australasian Journal of Philosophy* 88 (1): 1–19.

———. (2011) "Compatibilism without Frankfurt: Dispositional Analyses of Free Will," in R. Kane (ed.) *The Oxford Handbook of Free Will*, 2nd ed. (New York: Oxford Press): 153–74.

———. (2012) *Nature's Challenge to Free Will* (Oxford: Oxford University Press).

Braithwaite, R. B. (1957) *Scientific Explanation* (Cambridge: Cambridge University Press).

Carroll, J. W. (1990) "The Humean Tradition," *Philosophical Review* 99 (2): 185–219.

———. (1994) *Laws of Nature* (Cambridge: Cambridge University Press).

Earman, J. (1984) "Laws of Nature: The Empiricist Challenge," in R. J. Bogdan (ed.) *D.M. Armstrong* (Dordrecht: D. Reidel): 191–223.

Earman, J.; Roberts, J. T. (2004) "*Ceteris Paribus*, There is no Problem of Provisos," in J. W. Carroll (ed.) *Reading on Laws of Nature* (Pittsburgh: University of Pittsburgh Press) 207–49.

———. (2005a) "Contact with the Nomic: A Challenge for Deniers Humean Supervenience about Laws of Nature; Part I: Humean Supervenience," *Philosophy and Phenomenological Research* 71 (1): 1–22.

———. (2005b) "Contact with the Nomic: A Challenge for Deniers of Humean Supervenience about Laws of Nature; Part II: The Epistemological Argument for Humean Supervenience," *Philosophy and Phenomenological Research* 71 (2): 253–86.

Hitchcock, C. (2004) "Causal Processes and Interactions: What Are They and What Are They Good For?," *Philosophy of Science* 71 (5): 932–41.

Huemer, M. (2000) "Van Inwagen's Consequence Argument," *Philosophical Review* 109 (4): 25–44.

Hume, D. (1748) *An Enquiry Concerning Human Understanding* (Indianapolis: Hackett Publishing Company, 1977).

Lange, M. (2000) *Natural Laws in Scientific Practice* (Oxford: Oxford University Press).

Lewis, D. (1981) "Are We Free to Break the Laws?," *Theoria* 47 (3): 113–21 (reprinted in *Philosophical Papers 2* (Oxford: Oxford University Press, 1987: 291–98).

———. (1994) "Humean Supervenience Debugged," *Mind* 103: 473–89.

Mill, J. S. (1843) *A System of Logic, Ratiocinative and Inductive: Being a Connected View of the Principles of Evidence and the Methods of Scientific Investigation*, in vols. VII and VIII (1974) of Mill (1963–1991).

———. (1865) *An Examination of Sir William Hamilton's Philosophy and of the Principal Philosophical Questions Discussed in His Writings*, in vol. IX (1979) of Mill (1963–1991).

———. (1963–1991) *Collected Works of John Stuart Mill*, F.E.L. Priestly (gen. ed.), and subsequently J. M. Robson, 33 vols. (London/Toronto: Routledge and Kegan Paul/University of Toronto Press).

Nagel, E. (1961) *The Structure of Science* (New York: Harcourt Brace).

Ramsey, F. P. (1928) "Universals of Law and of Fact," in D. H. Mellor (ed.) *Philosophical Papers* (London: Routledge & Kegan Paul, 1990): 140–43.

Roberts, J. T. (2008) *The Law-Governed Universe* (New York: Oxford University Press).

———. (2010) "Some Laws of Nature are Metaphysically Contingent," *Australasian Journal of Philosophy* 88 (3): 445–57.

Tooley, M. (1977) "The Nature of Laws," *Canadian Journal of Philosophy* 7: 667–98.

———. (1999) "The Nature of Causation: A Singularist Account," in J. Kim and E. Sosa (eds.) *Metaphysics: An Anthology* (Oxford: Blackwell): 458–82.

van Fraassen, B. (1989) *Laws and Symmetry* (Oxford: Clarendon Press).

———. (2004) "Armstrong on Laws and Probabilities," in J. W. Carroll (ed.) *Readings on Laws of Nature* (Pittsburgh: Pittsburgh University Press): 112–34.

Woodward, J. (2000) "Explanation and Invariance in the Special Sciences," *British Journal for the Philosophy of Science* 51 (2): 197–254.

———. (2003) *Making Things Happen: A Theory of Causal Explanation* (New York: Oxford University Press).

Woodward, J.; Hitchcock, C. (2003) "Explanatory Generalizations, Part I: A Counterfactual Account," *Nous* 37: 1–24.

7 Mill on the Epistemology of Reasons
A Comparison with Kant

Christopher Macleod

It is perhaps still not fully appreciated that Mill's demonstration of the principle of utility in chapter 4 of *Utilitarianism* runs directly parallel to his vindication of the principle of induction in Book III of the *System of Logic*.[1] This is unfortunate: to the extent that we lose sight of the structural similarities of Mill's theory of practical reason and his theory of theoretical reason, we fail to appreciate the overall ambition of his account of normativity—and miss opportunities to draw on Mill's account of theoretical reason in examining puzzles surrounding his account of practical reason and *vice versa*.

I have, in two recent articles, offered an interpretation of Mill's architectonic, which attempts to do justice to this parallel, by providing an interpretation of his account of normativity.[2] I wish here to expand upon that account. In section I, I offer a reading of the arguments for the principles of induction and utility, which suggests that Mill does not attempt to move from a non-normative starting point to normative conclusions, but rather draws on the already normative character of pretheoretical dispositions to form beliefs and desires. In section II, I suggest that Kant employs the same strategy in his appeal to "common human reason," and I sketch the basic connection of this strategy in Kant's work to his transcendental idealism. Although they are closer in some regards than we are accustomed to think, Mill, of course, is no transcendental idealist. In section III, I attempt to outline what might justify *his* trust in our natural reasoning propensities.

I.

I.i. Mill on Theoretical Reason

III.iv.2 of the *System of Logic* is subtitled "Scientific induction must be grounded on previous spontaneous inductions." This subsection of the *Logic* contains a key claim:

> Need for Prior Inductions (NPI): "it is impossible to frame any scientific method of induction, or test of the correctness of inductions, unless on

the hypothesis that some inductions deserving of reliance have been already made."[3]

The claim separates inductive moves into two categories: scientific and pre-scientific inductions. Mill is not, of course, suggesting that the categories have neat boundaries. His point is, rather, that there is a distinction to be made between the consciously self-reflective methodology of science, and applications of reasoning "primitively pursued by the human understanding while undirected by science."[4] Science does not merely accumulate a body of knowledge by means of induction, but is also a practice that involves examination of the methods by which knowledge can be accumulated—and this is an examination that can be carried out, of course, only by means of the inductive method. Primitive inductions are, on the other hand, made without such reflective awareness and self-investigation.

In NPI, Mill makes two points. Firstly, that scientific inductions rely on the existence of previous inductive moves. The reason is clear to see: scientific inductions arise by inductively examining and refining pre-existent inductions. Once science is up and running, internal reflection upon, and refinement of, scientific inductions can take place. But in order to get science off the ground, reflection and refinement of some other mode of induction is necessary. And only primitive inductions are, at this stage, available. In the absence of primitive inductions, more refined modes of reasoning could not be established.

Secondly, and significantly, primitive inductions themselves are "deserving of reliance." Two accounts could be given of the origins of warranted beliefs. Mankind comes out of the cave, and starts—merely as a fact of empirical psychology—to have new beliefs triggered. Generalization, that is to say, is psychologically caused to happen and beliefs are automatically generated. Such generalizations are at this stage undeserving of reliance in the internalistic sense, even if they do in fact cause true beliefs to be formed; mankind is not capable, in principle, of acting in recognition of reasons, being merely another object moved around by causal forces. Later, man becomes sophisticated, and (somehow) reflects upon and evaluates that merely caused practice. Inductions from that stage become warranted, ceasing to be mere changes in belief profile caused by psychological factors, becoming justified moves made by reasoning agents. In this story, the pressure is on to show precisely how normative standards of evaluation arise from caused psychological acts; how one can escape characterizing such evaluations as anything other than further caused generalizations.

No matter, for this is not the story that Mill tells. Rather, Mill claims that primitive inductions are themselves "deserving of reliance" from the start. The first acts of induction, pursued "undirected by science" are themselves not brute happenings, but are already the adoption of beliefs that we take to be reasonable. We recognize uniformities (no less recognition, for being "involuntary recognition") and form beliefs on the basis of that recognition.

"[M]ankind learnt, as children learn, to expect the one where they found the other, long before they knew how to put their expectation into words by asserting, in a proposition, the existence of a connexion between those phenomena."[5] Primitive inductions are, that is to say, already acts in accordance with the norm of theoretical reason: beliefs formed on the basis of a realization that the results of primitive inductions are good beliefs to hold.

Mill, then, vindicates scientific induction by appealing to the fact that scientific induction is merely a sharpened form of an already warranted method of reasoning—primitive induction. This has in the past often been obscured by an over-reliance on Mill's *other* method of vindicating induction: the holistic appeal to the fact that past inductions have been successful. This is, to be sure, a vindication: induction is in this sense inductively self-supporting. But Mill is clear in NPI that the holistic justification will only be persuasive if there are already justified primitive inductions in place to which we can appeal.[6]

Scientific induction appeals to moves already recognized as reasonable—but we must consider how such prescientific inductions come to be seen as reasonable. A clue, as I have suggested, is given in Mill's repeated description of primitive induction as *spontaneous*.[7] On observing that $x_1, x_2, x_3, \ldots x_n$ are P, I spontaneously recognize that there is reason to believe that x_{n+1} is P: that such a belief is a good one to hold. Such a belief is not merely caused as a matter of fact, but held for a reason, and the normativity of beliefs is thereby established. With the knowledge that certain beliefs are reasonable, the possibility arises of metainductions generalizing over reasonable moves.

The key question is clearly what Mill means by "spontaneous" in this context, and how a belief's being spontaneously considered reasonable provides any assurance that it *is* reasonable—how spontaneity has any normative force. This question will be tackled below. For now, we might think of spontaneity by contrasting with it cases in which our response is conditioned in some manner. Such a response would be artificial, rather than spontaneous. Upon observing that $x_1, x_2, x_3, \ldots x_n$ are P, I spontaneously recognize that there is reason to believe that x_{n+1} is P. Had I been psychologically conditioned, I might well have had a different response—but such a response would not have been spontaneous, being rather a result of a nefarious influence.

Mill places initial trust in our natural reasoning propensities, as natural: spontaneous induction is afforded initial credibility on the grounds that it is the way that human beings unselfconsciously reason, and is asked to improve itself from there. Whether this is a viable move will concern us later. But we should note the assumption that our spontaneous—undistorted, uninterfered with—mode of reasoning is a good one is the position Mill is driven to as a thoroughgoing naturalist. "The laws of our rational faculty, like those of every other natural agency, are only learnt by seeing the agent at work."[8] If this mission statement is to be respected, and if the goal is the discovery of genuine norms of reasoning rather than mere description and prediction of practice, it must be that principles that we naturally reason with are—at some level—in basic conformity with valid principles of reasoning. Such principles of reasoning cannot, of course, themselves be proved by appeal to more fundamental principles, without regress: "To be incapable of proof by reasoning is common to all first principles; to the first premises of our knowledge, as well as to those of our conduct."[9] Without any mode of pure intuitive insight into the best ways of forming beliefs, the naturalist must hold that our natural propensities to form beliefs are basically reasonable, and seek to iteratively improve them—there simply is nothing else to go on. We might call this the *naturalistic drive to trust*.

I.ii.   Mill on Practical Reason

Whereas theoretical reason concerns what there is reason to believe, "Practical Reason" concerns "Teleology, or the Doctrine of Ends"[10]—those things that we have reason to desire. As noted, Mill's demonstration of the principle of utility runs parallel to his demonstration of the principle of induction. Mill's method is again anthropological: as norms of theoretical reason were uncovered by examining actual instances of theoretical reasoning, so too norms of practical reason are uncovered by examining actual instances of practical reasoning. As such, questions about the desirability "can only be determined by practised self-consciousness and self-observation, assisted by observation of others."[11] It can be easily missed that Mill does not, in *Utilitarianism*, set out to demonstrate a hitherto undiscovered moral principle; rather, he sets out to explicate, defend, and refine a principle of practical reasoning that has been in operation all along. "If the end which the utilitarian doctrine proposes to itself were not, in theory and in practice, acknowledged to be an end, nothing could ever convince any person that it was so."[12]

It would be impossible to construct any philosophic theory of the desirable, unless on the hypothesis that there were already objects regarded as desirable to appeal to, in an effort to refine our normative theory. In this sense, Mill holds Need for Prior Desirability (NPD) as a practical parallel of NPI. Just as in the theoretical case, Mill's argument is not addressed to someone who "set[s] out from the supposition that nothing had been already ascertained,"[13] but rather to the individual who takes it that there are things that are desirable, and seeks to refine his theory of the desirable.

As Mill assumes our prescientific modes of reasoning are basically warranted, so too he takes for granted that our prephilosophic desires are basically warranted. Such, of course, forms the basis for the first step of the "proof." "[T]he sole evidence it is possible to produce that anything is desirable, is that people do actually desire it."[14] As observation of our own practices makes explicit that we regard induction as reasonable, so observation of our practices makes explicit that we regard pleasure as desirable. "Human nature is so constituted as to desire nothing which is not either a part of happiness or a means to happiness."[15]

Mill does not use the term "spontaneous" in his demonstration of the principle of utility—a matter for regret. For it is, in fact, only on the supposition that we *spontaneously* regard pleasure as desirable that the evidence of desire could be of normative standing. I recognize that a sensation's being pleasurable is reason to desire that sensation, and I desire pleasure: in this sense, my desire for pleasure is already the adoption of a desire I see as warranted. If my desire for fame is entirely traceable to nefarious causal circumstances, then that desire is not good evidence for the desirability of fame. As with the theoretical case, such indoctrination is easy to imagine, and is in fact all that it means to be judging under the sway of ideology or false consciousness. Indeed, Mill anticipates just this when discussing the competence of judges:

> Of two pleasures, if there be one to which all or almost all who have experience of both give a decided preference, *irrespective of any feeling of moral obligation to prefer it*, that is the more desirable pleasure.[16]

The worry, clearly, is that judges might have their judgment disrupted by interfering factors. Indeed, this seems exactly Mill's diagnosis of the false consciousness of many of his moralizing contemporaries, indoctrinated into Victorian values. No doubt the Calvinistic virtues *are* genuinely desired by those espousing them: but this is only because their response has been conditioned by association.

The desire for pleasure, however, is different. It is not externally caused: our regard for pleasure as desirable has a "basis of powerful natural sentiment; and this it is which, when once the general happiness is recognised as the ethical standard, will constitute the strength of the utilitarian morality."[17] I spontaneously recognize that a sensation's being pleasurable is reason to desire it; this is not a brute happening, but already a desire formed in accordance with the norms of practical reason. Mill places trust in this initial propensity to find pleasure desirable, which, like our propensity to make inductive moves, does not present itself as a rule we choose to implement, but is nevertheless one we endorse. Spontaneous desires are afforded credibility on the grounds that this is the way that humans unselfconsciously desire, and this is the point from which a philosophic theory of ethics must depart. There is, once again, a *drive to trust*: without any direct *a priori* insight into the nature of the good or our obligations, and without an infallible God to guide us, we must assume that our natural dispositions to desire certain things are reasonable, and subject that norm to internal correction.

I.iii. The Naturalistic Fallacy

All of this goes some way toward clarifying why Mill was not guilty of committing the "naturalistic fallacy." We should, of course, remember that the naturalistic fallacy threatens theoretical norms just as much as practical norms. The reasonableness of primitive acts of induction cannot be claimed to *follow* from empirical matters of our psychology, any more than the desirability of pleasure *follows* from empirical matter of our psychology. This is merely another way of stating the Naturalistic Fallacy as applied to theoretical reason: Open Question Arguments threaten theoretical norms in just the same way as practical norms, and this is exactly the wedge that opens up the problem of induction. ("I know that you've seen one hundred elephants, all grey, and that you're therefore psychologically disposed to believe that Nelly is grey before you have seen her. But is that a *good* belief?")

Were Moore's arguments persuasive against Mill's account of the value of utility, they would hold equally against his account of induction. Of course, it is now generally taken to be the case that Moore misses his target when criticizing Mill, for Mill does not mean to claim that pleasure *is identical* to the practically good, or that the desired *is identical* to the desirable. Indeed, accentuating the theoretical parallel of such an identification perhaps makes it obvious just how strange such a belief would be—akin to holding that in the case of belief, the associatively generalized *is identical* to the warranted.

Most reconstructions of the "proof" now draw attention to the fact that Mill did not think it possible to *prove* his normative claims from psychological premises. Psychological premises are instead said to "determin[e] the intellect" in regard to normative conclusions.[18] This seems correct: Mill is explicit that only evidence, and not proof, could be given for his claims. But were the premises in question taken to be raw natural facts, it is not clear how an argument could be made that would even *evidence* normative claims—for this would still involve arguing from purely factual premises to normative conclusions.

I spontaneously recognize that there is reason to believe that x_{n+1} is P; I spontaneously recognize that a sensation's being pleasurable is reason to desire it. The judgments I make here are made on the basis of a recognition of these beliefs and desires as reasonable—at base, the spontaneously formed beliefs and desires Mill appeals to are already generated by acts of rule-following. To the extent that we take certain things as ends (things we have reason to pursue), and take certain things as warranted (things we have reason to believe), we are already engaged in a normative practice, and this is precisely the starting point of the "proof" and the vindication of induction. Mill does not attempt to move from factual to normative—and certainly not by any definitional sleight of hand—but is giving an account of norms we do actually endorse.

Mill holds that, prior to the philosophical defense of inductivism and utilitarianism, we do have knowledge of what there is reason to believe and to desire. The question, of course, is how that could be. How can we be assured that reasons that we spontaneously recognize reflect the genuine structure of value, or the genuine structure of the world? How are we to *defend* everyday reason? In order to explore Mill's answer to this question, it will be useful to compare Kant's response to the same question. For Kant is instructively similar in taking as his point of departure a non-revisionary attitude toward basic modes of practical and theoretical reasoning. Kant also holds that in everyday operations, we *do* achieve instances of moral and factual knowledge; like Mill, he operates under the assumption that we do, prior to philosophical intervention, successfully operate as reasoners. His task is to explore the conditions that must necessarily obtain in order for such success to even be possible, and use philosophical reflection to steady those faculties against both under and overextension. And like Mill, his account invokes the notion of spontaneity.

II.

II.i. Kant on Common Human Reason

In the *Critique of Pure Reason*, Kant tells us, that reason begins "with principles which it has no option save to employ in the course of experience, and which this experience at the same time abundantly justifies it in using."[19] We naturally draw on principles such as the principle of causation to understand the world—and such principles are "so unobjectionable that even common human reason readily accepts them."[20] Kant, like Mill, holds that we must place initial trust in the ability of such operations to achieve knowledge in everyday circumstances: his task is to investigate the conditions that must obtain in order for such knowledge to be possible. Investigation, Kant believes, shows that reason goes wrong when it strays into the terrain of metaphysical speculation. Prephilosophic reason naturally overreaches and attempts to apply concepts appropriate only *within* experience to metaphysical questions *beyond* experience. As such, we must check reason's tendency to go wrong—but such a project of sharpening reason can only take place by the internal process of reason's self-examination, a critique of reason by reason itself.

Kant's project, in this sense, is to investigate the claims of reason internally. Assuming that common human reason has basic warrant in the knowledge claims we start out with, to stabilize these claims with an explanation of the conditions of their possibility—and to show why *certain*, but not all, uses of theoretical reason are illegitimate.[21] As Robert Stern has put it, "[t]he key to Kant's strategy is to offer a way of allowing 'ordinary consciousness' to hang on to principles such as the principle of causation . . . but to argue that these principles are only valid for objects as they appear to us within experience, and so cannot be employed within any metaphysical speculations."[22] Thorough investigation allows us to refine our application of the principles that common human reason identifies, but philosophic reason "nonetheless respects our 'everyday' commitment to principles like the principle of causality."[23]

Kant's acceptance of everyday reason comes through even more clearly in his practical philosophy, and nowhere is it better on display than in the concluding section of *Groundwork* I.[24]

[C]ommon human reason . . . knows very well how to distinguish in every case that comes up what is good and what is evil, what is in conformity with duty or contrary to duty, if, without in the least teaching it anything new, we only, as did Socrates, make it attentive to its own principle; and that there is, accordingly, no need of science and philosophy to know what one has to do in order to be honest and good, and even wise and virtuous.[25]

Indeed, Kant is occupied in the vast majority of the *Groundwork* with an analytic exposition—not a synthetic derivation—of an already tacitly accepted moral principle. The work starts with a "transition from common rational to philosophic moral cognition" and from there moves on to found a "metaphysics of morals."[26] When he turns, in *Groundwork* III to attempt a deduction of morality—in an effort to ward off claims that morality might be a "chimerical idea"—he reaches the "extreme boundary of all practical philosophy."[27] To the extent that there was an attempt to derive practical laws from some non-practical perspective, this justification was later retracted, to be replaced with an appeal to the "fact of reason": that we do, by common consent, feel conscious of the moral law.[28]

Kant's moral philosophy starts from the claim that we *do* recognize moral claims—it is not an attempt offer a proof of the Categorical Imperative from a perspective external to practical reason, for nothing could convince someone who recognized no practical reasons *at all* that they were subject to such requirements. (This should bring to our mind Mill's claim that no moral philosophy would be possible, were it not for our prephilosophic recognition of some things as desirable.) Of course, Kant's claim that prephilosophic thinking has a basic level of competency in acting in accordance with valid practical norms does not imply that there is no place for philosophy. As he puts it, "[t]here is something splendid about innocence; but what is bad about it, in turn, is that it cannot protect itself very well and is easily seduced."[29] Common human reason is worthy of trust, but it is easily misdirected: in the practical case, philosophy is needed in order to check our tendency to imagine that reason's demands are negotiable, and in order to vindicate the claims of common reason when challenged by one who is unsure of their bindingness.[30] But for Kant, like Mill, philosophic work must take the form of defending and clarifying the demands of practical reason from the perspective that already accepts basic claims of practical reason—there is no attempt to derive normative claims from some non-normative perspective.

II.ii. Spontaneity in Kant

The challenge is to show how the reasons recognized by prephilosophic human reason are genuinely valid reasons. If our everyday move from an instance of constant conjunction to causation were justified, it might be claimed that justification could be strengthened by internal critique. Similarly, if our everyday application of a test of universalization had *some* degree of validity, analysis and critique could stabilize and improve such judgments. But some account needs to be given of why these operations of the mind are deserving of any reliance in the first place. This need not be a derivation of such norms—but some account that leads us to think them a source of basically trustworthy claims. Kant, like Mill, appeals to the fact that the application of this mode of reasoning is *spontaneous*—vindication is provided by the fact that human beings *spontaneously* apply the concept of causation to the world and *spontaneously* make moral judgments. Of course, Kant has a distinctive story to tell about the notion of the spontaneity.[31]

In forming beliefs, Kant notes we are receptive to sensible impressions. By way of our senses, we are presented with an intuition—but this chaotic array is itself unstructured. The process of making judgments and forming knowledge about the world, Kant explains, involves the mind taking up intuition and applying concepts.

> Our cognition arises from two fundamental sources in the mind, the first of which is the reception of representations (the receptivity of impressions), the second the faculty for cognising an object by means of these representations (spontaneity of concepts); through the former an object is given to us, through the latter it is thought in relation to that representation (as a mere determination of the mind).[32]

The application of concepts is, according to Kant, performed by the Understanding. As hinted at in the quote above, the Understanding acts "through a spontaneity of cognition (in contrast to the receptivity of the sensibility)."[33] In order to gain knowledge of the world, that is to say, an individual must be presented with sensible data, but the mind itself spontaneously applies concepts. Some are empirical concepts, themselves formed by the Understanding as abstractions from intuition—but in order for such to be formed, some more primitive concepts must be available to guide the abstraction of empirical concepts. Such pure concepts of the Understanding—the Categories—are our most basic modes of interpreting the world. Causation is one such concept—and this concept is spontaneously applied to interpret the manifold of intuition.

The characteristic feature of spontaneity in Kant's work, of course, is that it is empirically uncaused—when Kant discusses the freedom of the will in the Third Antinomy, he draws upon the notion: "[t]he transcendental idea of freedom . . . is that of the absolute spontaneity of an action."[34] And it is in the sense of being spontaneous that judgments of the Understanding are free: "If an appearance is given to us, we are still completely free as to how we want to judge things from it."[35] This process is one of active judging, and Kant notes "this spontaneity is the reason I call myself an intelligence."[36] Kant holds that were judgments not made freely, by the spontaneous application of concepts to intuition, they simply would not be my judgments: they would be mere changes in a belief profile, causally brought about. "When I say: I think, I act, etc., then either the word I is applied falsely, or I am free. Were I not free, then I could not say: *I* do it, but rather I would have to say: I feel in me a desire to do, which someone has aroused in me. But when I say: I do it, that means spontaneity in the transcendental sense."[37]

In order to see why judgments made spontaneously might be afforded a basic level of trust, we must observe that for Kant, the world to which concepts like causation apply—the phenomenal world, the world of appearances—is not itself mind-independent. This world is constructed by the mind. What constitutes correct judgment about that world is therefore intimately tied up with the functioning of our minds; objects of the phenomenal world must conform to our modes of understanding. If the phenomenal world is constructed by the mind, it is no surprise that concepts that are spontaneously applied by the mind to the world have some *prima facie* validity. (Of course, concepts such as that of causation do not apply to the *noumenal* world of things-in-themselves.) Categories that reflect the structure of the reasoning subject can be taken as appropriate to the phenomenal world, exactly because the structure of the phenomenal world is itself a reflection of the reasoning subject. And neither is the *freedom* of such judgments mysterious— after all, in their transcendental aspect, such judgments are *themselves* not empirically caused events, but acts of a non-empirical subject that is outside and prior to that causal nexus.

This account of theoretical spontaneity is the basis for Kant's account of practical spontaneity.[38] Kant's commitment to the reciprocal relation between morality and freedom is well known. "The autonomy of the will" is the "supreme principle of morality."[39] If morality is to take the form of a universal and necessary law—"for all rational beings as such, not merely under contingent conditions and with exceptions, but with absolute necessity"[40]—then its directives cannot be based on any particular willed end, but rather on the purely formal basis of law itself. "[N]othing is left but the universality of a law as such, with which the maxim of the action ought to conform," and such forms the basis for the derivation of the Categorical Imperative.[41] When one acts on a maxim that is in accordance with the Categorical Imperative, one is in this sense conditioned by no end, acting with autonomy—an individual's action is not subject to any "natural law of his needs."[42] Moral freedom is the property of the will such that "it can be efficient independently of alien causes determining it."[43] In this sense, the connection of ethical action to spontaneity is clear, and Kant draws out exactly this connection in the *Groundwork* III, when outlining how transcendental idealism could allow us to conceive of ourselves as free by locating man in the intelligible world.

Just as the phenomenal world is constructed by theoretical reason, so moral legislation is constructed by practical reason. "[T]he will is not just subject to the law, but subject in such a way that it must also be viewed as self-legislating, and just on account of this as subject to the law (of which it can consider itself the author) in the first place."[44] The free agent legislates the moral law, and as such, moral truth is deeply connected to the structure of the will of the free agent. It is of little surprise, then, that actions that exemplify human spontaneity—whether they are the products of philosophical reflection or are prior to such reflection—are actions under reasons. Free actions, which are not empirically caused when viewed from the transcendental perspective, are actions in recognition of reasons, and as such connected to the norms of practical reason. Spontaneous action itself already manifests a normative configuration.

None of this, of course, is to claim that spontaneity is a sufficient condition for truth. It is neither the case that all acts that have their root in spontaneous choice are morally good acts, nor that any belief formed spontaneously is warranted, just because they stem from free acts of the transcendental subject. *All activity* of the Understanding, and therefore all perception, involves spontaneity—not merely that which results in true beliefs. And heteronomous action, as action, involves the free adoption of some maxim.[45] Nevertheless, Kant provides a link between the world of reasons and the notion of spontaneity.

III.

III.i.   Can Mill Adopt Kant's Account?

A brief reminder of the state of play. Mill holds that in order to form any philosophic theory of what there is reason to desire or to believe, we must appeal to our presphilosophic practices. Such practice is grounded on our spontaneously taking certain things to be desirable or reasonably believed. I observe that $x_1, x_2, x_3, \ldots x_n$ are P, and I spontaneously recognize that there is reason to believe that x_{n+1} is P. Similarly I observe a sensation's being pleasurable, and I spontaneously recognize that there is reason to desire that sensation. The question we were left with at the end of section I was: how can we be assured that reasons that we spontaneously recognize reflect the genuine structure of value, or the genuine structure of the world? How are we to *defend* everyday reason?

Kant provides one possible answer to this question. With a similar account of the relationship between our philosophic theory of reasons and prephilosophic practice ("common human reason"), Kant too claims that we make theoretical and practical judgments on the basis of our spontaneous recognition of reasons. Kant's account of spontaneity offers a basic motivation to trust such judgments: they reflect the legislating moral agent, or the mind constructing the phenomenal world. Kant's transcendental idealism can offer an account of the fitness of our natural judgments by connecting the truth of those judgments to the operations of the mind. Moreover, the Kantian account of spontaneity can ground such an explanation with an account of how such judgments are not caused.

But of course, Mill is no transcendental idealist, and this debars him from accepting this solution. In his more considered moments Mill was a phenomenalist, believing matter to be no more than the permanent possibility of perception, and this connects him in interesting ways to the Idealist tradition.[46] But contra Kant, he nevertheless maintains a resolute commitment to philosophic supposition that activity of the mind must be treated as entirely within and subordinate to nature. Man is part of the natural world, and can be studied as such. In this sense, Mill is a committed naturalist about the mind.

For Mill, the spontaneous activity of our mind, then, can have no logical connection to how the world must be structured; there is no conceptual link between truth and our modes of apprehending the world. Such a position would require "that the universe of thought and that of reality, the Microcosm and the Macrocosm (as they once were called) must have been framed in complete correspondence with one another." But "an assumption more destitute of evidence could scarcely be made."[47] Such is Mill's criticism of intuitionism: that any attempted derivation of the way the world is from the way we are disposed to think about it is doomed to failure. From this direction, Mill's naturalism makes it difficult to see how any account of why our spontaneously thinking that certain beliefs and desires are reasonable could be worthy of any trust at all. This *naturalistic drive to doubt* clearly runs against the naturalistic drive to trust: and this is exactly what makes the problem seem intractable.

Worse still, within Mill's naturalistic picture, we perhaps even lack a clear conception of what spontaneity could be. I noted above that one way of framing Mill's account of spontaneity is by contrasting it with cases in which our response is in some sense conditioned, or artificial. Responses that are caused are not responses in recognition of reasons, but merely changes to my belief/desire profile. In contrast, when I spontaneously recognize that there is reason to believe that x_{n+1} is P, or reason to desire some pleasure, this response is not merely caused as a matter of fact, but held for a reason. It is clear that Kant's account of transcendental freedom provides a way to understand what this might mean. But Mill cannot appeal to a non-empirical agent behind the empirical causal order. For Mill, it is clear that even if the spontaneous judgments are not *merely* caused changes to my belief or desire profile, they nevertheless must still *be* caused. Let us first tackle this issue.

III.ii.   Millian Spontaneity

An account of spontaneity is, in essence, an account of what it means for the will to be free, and Mill offers a theory of such freedom in *Logic* VI.ii. Although this portion of the *Logic* has in general not been well received, it was central to Mill's thought—he recounts that the development of this portion of the *Logic* was "very important to myself . . . & even (if I may use the expression) critical in my own development."[48] The treatment offered is, of course, compatibilist.

No one who believed that he knew thoroughly the circumstances of any case, and the characters of the different persons concerned, would hesitate to foretell how all of them would act. Whatever degree of doubt he may in fact feel, arises from the uncertainty whether he really knows the circumstances, or the character of some one or other of the persons, with the degree of accuracy required: but by no means from thinking that if he did know these things, there could be any uncertainty what the conduct would be. Nor does this full assurance conflict in the smallest degree with what is called our feeling of freedom.[49]

Our actions are causally determined, but nevertheless we are free. Mill holds that a cause on a person with a character and a set of desires does causally necessitate an action. It is of course *not* true that if that person had some alternative character and set of desires that that same cause would necessitate that same action: this would be to hold that there was "some peculiar tie, or mysterious constraint exercised by the antecedent over the consequent."[50] Had that person had different desires, or a different character, he might well have acted differently. This, Mill concedes, would be of little consolation if our character and desires are beyond the control of an individual to influence. But, he points out, we *can* influence our character and desires. We can place ourselves in circumstances that modify our character, and we can practice better habits. Admittedly, this is itself merely another necessitated action, wholly determined. But we must keep in mind that *this* action will be determined as a function of external circumstances *and our character and desires.*

This is, Mill believes, enough. We are capable of modifying our character and controlling our reaction to stimulus, because the action of modification is in a large part determined by our own current character and desires. Mill does not overstate the case—a person is not in *full* control, and there can be no miraculous switching of dispositions.[51] But, nevertheless, the individual

has, to a certain extent, a power to alter his character. Its being, in the ultimate resort, formed for him, is not inconsistent with its being, in part, formed *by* him as one of the intermediate agents. His character is formed by his circumstances (including among these his particular organization); but his own desire to mould it in a particular way, is one of those circumstances, and by no means one of the least influential. We cannot, indeed, directly will to be different from what we are. But neither did those who are supposed to have formed our characters, directly will that we should be what we are.[52]

The view expressed is, of course, what we would now think of as a compatibilist theory of autonomy. As Gerald Dworkin puts it: "autonomy is conceived of as a second-order capacity of persons to reflect critically upon their first-order preferences, desires, wishes, and so forth and the capacity to accept or attempt to change these in light of higher-order preferences and values."[53] Although Mill does not use the term, it is clearly this notion that he appeals to in characterizing the feeling of moral freedom: "indeed, if we examine closely, we shall find that this feeling, of our being able to modify our own character *if we wish*, is itself the feeling of moral freedom which we are conscious of."[54]

It is necessary that we not be *overwhelmed* by causal antecedents: that our character and desires—including any higher-order desire to alter our character and desires—play a significant role in the determination of our behavior. It must be that we *ourselves* dictate our actions, not external circumstances. The extent to which our internal character determines our actions rather than external causal factors, of course, will be a matter of degree—in the vast majority of cases both will be present. But this is merely to say that we can be more, or less, free on any given occasion.

Judgments must live up to this standard too. A judgment can be spontaneous in the sense that it is not caused directly from the outside. Judgments must of course be part of the causal order—but they must emanate from the subject himself. It is in this sense that, prompted by experience, *I* must judge that x_{n+1} is *P*, in order for that to count as judgment; *I* must judge that pleasure is desirable. And, importantly, *were* I not to take the norm of induction or pleasure as providing good reasons to believe or to desire, I would have judged otherwise. Spontaneous judgments, that is to say, are judgments that are under the control of reason that I endorse and hold to be good reasons.

III.iii. Reason's Self Analysis

Clearly, however, nothing in this account of spontaneity can connect the fact that we spontaneously reason in a certain manner directly to the structure of the world. A defense of our spontaneous reasoning propensities therefore must take the form of a search for conditions under which the norms we find spontaneously compelling are *not* reliable: conditions under which we are particularly prone to be led astray. The only response, in other words, to the naturalistic drive to doubt must be an active process of charting the conditions under which those norms we find compelling lead to results at some way at odds with the world: where our natural reasoning propensities find themselves overreaching, we must correct our process of reasoning in light of these results. This cannot dispel the drive to doubt: but to the extent that it is successful in placating it, it transforms that drive from a negative and skeptical attitude into a genuinely critical one.

Like Kant, then, Mill turns reason upon itself to examine its own methods of belief and desire formation. This is exactly the project that is taken on—at least for theoretical reason—in the *System of Logic*. It too is an internal process of reason's self-examination: a critique of reason by reason itself.

[I]nduction by simple enumeration . . . though a valid process, it is a fallible one, and fallible in very different degrees: if therefore we can substitute for the more fallible forms of the process, an operation grounded on the same process in a less fallible form, we shall have effected a very material improvement. And this is what scientific induction does.[55]

Mill calls the process of refining and correcting our prephilosophic reason—finding instances in which prephilosophic reason leads us astray—the process of "ulterior revision." Failed instances of induction refine my willingness to trust any and all beliefs spontaneously regarded as reasonable, generating "ulterior revision of these spontaneous generalizations" and leading to "a stricter and surer method than that which they had in the first instance spontaneously adopted."[56] Reason charts its own capabilities, and revises its practices in light of these findings.

So, for instance, we spontaneously form the belief that *all* swans are white, upon seeing many and only swans that are white. The norm under which this belief was formed must be subject to ulterior revision, upon discovery that such a move is reasonable only in certain circumstances. Metainductions ranging over the conditions under which instances of induction have been faulty lead to improved practices of reasoning—as given by the Canons of Induction in *Logic* III.viii. Such ulterior revision corrects our understanding of what can give us reason to believe, internally. Of course, it must remain an open possibility that even our most central judgments will not withstand this process and must be disregarded: we might learn that the norms we spontaneously apply might fail *in their entirety* in certain situations (such as "distant parts of the stellar region"[57]) that are entirely foreign to our current experience.

It is only under the condition that faulty modes of reasoning are able to be isolated, and censured, that we could have any faith that the norms refined from our spontaneous tendencies lead to judgments that reflect the way that the world is. We can feel increased—though never total—confidence in norms that remain in place after such a process.

> The beliefs which we have most warrant for, have no safeguard to rest on, but a standing invitation to the whole world to prove them unfounded. If the challenge is not accepted, or is accepted and the attempt fails, we are far enough from certainty still: but we have done the best that the existing state of human reason admits of [. . .] we may rely on having attained such approach to truth, as is possible in our own day. This is the amount of certainty attainable by a fallible being, and this the sole way of attaining it.[58]

One might well object that, unanchored, this process requires just too much optimism: that the drive to trust is just *too* trusting. Whereas of course it is promising that reason does not undermine itself completely, but only in part—that an inductive examination of induction does not force us to abandon that practice as defective *tout court*, but only in specific circumstances—this can count for little. A basically capable mind, refining its modes of reasoning, can be assumed to achieve successful judgments, it might be admitted, but Mill does too little to show that the norms of reason we find spontaneously compelling are basically fit to interpret the world.

The worry does have bite, and can perhaps be pressed most forcefully in the case of practical reason, where Mill gives us little indication of what it would mean for us to find our norms in need of ulterior revision. That we can, from the inside, gain some measure of objectivity in our judgments, remains for Mill an article of philosophic faith. It is indicative of a distinctively liberal optimism, however—a hope that freedom, dialogue and honest inspection of the data, can, and will, eventually lead to truth—and under the naturalistic picture it is not entirely clear what, besides skepticism, the alternative is.[59]

NOTES

1. One author who makes this point explicit, however, is John Skorupski. See, for instance, Skorupski (1989: 286): "Mill's way of vindicating the claim that happiness is desirable, is exactly analogous to his way of vindicating the claim that enumerative induction is rational."
2. See Macleod (2013a and 2013b). The view proposed is roughly as follows. Mill is, contrary to common opinion, a cognitivist about normative statements. There is no firm textual evidence to support a noncognitivist reading, as has sometimes been argued. Indeed, such an interpretation suffers from the fault of anachronism and is difficult to reconcile with the clear commitment in *Utilitarianism* to the possibility of evidence being given for norms. I suggest that Mill holds that our belief in the reliability of inductive moves, as well as the desirability of pleasure, is vindicated by something akin to intuition. Although his endorsement of the normativity of these intuitions might seem to be in tension with the arguments he offers against the "intuitionist school," this tension is merely apparent.
3. Mill (1843, CW: VII.319). All references to Mill's works are to the authoritative edition of *Collected Works of John Stuart Mill* (Mill, 1963–1991—cited as CW, followed by volume and page number), unless otherwise indicated.
4. Mill (1843, CW: VII.318).
5. Mill (1843, CW: VII.318).
6. This account will perhaps raise the suspicion that I am misrepresenting Mill as a foundationalist, appealing to primitive inductive moves as warranted and sitting as the basis of all theoretical knowledge. But if the story I have told is foundationalist, it is only in a very loose sense of the term. Though primitive inductions could be described as foundational in terms of temporal ordering—coming first in time—they are not conceptually prior in justificatory terms, once other scientific inductions have been established. At that point, as much, if not more, support flows to primitive inductions from scientific inductions as from primitive induction to scientific inductions. They support, and are supported.
7. See Skorupski (1989: 192–95, 285–86).

8. Mill (1843, *CW*: VIII.833).
9. Mill (1861, *CW*: X.234).
10. Mill (1843, *CW*: VIII.949–50).
11. Mill (1861, *CW*: X.237).
12. Mill (1861, *CW*: X.234).
13. Mill (1843, *CW*: VII.318).
14. Mill (1861, *CW*: X.234).
15. Mill (1861, *CW*: X.237).
16. Mill (1861, *CW*: X.211, my emphasis).
17. Mill (1861, *CW*: X.231).
18. Mill (1861, *CW*: X.208).
19. Kant (*Critique of Pure Reason* Avii). In referring to Kant, I follow the convention of citing A/B editions in the case of the *Critique of Pure Reason*, and volume/page number of the *Academie* edition for all other works. Translations used are listed in the bibliography.
20. Kant (*Critique of Pure Reason* Avii). Kemp Smith translates *gemeine Menschenvernuft* as "ordinary consciousness"; Guyer/Wood opts for "ordinary common sense." It seems important, for purposes here, to retain consistency of translation between uses of *gemeine Menschenvernuft* between the *Critique* and the *Groundwork*, and I have therefore used the Gregor/Timmermann translation of "common human reason."
21. Kant's use of common human reason has of course been compared to the Scottish Common Sense tradition. See Kuehn (1987). Interestingly, such a comparison has also recently been made with Mill. See Miller (2010: 17ff).
22. Stern (2006: 110–11).
23. Stern (2006: 111).
24. K. Ameriks (2003) usefully draws attention to Kant's parallel use of common reason in the theoretical and practical cases. See also Guyer (2008).
25. Kant (*Groundwork*: 4.404).
26. Kant (*Groundwork*: 4.392).
27. Kant (*Groundwork*: 4.445, 402; *Groundwork*: 4.455).
28. Kant (*Critique of Practical Reason*: 5.31; 5.42). See Ameriks (2000: 189–233) on this reversal.
29. Kant (*Groundwork*: 4.404–05).
30. It is interesting to note that the misapplication of practical reason comes from its underextension: exactly the opposite tendency from the theoretical reason, which runs into difficulties when it overextends itself. Whereas the worry for theoretical reason is that it attempts to speak to matters beyond the boundaries of sense, the worry for practical reason is that it mistakenly takes heteronomous claims to apply when in fact moral claims do.
31. In what follows, I present a picture of Kant's account of spontaneity, and its relation to his transcendental idealism, which is at best un-nuanced. This is for the sake of brevity, and hopefully nothing said is too misleading. For useful accounts of spontaneity with a focus on the theoretical, see particularly Pippin (1997). Ameriks (1991); Allison (1990) and (1996) contain much useful material on practical spontaneity. Sgarbi (2012) also provides a useful overview.
32. Kant (*Critique of Pure Reason*: A50/B74).
33. Kant (*Critique of Pure Reason*: A126).
34. Kant (*Critique of Pure Reason*: A448/B476).
35. Kant (*Prolegomena*: 4.290.)
36. Kant (*Critique of Pure Reason*: B158).
37. Kant (*Lectures on Metaphysics*: 28.269).
38. Kant (*Groundwork*: 4.452). As Pippin points out, however, though it is tempting to equate the two, Kant is not committed to claiming that practical

and theoretical spontaneity are identical. (See Pippin, 1997: 52–54.) Nevertheless, Kant was committed to the claim that the moral individual exercises some form of spontaneity: see Allison (1990: ch. 3).

39. Kant (*Groundwork*: 4.440).
40. Kant (*Groundwork*: 4.408).
41. Kant (*Groundwork*: 4.421).
42. Kant (*Groundwork*: 4.439).
43. Kant (*Groundwork*: 4.446).
44. Kant (*Groundwork*: 4.431).
45. See Allison (1990: ch. 5).
46. Mill's account of matter as the "Permanent Possibility of Sensation" is given in Mill (1865: ch. 11). See N. Capaldi (2004: 310–14) for an account of Mill that connects him to the British Idealists. Capaldi perhaps overstates the case—see J. Skorupski (2007)—but there is more than a grain of truth to the claim that there is internal momentum in Mill's work toward his nineteenth century successors.
47. Mill (1865, CW: IX.68).
48. J. S. Mill to F. Nightingale, 10 Sept. 1860, CW: XV.706n. This letter is cited in E. Millgram (2010: 169). Though Millgram's account is quite different to that offered here, Millgram certainly seems to me correct in drawing attention to just how central Mill's theory of freedom was to his philosophic project.
49. Mill (1865, CW: VIII.837).
50. Mill (1865, CW: VIII.838).
51. Cf. Kant on the choice of our fundamental maxim to prioritize either morality or self-interest (*gesinnung*). Such a choice of fundamental maxim is radically free, as is the choice to *switch* maxim at any time. See Kant (*Religion within the Boundaries of Mere Reason*: 6.48).
52. Mill (1865, CW: VIII.840).
53. Dworkin (1988: 20).
54. Mill (1865, CW: VIII.841).
55. Mill (1843, CW: VII.568).
56. Mill (1843, CW: VII.318–19).
57. Mill (1843, CW: VII.574).
58. Mill (1859, CW: XVIII.232).
59. I owe thanks to Martin Sticker and Allison Stone for commenting on previous drafts of this chapter.

REFERENCES

Allison, H. E. (1990) *Kant's Theory of Freedom* (Cambridge: Cambridge University Press).
———. (1996) "Kant's Refutation of Materialism," in *Idealism and Freedom: Essays of Kant's Theoretical and Practical Philosophy* (Cambridge: Cambridge University Press).
Ameriks, K. (1991) "Kant on Spontaneity: Some New Data," in G. Funke (ed.) *Akten des Siebenten Internationalen Kant-Kongresses* (Bonn: Bouvier): 469–79.
———. (1982) *Kant's Theory of Mind*, 2nd ed. (Oxford: Oxford University Press, 2000).
———. (2003) *Interpreting Kant's Critiques* (Oxford: Oxford University Press).
Capaldi, N. (2004) *John Stuart Mill: A Biography* (Cambridge: Cambridge University Press).

Dworkin, G. (1988) *The Theory and Practice of Autonomy* (Cambridge: Cambridge University Press).

Guyer, P. (2008) *Knowledge, Reason and Taste* (Princeton, NJ: Princeton University Press).

Kant, I. (1929) *Critique of Pure Reason*, N. Kemp-Smith (trans.) (London: MacMillan).

———. (1997a) *Critique of Practical Reason*, M. Gregor (trans.) (Cambridge: Cambridge University Press).

———. (1997b) *Critique of Pure Reason*, P. Guyer and A. W. Wood (trans.) (Cambridge: Cambridge University Press).

———. (1997c) *Lectures on Metaphysics*, K. Ameriks and S. Naragon (trans.) (Cambridge: Cambridge University Press).

———. (1998) *Religion within the Boundaries of Mere Reason*, A. Wood and G. Giovanni (trans.) (Cambridge: Cambridge University Press).

———. (2004) *Prolegomena to Any Future Metaphysics*, G. Hartfield (trans.) (Cambridge: Cambridge University Press).

———. (2011) *Groundwork for the Metaphysics of Morals: A German-English Edition*, M. Gregor and J. Timmermann (trans.) (Cambridge: Cambridge University Press).

Kuehn, M. (1987) *Scottish Common Sense in Germany* 1768–1800 (Kingston: McGill-Queen's University Press).

Macleod, C. (2013a) "Mill, Intuitions, and Normativity," *Utilitas* 25 (1): 46–65.

———. (2013b) "Was Mill a Non-Cognitivist?" *Southern Journal of Philosophy* 51 (1): 206–23.

Mill, J. S. (1843) *A System of Logic, Ratiocinative and Inductive: Being a Connected View of the Principles of Evidence and the Methods of Scientific Investigation*, in vols. VII and VIII (1974) of Mill (1963–1991).

———. (1859) *On Liberty*, in vol. XVIII (1977) of Mill (1963–1991).

———. (1861) *Utilitarianism*, in vol. X (1969) of Mill (1963–1991).

———. (1865) *An Examination of Sir William Hamilton's Philosophy and of the Principal Philosophical Questions Discussed in His Writings*, in vol. IX (1979) of Mill (1963–1991).

———. (1963–1991) *Collected Works of John Stuart Mill*, F.E.L. Priestly (gen. ed.), and subsequently J. M. Robson, 33 vols. (London/Toronto: Routledge and Kegan Paul/University of Toronto Press).

Miller, D. E. (2010) *J. S. Mill* (Cambridge: Polity).

Millgram, E. (2010) "Mill's Incubus," in B. Eggleston, D. E. Miller and D. Weinstein (eds.) *John Stuart Mill and the Art of Life* (Oxford: Oxford University Press): 169–91.

Pippin, R. (1997) "Kant on the Spontaneity of Mind," in R. Pippin, *Idealism as Modernism: Hegelian Variations* (Cambridge: Cambridge University Press): 29–55.

Sgarbi, M. (2012) *Kant on Spontaneity* (London: Continuum).

Skorupski, J. (1989) *John Stuart Mill* (London: Routledge).

———. (2007) "The Philosophy of John Stuart Mill," *British Journal for the History of Philosophy* 15 (1): 181–97.

Stern, R. (2006) "Metaphysical Dogmatism, Humean Scepticism, Kantian Criticism," *Kantian Review* 11: 102–16.

8 Different Kinds of Pleasure

Jonathan Riley

INTRODUCTION: QUALITY AND QUANTITY

John Stuart Mill claims in *Utilitarianism* (1861) that there are different kinds of pleasant feelings, of different qualities, which can be accommodated consistently by classical hedonistic utilitarianism: "It is quite compatible with the principle of utility to recognise the fact, that some *kinds* of pleasure are more desirable and more valuable than others."[1] He regards any objections to his claim as absurd: "It would be absurd that while, in estimating all other things, quality is considered as well as quantity, the estimation of pleasures should be supposed to depend on quantity alone."[2]

Mill immediately goes on to indicate what he means by "difference of quality in pleasures" and says "there is but one possible answer."[3] I have argued elsewhere that the one possible answer is that, of two pleasant feelings, one is higher in quality if and only if it is felt and judged to be infinitely superior—superior to an unlimited degree—in relation to the other as pleasure by most if not all competent people: even a bit of the higher pleasure is more valuable, and thus a greater pleasure, than any quantity of the lower pleasure, no matter how large.[4] A qualitative difference is an intrinsic difference, regardless of quantity. This is my reading of Mill's statement: "If one of the two is, by those who are competently acquainted with both, placed so far above the other that they prefer it, even though knowing it to be attended with a greater amount of discontent, and would not resign it for any quantity of the other pleasure which their nature is capable of, we are justified in ascribing to the preferred enjoyment a superiority in quality, so far outweighing quantity as to render it, in comparison, of small account."[5]

Even those who dispute my reading must accept that, for Mill, a pleasure of higher quality often outweighs a more intense pleasure of lower quality. But they insist that it is extreme and unreasonable to assert that the higher kind of pleasant feeling *always* outweighs the lower kind, regardless of quantity. It is more attractive, they think, although the justification for their opinion remains unclear, to allow that sufficiently large quantities of a lower pleasure are more valuable as pleasure than small amounts of a higher pleasure. For them, differences of kind can be overturned by quantitative considerations. David Brink voices this opinion when he says: "One kind of pleasure might be preferred to another by a competent judge in the sense that he would prefer one unit of the first pleasure to several units of the second without its being true that there is no amount of the lower pleasure that would outweigh the higher pleasure."[6] As we shall soon see, this seemingly more attractive view is not Mill's. But at least it is a view that takes seriously his claim that there are different kinds of pleasures of different qualities, provided we read "pleasures" as "pleasant feelings" and do not conflate them (as we often do in the vernacular) with the activities and objects that are their sources.

Not many scholars do take Mill's claim seriously. Some are even inclined to reverse his remark about what is "absurd," throwing back at him their charge that it is nonsense to affirm that we experience different kinds of pleasant feelings of different qualities. Henry Sidgwick and his student G. E. Moore are pioneers of this sort of attack, and their scorn for Mill's extraordinary version of hedonistic utilitarianism continues to be influential. As a general matter, Sidgwick rejects what he sees as Mill's prescription of "an unqualified subordination of private to general happiness."[7] In his opinion, the arguments offered by Mill in *Utilitarianism* do not show why a prudent hedonist would take the community's total happiness as her ultimate end. In particular, he insists that Mill's "recognition of differences of quality in pleasures distinct from and overriding differences of quantity" is inconsistent with hedonism "since it is hard to see in what sense a man who of two alternative pleasures chooses the less pleasant on the ground of its superiority in quality can be affirmed to take '*greatest*' happiness or pleasure as his standard of preference."[8] Whereas it might be true that a harmony between individual and general happiness can be effected by assigning a superiority of quality to a moral kind of pleasure over a self-interested kind, he implies, the resulting doctrine is not genuine hedonistic utilitarianism but instead a complicated and perplexing doctrine that imports foreign values (e.g., perfectionist ideals) to constrain and subvert the greatest happiness principle. Moreover, "even after the introduction of this alien element, it cannot be said that Mill's utilitarianism includes an adequate proof that persons of all natures and temperaments will obtain even the best chance of private happiness in this life by determining always to aim at general happiness; indeed he hardly attempts or professes to furnish such a proof."[9]

Moore agrees and says that "Sidgwick has done very wisely to reject . . . [Mill's] doctrine of 'difference of quality in pleasures.'"[10] According to Moore, "if you say 'pleasure,' you must mean 'pleasure': you must mean some one thing common to all different 'pleasures,' some one thing, which may exist in different degrees, but which cannot differ in *kind*."[11] In other words, "pleasure" is a term that properly denotes a single kind of homogeneous feeling that can differ only in terms of quantity, that is, only in terms of more or less of the attribute of pleasantness that is common to all pleasant feelings. If we speak of different kinds of pleasures that differ in quality irrespective of quantity, however, some basic values besides pleasure must be smuggled in to distinguish higher from lower kinds of pleasures. For we cannot mean that a higher pleasure is more pleasant than a lower one, or "'more desired,' since, as we know, the degree of desire is always, according to Mill, in exact proportion to the degree of pleasantness."[12] But, then, Mill must be admitting that one thing can be more desirable than another even though the one is *not* more desired than the other and even though a greater degree of pleasant feeling is *not* expected from the one than from the other. He is therefore making an intuitive judgment that is independent of considerations of pleasure: "It is a direct judgment that one thing is more desirable, or better than another; a judgment utterly independent of all considerations as to whether one thing is more desired or pleasanter than another."[13] Thus, like Sidgwick, Moore claims that Mill ruins his hedonistic utilitarianism by insisting on differences of quality that require intuitive appeals to alien values: the intuitive judgments of quality undermine calculations of the greatest happiness.[14]

It never occurs to Sidgwick or Moore that, by differences of quality, Mill means intrinsic or infinite differences so that a higher kind of pleasure is greater than a lower kind to an unlimited degree, and that such differences are compatible with finite differences of quantity *within* any given kind of pleasant feeling.[15] As far as I can tell, neither of them ever consults Mill's *A System of Logic* (1843) to seek for clarification of his remarks in *Utilitarianism*. In any case, their view has become received wisdom: most scholars now either ignore Mill's doctrine of higher pleasures or give it an interpretation that is compatible with there being only a single kind of pleasant feeling, thereby allowing us to see him as a standard utilitarian (such as an act utilitarian or a rule utilitarian) or perhaps as a perfectionist. My main aim in this chapter is to make use of Mill's *Logic* to clarify what he means by different kinds of pleasures, and to confirm that, for him, a difference of quality is an infinite difference, that is, an intrinsic difference irrespective of quantity. I also want to show that such qualitative differences do not ruin hedonistic utilitarianism but instead enlarge and transform it in ways that make it a far more appealing doctrine than might at first glance seem possible.

Before proceeding, it is worth pausing for a moment to say a bit more about the anti-naturalistic views of Sidgwick and Moore, which have proved so influential within the academy. Indeed, they both reject hedonism in favor of ethical intuitionism. According to them, hedonism, to serve as an ethical doctrine, must be accompanied by an intuitive judgment, independent of the natural phenomenon of pleasure, that pleasure is the sole good. Otherwise, Moore says, the "naturalistic fallacy" arises, that is, "the contention that good *means* nothing but some simple or complex notion, that can be defined in terms of natural qualities."[16] He argues that Mill commits this fallacy and that "of all hedonistic writers, Prof. Sidgwick alone has clearly recognised that by 'good' we do mean something unanalysable, and has alone been led thereby to emphasise the fact that, if hedonism be true, its claims to be so must be rested solely on its self-evidence—that we must maintain 'Pleasure is the sole good' to be a mere *intuition*."[17] Whereas he grants that Sidgwick's "intuitionistic hedonism" is free from the naturalistic fallacy, however, Moore reports that he does not share Sidgwick's intuition and then tries to persuade us that pleasure is *not* the sole good. Nevertheless, he admits that resolving this clash of intuitions can prove nothing and that, for all he knows, ethical hedonism may be a true doctrine: "I shall try to shew [sic] you why my intuition denies [the proposition that pleasure alone is good], just as [Sidgwick's] intuition affirms it. It *may* always be true notwithstanding; neither intuition can *prove* whether it is true or not."[18]

Contrary to what Moore says, Sidgwick's "intuitionistic hedonism" is not hedonism at all. It appeals directly to some ethical value besides pleasure—some intrinsic value that Moore says cannot be defined but that he asserts is not a natural attribute or property of pleasure—to deem pleasure to be good, thereby destroying the hedonistic doctrine that pleasure *alone* is good. Sidgwick is properly viewed as a rational intuitionist, and his intuitions are dualistic insofar as he defends both universal hedonism (utilitarianism) and egoistic hedonism (ethical egoism). Indeed, hedonistic utilitarianism is said to be rational only to a limited extent: the rational faculty cannot determine how to resolve intuitive conflicts between utilitarianism and ethical egoism in some situations. Against Sidgwick, Moore rejects intuitionistic hedonism: he maintains that ethical egoism is a contradiction in terms so that it cannot ever be rational, and he also rejects utilitarianism in favor of his anti-hedonistic "principle of organic unities."[19] He defends what might be called an intuitionistic pluralistic idealism in which pleasure is only an ingredient of plural valuable organic unities, including complex mental states of appreciation of beautiful things and of personal affections that really exist, which cannot be summed together, and that are intuitively judged to be good by direct appeal to some "unanalysable" and "indefinable" intrinsic value or ideal.[20]

I shall proceed on the assumption that Mill's naturalistic version of hedonistic utilitarianism might be a true ethical doctrine. He fought against intuitionism throughout his life and even Moore admits that one person's self-evident intuitions may be another's arbitrary prejudices. Mill does not commit any naturalistic fallacy, I believe, even though he rejects the need for an independent ethical intuition that "pleasure is the sole good." He certainly does not think that an "ought" statement can be deduced solely from "is" statements, as his distinction between science and art illustrates.[21] Nor does he think that the proposition "pleasure alone is good" is merely a matter of intuition: "The subject is within the cognizance of the rational faculty; and neither does that faculty deal with it solely in the way of intuition."[22] Instead, he thinks that inferences can be drawn from experience that are "capable of determining the intellect" to give its assent to the proposition; "and this is *equivalent* to proof" in the usual sense.[23] Where critics such as Moore go astray is in supposing that distinct names such as "pleasure" and "good," or "desire" and "desirable," must always denote distinct things whereas in fact they may denote the same thing, to wit, the same feeling or state of consciousness. Different propositions such as "pleasure alone is ultimately desired" and "pleasure alone is good or desirable in itself and must or ought to be desired as an ultimate end" may be treated as logically distinct assertions because they express distinct moods of grammar, to wit, the indicative and the imperative moods, respectively. And yet it may be a reliable induction that they denote the same thing. The real issue is how to establish such a reliable inference, and this is perhaps the central concern of Mill's *Logic*. In short, the critics arguably confuse a question of linguistic usage with a question of what things exist, that is, a question of "physical and metaphysical" possibility.[24] But I cannot pursue that argument here.

I turn now to Mill's *Logic* with a view to clarifying his claim in *Utilitarianism* that hedonistic utilitarianism can consistently recognize differences of quality among pleasures, apart from differences of quantity.

I. REAL KINDS

In his *Logic*, Mill points out that we have an unlimited power to create distinct classes of things as long as there is any difference upon which to ground a distinction: "Take any attribute whatever, and if some things have it, and others have not, we may ground on the attribute a division of all things into two classes; and we actually do so, the moment we create a name which connotes the attribute."[25] A connotative name or term "denotes" a thing (also referred to as a subject or an object) and "implies [that is, connotes] an attribute."[26] A connotative term such as "white," "pleasant" or "human," for instance, is predicated of a thing and implies that the thing has, respectively, the attribute of "whiteness" or "pleasantness" or the attributes making up "humanity." Since some things have the property of whiteness and others do not, the connotative term "white" gives rise to a class of white objects as well as a distinct class of not-white objects. Indeed, in addition to positive connotative names, there are corresponding negative ones such as "not-white": it "denotes all things whatever except white things; and connotes the attribute of not possessing whiteness."[27]

For him, "whenever the names given to objects convey any information, that is, whenever they have properly any meaning, the meaning resides not in what they *denote*, but in what they *connote*."[28] Of concrete names, that is, names such as "John," "this table," "human," "white" or "pleasant" that denote a thing or a class of things, only the proper names of singular objects are not connotative: "A proper name is but an unmeaning mark which we connect in our minds with the idea of the object, in order that whenever the mark meets our eyes or occurs to our thoughts, we may think of that individual object."[29] Proper names tell us nothing about the attributes of the individual object itself but instead are "simply marks used to enable those individuals to be made the subject of discourse."[30] As he explains, however, all concrete general names are connotative and so are some concrete singular names (but not proper names). By contrast, abstract names, that is, terms such as "squareness," "humanity," "color," "whiteness" or "pleasantness" only denote an attribute or class of attributes. These names are typically not connotative. Yet even some of them are "justly considered as connotative," for example, a general term such as "fault," which denotes attributes and yet implies that those attributes have a secondary attribute "equivalent to *bad or hurtful quality.*"[31]

The claim that meaning resides in connotation is potentially misleading because it may seem that he is saying that abstract terms are typically meaningless.[32] But his real point is that the meaning of an abstract name is given by the connotation of the corresponding concrete name. He makes this clear when stating that a definition is a proposition that declares the meaning, that is, the connotation of a name: "we define a concrete name by enumerating the attributes which it connotes, and as the attributes connoted by a concrete name form the entire signification of the corresponding abstract name, the same enumeration will serve for the definition of both."[33]

Mill proposes to define the word "class" as "the indefinite multitude of individuals [things] *denoted* by a general name."[34] A general name (whether concrete or abstract) "is capable of being truly affirmed, in the same sense, of each of an indefinite number of things."[35] By contrast, "an individual or singular name is a name which is only capable of being truly affirmed, in the same sense, of one thing."[36] Strictly speaking, a singular term does denote something and so the definition of "class" might be modified accordingly. But such a modification of Mill's proposal seems of little interest. A singular name merely gives rise to a class consisting of a single object and a distinct class consisting of every other thing.

In any case, as Mill says, "the number of possible classes, therefore, is boundless; and there are as many actual classes (either of real or imaginary things) as there are general names, positive and negative together."[37] As an important aside, we should underscore his distinction between general names and collective ones: "A general name is one which can be predicated of *each* individual of a multitude; a collective name cannot be predicated of each separately, but only of all taken together."[38] "Happy" can be both a general name and a collective name. As a general term, "happy" denotes an indefinite number of individuals each of whom has the attributes connoted by "happy" and denoted by the abstract term "happiness." In contrast, as a collective name, "happy" refers to an attribute that a collection of individuals has as a collection but not as individual members of the group: the class of individuals when considered collectively is "considered as an aggregate whole."[39] In other words, "happy" in this collective sense denotes the group as a whole and connotes the attribute that the group as a whole has, to wit, "aggregate happiness." It denotes something that a collection of individuals has together but not as separate individuals. Aggregate happiness is not predicated of each individual. Indeed, we might predicate aggregate happiness of the group even if some of its members are not happy, although this is controversial since it raises the question of how aggregate happiness is related to each person's happiness. If each individual in the group is happy, however, then it is trivial to predicate aggregate happiness of the group. Moreover, each person's own happiness may have distinctive sources and yet the collection of persons together is properly said to have aggregate happiness, whatever the sources of individual happiness. If Sidgwick had attended to this distinction between a general name and a collective one, he would not have been so quick to read Mill as prescribing an "unqualified subordination" of individual happiness to aggregate happiness. Similarly, if Moore had attended to it, he could not have accused Mill of committing the fallacy of deducing that each individual desires the aggregate happiness from the proposition that each desires his own happiness.

After clarifying the idea of a class and emphasizing that the number of possible classes arising from general names is "unbounded," Mill argues that any classification, whether based on ordinary parlance or constructed for scientific purposes, must recognize that there is a crucial difference between two kinds of classes, to wit, classes that are properly considered real kinds and other classes that are not kinds. Real kinds are classes of things with an inexhaustible number of attributes in common whereas other classes share only some finite number of attributes:

> There are some classes [such as the class of white things], the things contained in which differ from other things only in certain particulars which may be numbered, while others [such as the class of animals] differ in more than can be numbered, more even than we need ever expect to know . . . It appears, therefore, that the properties, on which we ground our classes, sometimes exhaust all that the class has in common, or contain it all by some mode of implication [as in the case of white objects, which share only the property of whiteness and perhaps some other properties dependent on, or connected with, whiteness]; but in other instances [as in the case of animals or plants] we make a selection of a few properties from among not only a greater number, but a number inexhaustible by us, and to which as we know no bounds, they may, so far as we are concerned, be regarded as infinite.[40]

He points out that the Aristotelian logicians recognized this distinction between real kinds and other classes: "Differences which extended only to a certain property or properties, and there terminated, they considered as differences only in the *accidents* of things; but where any class differed from other things by an infinite series of differences, known and unknown, they considered the distinction as one of *kind*, and spoke of it as being an *essential* difference . . ."[41] Indeed, real kinds, "distinguished by unknown multitudes of properties, and not solely by a few determinate ones . . . are the only classes which, by the Aristotelian logicians, were considered as genera or species."[42] Mill endorses the schoolmen's "broad line of separation" between real kinds and other classes and says that he will "continue to express it in their language," with the important caveat that he drops talk of *essential* differences as a delusion of "metaphysics, that fertile field of delusion propagated by language."[43]

As a result, Mill embraces "the doctrine of the predicables . . . handed down from Aristotle, and his follower Porphyry," according to which "five different varieties of class-name" may be predicated of a thing, to wit, a genus, a species, a differentia, a proprium and an accidens.[44] He points out that such a classification is "not grounded as usual on a difference in [the] meaning [of general names of things], that is, in the attribute which they connote, but on a difference in the kind of class which they denote."[45] He also stresses that the five types of class-name are relative terms: animal is a genus with respect to man, for instance, but a species with respect to substance. Moreover, he follows the Aristotelians by classifying real kinds of things as species and genera, with the differentia being what distinguishes different species under the same genus. I will focus on these three varieties of class-name since they are the only ones that are used to classify real kinds of things.

More specifically, we can identify a proximate real kind as an *infima species*, that is, a species that has no sub-species as far as we can determine. A proximate kind cannot be a genus. If we can determine the proximate kind to which a thing belongs, every other real kind in which the thing can be classified must be a genus:

> When the *infima species*, or proximate kind, to which an individual [thing] belongs has been ascertained, the properties common to that kind include necessarily the whole of the common properties of every other real kind to which the individual can be referrible . . . And hence, every other kind which is predicable of the individual, will be to the proximate kind in the relation of a genus . . . ; that is, it will be a larger class, including it and more.[46]

We can, however, speak of any kind (not only the *infima species*) that is included in a larger kind as being in the relation of a species to a genus or family. Thus, Mill fixes "the logical meaning of these terms" as follows:

> Every class which is a real kind, that is, which is distinguished from all other classes by an indeterminate multitude of properties not derivable from one another, is either a genus or a species. A kind which is not divisible into other kinds, cannot be a genus, because it has no species under it; but it is itself a species, both with reference to the individuals [things] below and to the genera above . . . But every kind which admits of division into real kinds (as animal into mammal, bird, fish, &c., or bird into various species of birds) is a genus to all below it, a species to all genera in which it is itself included.[47]

A differentia "signifies the attribute which distinguishes a given species from every other species of the same genus."[48] And yet every real kind is distinguished from others by an infinite series of attributes so the question arises: which of the distinguishing properties does the differentia signify? Mill explains that the Aristotelians held that "the differentia must, like the genus and species, be of the *essence* of the subject [thing]" so that they claimed, for instance, rationality is the differentia of the species man, which distinguishes our species from others of the genus animal, even though the fact that we are the only animal that cooks its food is another of the attributes that could serve equally well as the differentia of our species.[49] Their notion of essence was vague, however, and became confused with the connotation of the general name of the thing being classified as a species:

> Their notion of the essence of a thing was a vague notion of a something which makes it what it is, *i.e.*, which makes it the kind of thing that it is—which causes it to have all that variety of properties which distinguish its kind. But . . . nobody could discover what caused the thing to have all those properties, nor even that there was anything which caused it to have them. [So] logicians . . . satisfied themselves with what made it to be what it was called.[50]

Logicians, confronted by "the innumerable properties, known and unknown, that are common to the class man," focused on the very small number of more obvious and supposedly more important attributes connoted by the name man, "and called them the essence of the species; and not stopping there, they affirmed them, in the case of the *infima species*, to be the essence of the individual too; for it was their maxim, that the species contained the 'whole essence' of the thing."[51] But their talk of essences exemplifies the metaphysical delusion of mistaking the connotation of a name for the nature of a thing. "On this account it was that rationality, being connoted by the name man, was allowed to be a differentia of the class; but the peculiarity of cooking their food, not being connoted, was relegated to the class of accidental properties."[52]

It emerges that the differentia, which signifies the property or class of properties that distinguishes a given species (real kind of thing) from others of the same genus (larger kind of thing), is rooted in the meaning of names and not in the essential nature of things.[53] So is the distinction between differentia, proprium and accidens: those terms connote distinct classes of attributes, respectively. Confining attention to the differentia, it is "that which must be added to the connotation of the genus, to complete the connotation of the species."[54] In other words, the attributes implied by the differential name must be added to those implied by the generic name to complete the meaning of the specific name. Mill also emphasizes that "a species, even as referred to the same genus, will not always have the same differentia, but a different one, according to the principle and purpose which preside over a particular classification."[55] One differentia such as rationality may be used to distinguish the species man from the genus animal for general purposes, for instance, whereas another differentia such as that of Linnaeus (i.e., possession of four incisors, solitary canine teeth and erect posture) may be employed for special or technical purposes: "The differentia, therefore, of a species may be defined to be, that part of the connotation of the specific name, whether ordinary or special and technical, which distinguishes the species in question from all other species of the genus to which on the particular occasion we are referring it."[56]

Two conclusions can be drawn immediately from this analysis of real kinds. First, when he refers to different kinds of pleasures, Mill is not talking about classes of pleasant objects and activities that are sources of pleasant feelings. A class of pleasant objects is not a real kind distinguished by an inexhaustible series of attributes and "parted off" from other kinds "by an unfathomable chasm."[57] Pleasant objects are not distinguished by any common properties except pleasantness and perhaps a few determinate others "dependent on, or connected with" pleasantness. As he makes clear, if anyone were to propose for investigation the common properties of all things that are pleasant, "the absurdity would be palpable."[58] There is no reason to believe that any such common properties exist, except for those, if any, which are derivable in some way from pleasantness itself.

Second, Mill is talking about real kinds of pleasant feelings *per se*. Feelings of pleasure are a genus, and different kinds of pleasant feelings are distinct species of the same genus or family.[59] Each species of pleasant feeling must be separated from the others by "an unfathomable chasm": the chasm must be unlimited in extent, "instead of a mere ordinary ditch with a visible [that is, limited or finite] bottom."[60] I shall next clarify why there is only one possible differentia for a given species of pleasure, that is, only one possible property that can distinguish that species from the others. This single attribute is what constitutes difference of quality between pleasant feelings. It is what Mill means when he says there is "but one possible answer" to the question of what is meant by difference of quality.

II. THE ONLY POSSIBLE DIFFERENTIA

Mill remarks that the names of feelings connote mere resemblance as an attribute of the given feeling:

> The names of feelings, like other concrete general names, are connotative; but they connote a mere resemblance. When predicated of any individual feeling, the information they convey is that of its likeness to the other feelings which we have been accustomed to call by the same name.[61]

When we call something "a sensation of white" or "a sensation of pleasure," for instance, we are asserting that the feeling resembles other feelings of that kind that we habitually call by that name, with the caveat that like feelings may differ in intensity or quantity. The relation of resemblance is itself a feeling. We may leave open whether the feeling of resemblance between two sensations of color or of pleasure is "a third state of consciousness, which I have *after* having the two sensations . . . or whether (like the feeling of their succession) it is involved in the sensations themselves."[62] In either case, these feelings of resemblance, and of dissimilarity, cannot be further analyzed. In short, the relation of resemblance is *sui generis*. It is an attribute that is nothing but our sensation or impression that two things are alike. That simple feeling, like the individual sensations of pleasure of which we predicate resemblance, is "peculiar, unresolvable, and inexplicable."[63]

Even if a thing only has a single attribute grounded on one of our simple feelings, the names both of the thing and of the attribute "still admit of definition: or rather, would do so if all our simple feelings had names."[64] We can define a white thing as "an object that excites the sensation of white," for instance, and a pleasant object as one that excites the sensation of pleasure. "Whiteness may be defined, the property or power of exciting the sensation of white," and analogously for pleasantness. But the names of the sensations themselves, although they are connotative names, cannot be defined "because their meaning is unsusceptible of analysis:"

> These are in the same condition as proper names. They are not indeed, like proper names, unmeaning; for the words sensation of *white* signify, that the sensation which I so denominate resembles other sensations which I remember to have had before, and to have called by that name. But as we have no words by which to recall those former sensations, except the very word which we seek to define, or some other which, being exactly synonymous with it, requires definition as much, words cannot unfold the signification of this class of names; and we are obliged to make a direct appeal to the personal experience of the individual whom we address.[65]

Similarly, the thing we name a sensation of pleasure connotes the single attribute of pleasantness and yet we cannot define either the thing or the attribute: we can only appeal to other people to confirm our feelings and our use of language to denote them.

Sensations are a species of feelings, sometimes called "bodily feelings," which differ from other species of the same genus feelings or states of consciousness. These other species include thoughts, emotions and volitions.[66] In contrast to the simple feelings named "sensations," and with the exception of simple thoughts or impressions that are mere copies of sensations, these other kinds of feelings are complex feelings. A complex feeling has ingredients in addition to sensations or their simple copies in memory or imagination.[67] A thought of something, for instance, contains, in addition to some assemblage or succession of sensations, an inference that these sensations constitute an object or activity, real or imaginary, which is commonly viewed as the source of the sensations. An emotion or sentiment is even more complex, and may contain in addition to various sensations and thoughts certain natural impulses and instincts of which we are not conscious. A volition is an intention or plan to produce an effect, and this mental state together with the effect it produces constitute an action.

These different kinds of compound feelings are mixtures of their ingredients, and each kind has its own distinctive properties. Indeed, as real kinds, the various species of feelings are separated from one another by innumerable properties, known and unknown. Which of the properties is employed to serve as the differentia of a given species depends on the principles and purposes of the particular classification. Moreover, the names of the complex feelings connote resemblance among the individual feelings denoted as such by that name, respectively, "thoughts," "emotions" and "volitions." Any complex feeling may be analyzed to recover its ingredients or parts, and it is an interesting issue how much similarity in the parts is needed to precipitate the feeling of resemblance between two individual complex feelings. But the feeling of resemblance itself is a simple feeling, "unsusceptible of analysis."

Whereas simple sensations of pleasure and their copies can be experienced by any sentient creature, complex pleasant thoughts, in which pleasure is inseparable from real or imagined objects and activities, and pleasant emotions or sentiments can only be experienced by those sentient creatures, notably humans, with the intellectual and moral capacities needed to experience them.[68] We may take a peculiar kind of mental pleasure in the thought of a vanilla latté or a bottle of Raveneau Chablis, for instance, and a peculiar kind of emotional pleasure in the beauty of a painting or a statue.[69] The pleasantness of a complex mental state such as an emotion is a property of that complex state: the pleasant feeling, although it is inseparably associated with the complex feeling, is a single attribute of that complex feeling. A pleasant aesthetic emotion or a pleasant moral sentiment, whereas it has the attribute or quality of pleasantness, is distinguished from a simple sensation of pleasure by innumerable properties. And yet we may focus attention on the complex mental state's single attribute or quality of pleasure, treating it as a simple feeling of pleasure in isolation, and yet keeping in mind that this simple feeling is not a sensation of pleasure but rather a feeling whose quality is inextricably bound up with the other attributes of the complex mental state.

If we focus on the simple feelings of pleasure alone and maintain that there are different kinds of them, then we can only mean that pleasant sensations differ in kind from the pleasant feelings that are properties of some complex mental states, and that the pleasant feelings that are qualities of pleasant thoughts differ in kind from the pleasant feelings that are properties of pleasant emotions.[70] Moreover, these different kinds of pleasant feelings must differ from one another to an unlimited degree. In other words, one kind must feel intrinsically superior to another as pleasure, regardless of quantity. That is implied by calling them real kinds of pleasures. The names of these different kinds of simple pleasant feelings, if they each had names, would connote mere resemblance between any two individual feelings of the same kind, with the caveat that these two feelings may differ in intensity or quantity. The kind of pleasantness connoted by each name would be the attribute or quality of that kind of pleasant feeling. Thus, differences of quality are infinite differences.

The only possible differentia of a given species of simple pleasant feeling is its quality in relation to the other species of the same genus. Since these various species of pleasure are real kinds, each species must be separated from the others by an infinite chasm. A classification of the various pleasures must therefore take the form of a hierarchy such that one kind of pleasant feeling is supreme in quality, a second kind is next in quality and so forth, down to the kind lowest in quality, where differences of quality are unlimited in degree and thus absolute. And yet we cannot define these different kinds of pleasant feelings. Our words can only denote them as we appeal to the direct experience of the people we address.

I submit that this is what Mill is saying when he claims that there is "only one possible answer" to the question of what is meant by differences of quality in simple feelings of pleasure. The *Logic* supplies the answer to the puzzle of what he is saying in *Utilitarianism*. The linkage is seamless and confirms yet again Mill's remarkable consistency, despite the dismissive remarks of Sidgwick, Moore and many others in the academy.

The reader may notice that I have said little about volitions and their relation to pleasure. As I understand him, Mill asserts that a volition or intention is a complex mental state with many ingredients, including a desire that, among our present desires, is strongest in degree. Any desire might be classified as an initiatory stage of volition. But a desire only becomes part of a volition if it is the most intense of our present desires. And yet what is a desire? Mill suggests that a desire for something is proportional to the amount of pleasure expected from the thing, with the caveat that experienced agents who are competently acquainted with the different kinds of pleasure will make proper allowance for kind. But that implies that desire for the thing is ultimately just a belief that the thing is a source of pleasure: the strength of desire is proportional to the amount of expected pleasure, with experienced (but not inexperienced) people making due allowance for kind of pleasure. Since "belief is a kind of thought," it seems that he agrees with his father that desire is a species of thoughts, more specifically, thoughts of pleasure associated with objects and activities.[71] This may be why he does not classify desires as a separate kind of feeling or mental state.[72]

A few additional remarks may be offered in support of my reading that, by differences of quality in pleasures, Mill means intrinsic differences, regardless of quantity. He tells us that "the properties of number, alone among all known phenomena, are, in the most rigorous sense, properties of all things whatever."[73] Since "all things are numerable," the properties of number by themselves do not, and cannot, distinguish one real kind of thing from another.[74] More of a thing feels unlike less of that same thing and yet this feeling of a difference in quantity itself feels dissimilar to the feeling of a difference in quality, that is, the feeling that two objects or attributes are different to an inexhaustible extent. The sensation of an infinite chasm between two kinds of things does not resemble the sensation of two different quantities of the same thing.[75] It is inexplicable why the one sensation of dissimilarity feels unlike the other, just as it is ultimately mysterious why a sensation of red feels unlike that of blue.

A closely related point is that the truths of mathematics, "the science of number," whereas they apply to all things, are independent of the kinds of things to which they are applied. We can add units of a thing together into a finite mass, for instance, without changing its kind. We can experience two different quantities of a sensation of pleasure and yet continue to feel that it is a sensation of pleasure. Consistently with this, Mill allows that some changes in kind may be a function of changes in quantity: "if it comes to be discovered that variations of quality in any class of phenomena [such as sensations], correspond regularly to variations in quantity either in those same or in some other phenomena; every formula of mathematics applicable to quantities which vary in that particular manner, becomes a mark of a corresponding general truth respecting the variations in quality which accompany them."[76] A sensation of pleasure may turn into a sensation of pain, for example, as the sensation or its source—say, heat—becomes more intense. A mathematical formula that covers the quantitative variations in sensation or heat then also marks the qualitative change in the feeling. But the formula per se does not alter the mystery of the two kinds of sensation. Our feeling of the change in quality cannot be reduced to the feeling of a change in quantity, even though the one feeling may regularly accompany the other: the feeling that there is an infinite gulf separating the two kinds of sensation is not explained by the awareness of a finite change in the quantity of heat or in the quantity of feeling produced by the heat. In any case, we never observe that variations in the quantity of a simple sensation transform it into a complex thought or an emotion. Indeed, the complex mental states are quasi-chemical compounds that cannot be decomposed into their various ingredients.[77]

A change in kind of pleasant feeling cannot be reduced to a change in quantity of pleasant feeling. We cannot say that a higher kind of pleasant feeling is worth, say, one hundred units of a lower kind so that one unit of the higher is qualitatively superior to ninety-nine units of the lower whereas one hundred and one units of the lower is qualitatively superior to the one unit of higher. By reducing difference of quality to difference of quantity in this way, we destroy the notion of a real kind. Since the difference is merely one of quantity, there is no reason grounded in the two feelings of pleasure themselves to conclude that one is superior in kind to the other. Thus, the switch point, at which one more unit of the lower pleasure renders the mass of lower pleasure superior to the higher as pleasure, is arbitrary when viewed through the lens of hedonism: it lacks any basis in the feelings of pleasure. Since this marginal unit is no different in quality than any other unit of the lower pleasure, it is impossible to understand how it, considered in isolation, transmits qualitative superiority to a finite mass of the lower pleasure over the higher pleasure. Instead, some value other than pleasant feeling must be brought in to account for qualitative superiority. The object or activity that is the source of pleasure must be judged more worthy in one case as compared to another, for instance, or some independent attitude must be used to adjust the importance of one pleasant feeling as compared to another. But such moves are incompatible with hedonism.

III.   CONCLUSION: QUALITATIVE HEDONISM

For Mill, pleasures of different qualities are different kinds of pleasant feelings, and real kinds are separated from one another by an infinite chasm. Many commentators argue otherwise but their arguments are fatally flawed as readings of Mill. Contrary to their assertions, he does not conflate higher pleasures with certain objects and activities that are judged more worthy sources of pleasant feelings themselves invariant in quality. Nor does he reject hedonism by importing alien attitudes and norms such as perfectionist values to distinguish between higher and lower kinds of pleasures.[78] Rather, he defends a consistent qualitative hedonism, as he repeatedly emphasizes he aims to do. It is long past time that there should be any doubts about this, and scholars ought to leave off attributing anti-hedonistic views to him.

I do not have space to assess the plausibility—as opposed to the consistency— of Mill's hedonistic utilitarian doctrine or even to flesh out in any detail the hierarchy of real kinds of pleasant feelings that he seems to think awaits discovery by human beings as they develop their capacities. But I have provided more extensive discussions of these matters elsewhere.[79] For now, I will merely say a bit more about the hierarchy and indicate in passing why such differences of quality are deserving of serious study.

As should already be clear, Mill holds that the lowest kind of pleasures, of least quality, are the inchoate physical sensations of pleasure registered by our body, that is, by our "animal nature" when assumed to be "disjoined" from our higher mental capacities.[80] Humans, like other animals, experience simple physical sensations automatically through the nervous system, independently of the will, the rational faculty and the creative imagination, including the ability to imagine oneself in the places of others and empathize with them. These elementary tingles and surges of pleasure, considered in isolation, are disjoined from any thoughts of objects and from any sentiments whose ingredients include various thoughts.

Mental pleasures are said to be superior in quality to the simple physical sensations of pleasure. Any mental pleasure is a quasi-chemical compound of various ingredients, including a thought of some object or activity together with physical sensations of pleasure, or their traces in memory and imagination, expected from that object or activity. These various ingredients melt together so that the mental pleasure feels like a whole new feeling with its own emergent properties, including the property of qualitative superiority over the pleasant physical sensations among its ingredients. The ingredients vanish from our consciousness as separate elements: the pleasant physical sensations become inseparably associated with the idea of the object or activity so that we are unaware that the pleasure and the idea are separate elements, unless the mental feeling is subjected to a psychological analysis.

Mill's stated view is that any person capable of experiencing the mental kind of pleasures will not voluntarily sacrifice even a bit of mental pleasure for any amount of the mere bodily kind of pleasure. Since mental pleasures are complex feelings that already include pleasant physical sensations or their traces among other ingredients, however, the only way mental and bodily kinds can come into conflict is when mental pleasure must be sacrificed altogether in return for a greater amount of the mere physical sensation of pleasure that is already a component of the mental pleasure.[81] In short, the issue is: would anyone who can exercise his mental faculties voluntarily give them up, along with the mental pleasure they make possible, in return for any amount of the purely sensual pleasure above and beyond that already contained in his mental pleasure? Mill's negative answer is plausible, keeping in mind his admonition that people may involuntarily sacrifice mental pleasures for mere physical sensations because they have become incapable of exercising their higher faculties or of making choices as a result of abuse, disease or neglect.[82]

Moreover, within the broad category of mental pleasures, some kinds of mental pleasures are qualitatively superior to others. Certain emotional kinds of pleasures are superior in quality to other mental pleasures. The latter pleasures might be named everyday mental pleasures, that is, a kind of pleasant mental feeling associated with objects or activities that we find useful or merely expedient for our daily life, keeping in mind that these things may relieve us of suffering as well as give us delight. In contrast, the emotional pleasures are far more complex and require more subtle and extensive exercise of our higher faculties. For example, Mill suggests that the kind of pleasant feeling associated with the moral sentiments, of which the sentiment of justice is the most important and sets the tone for the others such as the sentiment of charity or kindness, is qualitatively superior to any competing kinds of pleasures. This higher kind of pleasure, which he calls a feeling of "security," grows up around the idea of justice understood as a social code of fundamental rules, the "very groundwork" of our existence: the rules distribute and sanction equal rights and duties to a social group whose members each have a voice in the construction of the code. To competently experience this higher pleasure of justice and morality, the individual must develop his capacities to imaginatively sympathize with other people and even with other species of animals, to construct and obey rules designed to protect any human or any sentient creature from suffering harms reasonably judged to be wrongful, to direct resentment and punishment against those who intentionally, knowingly, recklessly or negligently break the moral rules, and so forth.[83]

Even so, the kind of pleasure associated with aesthetic emotions of beauty and sublimity may be qualitatively supreme if genuine aesthetic pleasures never conflict with moral pleasures. For Mill, aesthetic pleasure is apparently associated with lofty ideas or ideals of harmony, symmetry, infinity and so forth that direct our attention to an imaginary more perfect world or utopia or heaven that transcends the imperfect world of our experience.[84]

This ranking of the different kinds of pleasures in terms of increasing quality, from purely physical sensations through intellectual and moral feelings up to aesthetic emotions, deserves careful consideration.[85] It is a very special sort of ranking, namely, a lexicographical (or lexical) ranking. The lexical ranking is special because it captures the discontinuities of intrinsic value produced by the infinite superiority of higher pleasures over lower ones: no finite lower pleasure, however large, can ever be equal in value as pleasure to even a bit of higher pleasure.[86] A key implication of the ranking, for instance, is the absolute importance of social rules of justice within Mill's extraordinary version of hedonistic utilitarianism. Indeed, as I understand it, his doctrine confines the aggregation procedure to the higher pleasures of justice: as a social code of equal rights and duties is chosen in accordance with a democratic social choice process, individuals are free to pursue other kinds of pleasures in accordance with their recognized rights and duties.

In closing, I wish to stress that sensations of pleasure are a common element in the different kinds of pleasant feelings in the Millian hierarchy. Sensations of pleasure are among the ingredients of pleasant thoughts and emotions, although the sensations fuse with the other ingredients to form the more complex mental states. Considered in isolation, the simple feelings of pleasure that are properties of these more complex states of consciousness are higher in quality than mere physical sensations. But the fact remains that sensations of pleasure are involved in all of the different kinds of pleasant feelings. It is that fact that justifies classifying all of them as pleasures. Although the different kinds may not have their own distinctive names, the connotation of the generic name "pleasant feeling" encompasses them all. The definition of "pleasure" properly spells out this connotation or meaning of the generic name by pointing out the various kinds of simple pleasant feelings, of different qualities. Thus, the charges of Sidgwick, Moore and the hordes in their train are ill-considered.[87]

NOTES

1. Mill (1861, CW: X.211). All references to John Stuart Mill's works are to the authoritative edition of *Collected Works of John Stuart Mill* (Mill, 1963–1991—cited as *CW*, followed by volume and page number), unless otherwise indicated.
2. Mill (1861, CW: X.211).
3. Mill (1861, CW: X.211).

4. See, e.g., Riley (1999, 2003, 2008a, 2008b, 2009a).
5. Mill (1861, CW: X.211). Mill distinguishes "discontent" from unhappiness in sense of pain including absence of pleasure. He warns against confounding "the two very different ideas, of happiness, and content [or contentment]" (*ibid.*, 212). He also says that competent majorities must judge differences of quality (as well as differences of quantity) if there is not unanimity on the issue (*ibid.*, 213). Human nature cannot actually experience an infinite or unlimited pleasant feeling of any kind, and is not even "capable of" finite additions beyond some large quantity.
6. Brink (2013: 50). Brink provides an insightful survey of recent literature relating to Mill's higher pleasures doctrine, in the course of which he makes some telling criticisms of various readings. He defends a perfectionist account rather than a hedonistic account of Mill's idea of happiness, despite Mill's repeated endorsements of hedonism. See *ibid.*, 46–78.
7. Sidgwick (1902: 245).
8. Sidgwick (1902: 247, original emphasis).
9. Sidgwick (1902: 247).
10. Moore (1993: 129).
11. Moore (1993: 132, original emphasis).
12. Moore (1993: 130). Cf. Mill (1861, CW: X.237–38).
13. Moore (1993: 130).
14. See also Moore's discussion of the analogy between different kinds of pleasures and different kinds of colors as a way to illustrate his point: "if colour is our only possible end, as Mill says pleasure is, then there can be no possible reason for preferring one colour to another, red, for instance, to blue, except that the one is more of a colour than the other" (Moore, 1993: 131). The different kinds of color are supposedly just means to the end of color, and so one kind is no more valuable than another as color.
15. Infinity is not a determinate quantity or number.
16. Moore (1993: 125, original emphasis).
17. Moore (1993: 111, original emphasis).
18. Moore (1993: 126).
19. Moore (1993: 78–82, 147, 232–38).
20. Moore (1993: 238–73). For Moore's struggles with the notion of intrinsic value and the problem of defining such an attribute if it is unrelated to the natural properties of anything that supposedly has it, see, e.g., "The Conception of Intrinsic Value," in *ibid.*, 280–96.
21. Mill (1843, CW: VIII.943–52).
22. Mill (1861, CW: X.208).
23. Mill (1861, CW: X.208, emphasis added).
24. Mill (1861, CW: X.238).
25. Mill (1843, CW: VII.122).
26. Mill (1843, CW: VII.31). By contrast, "a non-connotative term is one which signifies a subject only [e.g., John, or London, or England], or an attribute only [e.g., whiteness, pleasantness, length]" (*ibid.*).
27. Mill (1843, CW: VII.41).
28. Mill (1843, CW: VII.34, original emphasis).
29. Mill (1843, CW: VII.35).
30. Mill (1843, CW: VII.33).
31. Mill (1843, CW: VII.32, original emphasis).
32. Mill explains in a note that his employment of the term "to connote" is distinctive and at odds with his father James Mill's usage of the same term in the *Analysis of the Phenomena of the Human Mind* (1829). He also argues that the schoolmen, from whom the term is adopted, support his sense of the term rather than his father's (Mill, 1843, CW: VII.40–41n).

33. Mill (1843, *CW*: VII.136).
34. Mill (1843, *CW*: VII.28, emphasis added).
35. Mill (1843, *CW*: VII.28).
36. Mill (1843, *CW*: VII.28).
37. Mill (1843, *CW*: VII.122).
38. Mill (1843, *CW*: VII.28, original emphasis).
39. Mill (1843, *CW*: VII.121).
40. Mill (1843, *CW*: VII.122–23).
41. Mill (1843, *CW*: VII.123, original emphasis).
42. Mill (1843, *CW*: VII.123).
43. Mill (1843, *CW*: VII.123, 127).
44. Mill (1843, *CW*: VII.123, 127).
45. Mill (1843, *CW*: VII.119).
46. Mill (1843, *CW*: VII.125, original emphasis).
47. Mill (1843, *CW*: VII.126). Note that since any real kind has an infinite series of properties in common, a classification of species and genera implicitly involves larger and smaller infinite sets of properties. A genus has an inexhaustible set of attributes in common and yet a species under it has all its properties and more.
48. Mill (1843, *CW*: VII.126).
49. Mill (1843, *CW*: VII.126, original emphasis).
50. Mill (1843, *CW*: VII.127).
51. Mill (1843, *CW*: VII.127, original emphasis).
52. Mill (1843, *CW*: VII.127). Despite his repeated dismissal of all talk of essences and of the nature of things in themselves, Mill is continually saddled by commentators with contrary metaphysical claims such as the claim that, by spontaneously choosing in accord with her own wishes and judgment, an individual reveals her unique essence or quiddity. He not only never makes such a claim but also expressly repudiates it. See, e.g., *ibid.*, 114–15; and Mill (1848, *CW*: II.319).
53. Although he adopts the Aristotelian doctrine of the predicables, Mill rejects the Aristotelian project in which definitions are supposed to expound a natural classification of things into real kinds (Mill, 1843, *CW*: VII.140–41). The definition of a kind cannot possibly enumerate all the properties of the kind since they constitute an infinite series. So this cannot be the purpose of a definition. All that can be required is that the definition spell out the connotation of the name, i.e., enough of the attributes to allow the kind to be distinguished from other classes.
54. Mill (1843, *CW*: VII.127). For clarification of the meaning of proprium and accidens, which connote properties not included in the connotation of the species or of the genus, see *ibid.*, 130–32.
55. Mill (1843, *CW*: VII.128).
56. Mill (1843, *CW*: VII.130).
57. Mill (1843, *CW*: VII.123).
58. Mill (1843, *CW*: VII.122). The case is analogous to that of white things.
59. Consistently with this, feelings of pleasure are a species in relation to the larger genus of feelings or mental states, a genus that includes sensations, thoughts, emotions and volitions. Moreover, although that larger genus might seem to be a species in relation to all nameable things, including mental states, substances (minds and external objects) and attributes (quantities, qualities and relations of coexistence, succession and resemblance), Mill argues that all we know of substances and attributes is contained in our mental states. As a matter of epistemology, then, there is no larger genus than that of mental states. For further discussion of the categories that he proposes to replace Aristotle's categories, see Mill (1843, *CW*: VII.46–77).

60. Mill (1843, CW: VII.123).
61. Mill (1843, CW: VII.104).
62. Mill (1843, CW: VII.70).
63. Mill (1843, CW: VII.70). Evidently, we can also predicate resemblance of two individual feelings that we are accustomed to naming "feelings of resemblance."
64. Mill (1843, CW: VII.136).
65. Mill (1843, CW: VII.136).
66. Mill (1843, CW: VII.51–55). Remarkably, Mill does not identify "desire" as a distinct kind of mental state. I shall come back to this point in due course.
67. Admittedly, the copies of sensations in memory or imagination are simple thoughts that are traces of the sensations themselves. So it is not the case that all thoughts are complex ones. But I ignore this point for ease of exposition. A simple thought of pleasure may differ in kind from an actual sensation of pleasure and yet there is no difference of quality in the pleasures concerned. A difference of kind in the mental state is necessary but not sufficient for a difference of quality in the pleasure that is an attribute of the mental state. As it turns out, for there to be a difference in quality of pleasant feelings, it is also necessary to have a complex mental state so that a quasi-chemical reaction can take place among its multiple ingredients, including sensations of pleasure or their traces, to generate a new kind of pleasant feeling as one of its properties.
68. Just as pleasant sensations are a species of the genus sensations, so pleasant thoughts are a species of the genus thoughts, and pleasant emotions are a species of the genus emotions.
69. Mill says, for example, that the attribute of beauty is "grounded on the peculiar feeling of pleasure which the statue produces in our minds; which is not a sensation, but an emotion" (Mill (1843, CW: VII.75).
70. I do not intend to deny that there are different sub-species of pleasant feelings under some of these species. While pleasant sensations form an *infima species*, there may be different species of emotional pleasures. In other words, pleasant emotions may be a genus with respect to, say, pleasant aesthetic emotions and pleasant moral sentiments. Indeed, I will suggest later in the text that this is the case. Perhaps these two species of pleasant emotions are also *infima species*. But I am not concerned to identify the various proximate kinds of pleasant feelings.
71. Mill (1843, CW: VII.75).
72. We should also recall that, according to Mill, the ingredients of a complex mental state such as a volition may disappear from consciousness if ever present in the first place. As a result of habit, the individual becomes unaware of the expectation of pleasure which originally constituted or triggered her desire for something, and desires the thing merely out of habit, independently of feelings of pleasure. "It is not the less true that will, in the beginning, is entirely produced by desire . . . [that is, by thinking of the thing] in a pleasurable light, or of its absence in a painful one . . . Will is the child of desire, and passes out of the dominion of its parent only to come under that of habit" (CW: X. 238–9).
73. Mill (1843, CW: VII.221).
74. Mill (1843, CW: VII.221).
75. Mill (1843, CW: VII.65–75).
76. Mill (1843, CW: VII.222).
77. Mill (1843, CW: VII.371–78, 434–42).
78. For examples and discussions of such flawed interpretations, see, among many others, Sumner (1996: 81–112); Feldman (2004 and 2010); Rawls

(2007: 258–65); Donner and Fumerton (2009: 16–32); Miller (2010: 34–36, 54–70); Brink (2013: 46–78).
79. See, e.g., Riley, (2009b and 2010a).
80. Mill (1861, CW: X.213).
81. Of course, different mental pleasures, in which the physical sensation of pleasure is fused with ideas of different objects or activities, may conflict so that an agent must choose one rather than another. Mental pleasures also differ in intensity so that the agent must also choose how much mental pleasure he wishes to enjoy from any given object or activity. But these decisions are not the ones under consideration.
82. Mill (1861, CW: X.211–14).
83. Mill (1861, CW: X.251). For Mill's analysis of the ingredients of the moral sentiment of justice and the pleasant feeling of security, which in his view is inseparably associated with it, see *ibid.*, 246–51; and Riley (2012).
84. For further discussion relating to the qualitative supremacy of the kind of pleasant feeling associated with genuine aesthetic emotion, see Riley (2010b and 2013).
85. A corresponding hierarchy of different kinds of pains and sufferings is implicit. Pleasant feelings and painful ones are heterogeneous phenomena, even though we can for convenience speak of pleasures including relief from pain.
86. Mill occasionally says that higher kinds of pleasant feelings are incommensurable with lower kinds. This is a valid usage of language, despite objections raised by critics such as Henry West (see West, 2004: 72n29). Strictly speaking, two pleasures or values may be said to be incommensurable if they cannot be compared in terms of a common scale of rational numbers. Since higher pleasures are superior to lower ones to an infinite extent, the two kinds of pleasures are properly said to be incommensurable. There are various forms of incommensurability, although a tendency exists in the literature to seize upon only one form of it, namely, incomparability *tout court*. Higher pleasures are evidently comparable with lower ones but the two kinds cannot be reduced to a common scale. Moreover, contrary to West, infinity is not a number: to say that one pleasure is superior to another to an unlimited degree does not imply that differences in quality are reduced to differences in quantity. Donner is also confused about these matters (See Donner and Fumerton, 2009: 32n2).
87. It is worth noting that whereas Mill is concerned with pleasant complex mental states, Moore intuits that "organic unities" are more valuable as a whole than any of their ingredients, which may but need not include pleasant sensations or their traces. Indeed, for Moore, a complex mental state may have great intrinsic value, even though each of its ingredients, considered in isolation, has no value at all.

REFERENCES

Brink, D. O. (2013) *Mill's Progressive Principles* (Oxford: Clarendon Press).
Donner W; Fumerton R. (2009) *Mill* (Oxford: Wiley-Blackwell).
Feldman, F. (2004) *Pleasure and the Good Life* (Oxford: Clarendon Press).
———. (2010) *What Is this Thing Called Happiness?* (Oxford: Clarendon Press).
Mill, J. S. (1843) *A System of Logic, Ratiocinative and Inductive: Being a Connected View of the Principles of Evidence and the Methods of Scientific Investigation*, in vols. VII and VIII (1974) of Mill (1963–1991).

————. (1848) *Principles of Political Economy with Some of their Applications to Social Philosophy*, in vols. II and III (1965) of Mill (1963–1991).

————. (1861) *Utilitarianism*, in vol. X (1969) of Mill (1963–1991).

————. (1963–1991) *Collected Works of John Stuart Mill*, F.E.L. Priestly (gen. ed.), and subsequently J. M. Robson, 33 vols. (London/Toronto: Routledge and Kegan Paul/University of Toronto Press).

Miller, D. E. (2010) *J. S. Mill: Moral, Social, and Political Thought* (Cambridge: Polity Press).

Moore, G. E. (1993) *Principia Ethica*, T. Baldwin (ed.) (Cambridge: Cambridge University Press).

Rawls, J. (2007) *Lectures on the History of Political Philosophy*, S. Freeman (ed.) (Cambridge, MA: Belknap Press of Harvard University Press).

Riley, J. (1999) "Is Qualitative Hedonism Incoherent?" *Utilitas* 11: 347–58.

————. (2003) "Interpreting Mill's Qualitative Hedonism," *Philosophical Quarterly* 53: 410–18.

————. (2008a) "Millian Qualitative Superiorities and Utilitarianism, Part I," *Utilitas* 20: 257–78

————. (2008b) "What Are Millian Qualitative Superiorities?" *Prolegomena* 7: 61–79

————. (2009a) "Millian Qualitative Superiorities and Utilitarianism, Part II," *Utilitas* 21: 127-43.

————. (2009b) "The Interpretation of Maximizing Utilitarianism," *Social Philosophy and Policy* 26: 286–325.

————. (2010a) "Mill's Extraordinary Utilitarian Moral Theory," *Politics, Philosophy & Economics* 9: 67–116.

————. (2010b) "Optimal Moral Rules and Supererogatory Acts," in B. Eggleston, D. Miller and D. Weinstein (eds.) *John Stuart Mill and the Art of Life* (Oxford: Oxford University Press): 185–229.

————. (2012) "Happiness and the Moral Sentiment of Justice," in L. Kahn (ed.) *Mill on Justice* (London: Palgrave Macmillan): 158–83.

————. (2013) "Mill's Greek Ideal of Individuality," in K. N. Demetriou and A. Loizides (eds.) *John Stuart Mill: A British Socrates* (Basingstoke: Palgrave Macmillan): 97–125.

Sidgwick, H. (1902) *Outlines of the History of Ethics for English Readers*, 5th ed. (Indianapolis: Hackett, 1988).

Sumner, W. (1996) *Welfare, Happiness, and Ethics* (Oxford: Clarendon Press).

West, R. H. (2004) *An Introduction to Mill's Utilitarian Ethics* (Cambridge: Cambridge University Press).

9   Mill, Informal Logic and Argumentation

Hans V. Hansen

This essay falls into two parts. The first part shows some of the ways in which Mill's work is an important precursor of the development in the late twentieth century of informal logic. There are important similarities in how Mill and the informal logicians conceive of logic, and Mill developed in greater detail than any of his predecessors two of the methods that are now widely used by informal logicians. The second part of the essay considers some of the ways Mill has contributed to the practice of argumentation. Affinities with the work of leading argumentation theorists are explored, and Mill's own interest in discussions as a means of persuasion is examined. Finally, the *Logic* and the *Liberty* are revealed to be connected by a common strand of concern for truth and the avoidance of error. Overall, the essay takes the view that Mill's contributions to informal logic and the study of argumentation are considerable.

I.   MILL'S CONTRIBUTIONS TO INFORMAL LOGIC

I.i.   Mill's and Informal Logic's Conceptions of Logic

I.i.a.   Definitions

Following Richard Whately's *Elements of Logic* (1826) Mill considers logic to be both an art and a science. The science studies the mental operations in reasoning, and the art formulates rules as an aid to reasoning well. However, he distances himself from Whately by insisting on a wider conception of logic to include inductive reasoning as well as deductive reasoning. From another direction he resists the too-broad idea that logic encompasses all that is relevant to the pursuit of truth, because this would include truths about our own mental states known immediately by intuition, and logic is devoted to inferences, or reasoning.[1] The subject of logic, for Mill, is the estimation of evidence. It is

> the science of the operations of the understanding which are subservient to the estimation of evidence: both the process itself of advancing from

known truths to unknown, and all other intellectual operations in so far as auxiliary to this. It includes, therefore, the operation of Naming; for language is an instrument of thought . . . It includes, also, Definition, and Classification.

. . . [and the bringing together of or framing of] a set of rules or canons for testing the sufficiency of any given evidence to prove any given proposition.[2]

This conception of logic embraces not only the empirical study of inferring, but also the auxiliary operations of (naming, definition and classification) needed for keeping our thoughts straight, and marshalling our facts when wanted to make arguments. Importantly, logic is also devoted to developing a set of rules for determining the sufficiency of evidence. What Mill takes logic to be about is inference or reasoning and "to reason is simply to infer any assertion, from assertions already admitted."[3] He holds that "logic takes cognizance of our intellectual operations, only as they conduce to our own knowledge, and to our command over that knowledge for our own uses."[4] But he is also ready to apply his logical principles to the arguments of others. So his remark about the scope of logic conducing only to one's own knowledge may be due more to Mill's empiricist epistemology than the intrinsic character of logic. (In this study I am taking Mill to be using "argument" and "inference" interchangeably.)

We will contrast Mill's conception of logic with one by given by Ralph H. Johnson and J. Anthony Blair who have taken a leading role in the development of informal logic since the late 1970s. They have several times forwarded a characterization of informal logic along these lines:

By "informal logic" we mean to designate a branch of logic whose task is to develop non-formal standards, criteria, procedures for the analysis, interpretation, evaluation, criticism and construction of argumentation in everyday discourse.[5]

Here informal logic has been indexed to *argumentation* rather than *arguments*; however, the surrounding discussion repeatedly reminds the reader that informal logic focuses on and is about *arguments*.[6] By "an argument" (as an entity and not a process), say the authors, is meant, "a set of reasons, more or less fully-developed, that is, has been, or might be, offered to another person with the intention of persuading them, or some audience, to modify their beliefs, attitudes or behaviour."[7] With this view of argument, and argument as the subject of informal logic, we can see that Mill and Johnson and Blair have different points of departure. Whereas Mill takes logic's first job to be the ordering of one's own reasoning, the informal logicians are primarily concerned with the logic of arguments that can be used to influence the cognitive and public behavior of others.

The definition of informal logic has several components. It shares with Mill's definition the function of developing standards and ways to evaluate inferences or arguments, but the other components—argument interpretation and construction—are different. Significantly, however, informal logic is, in the first instance, applied to arguments in everyday discourse and, it is added, to natural language argumentation in the special disciplines.[8]

I.i.b.   Practical Importance

Of paramount importance to informal logic has been the desire to provide intellectual tools that would have greater practical value in dealing with natural language arguments, especially those within the cultural and political spheres, than formal logic is thought to offer. According to Leo Groarke,

> Informal logic is an attempt to develop a logic that can assess and analyze the arguments that occur in natural language ("everyday," "ordinary language") discourse . . . [T]he overriding aim has been a comprehensive account of argument that can explain and evaluate the arguments found in discussion, debate and disagreement as they manifest themselves in daily life—in social and political commentary; in news reports and editorials in the mass media (in newspapers, magazines, television, the World Wide Web, twitter, etc.); in advertising and corporate and governmental communications; and in personal exchange.[9]

As we know, Mill was a leading public intellectual in his day, participating in the discussion of important issues that affected mid-nineteenth-century Europe. He also meant the logic he developed to be a useful tool for everyone to use. He expressed the need people have to know logical principles when he wrote:

> A few individuals, by extraordinary genius, or by the accidental acquisition of a good set of intellectual habits, may work without principles in the same way, or nearly the same way, in which they would have worked if they had been in possession of principles. But the bulk of mankind require either to understand the theory of what they are doing, or to have rules laid down for them by those who have understood the theory.[10]

Hence, there is a widespread need for logic to assist "the bulk of mankind" in what Mill calls "the great business of life"[11]—making inferences. In this respect the intentions of Mill and the informal logicians coincide.

I.i.c.   Formal/Informal

When informal logicians declare that it is non-formal standards, criteria and procedures they will develop, this shows a determination to eschew the use of logical forms, and the techniques used to deploy them, as means of analyzing and evaluating arguments, as proposed, for example, by Copi.[12] No argument will be found either worthy or wanting by informal logic because of its logical form.

Informal logic depicts itself as being in competition with formal logic with respect to the very same natural language arguments, and then claims that it is better at the job of analyzing and evaluating those arguments. Mill, however, thinks that informal and formal standards do not at all apply to the same parts of the reasoning process. He differentiates the logic of truth, the means whereby new knowledge is gained, from the logic of consistency, which is concerned only with logical consistency. Inductive inferences are the subject of the former and deductive ones of the latter.[13] The overall evaluation of inferences essentially includes deductive steps and Mill thinks that the logic of deduction (or ratiocination, as he calls it) is formal syllogistic logic. The role of formal logic is subservient to inductive logic, however, since it is only used to check on the validity of real, inductive inferences by drawing out the implications of generalizations (see below I.iii.b.). But since the logic of truth relies essentially on inductive inferences, whatever strength these inferences may have will not be a function of their logical form. In this way Mill's logic is informal.

Although Mill recognized the importance of formal logic, according to Francis Sparshott he had no interest in the further development of the subject.

> Mill lived to see the beginnings of the great revival of formal logic that has marked so deeply the face of philosophy in the last century. In this revival he took no part . . . partly no doubt because formal logic is a young man's game. What is more surprising is that he did not approve of it. It was too complicated. Logic was a necessary art, and therefore should be plain and simple, as Whately's had been. The elaboration of formal calculi was a distraction from the serious business of the mind. But that, after all, is the sort of thing elderly savants usually say about what the bright young men are doing.[14]

This remark should be balanced with Mill's repeated advocacy of the benefits of learning formal logic at an early stage of education.[15]

I.i.d. Standards

By "standards" in the definition of informal logic is meant logical standards of argument goodness, and by "criteria" ways of recognizing argument goodness; procedures are steps taken in analysis and evaluation *en route* to determining whether criteria have been satisfied. The three most general criteria of argument goodness that informal logic has developed are that (a) the premises of an argument must be acceptable independently of the conclusion, and (b) they must be positively relevant to and (c) sufficient for, the conclusion.[16] In terms of sufficiency informal logicians recognize both deductive and non-deductive standards. Among the latter they include not only the inductive standard (measured in terms of probability), they also explore standards for presumptive and plausible reasoning.[17]

Here we see only partial agreement with Mill's ideas. He does not discuss relevance apart from sufficiency and this is understandable since irrelevant premises are insufficient, and sufficient premises are relevant.[18] And, although Mill does not initially present his logic as including a standard of premise acceptability there is reason to think that he is committed to such a standard. His view is that, ultimately, all real inferences are from particular observations, and since he thinks there are fallacies of observation, (non-observation and mal-observation; see below I.iii.e.), it seems he must hold that there are standards for premises. But the main concern Mill shares with informal logic is that of premise or evidence sufficiency. He recognizes only two sufficiency standards, the inductive and deductive standards.

I.i.e.   Relation to science

Mill's view is that logic consists of both a science and an art, and that the art should be informed by scientific knowledge of how we actually do reason. Two of the results of his analysis of the mind at work in reasoning stand out and should be mentioned. First, contra Whately, he denied that general premises are needed for reasoning, and second, he observed that, unwittingly, we may be affected by biases when we reason. If we are prone to biases, as Mill thinks we are, then science must inform us of ways to detect them, and the art of logic must develop precepts that can be used to justify inductive inferences in the face of the existence of biases. Mill's inclusion of empirical considerations about our reasoning processes in his definition of "logic" puts him in conflict with most modern logicians who are "concerned only with the correctness" of the product and not at all with the psychological processes that brings the product about.[19]

The informal logicians seem to share this modern trend of separating logic from psychology but they nevertheless admit the importance of empirical research on reasoning such as that done by Nisbett and Ross (1980) and Mercier and Sperber (2011). But, with the exception of Maurice Finocchiaro (1980, 2005), few of the leaders in the field show any special interest in basing informal logic directly on empirical research.

I.i.f.   Revised Definition of "Informal Logic"

There are some important similarities between Mill's conception of logic and Johnson and Blair's conception of informal logic. Both parties oppose the idea that there is only one logic, formal deductive logic, and they are both advocates for the practical, social utility of their logics. They are furthermore alike in that they each conceive their logics as containing several non-illative sub-departments. Mill includes the processes of naming and defining, as well as the science of reasoning, in his definition of logic. Informal logicians include procedures for the interpretation and construction of arguments, matters that many consider to lie outside the scope of logic. Both conceptions of logic are, one might say, overloaded, but at the heart of each of them are two aspects that are essential to logic.

The first of these is expressed by Johnson and Blair when they refer to *procedures for evaluation*. Mill speaks instead of *practical methods* when he writes that "the general relation between the available means and the end . . . will constitute the general scientific theory of the art, from which its practical methods will follow as corollaries."[20] From the point of view of logical methodology rules and precepts must be built into a structured, repeatable procedure, or method, which can be used to determine whether criteria have been satisfied. In that way the application of standards such as consistency and sufficiency becomes systematic and the reliability of logical judgments is increased.

The second thing that is essential to logic and is shared by Mill and the informal logicians is the concern with illative evaluation. By "illative evaluation" we limit logic to questions concerning the premise-conclusion relationship: "does the conclusion reached *follow* from the premises used or assumed?"[21] And by "informal" is intended the exclusion of logical forms from the means of evaluation. Informal logicians have developed several methods of informal illative evaluation, among them the fallacies method, the argument schemes method, the deductive reconstruction method and the method of informal warrants.[22] Given these considerations, we can propose a pared-down definition of "informal logic" as *the set of methods of nonformal illative evaluation*. (Questions of premise acceptability are not included in illative evaluation; they belong to argument evaluation, of which logical evaluation is only a part.)

Considering informal logic in this way gives us a focus for studying Mill's contributions to informal logic. Which methods of non-formal illative evaluation did he advocate? The canons of induction,[23] sometimes referred to as "Mill's Methods,"[24] would be one such method, but it is too well-known to both Mill scholars and informal logicians to bear being repeated here, so we will instead pass it over and concentrate instead on two other methods found in *A System of Logic*, the method of warrants and the fallacies method.

I.ii.   Mill's Methods of Informal Logic

I.ii.a.   Mill's Method of Warrants

Mill argued that valid syllogistic reasoning begged the question: one could not know the generalization (every valid syllogism has one) without first knowing the conclusion. Syllogisms, therefore, at best, contained only apparent inferences. Accordingly, Mill held that it was a necessary condition of real inferences that whatever is inferred has some content that is not included in that from which it is inferred.[25] He took "the universal type of the reasoning process" to be that "certain individuals have a given attribute; an individual or individuals resemble the former in certain other attributes; therefore they resemble them also in the given attribute."[26] This kind of reasoning is analogical; it proceeds from particular cases to other particular cases without the intervention of generalizations. Generalizations have no role as either premises or conclusions here. Nevertheless, Mill thought they played an essential role in the justification of inferences. How does this work?

Mill combines his empirical findings about the nature of the reasoning process with an informal version of the principle of Universal Generalization:[27] "If that which has held true in our past experience will therefore hold in time to come, it will hold not merely in some individual case, but in all cases of some given description."[28] An indefinite number of inferences can be drawn from the same observations provided they fit "some given description." But to hold this thesis is not to hold that a general proposition is inferred, insists Mill (even though he sometimes lapses into that manner of speaking). "A general truth is but an aggregate of particular truths," he wrote, "a comprehensive expression, by which an indefinite number of individual facts are affirmed or denied at once."[29] A general proposition is a short hand expression that compresses "The results of many observations and [particular] inferences" already made, it also gives "instructions for making innumerable [particular] inferences in unforeseen cases."[30] So, the *process of generalizing* includes an inference to "unforeseen cases," and the unforeseen cases are of particular inferences that can be made. There are thus two different roles for generalizations:

> [A] proposition might be considered in two different lights, as a portion of our knowledge of nature or as a memorandum for our guidance. Under the former or speculative aspect an affirmative general proposition is an assertion of a speculative truth, *viz.*, that whatever has a certain attribute has a certain other attribute. Under the other aspect it is to be regarded not as a part of our knowledge but as an aid for our practical exigencies, by enabling us when we see or learn that an object possesses one of the two attributes to infer that it possesses the other, thus employing the first attribute as a mark or evidence of the second.[31]

The first of the two roles for generalizations is the speculative (or scientific) role. In it general propositions are expressions of information, and as such they may be considered to be descriptive statements. The second role of general propositions, in which they serve as an "aid for our practical exigencies" (i.e., as a help to our difficulties in evaluating inferences), is their memorandum or normative role. Having made this distinction between two functions of general propositions, Mill holds that in making inferences, generalizations function like memoranda; they are rules for making inferences, and conclusions are not drawn from such formulae, but according to them.[32] In their role as memoranda, generalizations are not a part of the material of inferences; they are rather something that stands apart from them, as licenses, or warrants, of inferences.

Sticking with his thesis that all inferences are from particulars, Mill sees that there are two courses of reasoning that lie open to the inferrer: the one is a particular-to-particular pattern of inference (P-P) and the other is the "up-and-down" pattern of inference that involves generalization as an intermediate step (P-G-P).

> I am unable to see why we should be forbidden to take the shortest cut from these sufficient premises to the conclusion and constrained to travel the "high priori road" by the arbitrary fiat of logicians. I cannot perceive why it should be impossible to journey from one place to another unless we "march up a hill and then march down again." It may be the safest road, and there may be a resting place at the top of the hill, affording a commanding view of the surrounding country, but, for the mere purpose of arriving at our journey's end, our taking that road is perfectly optional; it is a question of time, trouble, and danger.[33]

Thus, we have a choice; we do *not* have to infer in accord with a generalization. If, however, we have hesitation about a P-P inference we can recast it in the up-and-down mode that involves a generalization in its speculative role. P-G-P is "the form into which [an inference] *must necessarily* be thrown to enable us to apply to it any test of its correct performance."[34] The evaluation becomes a two-part process. Consider this argument:

(1) <u>Bertrand Russell is a man.</u>
     Bertrand Russell is a mathematician.

When there is a practical exigency or a suspicion of error in our P-P inferences, Mill advises us to recast as a P-G-P inference. We must therefore re-construct the argument as follows to include a generalization, perhaps like this:

(2a) Pythagoras was a man and a mathematician & Euclid was a man and a mathematician & Theaetetus was a man and a mathematician & <u>Descartes was a man and a mathematician.</u>
      Any man is a mathematician.[35]

(2b) Any man is a mathematician.
      <u>Bertrand Russell is a man.</u>
      Bertrand Russell is a mathematician.

The real inference lies in the first half of the two-step reconstruction, the move from particular cases to the generalization that "any man is a mathematician," a proposition that is shorthand for "any other men, in addition to those observed, are mathematicians too." If the evidence in 2a is a reason to think that the man Russell is a mathematician, it is equally a reason to think that "any man is a mathematician." We then continue to the second step in the P-G-P inference, which is shown in 2b. Here the generalization takes the speculative role and accordingly the conclusion 2b follows from the premises of 2b syllogistically. Mill does not consider this to be an inference but rather a hermeneutical act, an act of interpretation.[36] He thinks that the rules of the syllogism are rules to guide such interpretations.

Mill's view is that although all reasoning is of the P-P kind, the only way to evaluate reasoning is to recast it in the P-G-P mode. The inference in Argument 1 is a bad one. How can Mill's approach account for this? The focus of evaluation is in the first part of the P-G-P reconstruction where our attention is directed to the acceptability of the generalization. Mill sees two advantages to interposing the generalization. The first is that general propositions present "a larger object to the imagination than any of the singular propositions which it contains,"[37] and we are therefore more likely to exercise caution when we reason on the P-G-P model. The other reason is that through the use of generalizations we may become aware of our own biases that can undermine the validity of our reasoning. In those inquiries in which we have an interest

> there is very little to prevent us from giving way to negligence, or to any bias which may affect our wishes or our imagination, and, under that influence, accepting insufficient evidence as sufficient . . . [I]f the premises are insufficient, and the general inference, therefore, groundless, it will comprise within it some fact or facts the reverse of which we already know to be true, and we shall thus discover the error in our generalization by a *reductio ad impossibile*.[38]

We are then to perform a *reductio* step in order to see whether there are any counter-instances to the generalization. A generalization may be taken as true unless, together with other propositions known to be true, it leads to a contradiction. In our present test case, because it is known that Bob Dylan is a man and not a mathematician, and the generalization "any man is a mathematician" implies that he is a mathematician, a contradiction follows. Thus, by the *reductio* step, the generalization, "Any man is a mathematician" is shown to be false and must be rejected as a formula according to which one could infer from "Russell is a man" to "Russell is a mathematician." This is how the P-G-P pattern of reasoning is a method of illative evaluation that can be used to test the correctness of an inference from one particular proposition to another.

In everyday life, however, generalizations are not without exception. They tend to be of the form "Most S are P." Mill is aware of this and takes the view that, "For practical guidance . . . [approximate generalizations] are often all we have to rely on."[39] However, this poses a problem for the P-G-P method in which just one counter-example to a generalization will sink an inference. If the *reductio* step is used in conjunction with approximate generalizations, then the method will be much more difficult to apply, and in many cases it will not be efficient because it will be uncertain what is needed to refute the approximate generalization.

This then is Mill's method of illative evaluation by the use of warrants. It is not wholly an informal method because the hermeneutical step must accord with the rules of formal syllogistic logic. This is an unfortunate restriction in two ways. First, because in many cases it is possible to reason deductively without the aid of formal rules, and so insisting on syllogistic correctness seems arbitrary. Second, because syllogistic logic is only a part of deductive logic, there will be arguments outside the reach of the method because their deductive steps cannot be evaluated by the limited scope of the syllogism.

I.ii.b. *Toulmin's Method*

One of the most celebrated texts in the informal logic literature is Stephen Toulmin's *The Uses of Argument* (1958). Like Mill, Toulmin is also concerned with the "practical business" of arguments[40] and his analysis of everyday arguments bears a strong resemblance to Mill's P-G-P method.

Both authors take arguments with only particular propositions as premises and conclusions as their paradigm cases; furthermore, Toulmin makes a distinction very similar to Mill's between the memorandum and formula roles of generalizations when he writes that

> . . . the same English sentence may serve a double function: it may be uttered . . . in one situation to convey a piece of information, in another to authorize a step in an argument, and even perhaps in some contexts to do both these things . . . [T]he nature of the distinction is hinted at if one contrasts the two sentences, "Whenever A, one has found that B" and "whenever A, one may take it that B."[41]

A sentence such as "Everyone born in Bermuda is a British subject" can serve a double function. It can report on empirical findings, and then it should be taken to have the form "All A are B." The sentence may also be understood as a legal statute, "whenever A, one may take it that B." The phrase "one may take it that B" means the same as "one may infer that B." Toulmin further parallels Mill's P-G-P model when he distinguishes "inferring from" and "inferring in accord with." Suppose we interpret major premises as warrants, then

> A "singular premiss" expresses a piece of information *from* which we are drawing a conclusion, a "universal premiss" now expresses, not a

piece of information at all, but a guarantee *in accordance with* which we can safely take the step from our datum to our conclusion.[42]

So, on Toulmin's view, as on Mill's, conclusions are drawn *from premises* (the data, particular propositions) *in accordance with a warrant* (hypothetical propositions, the "major premise"). Warrants are not additional data or information, Toulmin insists. They are not premises at all. Rather they are "rules, principles, inference-licenses"; they are "general, hypothetical statements, which can act as bridges, and authorize the sort of step to which our particular argument commits us"[43] and they often remain unstated.

Toulmin and Mill agree not only on the role of generalizations, they also use much of the same terminology. There are more similarities between the views but also important points of difference. Mill develops his views from an epistemological perspective, holding that induction plays the central role in generating warrants with the commands of positive law being an important exception.[44] Toulmin's view is developed from a jurisprudential model of argumentation[45] and he thinks that warrants are field-dependent, i.e., that how a warrant is established depends on what field or subject it belongs to.[46] But at the level of generality where we use informal, (for the most part) contingent warrants as a license or rule to support our inferences or arguments, Mill's anticipation of Toulmin's work is clear, and consequently his contribution to informal logic. It is a wonder, given Toulmin's interest in the history of ideas, that in *The Uses of Argument*, he makes no reference to *A System of Logic*.

I.ii.c.   Mill's Fallacies Method

The second of Mill's informal methods of illative evaluation to consider is the fallacies method. Informal logic is often identified with the study of fallacies because, although there are other methods, several of the early informal logic textbooks used a fallacies approach to teach argument evaluation.[47] Moreover, since the 1980s there has been a wealth of research not only on individual fallacies, but also on theories of fallacies. Distinguishing themselves from the scholastic tradition, Johnson and Blair have developed a new inventory of fallacies especially relevant to contemporary popular discourse as well as a new classification scheme. It was their classification of fallacies as arguments having either unacceptable premises, irrelevant premises or insufficient premises that led to the conception of a good argument satisfying all three of the criteria mentioned in I.i.c. Accordingly, Johnson and Blair define a fallacy as a failure to satisfy one of these criteria.[48] This innovation in the catalogue and classification of fallacies is another step in a series of such attempts dating back to Aristotle's *Sophistical Refutations*.

Mill's contribution to fallacy studies has been undervalued. This is due in part to a shift of interest within the study of logic away from the evaluation of natural language arguments (where knowledge of fallacies is useful) toward the construction of formal systems that are less concerned with natural language, and not in need of supplementation against error by a list of fallacies. Hence, what has lately, for many, been the most convenient access to Mill's *Logic*—Ernest Nagel's *John Stuart Mill's Philosophy of Scientific Method* (1950), an abridged edition of the work—omitted Book V ("On Fallacies") altogether on the ground that "only materials of subordinate interest have been excluded, and nothing essential for the understanding of Mill's thought has been eliminated."[49] More recently, Charles Hamblin, who, in *Fallacies* (1970), stirred the late twentieth-century revival of scholarly interest in the fallacies, passed lightly over Mill's contribution, although he did credit him with an original classificatory scheme.[50]

In the book on fallacies (Book V) Mill introduces the idea of a Philosophy of Error. It has two divisions, one considering the moral causes of error (those due to human nature) and the other considering the causes due to misestimation of evidence (the fallacies). Biases and indifference to truth belong in the first category of error, and Mill treats them as predisposing causes of fallacies. Mill's treatment of fallacies is historically valuable, not only because he broadens the concept to include inductive fallacies, but also because of the wide range of non-trivial examples taken from science, religion and philosophy he uses when illustrating each of the fallacies. He also anticipated one of the modern developments in fallacy theory, to wit:

> Fallacies of Inference, or erroneous conclusions from supposed evidence, must be subdivided according to the nature of the apparent evidence from which the conclusions are drawn: or (what is the same thing) according to the particular kind of sound argument which the fallacy in question simulates.[51]

According to this view on which fallacies have a semblance to good arguments, there are argument kinds that can have both good and bad instantiations: some *post hoc ergo propter hoc* arguments are strong, some are fallacies; some appeals to authority are legitimate, others are fallacies. Mill wrote that "we never really know what a thing is, unless we are also able to give a sufficient account of its opposite."[52] So, our knowledge of fallacies will be advanced by knowing the corresponding good instances of the argument kind, and vice versa. This is an idea that has been worked out recently in some detail, especially by Douglas Walton.[53] It has the consequence that the fallacies are more than archaic curiosities inherited from the scholastic tradition: they exhibit the pathology of good arguments gone bad.

In the *Sophistical Refutations* Aristotle divided thirteen fallacies into two groups, those dependent on language and those not dependent on language. Those fallacies and their division remained the mainstay of fallacy scholarship until Jeremy Bentham made up a new list of political fallacies, which had four groups: fallacies of Authority, Danger, Delay and Confusion,[54] a classification thought lacking in logical sense by Whately, who proposed his own twofold division between logical and non-logical (material) fallacies just two years later in 1826.[55] Mill rejected Bentham's way of going about it as being largely arbitrary and also Whately's classification because it was too narrowly concerned with errors of ratiocination. For Mill, a fallacy occurs when apparent sufficient evidence is mistaken for sufficient evidence, in either the deductive or inductive part of the reasoning process, or the fault consists in failing to reason.[56] So, Mill is among those who think that having a misleading appearance is a necessary condition of being a fallacy. Interestingly, however, he does not subscribe to the requirement that all fallacies are inferences or arguments. His own five-fold classification of fallacies has a category of *a priori* fallacies. These consist of allegedly self-warranting kinds of beliefs both of the philosophical kind (there are souls) as well as folk beliefs (there are ghosts), held without benefit of inference.[57]

The rest of the Millian fallacies do involve inferences. They are divided into two classes, one in which the evidence is taken to be distinctly conceived and one in which it is indistinctly conceived. The former reflects the P-G-P pattern of reasoning, and it has three sub-classes. Fallacies of observation can arise due to non-observation or mal-observation, i.e., because of a failure to observe other instances that should have been observed, or to observing something as something it is not. Fallacies of generalization are mistaken inferences from particulars to general statements (e.g., *post hoc*, faulty analogy and hasty generalization). Fallacies of ratiocination are those that can occur in the deductive part of the reasoning process and would thus include undistributed middle, and the fallacy of four terms (Mill's view of deduction did not go beyond the syllogism). In the category of fallacies of evidence indistinctly conceived, also called fallacies of confusion, Mill places many of the Aristotelian fallacies, a move the Philosopher himself might not have objected to since he offers that all his fallacies can be seen as failures to distinctly understand the concept of refutation.[58]

No one before Mill had discussed fallacies in the same detail and with the same acuteness that he did. The fallacies he thought important were, despite his assurances to the contrary, connected to his epistemology and logic, and thus stand outside the tradition that sees fallacies as primarily having application in the field of popular discourse. What Hamblin said of the average modern textbook treatments of fallacies, that it is "debased, worn out, and dogmatic . . . [and] incredibly tradition-bound, yet lacking in logic and in historical sense alike"[59] can hardly be said of Mill's treatment of the fallacies.[60]

To reconstruct the knowledge of fallacies as a Millian method of illative evaluation we consider the logician armed with a list of defining conditions of all Mill's fallacies who sets about comparing each of the arguments before her to each of the definitions on the list. If any of the arguments match one of the fallacies defined on the list, the logician rejects the argument. That is the method. Of course, as one becomes more experienced in understanding arguments, and has internalized the defining characteristics of the fallacies, one uses the method more fluidly, quickly passing over unproblematic arguments. The fallacies method has great value in that it can keep one from accepting a fallacious argument; but it also has a serious drawback: it can only render negative judgments, and since the list of fallacies may not be complete, some bad arguments may go undetected. This is why some logicians think it best suited as a supplementary method, as Mill intended it.

II. MILL'S CONTRIBUTION TO ARGUMENTATION THEORY

II.i. Introduction

Mill does not have a theory of argumentation in the same explicit way in which he has a logic. The term "theory of argumentation," he observed, was traditionally used for that part of logic that treated of the syllogism.[61] The way the term is used in contemporary discussions is much closer to what Mill meant by "rhetoric" when he said that "the communication of . . . [our logical thinking] . . . to others falls under the consideration of Rhetoric, in the large sense in which that art was conceived by the ancients."[62] But there is not universal agreement nowadays that rhetoric and argumentation theory are one and the same thing. Although some do take an exclusively rhetorical approach to argumentation, most think that the emerging field of argumentation theory is an amalgamation of several sub-disciplines, including logic, linguistics, dialectics and rhetoric.[63] Here we will briefly review two contemporary approaches to argumentation, one by Alvin Goldman and the other by Frans van Eemeren and Rob Grootendorst, and show how Mill's work has affinities with both approaches.

II.ii. Truth and argumentation

II.ii.a. *Goldman on Argumentation*

In *Knowledge in a Social World* (1999), Alvin Goldman develops an approach to epistemology which is social and veritistic. It is social rather than individual or Cartesian because it focuses on the social paths to knowledge and it is veritistic (truth oriented) because it is concerned with knowledge and its contraries, error and ignorance, rather than mere belief or acceptance. The crucial question for social epistemology is "which [social] practices have a comparably favourable impact on knowledge as contrasted with error and ignorance?"[64] One such social practice (deserving a whole chapter) is argumentation, which is defined as follows:

> If a speaker presents an argument to an audience, in which he asserts and defends the conclusion by appeal to the premises, I call this activity *argumentation*. More specifically, this counts as *monological* argumentation, a stretch of argumentation with a single speaker . . . *[D]ialogical*

> argumentation . . . [is when] . . . two or more speakers discourse with one
> another, taking opposite sides of the issue over the truth of the conclusion.[65]

This view of argumentation is broad in the sense that it includes both mono-
logical and dialogical argumentation. Dialogical argumentation is a two-or-
more-person activity in which there is a protagonist presenting his or her
argument and a critic making responses. The veritistic value of this activity
accrues primarily to the participants in the dialogue as they either inform or
correct each other. This may be distinguished from a kindred kind, debate,
in which dialogical argumentation is done for the sake, at least partly, of an
audience; it has increased possibilities for the spread of truth since people
can benefit from overhearing other people argue with each other.[66] The normative dimension of argumentation enters through a set of fourteen rules
Goldman develops for how argumentation can profitably serve the end of
knowledge. The last of these "folk rules" is that

> When there are existing or foreseeable criticisms of one's main argu-
> ment, a speaker should embed that argument in an extended argumen-
> tative discourse that contains replies to as many of these (important)
> criticisms as possible.[67]

Rules like these are not rules of logic but rather rules that direct speakers on
how to argue when the practice of argumentation is in the service of increasing knowledge.

Goldman distinguishes arguments from argumentation on the basis that
arguments are sets of sentences or propositions considered independently
of speakers and audiences whereas argumentation is the endorsement or
criticism of arguments by speakers.[68] This way of marking the difference
points to a way of telling the difference between logic and argumentation
theory: logic is about arguments, argumentation theory is about argumentation. When, above (in I.i.a.), we considered Johnson and Blair's definition of "informal logic" we noticed that they did not clearly distinguish
arguments from the use of arguments to affect others. Many informal logicians share this ambivalence: they straddle the argument-argumentation
divide.

II.ii.b.   Mill on Truth

Mill's *Logic* is an example of what Goldman would consider an individual
veritistic epistemology, but chapter 2 of *On Liberty* fits his conception of
a social epistemology. In this celebrated chapter Mill is concerned with the
promotion of truth and the avoidance of error through the means of unrestricted argumentation with others, seeing it as necessary for the testing and
maintaining of true beliefs.

Let us consider argumentation as an art on Mill's terms.[69] As such it will
have a purpose, rules and be informed by sciences, and it will rest ultimately

on the Principle of Utility for its normative dimension. But, it may be thought that utility will sometimes trump truth, and so the purpose of argumentation would not always be the promotion of truth. Mill resists the argument that because some false beliefs could have great importance to society (utility) they should be held immune from free discussions, insisting that "the truth of an opinion is part of its utility,"[70] and that ultimately, there is no conflict between truth and utility.

Although Goldman and Mill share the promotion of truth and avoidance of error as the value of argumentation, we must note an important difference. Goldman limits himself to giving an account of factual argumentation, concerned with beliefs rather than with what to do.[71] In *On Liberty* Mill takes a wider view: all subjects, scientific as well as "morals, religion, politics, social relations and the business of life" can and should be the subject of argumentation.[72] Thus the role of argumentation that Mill develops in *On Liberty* has wider scope than does Goldman's epistemological argumentation.

II.iii.   The Concept of "Discussion"

II.iii.a.   *Van Eemeren and Grootendorst on Argumentation*

The Pragma-dialectical approach to argumentation has its roots not in epistemology but in discourse analysis. As communication the main function of argumentation is to convince people by overcoming their doubt regarding a position, or their doubt about the criticism of a position. The theory is comprehensive and constitutes an expanding research program as can be seen from van Eemeren and Grootendorst's *A Systematic Theory of Argumentation* (2004). In this overview we can only mention two aspects of the theory. The one is that it puts convincing by argumentation in the service of resolving interpersonal disagreements, rather than promoting truth; the other distinguishing feature that Pragma-dialectics has developed is the concept of a *critical discussion* as an ideal model, useful both for the analysis and evaluation of argumentation. By this model "all argumentation is regarded as part of a critical discussion between parties that are prepared to abide by an agreed discussion procedure."[73] Used heuristically the model analyzes argumentation as falling into four stages: the confrontation stage, the opening stage, the argumentation stage and the resolution stage. Each of these stages is governed by certain norms that, taken together, constitute a set of rules that provide the standard for the evaluation of argumentation. Two of the ten rules are:

> (R1) Discussants may not prevent each other from advancing standpoints or from calling standpoints into question.[74]

> (R9) Inconclusive defenses of standpoints may not lead to maintaining these standpoints, and conclusive defenses of standpoints may not lead to maintaining expressions of doubt concerning these standpoints.[75]

Clearly these are not rules of logic, but rules for how argumentation should be conducted in the interest of resolving disagreements.

II.iii.b.   Mill on Discussions

The concept of "discussion" is also central to Mill's views on argumentation as these can be gleaned from *On Liberty*. His views are not as sharply presented on this question as is the Pragma-dialectical position, but we can see that in using the term "discussion," Mill is signaling a certain attitude toward argumentation. "Discussion" conjures up images of civility, politeness, turn-taking and good will; it does not connote violence, deceit or coercion, but rather a certain openness, tentativeness and bilateralism. And although discussions can be manipulated by people of ill will, Mill is advocating "free and equal discussions,"[76] "free discussions,"[77] which must also be "fair discussions,"[78] and "fair and thorough discussions."[79] In urging that discussions should have these qualities, Mill is not only rejecting authoritarian views that would make discussions pointless, he is prescribing a mode of intellectual intercourse that is a means of testing ideas as well as a vehicle of persuasion. Thus, his views of argumentation share something with both Goldman's veritistic approach and van Eemeren and Grootendorst's disagreement resolution approach.

Interestingly, for Mill, we should not equate "discussion" and "debate." Several authors have made the assimilation. "In his classic book *On Liberty*, John Stuart Mill gives . . . his theory of debate," say Woods, Irvine and Walton.[80] Earlier Willmoore Kendall had criticized Mill for presenting an unworkable model for society. "Mill's proposals," he wrote, "have as one of their tacit premises a false conception of the nature of society . . . They assume that society is, so to speak, a *debating club* devoted above all to the pursuit of truth, and capable therefore of subordinating itself—and all other considerations, goods, and goals—to that pursuit."[81] We should be wary of these readings of Mill since the word "debate" does not occur in any chapter of *On Liberty*, *Utilitarianism* or *The Subjection of Women*, works in which Mill practices and comments on argumentation. However, as we know from his autobiography,[82] Mill was well familiar with debates, acknowledging his own participation in some and using the term "debate" freely when referring to the activities of others. Why then is the term so strangely absent from Mill's popular and influential essays? According to Helen McCabe, Mill grew disenchanted with the model of persuasion he had learned from his father, James Mill, for several reasons. After his "mental crisis" in the mid-1820s, and especially after an unhappy debate experience with a close friend, Mill came to believe that argumentative debate made people associate changing their mind with the feeling of defeat, and thus made them "through misplaced pride, cling to their existing beliefs."[83] Moreover, debate allowed no chance of compromise or complementarity as an outcome, a possibility Mill thought should always be on the table.[84]

There is, of course, a difference between formal and informal debate, but Mill seems to have been backing away from even a relaxed kind of debating format as a means of persuasion. We are then not to think of Millian discussions as being debates, but rather as talk-exchanges in which participants can change their minds or modify their views in response to arguments and argument criticisms without feeling that they are in competition with their discussants.[85]

II.iv.   Functions of Argumentation

II.iv.a.   *Mill's Argumentation Practices*

Mill does not discuss argumentation (or rhetoric, as he might call it) as an art in the way that he gives a detailed treatment of logic and ethics. Yet, he has definite and identifiable views about how argumentation should be done to best advantage. We can find those views by extracting them from his argumentation practice, in particular those in which he shows a self-awareness of being engaged in argumentation. It eventuates that he had two different but related roles for argumentation; the one is the persuasion of others, the second is the justification of one's own beliefs.

A recent biography of Mill comments that, "Mill rarely wrote merely for the sake of philosophical exactness. He wrote, especially in his essays, to persuade."[86]And Helen McCabe remarks that "Mill wrote primarily for a public audience, with the intent of affecting political outcomes through mobilizing public opinion either to bring weight to bear on elected politicians, or to change social mores."[87] This is most evident in three of his best known essays. In *The Subjection of Women*, chapter 1, Mill is trying to persuade lawmakers to change the laws that make women subordinate to men. In chapter 2 of *On Liberty* he writes to persuade society that it should not interfere with the freedom of thought and discussion of its members. *Utilitarianism* is addressed to a narrower audience, one interested in philosophical questions about the foundations of morality, and Mill's aim there is to persuade his readers of the truth of the utilitarian theory; but the general pattern of argumentation here employed by Mill is much the same as it is in the other essays.

These three chapters are all paradigms of extended argumentation. The general pattern that emerges is that Mill spends most of his efforts on showing that objections to his position can be refuted. He even says, "when we turn to subjects infinitely more complicated, to morals, religion, politics, social relations, and the business of life, three-fourths of the arguments for every disputed opinion consist in dispelling the appearances which favour some opinion different from it."[88] He is thus self-aware of his practice of putting much more effort into dealing with objections than putting forward supporting arguments. We must ask why this is his argumentation practice.

Mill would have known that Whately (whom he admired for his *Elements of Logic*) had revived the legal notions of presumption and burden of proof as part of his analysis of argumentation in his *Elements of Rhetoric*.[89] Moreover, Mill had a legal turn of mind. He is aware that there is a presumption for freedom and against restrictions; hence there is a presumption for the views that he defends in *On Liberty*. And there is a presumption for equality and against inequality, and so there is a presumption for the view he maintains in *The Subjection of Women*. Yet popular opinion was opposed to these presumptions. Hence, if the objections to these views that sustain the prejudice against them can be turned away or softened, then the theses upheld by Mill, having presumption in their favor, would be left standing and would, in strictness, not require any argument at all in their support. Nevertheless, Mill believes that supporting arguments are also wanted, but they take up less of the overall argumentation than does the dealing with objections. As for why this is the general pattern in the second chapter of *Utilitarianism*, we must have another answer, for it cannot be said that there is a presumption in favor of utilitarianism. Mill does give an argument in support of the Principle of Utility,[90] but he cautions that "questions of ulti- mate ends are not amenable to direct proof"[91] and he knew that his argu- ment in favor of utilitarianism would not suffice unless the entrenched views opposing it were shown to be mistaken; hence, to make the view acceptable, he puts his efforts into overcoming objections to it in chapter 2. Thus, Mill's method of argumentation has a general pattern which puts most of the labor into answering arguments that are obstacles to the view proposed.

II.iv.b.   *Socratic Function of Argumentation*

It is clear from *On Liberty* that persuading others is not the only function of argumentation. It also has a self-regarding function requiring each person to test their opinions through argumentation with others. One should not commit to an opinion until one has proactively taken extensive steps to see whether or not it can withstand criticism and objections.

> The steady habit of correcting and completing his own opinion by col- lating it with those of others, so far from causing doubt and hesitation in carrying it into practice, is the only stable foundation for a just reli- ance on it: for, being cognizant of all that can, at least obviously, be said against him, and having taken up his position against all gainsayers knowing that he has sought for objections and difficulties, instead of avoiding them, and has shut out no light which can be thrown upon the subject from any quarter—he has a right to think his judgment better than that of any person, or any multitude, who have not gone through a similar process.[92]

Here Mill is using "right" in an epistemic sense and pointing to the correla- tive obligations that comes with having such a right, which are, accord- ing to Mill, that one has to proactively go looking for objections to one's view and that one must be able to answer them. We are reminded here of Socrates' quest to find the meaning of what the Delphic oracle had said to him by conducting an exhaustive list of interviews with the wise, one person after another, the poets and the craftsmen.[93] This is a very high standard by which most of us would have a right to only very few opinions. Later in the same chapter, Mill seems to soften the demand a little when he says that we ought to be able to defend at least against the "common objections."[94]

In summary, we see that Mill sees a dual function for argumentation: it is an activity for the persuasion both of others and self. The method is to support a thesis, not only by giving arguments for it but also by dealing with objections that are opposed to it. Addressing and defusing relevant objections serves a dual purpose. First, it weakens the normative support perceived to be against the thesis; second, it has an eroding effect on the entrenched biases that make people hold to their views even as supporting evidence is washed away. Addressing this psychological concern is a necessary factor in persuasion. When the argumentation is Socratic, it is also a way of uncovering our own entrenched biases and prejudices.

II.v. Argumentation and Error

II.v.a. Error and On Liberty

Although Mill seldom makes explicit mention of fallacies in *On Liberty*, one of the dominant themes of the chapter on freedom of thought and discussion is the detection and prevention of error. In fact, in that chapter, the word "error" (or "erroneous") occurs twenty-five times. Interestingly, our neglect of Mill's work on fallacies, thinks Frederick Rosen, has caused us to overlook the continuity of the *Logic* and *On Liberty*.

> It is clear from the opening paragraphs [of *On Liberty*] that Mill's philosophy of error was lurking in the background. The pursuit of truth, which liberty would facilitate, was inconceivable for Mill without the presence and beneficial use of error. If liberty was denied, an erroneous opinion could not be exchanged for a true one; but if an original opinion was true, the denial of liberty meant that one could not benefit from "the clearer perception and livelier impression of truth, produced with a collision with error" ... The study of fallacies was one important way of encouraging the beneficial dialogue between truth and error, which enabled truth ultimately to replace error in inference, deduction and in argument generally.[95]

Rosen takes the continuity of the *Logic* and *On Liberty* a step further. Whereas Mill, in the *Logic*, held that "the bulk of mankind require either to understand the theory of what they are doing, or to have rules laid down for them,"[96] in *On Liberty* his concern is with enabling ordinary human beings to detect and correct error. It is indispensable, he wrote "to enable average human beings to attain the mental stature which they are capable of."[97] Although few will be great philosophers, all human beings can learn to correct errors and in that way, at least, they can defend themselves against spurious views.[98] So, that we are corrigible, and that we can learn to detect errors and fallacies, makes everyone a possible contributor to the elimination of falsehoods. Thus the "opportunity of exchanging error for truth" may be seen as depending on two conditions: unrestricted access to information, and logical knowledge, including knowledge of the fallacies. In this way Rosen finds a thematic connection between *A System of Logic* and *On Liberty*.

Looking at it this way, we can think of the *Liberty* as taking the *reductio* step in the P-G-P method to the limit: not only do we have to consider any exceptions within our ken in order to avoid error, we have to be free through unrestricted inquiry to find any exceptions to our generalizations that there might be. As Toulmin remarks, "general ethical truths can aspire at best to hold good in the absence of effective counter-claims."[99]

II.v.b.   Errors of Argumentation

The fallacies in the *Logic* are (excepting those of simple inspection) fallacies of inference and argument. Insofar as arguments are components of argumentation, fallacies in arguments will also be fallacies of argumentation. But, we might ask, does Mill identify any errors that belong uniquely to argumentation? I will mention just three.

Most obvious is the *argumentum ad verecundiam*, originally identified by John Locke and now known as "appeal to authority." Locke observed that authority was sometimes used in lieu of "proofs drawn from any of the foundations of knowledge and probability" in order to get people to agree.[100] Mill's chapter 2 of *On Liberty* is an extended critique of the use of authority to this end. That an authority declares something to be true is not a guarantee that it is true and, by restricting discussion, authorities prevent the knowing by others of the grounds of both true and false opinions, something that has significant negative implications for both the welfare of society and individuals. When Locke's "kind of argument" was used unfairly, thought Whately,[101] it was a fallacy. Since then it has become the standard practice to distinguish legitimate and fallacious appeals to authority. There are several senses of "authority" and it can on occasion be appropriate to respond positively to one of them. Goldman, for example, and others do not see the *ad verecundiam* as always fallacious when "authority" has the sense of expertise.[102] Mill's objection is to the use of political authority in matters epistemological, but he does not call the error a fallacy.

Similarly, Mill has reservations about *argumentum ad populum*. "Popular opinions, on subjects not palpable to sense, are often true," he said, "but seldom or never the whole Truth."[103] Both the appeals to authority and popular opinion are questionable ways of supporting a thesis but, more importantly, they are ways of getting interlocutors to abandon their epistemic obligations to test their beliefs through argumentation with others. Using such arguments is an error and antithetical to the high standard Mill set in *On Liberty*.

As a last example of an error of argumentation, we return to Mill's remarks regarding the shifting of the burden of proof (II.iv.a.). In his discussion of the situation in which he finds himself when he wants to argue the case for women's equality, he remarks that it is unfair that the burden of proof is placed on him because, since there is a presumption for the view he is arguing, the burden should be on those who think the rights of women should be restricted.[104] The error in argumentation here is that of failing to appreciate where the burden of proof lies.[105]

There are other kinds of moves in argumentation that Mill thinks are errors, and unproductive of truth. We cannot catalogue them here and they must await another occasion.

III. CONCLUSION

We have contrasted Mill's conception of logic with that of two leading informal logicians, and found that their views are alike in two important respects: the focus on illative evaluation and the commitment to non-formal methods. Mill contributed significantly to the articulation and development of two of the most widely used methods of informal logic, the method of warrants and the fallacies method. His contributions have been overlooked, or hastily dismissed, by those who should have acknowledged them.

We also found that Mill had views about argumentation similar to those of some contemporary argumentation theorists. His focus on the value of truth as an outcome of argumentation fits remarkably well with Goldman's veritistic approach, and his concern with discussions as the vehicle for justification of opinions has many similarities with the theory of argumentation being proposed by van Eemeren and Grootendorst. Finally, through the work of Fred Rosen, we are made to see that the concern for truth and avoidance of error at the heart of the *Logic* is also what drives the approach to argumentation in *On Liberty*. Mill's *Logic* and essays are a rich vein to mine for both those interested in the history of ideas as well as those developing theories of informal logic and theories of argumentation.[106]

NOTES

1. Mill (1843, CW: VII.6–9). All references to Mill's works are to the authoritative edition of *Collected Works of John Stuart Mill* (Mill, 1963–1991—cited as CW, followed by volume and page number), unless otherwise indicated.
2. Mill (1843, CW: VII.12).

3. Mill (1843, CW: VII.4).
4. Mill (1843, CW: VII.6).
5. Johnson and Blair (2002: 358). Compare: "We believe that informal logic is best understood as the normative study of argument. It is the area of logic which seeks to develop standards, criteria and procedures for the interpretation, evaluation and construction of arguments and argumentation used in natural language" (Blair and Johnson, 1987: 148). Notice here the absence of "non-formal" and the presence of "argument."
6. Johnson and Blair (2002: 359–60).
7. Johnson and Blair (2002: 361).
8. Johnson and Blair (2002: 359).
9. Groarke (2011).
10. Mill (1843, CW: VII.11).
11. Mill (1843, CW: VII.9).
12. Copi (1961: 253ff.).
13. Mill (1843, CW: VII.206–08).
14. Sparshott (1978: xvii).
15. See (i) Mill (1843, CW: VII.13–14), (ii) Mill's *Autobiography*, chapter 1, paragraph 12 (1873, CW: I.21, 23), as well as (iii) references to Mill's "Inaugural Address" in Rosen (2006: 122).
16. Johnson and Blair (2002: 370).
17. See, for instance, Walton (1992).
18. Informal logicians find the relevance criterion useful, since insufficient premises may still be relevant.
19. Copi (1961: 6).
20. Mill (1843, CW: VIII.947).
21. Copi (1961: 6).
22. Hansen (2012).
23. Mill (1843, CW: VII.388–433).
24. See, e.g., Copi (1961: 363).
25. Mill (1843, CW: VII.172–75).
26. Mill (1843, CW: VII.202–03).
27. See, e.g., Copi (1961: 318–19).
28. Mill (1843, CW: VII.196).
29. Mill (1843, CW: VII.186).
30. Mill (1843, CW: VII.187).
31. Mill (1843, CW: VII.180); see also Mill (1843, CW: VII.97–99).
32. Mill (1843, CW: VII.193–95).
33. Mill (1843, CW: VII.187).
34. Mill (1843, CW: VII.202; italics added). See also Mill (1843, CW: VII.198): "An induction from particulars to generals, followed by a syllogistic process from those generals to other particulars, is a form in which we may always state our reasonings if we please. It is not a form in which we *must* reason, but it is a form in which we *may* reason and into which it is indispensable to throw our reasoning when there is any doubt of its validity . . ."
35. Mill prefers to express generalizations with "any" as a quantifier, rather than "all" or "every" because "any" is better at keeping with the idea that it is only particulars that are inferred. See Mill (1843, CW: VII.198n).
36. Mill (1843, CW: VII.194).
37. Mill (1843, CW: VII.196).
38. Mill (1843, CW: VII.197).
39. Mill (1843, CW: VII.592). See also Ryan (1970: 19).
40. Toulmin (1958: 95).
41. Toulmin (1958: 99).

42. Toulmin (1958: 114; see also 128).
43. Toulmin (1958: 98).
44. Mill (1843, CW: VII.193–95).
45. Toulmin (1958: 7).
46. Toulmin (1958: 112).
47. Johnson and Blair (2002: 370).
48. Johnson and Blair (2002: 370).
49. Nagel (1950: xlix).
50. Hamblin (1970: 48).
51. Mill (1843, CW: VIII.741).
52. Mill (1843, CW: VII.735).
53. See Walton (2005).
54. Bentham (1824).
55. Whately (1826: III.§4).
56. Mill (1843, CW: VIII.737–39).
57. Mill (1843, CW: VII.746–47).
58. Aristotle (*Soph Ref.* 168a18).
59. Hamblin (1970, 12).
60. It isn't possible to review Mill's work on the fallacies in detail in the present chapter. The reader is referred especially to Rosen (2006) for an excellent overview.
61. Mill (1843, CW: VII.5).
62. Mill (1843, CW: VII.6).
63. See, e.g., Tindale (1999) and van Eemeren and Grootendorst (2004).
64. Goldman (1999: 5).
65. Goldman (1999: 131).
66. Goldman (1999: 131).
67. Goldman (1999: 144).
68. Goldman (1999: 132).
69. See Mill (1843, CW: VIII.943–45).
70. Mill (1859, CW: XVIII.233).
71. Goldman (1999: 132).
72. Mill (1859, CW: XVIII.244–45).
73. Van Eemeren and Grootendorst (2004: 16).
74. Van Eemeren and Grootendorst (2004: 190).
75. Van Eemeren and Grootendorst (2004: 195).
76. Mill (1859, CW: XVIII.224).
77. Mill (1859, CW: XVIII.233, 246, 247, 250).
78. Mill (1859, CW: XVIII.234, 258).
79. Mill (1859, CW: XVIII.242).
80. Woods, Irvine and Walton (2004: 29).
81. Kendall (1960: 36).
82. "Debate" does occur over two dozen times in Mill's *Autobiography* (1873), especially in chapters 4 and 5.
83. McCabe (2014: 47).
84. Mill (1859, CW: XVIII.257–58).
85. In this paragraph, I am much indebted to McCabe.
86. Reeves (2007: 118–19).
87. McCabe (2014: 38).
88. Mill (1859, CW: VII.244–45).
89. Whately (1846: I.iii.2).
90. Mill (1861, CW: X.234).
91. Mill (1861, CW: X.207).
92. Mill (1859, CW: XVIII.232).

93. Plato (*Apology*: 21b–23c).
94. Mill (1859, CW: XVIII.244).
95. Rosen (2006: 129). See, Mill (1859, CW: XVIII.228–9)
96. Mill (1843, CW: VII.11).
97. Mill (1859, CW: XVIII.243).
98. Rosen 2006 (131).
99. Toulmin (1958: 109).
100. Locke (1690: IV.xvii 22).
101. Whately (1826: III.§15).
102. Goldman (1999: 150–51)
103. Mill (1859, CW: XVIII.252).
104. Mill (1869, CW: XXI.261–62).
105. Pragma-dialectics holds that illegitimate shiftings of the burden of proof is a fallacy (van Eemeren and Grootendorst, 2002: 140–41). The theory, however, subscribes to a very broad notion of fallacy.
106. I am grateful to J. A. Blair, R. H. Johnson and C. W. Tindale, three of my colleagues in the Centre for Research in Reasoning, Argumentation and Rhetoric (CRRAR) at the University of Windsor, to M. A. Finocchiaro and to the editor of this volume, Antis Loizides, for their suggested corrections to an earlier draft of this essay.

REFERENCES

Bentham, J. (1824) *The Handbook of Political Fallacies*, H. A. Larrabee (ed.) (New York: Harper and Brothers, 1962).
Blair, J. A., and Johnson, R. H. (1987) "The Current State of Informal Logic," *Informal Logic* 11: 147–51.
Copi, I. (1961) *Introduction to Logic*, 2nd ed. (New York: MacMillan).
Finocchiaro, M. (1980) *Galileo and the Art of Reasoning* (Dordrecht: Reidel).
———. (2005) *Arguments about Arguments* (New York: Cambridge University Press).
Goldman, A. (1999) *Knowledge in a Social World* (Oxford: Clarendon Press).
Groarke, L. (2011) "Informal Logic," *The Stanford Encyclopedia of Philosophy*, E. N. Zalta (ed.), Spring 2013 Edition (http://plato.stanford.edu/archives/spr2013/entries/logic-informal).
Hamblin, C. L. (1970) *Fallacies* (London: Methuen).
Hansen, H. V. (2012) "An Enquiry into the Methods of Informal Logic," in H. J. Ribeiro (ed.) *Inside Arguments: Logic and the Study of Argumentation* (Newcastle upon Tyne: Cambridge Scholars Publishing): 101–16.
Johnson, R. H.; Blair, J. A. (1983) *Logical Self-Defence*, 2nd ed. (Toronto: McGraw-Hill Ryerson).
———. (2002) "Informal Logic and the Reconfiguration of Logic," in D. M. Gabbay, R. H. Johnson, H. J. Ohlbach and J. Woods (eds.) *Handbook of the Logic of Argument and Inference: The Turn towards the Practical* (Amsterdam: Elsevier): 339–96.
Kendall, W. (1960) "The 'Open Society' and its Fallacies," in P. Radcliff (ed.) *Limits of Liberty* (Belmont: Wadsworth): 27–42.
Locke, J. (1690) *An Essay Concerning Human Understanding*. [Widely reprinted.]
McCabe, H. (2014) "John Stuart Mill's Philosophy of Persuasion," *Informal Logic* 34 (1): 38-61.
Mercier, H.; Sperber D. (2011) "Why Do Humans Reason? Arguments for an Argumentative Theory," *Behavioral and Brain Sciences* 34: 57–111.

Mill, J. S. (1843) *A System of Logic, Ratiocinative and Inductive: Being a Connected View of the Principles of Evidence and the Methods of Scientific Investigation*, in vols. VII and VIII (1974) of Mill (1963–1991).

———. (1859) *On Liberty*, in vol. XVIII (1977) of Mill (1963–1991).

———. (1861) *Utilitarianism*, in vol. X (1969) of Mill (1963–1991).

———. (1869) *The Subjection of Women*, in vol. XXI (1984) of Mill (1963–1991).

———. (1873) *Autobiography*, in vol. I (1981) of Mill (1963–1991).

———. (1963–1991) *Collected Works of John Stuart Mill*, F.E.L. Priestly (gen. ed.), and subsequently J. M. Robson, 33 vols. (London/Toronto: Routledge and Kegan Paul/University of Toronto Press).

Nagel, E., ed. (1950) *John Stuart Mill's Philosophy of Scientific Method* (New York: Hafner).

Nisbett, R.; Ross, L. (1980) *Human Inference* (Englewood Cliffs: Prentice Hall).

Reeves, R. (2007) *John Stuart Mill: Victorian Firebrand* (London: Atlantic Books).

Rosen, F. (2006) "The Philosophy of Error and the Liberty of Thought: J. S. Mill on Logical Fallacies," *Informal Logic* 26: 121–47.

Ryan, A. (1970) *The Philosophy of John Stuart Mill* (London: MacMillan).

Sparshott, F. E. (1978) "Introduction," in J.M. Robson (ed.), *Collected Works of John Stuart Mill*, vol. XI (London/Toronto: Routledge and Kegan Paul/ University of Toronto Press): vii–lxxvi.

Tindale, C. W. (1999) *Acts of Arguing* (Albany: State University of New York Press).

Toulmin, S. E. (1958) *The Uses of Argument* (Cambridge: Cambridge University Press).

Van Eemeren, F. H.; Grootendorst R. (2004) *A Systematic Theory of Argumentation* (Cambridge: Cambridge University Press).

Walton, D. (1992) *Plausible Argument in Everyday Conversation* (Albany: State University of New York Press).

———. (2005) Justification of Argument Schemes, *Australasian Journal of Logic* 3: 1–13.

Whately, R. (1826) *Elements of Logic*, 9th ed. (London: Longmans, Green, 1875).

———. (1846) *Elements of Rhetoric*, 7th ed., reprint (Carbondale: Southern Illinois University Press, 1963).

Woods, J.; Irvine A.; Douglas W. (2004) *Argument: Critical Thinking, Logic and the Fallacies*, 2nd ed. (Toronto: Pearson/Prentice Hall).

10 Mill on the Method of Politics

Antis Loizides

In 1891, Henry Sidgwick (1838–1900) argued that the method of politics is primarily deductive; "certain general characteristics of social man" are assumed in the process of seeking out laws and institutions that are conducive to "the welfare of an aggregate of . . . [civilized] beings living in social relations."[1] According to Sidgwick, both Jeremy Bentham (1748–1832) and James Mill (1773–1836) employed this method.[2] It is well known that John Stuart Mill (1806–1873) disagreed with his utilitarian predecessors on the method of politics. In *A System of Logic* (1843), the younger Mill argued that the deductive method of the "interest-philosophy" of the Bentham school had to give way to an "inverse deductive" or a "historical" method in the study of complex political phenomena. However, Sidgwick argued that when the younger Mill, in his *Considerations on Representative Government* (1861), "came to treat with a view to practical conclusions the question of the best form of Government, he certainly dealt with it by a method not primarily historical: a method in which history seems to be only used either to confirm practical conclusions otherwise arrived at, or to suggest the limits of their applicability." Thus, Sidgwick claimed, whether consciously or not, Mill had abandoned "the general conception of the relation of Politics to History," which one finds in his *Logic*, for the sake of the deductive method of Bentham and James Mill.[3] This was an important claim, made by someone who matched Mill "in the attention he devoted to questions of method."[4] Agreeing with Sidgwick, commentators argue that Mill seemed to revert, in the last fifteen years of his life, "to some of those traditional ways of approaching the study of politics which he had most seemed to scorn" on evidence of his *A System of Logic.*[5]

In this chapter, I argue that the claim that Mill reverted to his utilitarian predecessors' method of treating political phenomena ignores the nuances of Mill's discussion of deductive reasoning as applied in practical affairs. To this effect, I turn, first, to the difference between science and art, i.e., theoretical and practical knowledge, as applied to ethics and politics; second, to the method that is appropriate to each domain of knowledge; third, to Mill's analysis and criticism of traditional methodological approaches to politics; fourth, to Mill's delineation of the proper method of studying social phenomena; and, finally, to Mill's method as applied in his *Representative Government*. In attempting to develop a "philosophy of government" in *Representative Government*, Mill sought out and defined the "middle principles" between specific experience and psychological and ethological laws that ground the theorems his method produces—the key move was defining the criteria of good government in the "educative" and "administrative" functions of government. A closer look at Mill's *Logic* and *Representative Government* suggests that these works were more consistent than Mill's critics allow.[6] As Alan Ryan has argued, Mill modified "the utilitarianism he had inherited by the historicism he had acquired, allowing himself room to talk usefully about institutional arrangements, but confining himself tightly enough to see that what he wrote was not Utopia-building."[7]

I.

John Stuart Mill argued that ethics and politics are both an art and a science. Science, according to Mill, determines what is; art prescribes what should be—the difference is between theoretical and practical knowledge. The theoretical part of ethics consists of the theory of the moral sentiments, i.e., the part of human nature relevant to ethics that can be subject to scientific study, as well as the conditions of human well-being; its practical part consists of rules or precepts for the attainment of the chosen end, but it also consists of the choice of the end itself, i.e., securing those conditions of human well-being identified by the theoretical part. Likewise, the theoretical part of politics refers to a study of human nature, but, this time, human nature under social arrangements; it involves the laws of political phenomena. The practical part of politics has to do with rules or precepts for the "right guidance and government of the affairs of society." As Mill argued in 1836, "[s]cience takes cognizance of a *phenomenon*, and endeavours to discover its *law*; art proposes to itself an *end*, and looks out for *means* to effect it."[8]

In more detail, on one hand, science according to Mill is a system of truths, i.e., a body of propositions asserting matters of fact—simple existence, co-existence, succession (sequence or causation) and resemblance. Simply put, Mill argued, "[t]he language of science is, This is, or, This is not; This does, or does not, happen."[9] The proposition "Prudence is a virtue" asserts that "a correct foresight of consequences, a just estimation of their importance to the object in view, and repression of any unreflecting impulse at variance with the deliberate purpose" is "a mental quality beneficial to society" (which is one possible definition of virtue).[10] A series of inductions or of deductions prove whether this proposition is true or not.

On the other hand, art is a system of precepts, i.e., a body of directions for conduct; "[t]he language of art is, Do this; Avoid that."[11] These propositions are not of the same kind as those of science; they are, Mill argued, "generically different." Propositions of art "enjoin or recommend that something should or ought to be." Even though the proposition "You should avoid imprudent conduct" or "Avoid imprudent conduct" states—as a matter of fact—a feeling of approbation on part of the speaker (or of society), the feeling itself is not sufficient reason for action, as it requires justification— justification with recourse to a higher principle, a general major premise "which enunciates the object aimed at, and affirms it to be a desirable object."[12] Thus, we may prove to someone that prudence is beneficial to society and that benefiting society will gain her/him our approbation or the approbation of esteemed members of society or of society in general, but, unless s/he already finds the approbation of others a worthy and desirable end, that approbation itself is not sufficient reason for her or him to act as recommended.[13] As Mill noted, "[f]or the purposes of practice, every one must be required to justify his approbation: and for this there is need of general premises, determining what are the proper objects of approbation, and what the proper order of precedence among these objects."[14] However, ends do not fall within the domain of science; and if ends may be justi- fied through recourse to higher principles or higher ends, no argument can prove *final* ends, that is, *first* principles. In 1833, Mill had reserved for pos- terity the task of proving Jeremy Bentham right on the *philosophia prima* of conduct—having just noted that no proof can be given "that we ought to regulate our conduct by utility." Thirty years later, Mill's *Utilitarianism* (1861) did attempt to provide the "sounder and profounder metaphysics" needed for passing judgment on rival ethical doctrines as well as providing whatever proof there could be for the principle of utility.[15]

II.

The method then for ethics and politics partakes of the method of theory and that of practice. As already suggested, the theoretical part of ethics and politics refers to a scientific study of human nature. According to Mill, an exact science of human nature enables "us to foretell how an individual would think, feel, or act, throughout life, with the same certainty with which astronomy enables us to predict the places and occultations of the heavenly bodies." Such exactness and such certainty are impossible for various rea- sons in the study of human nature; still the most important effects of human conduct, the modes of thinking, feeling and acting, can be controlled and foretold—at least, when we are working with large bodies of men. These predictions gain scientific credence when the approximate generalizations, the empirical laws suggested by observation or through a study of history, on which they are based, are connected deductively with the universal laws of human nature.[16]

The predictability afforded by the existence of universal laws does not mean, according to Mill, that individuals have no control over social pro- cesses. The underlying assumption is that the conduct of human beings is subject to invariable laws;[17] but conduct is a joint result of external circumstances and of inward circumstances, i.e., of individual character.[18] Equipped with self-reflection and awareness of associationist psychology and of ethological laws, individuals can predict and control, e.g., alter, their own (as well as others') thoughts, feelings and actions, by intervening in the sequences in which social phenomena are embedded, as well as in those through which one's own character is formed.[19] First, Mill referred to two general laws of Psychology: a. that every mental impression has its idea; through this idea, individuals can later revisit past experiences, though with less intensity than the original impression, and b. the secondary mental states may be excited either by impressions or other ideas following the Laws of Association.[20] However, simple ideas may either generate or compose complex ideas—a complex idea may be incapable of being analyzed into simpler ones, when the latter are indistinguishable from one another or even when they combine to form something completely different from themselves.[21]

Second, Mill argued that in contrast to psychology, the laws of character formation had only been studied cursorily in his time. According to Mill, Ethology was *"la théorie de l'influence des diverses circonstances extérieures, soit individuelles, soit sociales, sur la formation du caractère moral et intellectuel."*[22] As a science, Ethology could determine "the kind of character produced . . . by any set of circumstances, physical and moral." As far as the implications of Ethology for ethics and politics are concerned, the knowledge of personal and social circumstances, Mill argued, would afford the "power as to establish in the mind of every individual an indissoluble association between his own happiness and the good of the whole."[23] In short, Ethology would study both the rational and the emotional nature of man; it was to be the science that discovers those general laws of human nature to be used in training and instruction; Ethology constituted the theoretical part of the art of education.[24] Ethology would thus allow for stricter regulation of the development of stable dispositions which direct feelings and desires (i.e., one's character, defined as *êthos*) in accordance to what they have reason to value. It is important for individuals to master this process in order to set and to pursue what they themselves consider worthwhile (which underlies the possibility of freedom of will).[25]

Ethological laws were deduced from the general laws of the mind and were verified by observation of the behavior of individuals in actual conduct and actual social circumstances.[26] Although the complexity of each individual case renders impossible the collection of all the data required for a precise prediction, the degree of prediction that can be achieved by a combined study of Psychology and Ethology is not devoid of practical worth, either in ethics or in politics; as Mill argued, "[i]t is enough that we know that certain means have a *tendency* to produce a given effect, and that others have a tendency to frustrate it."[27] For most practical purposes, in social and political sciences, Mill argued, approximate generalizations were equivalent to exact ones: "that which is only probable when asserted of individual human beings indiscriminately selected, being certain when affirmed of the character and collective conduct of masses."[28]

Ethology was to reach its conclusions through a double process: first, the deduction of "ethological consequences of particular circumstances of position," which would then be tested against experience; and, second, a "reverse operation": a careful collection of experiential data regarding different types of human character, which, with the help of psychological laws, would account for the different characteristics or manifestations of individual character by the peculiarities of the circumstances. Ethological laws, as the *axiomata media* of the science of human nature, offered a safer foundation and "a more deepened theory of human nature" in any study of individuals under social conditions.[29]

III.

As we saw, the scientific, or theoretical, part of ethics and politics consists of the laws of Psychology and of Ethology combined with a study of "time, place and circumstance."[30] The logic of practice similarly involves both induction and deduction. There are two types of method as regards practice. The first has to do with following a pre-established rule of conduct; the second involves finding or constructing the rule by which individuals are to guide their conduct—that is, develop the rule through induction (or a prior deduction, itself based on induction), and then deductively reason from it.[31] Theoretical reasoning has direct implications for the second type of method rather than the first.

Correct use of the first type of method concerning practical reasoning, i.e., following a pre-established rule, is a matter of consistency: of correctly arguing down from general premises to the particular case at hand.[32] The general premise, the rule itself, in this type of method is final—it is taken as granted that the evidence for it has been carefully weighted and deemed sufficient. "The only point to be determined," Mill argued, "is whether the authority which declared the general proposition, intended to include this case [i.e., the particular case at hand] in it." Hence, according to Mill this method refers to a process of interpretation. Since the major premise, rule or general proposition, is final, the conclusion follows once one has established through observation (e.g., testimony or investigation) that the case at hand (the minor premise) possesses those marks that would justify bringing it under the general formula. The rule states that "Attribute A is a mark of attribute B"; the conclusion that "the given object has the attribute B" is established when one has shown that "the given object has the mark A". The role of the practitioner in this process is to examine whether the specific object, in the case at hand, has the marks that are considered sufficient evidence (i.e., actually possessing attribute A) for the presence of attribute B.[33] The process may be tricky, since it may happen that for the establishment of the minor premise itself, a previous inference (and/or interpretation) must have been already established.

By contrast, when following the second method, the practitioner does not take the rule for granted or as final, but attempts to discover the scientific laws that ground the rule itself. What is more, the reasons for rules of conduct need to be sought out in the "complicated affairs" of the lives of individuals, societies and states, because the rules in these affairs (contrary to manual arts) can never be constructed in an ideal manner: that is, one cannot ascertain the whole of the conditions (both positive and negative) on which an effect depends. To act according to rules of art, one needs to remember them; attempting to make a rule of art (in complicated affairs) perfect or complete, rather than provisional, requires taking under consideration all counteracting contingencies (to deal with exceptions or rarities), which would make the rule too complicated to remember (and thus impractical). However, having the capacity to refer to the theoretical grounds of the rule allows the practitioner to make modifications to suit each particular case, since the practitioner would then know "what combinations of circumstances would interfere with, or entirely counteract," the intended effects that the rule of art, the major premise, is meant to serve as a memorandum or a formula to be interpreted.[34] Thus, according to Mill, the proper procedure in complicated affairs, where the conditions of effects are numerous and neither "plain to common observation" nor "speedily learnt from practice,"[35] is:

> The art proposes to itself an end to be attained, defines the end, and hands it over to the science. The science receives it, considers it as a phenomenon or effect to be studied, and having investigated its causes and conditions, sends it back to art with a theorem of the combinations of circumstances by which it could be produced. Art then examines these combinations of circumstances, and according as any of them are or are not in human power, pronounces the end attainable or not.[36]

In this way, strictly speaking, ethics and politics are not both arts and sciences; they are arts, whose practical maxims draw on scientific theorems—whose ultimate foundation is induction. This was an important feature of Mill's treatment of the logic of art.[37]

IV.

In 1843, Mill was praised by Edward Lytton Bulwer for the proposition that morality is an art, not a science; Mill replied that this proposition followed "as a necessary corollary from my particular mode of using the word Art, but at bottom I fancy it is merely what everybody thinks, expressed in new language."[38] However, Mill did more than express what everybody thought

in new language. When he published *A System of Logic*, more than a decade
had passed since the Reform Act of 1832. And already by 1832, there had
been a long history of debate in and out of the Parliament concerning parliamentary reform, in which two schools of thought with regard to the method
of politics, the *a priori* and the *a posteriori*, seemed to have formed: Jeremy Bentham and James Mill on one side, James Mackintosh and Thomas
Babington Macaulay on the other (the latter two replying with reviews of
works by the former two in the *Edinburgh Review*). Suffice it to say, the
methodological differences between them led to disagreements as to whether
reform should have been extensive or moderate.[39] From Mill's perspective,
all of them had been in the wrong; according to his *Autobiography* (1873),
Mill came to realize in the early 1830s

> that a science is either deductive or experimental, according as, in the
> province it deals with, the effects of causes when conjoined, are or are
> not the sums of the effects which the same causes produce when sep-
> arate . . . It thus appeared, that both Macaulay and my father were
> wrong: the one in assimilating the method of philosophizing in politics
> to the purely experimental method of chemistry: while the other, though
> right in adopting a deductive method, had made a wrong selection of
> one, having taken as the type of deduction, not the appropriate process,
> that of the deductive branches of natural philosophy, but the inappro-
> priate one of pure geometry, which not being a science of causation at
> all, does not require or admit of any summing-up of effects.[40]

Thus, the key to the proper method of politics (and ethics) was seeing that
the laws of social phenomena "are, and can be, nothing but the laws of the
actions and passions of human beings united together in the social state."
The reasons or grounds for the rules (the maxims of policy) of the art of politics are to be sought in the laws of individual human nature and ethological
laws, since "[m]en are not, when brought together, converted into another
kind of substance, with different properties."[41]

For Mill, the proponents of the *a posteriori*, i.e., the Chemical, or Experimental, method argued that little could be gained by looking at individuals
in the abstract; the key to deciphering political phenomena was looking
at specific experience.[42] However, even though neither Mackintosh's nor
Macaulay's view was as simple as that, they did not acknowledge the limitations of the experimental methods in political phenomena.[43] In 1820, James
Mackintosh tried to provide the reasons for moderate reform in the House
of Commons on the basis of adequate representation of the various interests
residing in the state. Mackintosh, by citing "ancient examples," aimed to
show that in key moments in British parliamentary history there was no
concern with the number itself of voters as regards representation.[44] What
seemed to suggest itself as the general principle of the English constitution
was that "the interests of every unrepresented district are in danger of being

overlooked or sacrificed." This meant that representation of the separate interests of society in Parliament would have protected all citizens, not an increase of voters. This was a useful maxim of constitutional policy, according to Mackintosh, not an unbending rule or "axiom of a science." In the application of political maxims, Mackintosh added, it "was often necessary to yield to circumstances, to watch for opportunities, to consult the temper of the people, the condition of the country, and the dispositions of powerful leaders."[45] Principles such as the one just noted form the middle principles of politics, the ones that "connect its most general principles with the variety and intricacy of the public concerns." Abstract principles, which may be applicable to all governments, at any time and situation, "shed too faint a light to guide us on our path; and can seldom be directly applied with any advantage to human affairs."[46] More strongly, Macaulay argued that "it is utterly impossible to deduce the science of government from the principles of human nature."[47] The method of Induction, Macaulay added, was the only suitable method for arriving at just conclusions in politics, i.e.,

> by observing the present state of the world,—by assiduously studying the history of past ages,—by sifting the evidence of facts,—by carefully combining and contrasting those which are authentic,—by generalizing with judgment and diffidence,—by perpetually bringing the theory which we have constructed to the test of new facts,—by correcting, or altogether abandoning it, according as those new facts prove it to be partially or fundamentally unsound.[48]

The question was, according to Mill, whether the conditions for a real induction concerning the causes of political effects could be ever satisfied in social phenomena. As we saw, Mill thought that the universal law of social phenomena was the composition of causes, i.e., that the joint effect of several causes was identical with the sum of their separate effects.[49] However, because of the complexity of social phenomena, none of the inductive methods was of any use to the social scientist; the causes of social phenomena such as "security, wealth, freedom, good government, public virtue, general intelligence, or their opposites, are infinitely numerous, especially the external or remote causes, which alone are, for the most part, accessible to direct observation."[50] The *a posteriori* method takes the whole collection of causes that produced the effect as one single cause, and tries to identify it by comparing different instances.[51] But controlled, artificial experiments, which could eliminate the potential influence of unknown circumstances in the attempt to establish causation, cannot be performed; the social scientist can only rely on natural experiments, i.e., historical events with enough similarities which would allow drawing conclusions.[52] Still, trying to compare the state of things following the (natural) experiment with that which preceded it is to no avail, since other causes than that whose effect is being determined have been in operation all along—it is not enough that no unknown circumstances are present in the phenomenon under scrutiny, all conditions capable of influencing the effect need to be inoperative, in order to establish causation. Thus, the experimental method is even less applicable in the "phenomena of politics and history," Mill argued, than physical sciences in which complex phenomena (i.e., phenomena with "plural causes" and "intermixed effects") take place.[53]

Mill agreed with Sidgwick that practical reasoning was essentially deductive; the deductive method was capable of addressing the problem of complexity in social phenomena. However, the deductive method Mill was speaking of consisted of three parts: induction, deduction and verification—it was not deduction *simpliciter*. The "theorists" of reform, Bentham and James Mill, according to the younger Mill, had supposed that each social phenomenon resulted from only one source, "one single property of human nature."[54] Not only did they neglect to consider the possibility of conflicting forces in society,[55] they also followed the wrong type of practical reasoning—i.e., arguing from unbending practical maxims—even though they knew the difference between science and art: "that rules of conduct must follow, not precede, the ascertainment of law of nature, and that the latter, not the former, is the legitimate field for the application of the deductive method."[56]

The "interest-philosophy of the Bentham school" seemed to base their theory on the comprehensive premise: "Men's actions are always determined by their interests."[57] Notwithstanding the imprecision in the term "interest," Mill argued that the actions of human beings are not always so determined.[58] However, the younger Mill argued, even if we grant that Benthamites seemed to hold a more rational version of this principle, "[a]ny succession of persons, or the majority of any body of persons, will be governed in the bulk of their conduct by their personal interests,"[59] their fundamental theorem of political science, consisting of three syllogisms,[60] depended

> chiefly on two general premises, in each of which a certain effect is considered as determined only by one cause, not by a concurrence of causes. In the one, it is assumed that the actions of average rulers are determined solely by self-interest; in the other, that the sense of identity of interest with the governed, is produced and producible by no other cause than responsibility.

However, according to Mill, neither were the premises true nor the fundamental theorem.[61] In short, the foundation of the Philosophic Radicals' theory, a theory caught up in the "mere polemics of the day," was not sufficiently broad.[62] Despite different conclusions, the premises of the Philosophic Radicals were often common with conservative thinkers;[63] according to David Hume, laws and forms of government have "little dependence . . . on the humours and tempers of men," and "consequences almost as general and certain may sometimes be deduced from them, as any which the mathematical sciences afford us."[64] Mill thought that the error of the eighteenth-century philosophers was deducing

> politics like mathematics from a set of axioms & definitions, forgetting that in mathematics there is no danger of partial views: a proposition is either true or it is not, & if it is true, we may safely apply it to every case which the proposition comprehends in its terms: but in politics & the social science, this is so far from being the case, that error seldom arises from our assuming premises which are not true, but generally from our overlooking other truths which limit, & modify the effect of the former.[65]

They thus mistook "the perfect coherence and logical consistency of . . . [their] system, for truth."[66]

V.

Both "traditional" methods pretended to establish a science of government; however, neither had studied "all the determining agencies" with equal consideration.[67] Despite the great number and variety of agencies at play in social phenomena, it is possible to get a grip on the process since these agencies come together under a small number of laws, i.e., psychological and ethological laws, "which govern the action of circumstances on men and of men on circumstances,"[68] since "whatever influence any cause exercises upon the social phenomena, it exercises through those laws." When these laws are sufficiently known, one can distinguish tendencies of causes in determining effects—as we saw, determining tendencies in complex phenomena is sufficient for practical purposes. What is more, according to Mill, "[t]he aim of practical politics is to surround any given society with the greatest possible number of circumstances of which the tendencies are beneficial, and to remove or counteract, as far as practicable, those of which the tendencies are injurious." Once these *a priori* results of reasoning are compared to *a posteriori* observations on social phenomena, the reasoning will be verified, given that the cause or causes will have been correctly identified; once causal connections (or strong indications of causal connections) between phenomena have been identified, as we saw, then rules can be made for the "right guidance and government of the affairs of society."[69]

Thus, the Deductive Method combines induction and ratiocination as well as a process of verification. The first step is to investigate the laws of human action as well as the properties of external circumstances which influence human actions in society. It is an inductive step in the sense that these laws are determined by observation, experiment or a prior deduction (complex laws derived from simpler ones), which was itself ultimately established by observation or experiment. According to Mill, it is an undeniable fact that social phenomena depend on acts and mental impressions of individuals; the problem was correctly defining those laws that govern impressions and actions.[70] The second step aims to determine the effects to be expected in known circumstances (i.e., the complex combination of causes that are at any time present in a society) or the antecedent conditions under which a complex effect will occur (i.e., as we saw, when one sets an effect as a worthy and desirable end).[71] The final step is making sure that the above two steps were correctly performed; the only way to verify their results is by testing them against all known cases where the given combination of causes have actually existed or the desired effect to be produced had taken place; if and when that verification process fails, one needs to be able to explain why, e.g., when the expected effect did not follow, one needs to show what agencies were at play that could have prevented it from happening.[72]

However, the Deductive Method can be applied only to classes of social phenomena in which the directly determining causes are primarily those that act through a limited number of laws of human nature (and from those outward circumstances that operate through those laws). Once the effects are ascertained through this universally applicable method, one may tinker with them, making room for modifying circumstances or for varying premises, so that the results hold for the locality to which the method is applied.[73] However, according to the younger Mill, "there can be no separate Science of Government," since "[a]ll questions respecting the tendencies of forms of government must stand part of the general science of society"; the reason is that forms of government are "most mixed up, both as cause and effect, with the qualities of the particular people or the particular age."[74] Political phenomena are not of the same nature as those of political economy or "Political Ethology," that is "the theory of the causes which determine the type of character belonging to a people or to an age."[75] There has been such a long series of actions and reactions between human beings and their circumstances, from the infancy of human race up to the present time, that it is impossible "to determine *à priori* the order in which human development must take place, and to predict . . . the general facts of history up to the present time."[76] Now, the appropriate method for the comprehensive or "general science of society" is the Inverse Deductive Method. As the name suggests, this method begins with drawing empirical laws from history; but it only gains scientific credence, when these empirical laws are verified by connecting them with ultimate laws, i.e., ethological and psychological laws. This process then converts the empirical law into a scientific one—upon which political actions can rely.

As we saw at the beginning, there are two issues that stand out in Sidgwick's criticism of Mill's method in *Representative Government*: a. the role of history in it, and b. whether Mill was employing the Direct Deductive Method or the inverse deductive method. As regards the first issue, Mill told the students of St. Andrews in 1867 that "[a]ll true political science is, in one sense of the phrase, *à priori*, being deduced from the tendencies of things, tendencies known either through our general experience of human nature, or as the result of an analysis of the course of history, considered as a progressive evolution."[77] Three decades earlier, while engaged in writing the *Logic*, Mill noted in his "Rationale of Representation" (1835) that "[t]here is not a fact in history which is not susceptible of as many different explanations as there are possible theories of human affairs." History is not the source of political philosophy, according to Mill, "but the profoundest political philosophy is requisite to explain history; without it all in history which is worth understanding remains mysterious." In social science, Mill added in 1859 (when he revised the "Rationale"), history suggests, corroborates, and verifies rather than grounds political truths; the proof of these truths "is drawn from the laws of human nature; ascertained through the study of ourselves by reflection, and of mankind by actual intercourse with them."[78] As Mill noted in *Logic*, history "does, when judiciously examined, afford Empirical Laws of Society."[79] Depending on the method employed, these empirical laws will either constitute the third step of the method, i.e., providing verification of the combination of psychological and ethological laws and outward circumstances, or the first step of the method, i.e., requiring verification through the combination of psychological and ethological laws and outward circumstances. Hence, contra Sidgwick, "Theoretical Politics," which in Mill's discussion of art and science refer to the theorems of science that ground the rules of art, do not consist solely in the "application of the Science or Philosophy of History."[80]

In reference to the second issue, as Mill noted in his rectorial address in 1867, the study of political phenomena requires both deduction and induction.[81] The original statement of this idea is found twenty-seven years earlier. In 1840, prior to the publication of his *Logic*, Mill reviewed the second part of Alexis de Tocqueville's *De la Démocratie en Amérique* (1835–1840). In that review, Mill noted that Tocqueville's "method is, as that of a philosopher on such a subject must be—a combination of deduction with induction." The "true Baconian and Newtonian method applied to society and government" combines evidence from laws of human nature and from historical examples—the "conclusions never rest on either species of evidence alone."[82] However, both methods, the direct and the inverse deductive methods, make this combination; so which method did Mill think that Tocqueville used? A clue to this may be found in an even earlier work by Mill. According to Mill, "[t]he most important contribution which has been made for many years to the Philosophy of Government" was Tocqueville's.[83] This gives us an important clue, because for Mill, the "philosophy of government," was "a most extensive and complicated science," involving

a complete view of the influences of political institutions; not only their direct, but what are in general so little attended to, their indirect and remote influences: how they affect the national character, and all the social relations of a people; and reciprocally, how the state of society, and of the human mind, aids, counteracts, or modifies the effects of a form of government, and promotes or impairs its stability.[84]

Mill's "Philosophy of Government" as described in 1835, corresponds to the comprehensive science of society, developed more fully in *Logic*. And the method applicable to the complex phenomena of the social science is the Inverse Deductive Method.

Mill argued that the idea of obtaining the generalizations of the Deductive Method by a reverse order, i.e., "by a collation of specific experience, and verif[ying] them by ascertaining whether they are such as would follow from known general principles," was one entirely owed to Auguste Comte (1798–1859)—only at the turn of the decade did Mill fully realize the possibilities of this method.[85] But soon enough Mill found this method put to good use in Tocqueville's work,[86] claiming however that there was "much which will be better done by those who come after him, and build upon his foundations."[87] What is more, in 1835, Mill noted that an exposition of the "advantages of a representative government" as well as "the principles on which it must be constructed in order to realise those advantages" would form only part of the philosophy of government: "so far as one branch can be considered separately from the rest," this branch of the inquiry can be "regarded as nearly perfect,"[88] and thus it only needs to "borrow from political philosophy . . . its general principles."[89]

To return to the debate on the appropriate method of politics, it should be clear that John Stuart Mill's position was no compromise between the two "traditional" methods.[90] According to Sidgwick, James Mill's "Government" had followed the Direct Deductive Method.[91] Indeed, James Mill did follow the method of "abstract speculation" since he recognized that, as the younger Mill put it, "it is vain to hope that truth can be arrived at, either in Political Economy or in any other department of the social science, while we look at the facts in the concrete, clothed in all the complexity with which nature has surrounded them, and endeavour to elicit a general law by a process of induction from a comparison of details."[92] However, James Mill seemed to treat politics as one "department of the social science," which was unacceptable to John Stuart Mill. The elder Mill's premises were not sufficiently broad. Hence, in the succession of steps of the Direct Deductive Method, James Mill's "Government" was confined to the second, *a priori*, step. Not only did James Mill ignore the first step—the inductive foundation—but also he treated social phenomena as ones of "co-existence," not of "sequence," i.e., considering only society to be static and not dynamic as well.[93] The psychological and ethological laws employed by the Bentham School were insufficient to account for the complexity of political phenomena. Of the two deductive ways of reasoning on matters of art, the Bentham School followed the wrong one—reasoning from unbending practical maxims. Thus, their method was not even comparable to the method of Political Economy, which was deductive in the appropriate sense, i.e., combining induction, deduction and verification.[94] What is more, the "Inverse Deductive Method," in particular, paid close attention to "Political Ethology," something that Mill thought Bentham in particular had completely ignored.[95]

Likewise, the use of the inductive principles defined by Mackintosh and Macaulay, i.e., the empirical laws that direct observation and collation of instances supply, corresponded only to the third step of the Direct Deductive Method, i.e., as verification of *a priori* reasoning. Moreover, notwithstanding the value empirical laws had in the "Inverse Deductive Method," i.e., providing its first step, empirical laws themselves are required, Mill argued, to be accounted for. Empirical laws are derivative laws, whose derivation "is not yet known." As the causes of the empirical laws are not known, the conditions under which they would cease to be fulfilled are also not known. For this reason, empirical laws cannot be relied "upon in cases varying much from those which have been actually observed."[96] The truth of an empirical law cannot thus be extended beyond "time, place and circumstance."[97] However, if these empirical laws are connected with psychological and ethological laws (which would identify both the ultimate laws and appropriate modifications of the component elements of any particular social phenomenon),[98] then, Mill argued, the theory in question would be most effectively verified.[99] Mackintosh's and Macaulay's empirical laws, contrary to what they argued, were not the "middle principles" of the method of politics. For Mill, the *axiomata media*, the link between empirical laws and elementary laws of human nature, are supplied by ascertaining the conditions of stability and the law of progress in the social union, and combining them.[100] Contrary to what its name misleadingly suggests, the key to the "Historical Method" is this combination, and the subsequent verification of empirical laws with psychological and ethological laws, not the empirical laws drawn from history on their own accord.[101]

VI.

Frederick Rosen has recently examined the implications of the "science of Ethology" for Mill's *Representative Government*,[102] convincingly illustrating how "Political Ethology" and "character," notwithstanding the limitations of Mill's exposition of active and passive character, provide the background on which Mill developed his "comprehensive science or art of government."[103] As Rosen argues, "[p]ut simply, Mill followed the pattern sketched out in the *Logic* to establish representative government as 'the ideally best form of government' both as a consequence for his analysis of character and in terms of the consequences of representative government for the development of character."[104] However, the argument by Collini, Winch and Burrow that Mill reverted to the traditional ways of approaching the study of politics in *Representative Government* anticipates Rosen on precisely the point of Mill's use of "character":

> [b]y contrast to the universalist prescriptions of deductive Utilitarianism this [i.e., Mill's use of "character" and "national character" as

explanatory concepts] does have a certain relativising tendency, but unless it is resolved into some more fundamental set of determinants (which Mill never saw his way to doing), it remains within a strongly moral-political vocabulary.[105]

The "state of society," i.e., "the simultaneous state of all the greater social facts or phenomena," would have been a better explanatory concept, according to Stefan Collini, Donald Winch and John Burrow.[106] Although Mill had defined the "state of society" ambitiously broadly in *Logic*, "in practice in *Representative Government* it always turns out to be confined to 'the qualities of the human beings composing the society over which the government is exercised'." Mill's question of the adaptability of forms of government to "states of society" focuses primarily on the effects of forms of governments on the (moral and intellectual) progress of a people.[107] However, as we saw, Mill thought that his father's theory was a remnant of the eighteenth-century mode of proceeding in questions of politics. In the eighteenth century, Hume had already "established" that "politics admit of general truths, which are invariable by the humour or education either of subject or sovereign."[108] Thus, Mill's focus precisely on the education, "humour and temper" of a state of society, even if by that he remained within a moral-political vocabulary, was supposed to provide the other half of the truth—i.e., what the nineteenth-century reaction to the previous century had brought to the study of politics.

Furthermore, according to the commentators, Mill's selective use of historical examples vitiated his attempt to ground laws of human nature in history, which led Mill to develop a form of government abstracted from particular historical conditions—in contrast to his claims in *Logic*.[109] However, the theory of development sketched in *Logic* informs *Representative Government* in several ways.[110] First, Mill recognized the possibility of change of the form of government by human design. Collini, Winch and Burrow argue that the "striking voluntarist conclusion" in *Representative Government*, that institutions and forms of government are a matter of choice, draws on Mill's intellectualist account of historical change.[111] Indeed, in *Logic*, Mill argued that the fundamental theorem of the social science was that there is "a progressive change both in the character of the human race, and in their outward circumstances so far as moulded by themselves."[112] But it was important to recognize that "[t]he order of the developement of man's faculties, is as various as the situations in which he is placed" limited that fundamental theorem.[113] What is most important, there is one element in the "complex existence of social man," according to Mill, which is "preeminent over all others as the prime agent of the social movement": the state of the speculative faculties of mankind.[114] As Mill argued in 1829, "Government exists for all purposes whatever that are for man's good: and the highest & most important of these purposes is the improvement of man himself as a moral and intelligent being."[115] In 1850, Mill would be more explicit in arguing that political progress depended upon the "intellectual & moral state of all classes."[116] Being an exposition of this "prime agent," Mill's argument in *Representative Government* did draw on an intellectualist account of historical change; its foundations however had been in place long before the publication of *Representative Government*. As Mill noted in *Autobiography*, "any general theory, or philosophy of politics supposes a previous theory of human progress, and that this is the same thing with a philosophy of history."[117]

The charge that Mill's *Representative Government* did "exemplify that 'vulgar mode' of citing presumed parallels or isolated and under-analysed illustrations" from history is well founded.[118] However, it does not have direct bearing on the question of Mill's method. Mill's historical examples (i.e., examples of specific experience) did not mean to *ground* "the controlling laws of social development,"[119] i.e., the conditions of stability and the law of progress which formed the *axiomata media* of the method of politics. Mill's examples merely suggested empirical laws themselves needing verification from psychological and ethological laws. The "middle principles," the conditions of stability and the law of progress, seemed to bridge the gap between specific experience and "abstract speculation," i.e., ethological and psychological laws. However, the suggestion that Mill belonged in the previous generation of political writers, the *a priori* rather than the comparative school, as we saw at the beginning, seems right: the fundamental theorem upon which Mill developed social science was "the progressiveness of man and society." However, unless there was a combined study of Social Statics and Social Dynamics, that fundamental theorem would remain an empirical law.

Unlike his utilitarian predecessors, Mill did not develop a deductive argument and then consider various modifying circumstances; fulfilling the historicist requirement, Mill "reasoned back from an enlarged collection of facts to principles,"[120] and then went on, through "middle principles," to verify these results through ethological and psychological laws. It usually goes unnoticed that, right at the outset of *Representative Government*, Mill considered the use of the Direct Deductive method, but rejected it.[121] The methodological framework that Mill developed in *Logic* combined a study of Social Statics, the science of the coexistences of social phenomena, with Social Dynamics, the science of the sequence of social phenomena. Beginning from the former, Mill argued that, it provides "the necessary correlation between the form of government existing in any society and the contemporaneous state of civilization." Social Dynamics aim "to observe and explain the sequences of social conditions."[122] The "Historical Method" proceeds to combine

the statical view of social phenomena with the dynamical, considering not only the progressive changes of the different elements, but the contemporaneous condition of each; and thus obtain empirically the law of correspondence not only between the simultaneous states, but between the simultaneous changes, of those elements. This law of correspondence it is, which, duly verified *à priori*, would become the real scientific derivative law of the development of humanity and human affairs.[123]

In *Representative Government*, Mill did in fact proceed to "inquire into the best form of government in the abstract," having first considered three limiting conditions, that is, a. "the people for whom the form of government is intended must be willing to accept it," b. [t]hey must be willing and able to do what is necessary to keep it standing," and c. "they must be willing and able to do what it requires of them to enable it to fulfil its purposes."[124] However, Mill's criteria of good government were in fact based on a theory of development, which is a second way in which Mill's *Representation Government* drew on the *Logic*.[125] After considering a popular division of the interests of society (i.e., of Progress and of Order) to be pursued by government, and rejecting it, Mill concluded that evaluations of the merit of political institutions "consists partly of the degree in which they promote the general mental advancement of the community, including under that phrase advancement in intellect, in virtue, and in practical activity and efficiency," i.e., an educative function, "and partly of the degree of perfection with which they organize the moral, intellectual, and active worth already existing, so as to operate with the greatest effect on public affairs," i.e., an administrative function.[126]

The first, according to Mill, the moral and intellectual excellence as well as activity of the governed, supplies the "moving force which works the machinery"; as such it varies in different states of civilization or different forms of government. The second refers to the "quality of the machinery itself"; but since that quality consists in the ability to make the good qualities of the governed, collectively and individually, instrumental to the right purposes, it does not depend, as the educative function does, so much on different states of civilization or different forms of government.[127] Thus, though it may not appear as such on first sight, the reference to social power that is active in society in the first instance and the ability to use that power as instrument to the right purpose, i.e., to move the society forward "rapidly into a higher state," in the second instance, seem to correspond to the combined study of Social Statics and Social Dynamics—Mill's "Inverse Deductive Method" had defined Social Dynamics especially as the *axiomata media* of "General Sociology," i.e., the comprehensive social science.[128] What is more, Mill noted that the difference between the educative and administrative functions is a difference in *kind*, not one of *degree*, which, though not exactly clear, may refer to the classification of social phenomena involved in Social Statics and Social Dynamics as ones of co-existence and ones of sequence, as we saw.[129] Thanks to Comte's "great law," Mill had limited his task in making the principles of statics more explicit rather than those of dynamics.[130] Mill argued that "the one indispensable merit of a government, in favour of which it may be forgiven almost any amount of other demerit compatible with progress, is that its operation on the people is favourable, or not unfavourable, to the next step which it is necessary for them to take, in order to raise themselves to a higher level."[131] But to know, and to take, the step needed to advance to a higher state of society, not only must one already know the next, and "all the steps which society has yet to make,"[132] but also one must already know "the immediate or derivative laws according to which social states generate one another as society advances."[133] Mill's confidence in the existence and possibility of identification of such laws may strike one as strange. The first chapters of *Representative Government* exhibit Mill's attempt to build on the *Logic*'s foundation rather than its conscious or unconscious abandonment—whether that foundation was sufficient or not is a different question.

Collini, Winch and Burrow argue that Mill's attempt to judge "of the merits of forms of government" through the construction of an ideal form of government, "that is, which, if the necessary conditions existed for giving effect to its beneficial tendencies, would, more than all others, favour and promote not some one improvement, but all forms and degrees of it,"[134] constituted a straightforward "stride forward into the Promised Land of prescriptive political theory."[135] However, the art of politics is by definition prescriptive. As we saw at the beginning, to follow a rule of art, individuals must already desire the end(s); thus, the development of rules of politics must be grounded on psychological and ethological laws. Moreover, if by the remark on Mill's "stride," it is meant that Mill abandoned the historical method for the direct deductive method, then we need to recall that even though the *a priori* step in both deductive methods was the same, it served a different function. Once Mill acquired the empirical laws of good government, he proceeded to verify them through *a priori* ethological and psychological laws (taking into account, as we saw, the "middle principles" of the laws of social development) by supposing a given set of circumstances—an ideal set in the case at hand—and then considering what, according to psychological and ethological laws, would have been the influence of those circumstances on the mental, intellectual and active faculties of human beings. If the results were the same with those suggested by the empirical laws of society, then those laws could gain scientific credence. If the results were different then there was a basis on which reform could be based or a less ideal form of government could be put into effect.[136]

According to Mill, "[w]hen the circumstances of an individual or of a nation are in any considerable degree under our control, we may, by our knowledge of tendencies, be enabled to shape those circumstances in a manner much more favourable to the ends we desire, than the shape which they would of themselves assume."[137] In *Representative Government*, Mill reminded his readers that "the ideally best form of government . . . does not mean one which is practicable or eligible in all states of civilization, but the one which, in the circumstances in which it is practicable and eligible, is attended with the greatest amount of beneficial consequences, immediate and prospective."[138] Mill's attempt to "judge" the criteria of good government via an *a priori* procedure, i.e., connecting the criteria of good government with the importance of active character for social advancement (ideal circumstances being assumed) was in agreement with the *Logic*'s sketch of the inverse deductive method—it was the only way, according to Mill, to safely provide practical rules in the complex affairs of "social man."

CONCLUSION

In *Representative Government*, Mill defined what the goals of political institutions are—i.e., the end to be attained—and looked out for means to achieve those ends—i.e., which institutional arrangements were more likely to bring about the desired ends. The political institutions, that is, the institutional arrangements that support the particular form of government, and the form of government itself, for which Mill was arguing, are considered desirable as well as justified by virtue of their contribution to the progressiveness of mankind. In this respect, Mill's argument was teleological. Even though individuals find themselves in established political institutions, institutions are still man-made—as such they ought to serve the "permanent interests of man as a progressive being."[139] The question was how to make them more effective in fulfilling those goals; effectiveness is achieved by understanding "the controlling laws of social development," which ground, verify and explain the empirical laws concerning good government drawn from history—these controlling laws are the *axiomata media* and are themselves traced back to the elementary laws of ethology and psychology. If the approximate generalizations drawn from history are not so grounded and verified, they are not to be relied upon to make the necessary changes in the institutions to improve effectiveness in the pursuits of human beings under social conditions—such knowledge is necessary to prevent deterioration and achieve advancement. Collini, Winch and Burrow point out that when Mill argued that "the maxim, that the government of a country is what the social forces in existence compel it to be, is true only in the sense in which it favours, instead of discouraging, the attempt to exercise, among all forms of government practicable in the existing condition of society, a rational choice,"[140] he was essentially begging the question. However, as we saw, this maxim was founded on a previous discussion in *Logic*, in which Mill identified the speculative capacities of individuals as the "prime agent" of "social progression" toward a "better and happier state."[141]

NOTES

1. Sidgwick (1891: 11). All references to John Stuart Mill's works are to the authoritative edition of *Collected Works of John Stuart Mill* (Mill, 1963–1991—cited as CW, followed by volume and page number), unless otherwise indicated. I am greatly indebted to Georgios Varouxakis and Elijah Millgram for extremely helpful advice on earlier drafts of this chapter.

I would also like to thank Fred Rosen, Gregoris Molivas and Kyriakos Demetriou for stimulating discussions on Mill's method.

2. For example, James Mill had argued, almost three quarters of a century earlier, that "the whole science of human nature must be explored to lay a foundation for the science of government" (J. Mill, 1820: 491).

3. Sidgwick (1891: 11n1).

4. Collini, Winch and Burrow (1983: 130). Mill's method in *Representative
Government*, especially in reference to the *Logic*, has not been subjected to
much scrutiny (e.g., Garforth, 1980; Skorupski, 1989; Urbinati, 2002; Miller,
2010). Interestingly, neither did Mill's reviewers pay any attention to Mill's
method (e.g., [Anon.] 1861; Lorimer, 1861; Johnson, 1861). Ryan (1970,
1974) and, especially, Thompson (1976) and Rosen (2013) have discussed
Mill's method as regards *Representative Government*, but with different ends
in mind; the exposition advanced here is indebted to the work of Rosen, Ryan
and Thompson. Skorupski (1989: ch. 8) has provided one of the clearest discussions of Book VI of Mill's *Logic*, but has not attempted any comparison
with *Representative Government*.

5. Collini, Winch and Burrow (1983: 135, 150–55, 156).

6. As Mill himself argued, coherence should not be mistaken for "truth" (Mill,
1843, CW: VIII.822); consistency between the two works does not mean
that Mill's "Historical Method" was sufficiently historical. Collini, Winch
and Burrow (1983: 145) do well to point out that Mill was classified by his
contemporaries, or near contemporaries, as a pre-"Comparative and Historical Method" political writer (cf. Ryan, 1970: ch. IX). It does not thus come
as a surprise to find that in Charles Merriam's (1925: 49) famous "lines of
development" of the methods of political theory, Mill's "Inverse Deductive
Method" falls in the first one, the *a priori* and deductive method; between
1850 and 1900, the historical and comparative method was dominant. Notwithstanding the limitations of Mill's historicism, Ryan (1974: 198–200)
has noted, Mill's "utilitarian case" owes almost nothing to the *a prioristic*
approach of his utilitarian predecessors, especially that of his father.

7. Ryan (1974: 197). Interestingly, a reviewer of Mill's *Representative Government* did find Mill's scheme utopian ([Anon.], 1861: 538).

8. Mill (1836, CW: IV.310–12; 1843, CW: VIII.943ff; 1865, CW: IX.350–51).

9. Mill (1843, CW: VIII.949; 1836, CW: IV.312).

10. Mill (1843, CW: VII.106–07).

11. Mill (1836, CW: IV.312; 1843, CW: VIII.949).

12. Mill (1843, CW: VIII.949).

13. Mill (1834, CW: XI.150).

14. Mill (1843, CW: VII.949).

15. Mill (1833, CW: X.6). See further, Mill (1861b, CW: X. ch. IV).

16. Mill (1843, CW: VIII.846–48).

17. Mill (1843, CW: VIII.835).

18. Mill (1843, CW: VIII.847).

19. Mill (1843, CW: VIII.842, 869–70).

20. The Laws of Association are: i. Similar ideas tend to excite one another. ii. An
impression, or an idea, tends to excite other ideas (or ideas of impressions),
which have been frequently experienced (or thought of) together, either
simultaneously or in immediate succession. iii. Greater intensity in either or
both impressions is equivalent, in rendering them excitable by one another,
to a greater frequency of conjunction.

21. Mill (1843, CW: VIII.852–53).

22. J. S. Mill to A. Comte, 30 Oct. 1843, CW: XIII.604 and 8 Dec. 1843, CW:
XIII.616.

23. Mill (1843, CW: VIII.869; 1861b, CW: X.218). As Garforth puts it (1979: 60): "if *a* is a psychological law, *x* a pattern of circumstances and *y* a form of behavior, one might generalise that a + x = y, and this equation would constitute a universal law of the formation of character."

24. J. S. Mill to A. Comte, 30 Oct. 1843, CW: XIII.604; Mill (1843, CW: VIII.869, 889).

25. See Rosen (2013) for a serious attempt to study the bearing of Ethology on a number of aspects of Mill's thought. For a discussion on character as *êthos*, see Loizides (2013: ch. 8).

26. Mill (1843, CW: VIII.862, 864, 869) and Mill (1836, CW: IV.327–29).

27. Mill (1843, CW: VIII. 847, 869–70).

28. Mill (1843, CW: VIII. 847–48; VII.603).

29. Mill (1843, CW: VIII.873–75). See also, J. S. Mill to A. Comte, 26 Mar. 1846, CW: XIII.698; Bain (1843: 453). For more detailed discussions of ethology, see *infra*, chapter five; Capaldi (1973); Feuer (1976); Ball (2000 and 2010).

30. Mill (1843, CW: VIII.862).

31. Mill (1843, CW: VIII.944).

32. Mill (1843, CW: VIII.944).

33. Mill (1843, CW: VII.193–94, 177–81).

34. Mill (1843, CW: VIII.943–46).

35. Mill (1843, CW: VIII.945).

36. Mill (1843, CW: VIII.944).

37. Rosen notes that Mill's *Logic* was primarily engaged in establishing the correct process of scientific reasoning, and adds: "[o]nly the brief final chapter of the *Logic*, added in the third edition of 1851, almost as an afterthought, is devoted to the arts" (Rosen, 2013: 77). However, the final chapter, on the logic of art, was not added in the third edition—only parts of it (mainly the parts concerning the "Art of Life").

38. See J. S. Mill to E. Lytton Bulwer, 27 Mar. 1843, CW: XIII.579.

39. Bentham (1817); Mackintosh (1820); J. Mill (1820); Macaulay (1829). For the debate between Radicals and Whigs (and main texts), see Lively and Rees (1978). See also, Thomas (1979).

40. Mill (1873, CW: I.167, 169).

41. Mill (1843, CW: VIII.879). By making this statement, Ryan (1970: 136) has argued, Mill essentially decided in advance which method was suitable for politics. Also, there seems to be a missing step (the "composition law") in Mill's reasoning that undermines his whole case; as Fred Wilson (1990: 92) has argued: "It is *not* true that from a knowledge of the laws of the simple system, that is, from this knowledge *alone*, one can arrive *deductively* at the law for the complex system."

42. Mill (1843, CW: VIII.879).

43. Mill (1843, CW: VIII.880). According to Mill, "[t]he vulgar notion, that the safe methods on political subjects are those of Baconian induction that the true guide is not general reasoning, but specific experience will one day be quoted as among the most unequivocal marks of a low state of the speculative faculties in any age in which it is accredited" (Mill, 1843, CW: VII.452). Mill went on to illustrate the limitations of all inductive methods when applied to social phenomena (1843, CW: VIII.881ff). Moreover, Mill had been critical of "practical men," who also employed the "Chemical Method," from his youth, considering them to be the worst authority and the "most unsafe of all guides" in any political matter (see Mill, 1824, CW: IV.16); soon after Macaulay's criticism to James Mill's method, the younger Mill also made critical remarks that some individuals ("having a

little cleverness and a large stock of self-conceit") thought "the science of politics is fixed and unchangeable, like a system of abstract truth, instead of being, as we consider it, progressive with civilization, and fluctuating with the exigencies of society" (see Mill, 1832, CW: XXIII.404). For the limitations of Mill's critique to the "Chemical Method," see Ryan (1970: 136ff).

44. Mackintosh (1820: 469–71, 471ff).
45. Mackintosh (1820: 474–75).
46. Mackintosh (1820: 476). As Mackintosh tried to explain with reference to Hobbes, the "geometrical method" committed "the double error of hastily applying . . . general laws to the most complicated processes of thought, without considering whether these general laws were not themselves limited by other not less comprehensive laws, and without trying to discover how they were connected with particulars, by a scale of intermediate and secondary laws." See Mackintosh (1821: 241–42).
47. Macaulay (1829: 185).
48. Macaulay (1829: 188–89).
49. Mill (1843, CW: VIII.879; VII.371).
50. Mill (1843, CW: VIII.884). However, George Cornewall Lewis (1850: I.341ff) tried to show how Mill's inductive methods could be used in politics.
51. Mill (1843, CW: VII.446).
52. Mill (1843, CW: VIII. 879–83).
53. Mill (1843, CW: VII.449–50).
54. Mill (1843, CW: VIII.888). See further, Ryan (1970: 140, 144–45).
55. Mill (1843, CW: VIII.887–88, 889).
56. Mill (1843, CW: VIII.890).
57. Mill (1843, CW: VIII.890).
58. David Ricardo himself had pointed out this limitation of James Mill's theory of government to James Mill himself several times during their friendship. He criticized the elder Mill of being "unjustly severe" in refusing to acknowledge the influence of "public opinion" as a counteracting force on the actions of public men. See, D. Ricardo to J. Mill, 30 Aug. 1815; 25 Oct. 1815; 30 Dec. 1817; in Sraffa (1951–1977: VI.263–64, 310–11; VII.236–37).
59. Mill (1843, CW: VIII.890). David Ricardo seemed to allow James Mill such a restatement of the comprehensive premise of the "interest-philosophy" in the latter's *Essay on Government*. See, J. Mill (1820); D. Ricardo to J. Mill, 27 July 1820; in Sraffa (1951–1977: VIII.211).
60. See Mill (1843, CW: VIII.890–91).
61. Mill (1843, CW: VIII.891).
62. Mill (1843, CW: VIII.891). The mode in which James Mill delivered his arguments was not random, as this was a question that he had long thought on: "The only question for us is—whether the argument, being conclusive, has any thing in its mode of being put, which is more likely to silence our adversaries, and convince those who are not our adversaries, than the mode in which it has been put by any other body." See J. Mill to D. Ricardo, 15 Oct. 1811, in Sraffa (1951–1977: VI.59).
63. See further, Loizides (2014).
64. Hume (1742: 15–16).
65. J. S. Mill to G. D'Eichthal, 8 Dec. 1829, CW: XII.36.
66. J. S. Mill to G. D'Eichthal, 8 Dec. 1829, CW: XII.35. See also Mill (1843, CW: VIII.822). For an example of John Stuart Mill naming James Mill as an eighteenth-century philosopher, see Mill (1873, CW: I.213).
67. Mill (1843, CW: VIII.891).
68. Mill (1843, CW: VIII.914).
69. Mill (1843, CW: VIII.896–97, 898; 1865, CW: IX.351).

70. Mill (1843, CW: VII.454–55).
71. Mill (1843, CW: VII.459–60). As Mill noted in 1837, "those whom . . . we call philosophic radicals, are those who in politics observe the common practice of philosophers—that is, who, when they are discussing means, begin by considering the end, and when they desire to produce effects, think of causes" (1837b, CW: VI.353).
72. Mill (1843, CW: VII.460–61).
73. Mill (1843, CW: VIII.901, 904). I take up this opportunity to note that Mill here anticipates one of the objections of Collini, Winch and Burrow (1983: 152) that, in *Representative Government*, Mill "asserts (rather than argues) that the successful fulfilment of the latter [i.e., administrative] function [of government, through separate, deductive, branches of the comprehensive art of government, such as jurisprudence and political economy] is not significantly affected by historically variable circumstances" (on Mill, 1861a, CW: XIX.393). Mill had provided the justification of said thesis in *Logic*— which already suggests the interconnectivity of *Representative Government* with his earlier *magnum opus*.
74. Mill (1843, CW: VIII.906). It seems that political science and social science are interchangeable terms in Mill, at least, this is his contemporaries' thought: "Human society, to the philosophic inquirer, is political society; and therefore the 'social science' or 'sociology' of which Mr. Mill has so well described the limits and object, and for the investigation of which he has laid down the conditions with so much precision, appears to be in fact no other than political science" (Lewis, 1850: I.51).
75. Mill (1843, CW: VIII.907; 1867, CW: XXI.245). Political Ethology, as the science of national character, was the most important branch of social science (see Varouxakis, 2002: 54–60).
76. Mill (1843, CW: VIII.915–17).
77. Mill (1867, CW: XXI.237).
78. Mill (1835b, CW: X.44–45). As Mill argued in his "Inaugural Address," specific experience, in contrast to empirical laws, is often insufficient even to verify the conclusions of reasoning (Mill, 1867, CW: XXI.237).
79. Mill (1843, CW: VIII.916).
80. Sidgwick (1891: 5).
81. Mill (1867, CW: XXI.237).
82. Mill (1840, CW: XVIII.157).
83. Mill (1835a, CW: XVIII.18n).
84. Mill (1835a, CW: XVIII.18).
85. Mill (1873, CW: I.219).
86. Mill (1840, CW: XVIII.159–67). See further, Jones (1999). David Lewisohn (1972: 324) suggests that Mill had made a rough sketch of the Inverse Deductive Method in essays around 1835, which may be indebted to his exposure to French historians, since, as Lewisohn puts it "Comte may have been the first to describe Inverse Deduction but it was in general use among philosophically-minded historians." See also Varouxakis (1999) for the view that Mill's interest in Guizot prepared the ground for his excitement with Tocqueville.
87. Mill (1840, CW: XVIII.157). Siedentop (1994: 111–12) notes that Tocqueville was not so enthusiastic with Mill's methodological project in the social sciences; however this is not the impression Tocqueville gave to Mill. See J. S. Mill to A. de Tocqueville, 3 Nov. 1843, CW: XIII.612.
88. Mill (1835a, CW: XVIII.219).
89. Mill (1861a, CW: XIX.396).
90. Cf. Kort (1952: 1146ff).

91. See J. Mill (1820). Sidgwick (1891: 6) argued that the study of politics was similar to that of political economy; he admitted that the deductive method is not perfect, but he argued that taking into consideration modifying principles such as psychological and ethological ones offered the best countermeasure for its imperfection (Sidgwick, 1891: 13–15). Importantly, James Mill was criticized for neglecting to consider "middle principles" in his treatment of political economy (Winch, 1966: 188–89), something which Collini, Winch and Burrow do acknowledge (1983: 143).

92. Mill (1836, CW: IV.329). See also, J. Mill (1820: 494).

93. Mill (1843, CW: VIII.887).

94. For an example of the two methods of practical reasoning that Mill had identified being ignored in discussions of Mill's philosophical method, see Collini, Winch and Burrow (1983: 148ff).

95. See Mill (1833, CW: X.9; 1838, CW: X.99, 105).

96. Mill (1843, CW: VII.516).

97. Mill (1843, CW: VII.519).

98. Mill (1843, CW: VII.518).

99. Mill (1843, CW: VII.461).

100. Mill (1843, CW: VIII.917–25). This is an aspect of Mill's analysis that Collini, Winch and Burrow seem to neglect to consider. They highlight two features of Mill's "ideal" philosophy of government: "first that it was informed by 'certain conceptions of history considered as a whole, some notions of a progressive unfolding of the capabilities of humanity—of a tendency of man and society towards some distant result—of a *destination*, as it were, of humanity'; and second, that it had grasped that 'underneath all political philosophy there must be a social philosophy—a study of agencies lying deeper than forms of government, which, working through forms of government, produce in the long run most of what these seem to produce, and which sap and destroy all forms of government which lie across their path.'" (Collini, Winch and Burrow, 1983: 132 quoting Mill, 1845, CW: XX.260; and Mill, 1837a, CW: XX.183–84). However, the "progressiveness of Man and Society," the first feature identified above, unless combined with the "middle principles" of social development, i.e., "Social Statics" and "Social Dynamics," was only an empirical law, and hence insufficient to base upon a philosophy of government (see Mill, 1843, CW: VIII.914, 925). Therefore, contra Collini, Winch and Burrow (1983: 132), to the extent that Tocqueville did ground this empirical law on psychological and ethological foundations, there was nothing "odd" with regard to Mill's praise to his method.

101. Collini, Winch and Burrow (1983: 138–39) do go some way toward recognizing this fundamental aspect of Mill's "Historical Method," but this recognition does not seem to influence their argument that Mill abandoned that method in *Representative Government*.

102. Rosen (2013: ch. 4).

103. Mill (1861a, CW: XIX.393).

104. Rosen (2013: 88).

105. Collini, Winch and Burrow (1983: 151).

106. These "social facts" would be: "the degree of knowledge, and of intellectual and moral culture, existing in the community, and in every class of it; the state of industry, of wealth and its distribution; the habitual occupations of the community; their division into classes, and the relations of those classes to one another; the common beliefs which they entertain on all the subjects most important to mankind, and the degree of assurance with which those beliefs are held; their tastes, and the character and degree of their aesthetic

242 *Antis Loizides*

development; their form of government, and the more important of their laws and customs" (Mill, 1843, CW: VIII.912).

107. Collini, Winch and Burrow (1983: 151).
108. Hume (1742: 18).
109. Collini, Winch and Burrow (1983: 154).
110. I draw here on Thompson (1976: ch. 4).
111. Collini, Winch and Burrow (1983: 155); Mill (1861a, CW: XIX.375).
112. Mill (1843, CW: VIII.914).
113. J. S. Mill to G. D'Eichthal, 8 Dec. 1829, CW: XII.37; Mill (1843, CW: VIII.914).
114. Mill (1843, CW: VIII.925–26).
115. J. S. Mill to G. D'Eichthal, 8 Dec. 1829, CW: XII.36.
116. J. S. Mill to E. Herford, 22 Jan. 1850, CW: XIV.45. Cf. J. S Mill to T. D. Acland, 1 Dec. 1868, CW: XVI.1499. "Those who are acquainted with Mr Mill's other writings," a reviewer noted, "will not be surprised to be told that the improvement to which he attaches the greatest value, and with a view to the promotion of which his preference of one form of government over another is guided, is the moral and intellectual development of the citizen." See Lorimer (1861: 544).
117. Mill (1873, CW: I.169).
118. Collini, Winch and Burrow (1983: 155). However, once again, Mill's discussion on "belief" as a social force (Mill, 1861a CW: XIXI.381–82) did seem to draw on *Logic* (Mill, 1843, CW: VIII.936–37).
119. Collini, Winch and Burrow (1983: 154).
120. Macaulay (1829: 162).
121. Mill (1861a, CW: XIX.383–84) wrote:

> It would be a great facility if we could say, the good of society consists of such and such elements; one of these elements requires such conditions, another such others; the government, then, which unites in the greatest degree all these conditions, must be the best. The theory of government would thus be built up from the separate theorems of the elements which compose a good state of society.
>
> Unfortunately, to enumerate and classify the constituents of social well-being, so as to admit of the formation of such theorems, is no easy task. Most of those who, in the last or present generation, have applied themselves to the philosophy of politics in any comprehensive spirit, have felt the importance of such a classification; but the attempts which have been made towards it are as yet limited, so far as I am aware, to a single step.

What is most interesting, and also has gone unnoticed, Mill did not seem to reject this mode of proceeding in treating ethics. See J. S. Mill to H. Jones, 13 Jun. 1868, CW: XVI.1414.
122. Mill (1843, CW: VIII.917, 924). Skorupski (1989: 260) has identified four levels in the structure of the moral sciences: i. psychological laws, ii. ethological laws, iii. empirical laws of human nature and empirical laws of society, iv. observation of behavior in concrete historical and social circumstances (although Mill argued that "[t]here is no Art of Observing". See Mill, 1843, CW: VII.380). Social Statics and Social Dynamics would belocated on the third level.
123. Mill (1843, CW: VIII.925). The "principle of antagonism" that safe keeps the progressiveness of democratic societies could be verified by a similar process. See J. S. Mill to A. Comte, 25 Feb. 1842, CW: XIII.502 and 22 Mar. 1822, CW: XIII.508; see also Mill (1845, CW: XX.269–70; 1849, CW: XX.358–59).

124. Mill (1861a, CW: XIX.376). As we saw, Collini, Winch and Burrow (1983: 151) have acknowledged these "relativising" tendencies in their discussion of Mill's method.
125. The position advanced here differs slightly from Thompson (1976: ch. 4).
126. Mill (1861a, CW: XIX.392). I follow Collini, Winch and Burrow (1983: 152) in the use of the terms "educative" and "administrative."
127. Mill (1861a, CW: XIX.390–91, 393).
128. Mill (1861a, CW: XIX.924).
129. Mill (1861a, CW: XIX.392). Miller (2010: 172) notices the static and dynamic elements of Mill's account, but does not engage in a discussion of Mill's method. Even though social statics and social dynamics deal with different kinds of phenomena, the former "depend on"—rather than being "subordinate to," as Halliday (1976: 73) argues—the latter. See J.S. Mill to J.E. Cairnes, 20 Sept. 1871, CW: XVII.1833; also, Thompson (1976: 142).
130. J. S. Mill to A. Comte, 17 Jan. 1844, CW: XIII.620).
131. Mill (1861a, CW: XIX.394).
132. Mill (1861a, CW: XIX.397).
133. Mill (1843, CW: VIII.924).
134. Mill (1861a, CW: XIX.398).
135. Collini, Winch and Burrow (1983: 152).
136. Mill (1861a, CW: XIX.398).
137. See Mill (1843, CW: VIII.869–70).
138. Mill (1861a, CW: XIX.404).
139. Mill (1859, CW: XVIII.224).
140. Mill (1861a, CW: XIX.382).
141. Mill (1843, CW: VIII.926, 914). Cf. Ryan (1972: 101).

REFERENCES

[Anon.] (1861) "*Considerations on Representative Government* by John Stuart Mill," *Critic* 22 (564; 27 Apr. 1861): 537–38.

[Bain, A.] (1843) "A System of Logic: By John Stuart Mill," *Westminster Review* 39 (2): 412–56.

Ball, T. (2000) "The Formation of Character: Mill's 'Ethology' Reconsidered," *Polity* 33 (1): 25–48.

———. (2010) "Competing Theories of Character Formation: James vs. John Stuart Mill," in G. Varouxakis and P. Kelly (eds.) *John Stuart Mill: Thought and Influence* (London and New York: Routledge): 35–56.

Bentham, J. (1817) *Plan of Parliamentary Reform, in the Form of a Catechism, with Reasons for Each Article, with an Introduction, Shewing the Necessity of Radical, and the Inadequacy of Moderate, Reform* (London: R. Hunter)

Capaldi, N. (1973) "Mill's Forgotten Science of Ethology," *Social Theory and Practice* 2 (4): 409–20.

Collini, S.; Winch, D.; Burrow, J. (1983) *That Noble Science of Politics: A Study in Nineteenth-Century Intellectual History* (Cambridge: Cambridge University Press).

Feuer, L. S. (1976) "John Stuart Mill as a Sociologist: The Unwritten Ethology," in J. M. Robson and M. Laine (eds) *James and John Stuart Mill: Papers of the Centenary Conference* (Toronto: University of Toronto Press): 86–110.

Garforth, F. W. (1979) *John Stuart Mill's Theory of Education* (Oxford: Martin Robertson).

———. (1980) *Educative Democracy* (Oxford: Oxford University Press).

Halliday, R. J. (1976) *John Stuart Mill* (London and New York: Routledge).

Hume, D. (1742) "That Politics May be Reduced to Science," in *The Philosophical Works of David Hume*, vol. 3. (Edinburgh: Adam Black and William Tait, 1826): 14–30.

Jones, H. S. (1999) "'The True Baconian and Newtonian Method': Tocqueville's Place in the Formation of Mill's *System of Logic*," History of European Ideas 25 (3): 153–61.

[Johnson, A.] (1861) "Mr Mill on Representative Government," *Westminster Review* 20 (1): 91–114.

Kort, F. (1952) "The Issue of a Science of Politics in Utilitarian Thought," *American Political Science Review* 46 (4): 1140–52.

Lewis, G. C. (1850) *A Treatise on the Methods of Observation and Reasoning in Politics*, 2 vols. (London: John W. Parker).

Lewisohn, D. (1972) "Mill and Comte on the Methods of Social Science," *Journal of the History of Ideas* 33 (2): 315–24.

Lively, J.; Rees, J., eds. (1978) *Utilitarian Logic and Politics* (Oxford: Oxford University Press).

Loizides, A. (2013) *John Stuart Mill's Platonic Heritage: Happiness through Character* (Lanham, MD: Lexington Books).

———. (2014) "George Grote and James Mill: A Defense of 'Theoretic Reform'," in K. N. Demetriou (ed.) *George Grote and the Classical Heritage: A Brill Companion* (Leiden: Brill, forthcoming).

[Lorimer, J.] (1861) "Mr Mill on Representative Government," *North British Review* 35 (60): 534–63.

[Macaulay, T. B.] (1829) "Mill's Essay on Government: Utilitarian Logic and Politics," *Edinburgh Review* 49 (97): 159–89.

[Mackintosh, J.] (1820) "Parliamentary Reform," *Edinburgh Review* 34 (68): 461–501.

[———.] (1821) "Stewart's *Introduction to the Encyclopaedia*," part 2, *Edinburgh Review* 36 (71): 220–67.

Merriam, C. E. (1925) *New Aspects of Politics*, 2nd ed. (Chicago: University of Chicago Press, 1931).

[Mill, J.] (1820) "Government," in M. Napier (ed.) *Supplement to the IV, V, and VI Editions of the Encyclopaedia Britannica*, vol. 4, part 2 (Edinburgh: Archibald Constable): 491–505.

Mill, J. S. (1824) "War Expenditure," in vol. IV (1967) of Mill (1963–1991): 3–22.

———. (1832) "Hickson's The New Charter," in vol. XXIII (1986) of Mill (1963–1991): 404–5.

———. (1833) "Remarks on Bentham's Philosophy," in vol. X (1969) of Mill (1963–1991): 5–18.

———. (1834) "Plato's *Gorgias*," in vol. XI (1978) of Mill (1963–1991): 97–150.

———. (1835a) "Rationale of Representation," in vol. XVIII (1977) of Mill (1963–1991): 17–46.

———. (1835b) "Sedgwick's Discourse," in vol. X (1969) of Mill (1963–1991): 33–74.

———. (1836) "On the Definition of Political Economy; and on the Method of Investigation Proper to It," in vol. IV (1967) of Mill (1963–1991): 309–39.

———. (1837a) "Armand Carrel," in vol. XX (1985) of Mill (1963–1991): 169–215.

———. (1837b) "Fonblanque's England under Seven Administrations," in vol. VI (1982) of Mill (1963–1991): 349–80.

———. (1838) "Bentham," in vol. X (1969) of Mill (1963–1991): 77–115.

———. (1840) "De Tocqueville on Democracy in America," in vol. XVIII (1977) of Mill (1963–1991): 155–204.

———. (1843) *A System of Logic, Ratiocinative and Inductive: Being a Connected View of the Principles of Evidence and the Methods of Scientific Investigation*, in vols. VII and VIII (1974) of Mill (1963–1991).

———. (1844) *Essays on Some Unsettled Questions of Political Economy*, in vol. IV (1967) of Mill (1963–1991): 229–339.

———. (1845) "Guizot's Essays and Lectures on History," in vol. XX (1985) of Mill (1963–1991): 259–94.

———. (1849) "Vindication of the French Revolution of February 1848," in vol. XX (1985) of Mill (1963–1991): 319–63.

———. (1859) *On Liberty*, in vol. XVIII (1977) of Mill (1963–1991).

———. (1861a) *Considerations on Representative Government*, in vol. XIX (1977) of Mill (1963–1991).

———. (1861b) *Utilitarianism*, in vol. X (1969) of Mill (1963–1991).

———. (1865) *An Examination of Sir William Hamilton's Philosophy and of the Principal Philosophical Questions Discussed in his Writings*, in vol. IX (1979) of Mill (1963–1991).

———. (1867) "Inaugural Address Delivered to the University of St. Andrews," in vol. XXI (1984) of Mill (1963–1991): 217–57.

———. (1873) *Autobiography*, in vol. I (1981) of Mill (1963–1991).

———. (1963–1991) *Collected Works of John Stuart Mill*, F.E.L. Priestly (gen. ed.), and subsequently J. M. Robson, 33 vols. (London/Toronto: Routledge and Kegan Paul/University of Toronto Press).

Miller, D. E. (2010) *J. S. Mill* (Cambridge: Polity Press)

Rosen, M. (2013) *Mill* (Oxford: Oxford University Press).

Ryan, A. (1970) *The Philosophy of John Stuart Mill*, 2nd ed. (New Jersey: Humanities Press International, 1990).

———. (1972) "Two Concepts of Politics and Democracy: James and John Stuart Mill," in M. Fleisher (ed.) *Machiavelli and the Nature of Political Thought* (New York: Atheneum): 76–113.

———. (1974) *J. S. Mill* (London and Boston: Routledge and Kegan Paul).

Sidgwick, H. (1891) *The Elements of Politics*, 4th ed. (London: Macmillan and Co., 1919).

Siedentop, L. (1994) *Tocqueville* (Oxford: Oxford University Press).

Skorupski, J. (1989) *John Stuart Mill* (London and New York: Routledge).

Sraffa, P., ed. (1951–1977) *The Works and Correspondence of David Ricardo*, 11 vols. (Indianapolis: Liberty Fund, 2004).

Thomas, W. (1979) *The Philosophic Radicals; Nine Studies in Theory and Practice 1817–1841* (Oxford: Clarendon Press).

Thompson, D.F. (1976) *John Stuart Mill and Representative Government* (Princeton: Princeton University Press).

Urbinati, N. (2002) *Mill on Democracy: From the Athenian Polis to Representative Government* (Chicago: University of Chicago Press).

Varouxakis, G. (1999) "Guizot's Historical Works and J. S. Mill's Reception of Tocqueville," *History of Political Thought* 20 (2): 292–312.

———. (2002) *Mill on Nationality* (London and New York: Routledge).

———. (2012) *Liberty Abroad: J. S. Mill on International Relations* (Cambridge: Cambridge University Press).

Wilson, F. (1990) *Psychological Analysis and the Philosophy of John Stuart Mill* (Toronto: University of Toronto Press).

Winch, D., ed. (1966) *James Mill: Selected Economic Writings* (Edinburgh and London: Oliver and Boyd).

11 *A System of Logic* and the "Art of Life"

Alan Ryan

For much of the twentieth century, John Stuart Mill's *Utilitarianism* (1861) seemed to exist only to provide an opportunity for beginning philosophy students to cut their teeth on the problems associated with his notorious "proof" of the principle of utility. G. E. Moore's dismantling of what he termed "the naturalistic fallacy" embraced more targets than Mill's proof alone, and on closer inspection revealed as many problems in Moore's conception of definition as in the moral theories he criticized; nonetheless, it was an effective piece of demolition that set the tone for the discussion of Mill's little essay in the first half of the twentieth century.[1] The wish to see what might be rescued of Mill's argument was one thing that drew me to the discussion of the "Art of Life" in Book VI of the *A System of Logic* (1843). An equally important motive was the belief that Mill had more resources than most critics supposed for deriving the libertarian doctrines of *On Liberty* (1859) from (what he understood as) utilitarian premises.[2] Even if there remained unresolved tensions between the absolutism of the defense of individual liberty in the one essay and the flexibility inherent in the teleological and maximizing thrust of the utilitarianism defended in *Utilitarianism*, I was unwilling to follow Isaiah Berlin in disregarding Mill's own insistence that his defense of liberty rested on utilitarian foundations.[3] It appeared from Mill's essay on Jeremy Bentham (1838) that he had a more complex understanding of utilitarianism than a simple appeal to the greatest happiness principle might suggest, and that the apparatus that underpinned that understanding was also to be found in the *Logic*, although it was explained very briefly, and its bearing on *Liberty* not brought out in the discussion in the *Logic*.[4] My wider concern with Mill stemmed from my interest in the philosophy of the social sciences, and this embraced a curiosity about Mill's references to his moral philosophy as "inductive" in distinction to the *a priori* morality of the intuitionists represented by William Whewell.[5] As the *Autobiography* (1873) insists, Mill thought of utilitarianism as "progressive," again in distinction to the conservativism of an intuitive ethics committed to the existence of fixed and timeless moral truths known to a moral sense, or in the alternative held to be indubitable however they were known because their falsity was "inconceivable." The fact that utilitarianism was "inductive" was connected in Mill's mind to the fact that it was "progressive." A belief in progress and a commitment to Millian empiricism are by no means logically connected, however. One might, as Whewell perhaps did, believe that the fundamental truths of the natural sciences are true *a priori*, and their falsity inconceivable once they are clearly apprehended, but believe nonetheless that their discovery involves a slow process of uncovering what they are. Only after they are clearly apprehended can they be seen to be necessarily true; the test of their truth may be the inconceivability of their falsity, but uncovering the deep truth about the natural order of things is an experimental process, and our confidence that there are such truths to be uncovered rests on the evidence that we are making progress in uncovering them. Nor need an intuitionist in the philosophy of science believe that *all* scientific truths are self-evidently true when clearly understood; there may be innumerable partial generalizations, accepted as useful rules of thumb, true for the most part, but neither self-evident nor indubitable. It is the true laws of nature underlying them that are, when properly understood, self-evident and indubitable.

This thought exposes a difference between intuitionism as a philosophy of science and ethical intuitionism, however. Many defenders of the intuitive school in ethics believed that the truths of morality were already known to us, whereas the truths of the physical sciences reveal themselves only little by little. This suggests that the truths of morality are not on all fours with those of the natural sciences; philosophers have sometimes held that the truths of geometry and mathematics are the object of immediate apprehension in more nearly the same way as the truths of morality, whereas the laws of the physical universe are not, since even if the latter are necessarily true, they do not wear their necessity on their face. That may have motivated Mill's desire to drive intuitionism from its stronghold in mathematics and geometry, as he attempted to do both in the *Logic* and in his *Examination of Sir William Hamilton's Philosophy* (1865); conversely the feeling that they needed to defend intuitionism across the board provoked Mill's critics to defend Hamilton and intuitionism, so Mill remarked, "as *pro aris et focis*."[6] Whatever the strengths and weaknesses of Mill's anti-intuitionism, his opponents shared his view that the survival of a worldview friendly to conventional ethical and religious convictions was assisted by intuitionism and threatened by Mill's arguments. The young John Dewey, learning philosophy at the University of Vermont, suspected that his teacher, H.A.P. Torrey, an intuitionist in the mould of Hamilton, Mansel and McCosh, would not confront intuitionism's empiricist critics because he dared not, and that what he feared was the erosion of the students' Christian faith.[7]

It would be foolish to suggest that *A System of Logic* builds inexorably towards Book VI, chapter XII (chapter XI in the first four editions) on "The Logic of Practice or Art; Including Morality and Policy," not foolish to suggest that an important motive for providing a persuasive account of the logic of the physical sciences was that it was needed to underpin the account of the "moral sciences" that Book VI provides.[8] It may or may not be significant that Mill's account of the origins of the *Logic* in his *Autobiography* pairs his first thoughts about logic in the narrow sense—that covered by the term "ratiocinative" in the full title *A System of Logic Ratiocinative and Inductive*—with coming to see that T. B. Macaulay's attack on James Mill's essay "Government" (1820) had shown that a "geometrical" approach to political theorizing would not do. James Mill was right to think that mere rule of thumb empiricism of the sort Macaulay seemed to be espousing would not do either, but these were not the only alternatives.[9] It is never wise to take John Stuart Mill's retrospective accounts of his intellectual development unskeptically; no more than most of us, was he an infallible witness to events of thirty years before. Much more than most of us, too, he was concerned to give his intellectual life a "progressive" shape, doing justice to his debts to his early education in "Benthamism" and reinforcing the message that his new openness to French and German ideas about historical change and the importance of culture did not mean the wholesale rejection of what he had been taught earlier.

There are difficulties in the way of providing a simple account of what Mill thought about the logic of practice, of which the most obvious is that two of the most explicit accounts, in *Logic* and "Bentham," are very short and not entirely like each other. The account in "Bentham" is intended on the one hand to insist against Bentham himself that the cultivation of our own better selves is a proper object of ethical, though not of narrowly moral, concern, and on the other to provide a brief account of the dimensions of the appraisal of action and character that Bentham omitted. The account in the *Logic* is not directed against Bentham so much as against Comte when against anyone in particular, but it widens the issue to the logic of practice in general. Coming to a view of just what Mill had in mind requires more inference than a commentator should be happy with. It is not hard to see in outline what Mill was arguing, but more difficult to see in detail how the apparatus he provides is intended to work. Happily, there has been some impressive and sophisticated recent discussion of Mill's project, on which I shall rely.[10] A second problem is that there was a surprisingly long interval between Mill's essay on Bentham published in 1838 and the revision of the final sections of chapter XII in the third edition of the *Logic*. There was an even longer interval between Mill's appeal to the distinction between the science and the art of economics in his essay "On the Definition of Political Economy and the Method of Investigation Proper to It," published in 1836, but written some five years earlier, and the discussion in the third edition of *Logic*. The third edition of the *Logic* appeared only in 1851, and the new sections 6 and 7 that replaced the former section 6 are quite different from what they replace. In what follows, I briefly recapitulate what I initially thought the implications of Mill's discussion of "the art of life" were, and why I agree with critics of some aspects of my reading. I am, of course, happy that other aspects seem generally agreed to be right. I then go on to link the discussion of the art of life to Mill's contrast between progressive morality and its alternatives; that allows me to tie the defense of individual liberty to utilitarianism as Mill understood it in a rather different way from what I suggested fifty years ago. The problem to which I have no resolution is familiar, though not even now perhaps discussed as often as it should be, namely whether Mill's conception of "progress" implies an eventual convergence on an understanding of human nature in much the way that most theorists assume that progress in physics implies an eventual convergence on a single wholly adequate physical theory, or whether it is nearer to progress in the arts, where we can discern a direction of travel, but not the convergence expected of the physical sciences.[11]

"THE ART OF LIFE"

Mill's insistence in *Logic* that "art" and "science" are essentially different is neither the only nor the first place where he draws the distinction as he does there. In his essay on definition and method in political economy, he says firmly that the notion that political economy is the science that shows a nation how to become wealthy confuses the science of political economy with the art of becoming wealthy.[12] In making the point, he criticizes Adam Smith's seeming conflation of the two in his *Wealth of Nations* (1776),[13] but he also insists on the necessity of an adequate scientific basis for any successful art. The defect of doctrinaires is that they try to deduce detailed rules of practice from one simple premise, whereas what we need is instruction that takes into account all the occasions when a *prima facie* rule needs to be supplemented or ignored; in *Logic* this thought sustains the argument that art cannot be deductive. It is in the discussion in "Definition and Method" that Mill says that art employs the imperative mood rather than the indicative; it issues hypothetical or categorical imperatives, not propositions in the ordinary sense.

> Science is a collection of *truths*, art a body of *rules*, or directions for conduct. The language of science is, This, or, This is not; This does, or does not, happen. The language of art is, Do this; Avoid that. Science takes cognizance of a *phenomenon* and endeavours to discover its *law*; art proposes to itself an *end*, and looks out for *means* to effect it.[14]

He takes over exactly this formulation in *Logic*.[15] In the discussion that leads up to his insistence on the difference between science and art, Mill also argues that so-called first principles are commonly the last to be discovered; anticipating Karl Popper's assault on an obsession with definition many years afterwards, Mill points out that scientific inquiry never begins with definitions of terms; only late in the process of investigation and discovery do we converge on definitions.[16] This may be one reason why Mill was so cavalier about the "proof" of the principle of utility.[17] If the history of the sciences is initially marked by the accumulation of explanations and partial laws that are more nearly rules of thumb than laws of nature,[18] so that the first principles of any particular science emerge late in its history, one might think by analogy that much of our morality will consist of precepts that are regularized only under pressure, whether the pressure of events or the dialectical pressure to which Socrates subjects his interlocutors in the Platonic dialogues. Mill's claim in *Utilitarianism* that such coherence as human morality displays reflects the influence of a standard not acknowledged, namely utility, is consonant with that view. The distinction Mill has in mind between art and science does not appear to vary between one context of discussion and another. "Art" as the reference to the Greek *technê* suggests, consists of instructions to be followed to achieve some end or other, based on the knowledge provided by the corresponding science, and one can see the impact of Mill's exasperated reaction to Macaulay's criticism of a scientific approach to political analysis when he follows Plato in distinguishing *empeiria* or mere empiricism from philosophically sophisticated *technê*.[19]

The implication on which I first seized was that the imperatives of an art are not strictly speaking objects of proof, so that Mill could not have thought himself obliged to prove them. "Facts of the matter" susceptible of proof and disproof enter at two points, however; firstly, offering instructions to whomever we might offer them presupposes that their mind is already directed to the end that following the instructions will achieve. "Tighten the bolts from left to right" presupposes that we have it in mind to achieve the result that tightening the bolts in the right order will bring about; if we do not care about the end result the advice presupposes, we will ignore the advice, or find it irrelevant. "Irrelevance" is not disproof, but we may think that it is a defect in an imperative analogous to falsity as a defect in a factual proposition. We may not, of course—we may think it good advice, but for someone else, whereas falsity is in that sense person-invariant. Secondly, an imperative can suffer from a defect much more directly related to falsity. If the factual truths that the instruction presupposes are not in fact true the imperative will not be one to follow; if tightening the bolts from left to right will result in the piece of machinery failing to function as it ought, the imperative is not falsified but is certainly undermined, and the undermining is person-invariant. "That won't work" knocks an instruction on the head. This opens the way for the interpretation I wanted to offer of Mill's conception of his project in *Utilitarianism*. If morality consists of rules—what sort of rules is a further difficult subject—Mill was not proving them in the way Moore supposed. Moore's notion of what was at issue was that the "proof" offered by Mill rested on *defining* goodness as pleasure, and on Moore's view, goodness was a simple, unanalyzable, non-natural property unsusceptible of definition.[20] Mill's argument is remote from a concern with definition, and relies on claims about what it is psychologically possible and impossible to want that have themselves been sharply criticized. The part of the "proof" that aroused the most criticism from the beginning, however, was the move from the claim that each person pursues his own happiness, which is therefore a good to him, to the claim that we *should* pursue the general happiness, which is a good to all of us. I shall not try to rescue Mill from the complaint that he commits the fallacy of composition. His own response to the criticism was unhelpful.[21] Observing that he meant to say that if we find our own happiness a good to us, we must acknowledge that the happiness of everyone is at least *a* good does not remove the difficulty: if "good" always means "good in the eyes of" whomever it may be, there is no such thing as "a good" *tout court*. If there is not, we cannot make the move that Mill requires from my thinking that my own happiness is a good (for me) to thinking that everyone else's happiness is a good (for me). There is a longer and more indirect route that Mill may well have had in mind, the essence of which is an appeal to the terms on which rational creatures can sustain social life, but this is not the place to spell it out. I shall try only to explain how an emphasis on morality as an art, which is to say a set of rules, illuminates what Mill might have been doing. In retrospect, I think I exaggerated the centrality of the distinction between science and art to Mill's view of what kind of proof the principle of utility might be susceptible of. It is clear that one cannot literally prove an imperative, not clear how far Mill relied on that fact when admitting that ultimate principles cannot be proved. Mill more obviously relies on the thought that first principles are unsusceptible of proof because proof is a process of derivation from prior principles, and *ex hypothesi* first principles cannot be derived from something prior to them.[22] Oddly enough, the *Logic* itself repudiates that view of proof; Mill's account of syllogistic reasoning presents proof as a process of inference *according to* the major premise, not *from* it, and relies on that model to give a novel solution to the problem of induction, by arguing that every successful prediction is both a success for the particular causal claim and for the inductive method itself.[23] It is inference from particulars to particulars according to the principle embodied in the major premise. It is tempting to think that moral reasoning might yield to the same analysis, but Mill never suggests it. Mill may himself have been uncertain which of the many points he wished to make he should give priority to. For he was usually less anxious to argue for the importance of first principles than to argue for that of *axiomata media*, the middle level principles that he thought Bentham was especially good at seeking out, and whose importance in the physical sciences he credited Francis Bacon with emphasizing many years earlier.[24] Readers today might think that the most interesting implication of an emphasis on *axiomata media* is what it means for establishing a practical consensus on social and political rights in the absence of agreement on moral or metaphysical first principles, but Mill was writing a century before John Rawls's discussion of the "overlapping consensus" that he thought could provide the basis for a liberal political system in the absence of an agreement on ultimate principles, and although Mill's emphasis on *axiomata media* may look like an anticipation of Rawls's thought, it is anything but.[25] Mill's claim is the reverse of Rawls's. When he says that whatever steadiness there is in the world's moral judgments stems from mankind's unacknowledged adoption of a utilitarian standard they might explicitly repudiate, he is arguing on behalf of utilitarianism, not trying to persuade his readers that they can be political liberals while holding many different views about ethics. That is, he is arguing that we in fact steer our conduct by something like the utilitarian standard, no matter what other reasons we give for what we do. Why this might be true in many instances is obvious enough. The reasons why it might not be true in some important instances will emerge toward the end of this discussion.

The considerations "capable of determining the intellect" to which Mill refers[26] must be sought in two places, both lying in the orientation of the will, though not there alone. The first is that if the imperative "seek the general happiness" is to be grounded, it must be grounded in something we desire already. This is the obvious gloss on Mill's long argument to show that when we desire something we desire it as something that will make us happy; and it runs into the familiar difficulty that we seem to desire all sorts of things for their own sakes and not obviously for the sake of the happiness, let alone the pleasure, that they yield. The man who seeks to reach the top of Everest, knowing that there is a one in six chance of death in the course of the expedition, wants to reach the top of Everest rather than to make himself happy by doing so. Were he to take Mill's definition of happiness as pleasure and the absence of pain absolutely literally, and compare the pleasure and absence of pain he will derive from risking frostbite or death in a fall on Everest with that to be derived from sitting by a warm fire, it seems unlikely that Everest would be the winner. Nonetheless, we say he is happy to take the risk, he would be made unhappy if prevented from going on the expedition and so familiarly on. Mill assembles reminders of these obvious points to provide the motivational background to the imperative he wants us to accept as the major premise of the art of life. The second aspect of Mill's case also rests on a presumed aspiration of the reader. We are assumed by Mill to have a desire for security that is both a first-order and a second-order desire: we directly want immunity from the coercive or violent measures of other persons whether organized in institutions or merely acting on their individual initiative, which is to say freedom from fear, and we want to be able to plan our future actions in the knowledge that whatever we may wish to do in the future we can attempt to do without coercive interference by others. Freedom from fear is a good in itself, and security is a second-order good inasmuch as whatever we might wish to do we must rationally wish to be uninterfered with in doing it. This is why it grounds Mill's account of justice and is fundamental to his account of liberty.[27] If it is true that we are disposed to pursue happiness and desire to be secure in that pursuit, we are motivationally aligned to accept the imperatives flowing from the art of life as Mill construes it. Its injunctions are not undermined by irrelevance.

A further aspect of this argument is that it allows us to understand how two very different kinds of utility may be of overriding importance in Mill's theory: security is the ground of social existence and grounds what one might call the defensive theory of rights proposed in *Liberty*. The pursuit of an ideal nobility of character is what Mill has in mind as the realm of the aesthetic, and it gives a point to human existence that it would otherwise lack. The right to pursue our own conception of our own highest good grounds the positive theory of rights in *Liberty*. It is a view that remains attractive to writers of a very different metaphysical persuasion from Mill.[28] This much of what I believed that Mill was arguing, I still think is right as an account of Mill's argument.

Where I followed my view of what he *should* have been doing too far was in my interpretation of the gloss to be placed on the several departments of the art of life. My initial thought was that Mill's discussion in *Logic* where the art of life is divided into morality, prudence and aesthetics lined up the art of life into duties to others, care of oneself and the exploration of ultimate ends; this has the advantage of making morality enforceable by psychological sanctions, prudence "enforceable" by the natural consequences of our actions, and aesthetics the pursuit of ideals of character to be encouraged or deplored by others, but not enforced by coercion nor necessarily sanctioned by naturally caused consequences. They may yield disappointment or elation, but not necessarily the benefits and harms that accrue independently of our attitudes to which prudence attends. If we cannot abide Picasso's Blue Period paintings, no matter how hard we try, we may have wasted money on museum admissions charges, or purchasing books on the merits of Picasso, and in that sense we shall have been imprudent in vainly pursuing a particular experiment in living; but the central unhappiness has nothing to do with these losses, but with the frustration of the attempt to enlarge our tastes. Lining up the several considerations of the art of life as I did reflects Mill's insistence in *Liberty* that duties should be strictly enforced, both by the pressure of opinion and the agent's conscience, that imprudent conduct should not be coercively interfered with and that natural ill-consequences were not punishment, and the point of constraining coercive interference by reference to the harm principle was to allow and encourage individuals to explore ways in which they might better exemplify an ideal of human life. However, it seems that whatever the virtues of this way of organizing the art of life, Mill was doing something different; in *Logic*, he writes of "policy" rather than "prudence," and it seems that he has in mind something closer to the classical distinction between the *honestum* and the *utile* than my reading of the distinction as other-regarding and self-regarding. It is the distinction between the right and the expedient—as Mill himself says—rather than what I was looking for. This distinction seems to be one that Mill encountered, not in Cicero's discussion in *De Officiis*, but in Plato, whose dialogues Mill translated, and whose work he complained the universities of Oxford and Cambridge insisted on treating as literature when its real value was philosophical.[29] Plato's conviction that a man would *necessarily* do better by practicing justice rather than injustice was not one that Mill could share, of course. Mill's starting point was a version of the self-interest axiom, even if his conclusion was not so remote from Plato's. We could make ourselves, and be made by others, into creatures whose happiness lay in pursuing the general happiness, but this is a process in which we take the raw materials of nature and use them for our own purposes. This is very far from the claim that *nomos* and *phusis* are in harmony and reason will reveal that harmony to us; Mill's essay "Nature" (1874) is a notably bleak piece of work. Nonetheless, the claim that we can find our own happiness in pursuing the happiness of all sentient creatures (among many other goals) is central to Mill's moral philosophy. In outline, Mill's picture of moral development supposes that children come to associate their own happiness with pleasing the adults who rear them; the association is internalized as conscience. Adults, both ourselves and others, can and should reflect on this process and reinforce it where appropriate and work against it where second thoughts suggest that we have been brought up to overvalue some goods and undervalue others. *Positive* morality on this view is the set of rules current in a given society at a given time that is enforced by public opinion and internalized as conscience. *Critical* morality is the set of rules that would, if so instituted and internalized, maximize the happiness of everyone affected. Mill's conviction that the defense of freedom in his essay on liberty was a utilitarian defense is the claim that the optimific set of rules would confer on individuals the rights to freedom of thought and action that *Liberty* defends. Mill's methodological difficulty is that the apparatus that socializes children into their new role as moral agents appears to leave too little room for reflection by the children so socialized once they grow up. Bentham's notorious description of his Panopticon as "a mill for grinding rogues honest, and idle men industrious" is just what Mill resisted, as he did the claim of Robert Owen that society may give individuals any character it chooses, "from the best to the worst," although Owen's offence lay less in emphasizing the omnipotence of social training than in apparently thinking that individuals were simply stuck with whatever character they had been given by this process. Mill wanted the reflective desires and aspirations of the individual himself to be part of a process that could re-create his character, and thought that his discussion in *Logic*, Book VI, chapter 2, had provided the necessary freedom of maneuver for this. It is easy to imagine that Mill felt himself to have been "manufactured" by his strong-willed father, but in any case, if he was to have any room for the concept of self-development as he learned it from reading Coleridge and Carlyle, or for the idea of autonomy as he was learning it from Harriet Taylor, herself as strong-willed as his father, the agent's own understanding of the person he might make of himself must be part of the causal process by which he can come to have the character he hopes. This is not the place to consider how far Mill was successful in developing his compatibilist account of the freedom of the will, only to observe that he was happy to rest on it for the rest of his life, and to dismiss the problem of the freedom of the will when writing *Liberty*.[30]

It is time to turn to Mill's discussion in *Logic*, Book VI. In the first two editions of the work, chapter xii, section 6 provides a compressed account of the application of the distinction between science and art to the particular case of morality. Mill focuses on a subject that bears very directly on the idea of a progressive morality; he observes that in many cases, what we ought to do is to comply with a simple rule. Thus, if it is a matter of telling the truth or telling a lie, we follow the injunction "tell the truth." The value of following rules is that it gives everyone else certainty about our behavior, so if the rule is well-chosen—"tell the truth" is very firmly supported by considerations enshrined in the factual claim that we can only conduct our lives with any degree of success if we can rely on one another's veracity—it will generally achieve the good we aim at, *and* the knowledge that we are likely to follow the rule rather than make up some *ad hoc* principle increases another person's ability to predict our behavior and organize their own reactions to it. But Mill insists we are not to succumb to rule-worship. There may have been doctors who preferred their patients to die by the book rather than survive on the basis of a novel treatment, but that was the frame of mind that utilitarianism repudiated. Utilitarians should always look to the ends that morality served. Sometimes, we are like judges applying rules, and sometimes like legislators; in the latter case, we should be guided by the merits of the case.[31] Among twentieth century moral theorists, R. M. Hare came to hold a similar view, and although he was best known for introducing or reintroducing the concept of "universalizability" into modern moral philosophy, he thought of himself as a utilitarian in consequence.[32] A marked feature of Mill's argument, and one that persists, is the insistence that we need principles if we are to bring order to our moral convictions. Veracity is overwhelmingly likely to be the rule we should follow, but not always; to decide when it is right to lie rather than to tell the truth, we need some further principle. Intuitionists, he thought, either had some such principle to which they accorded self-evidence, or they believed that their particular intuitions came accompanied by intuitions about how to weigh one against another.[33]

Section 6 was replaced in its entirety by the more elaborate sections 6 and 7. Much of the thrust of the previous discussion remained, but amplified by the discussion of the art of life under the general heading of *Teleology or the Doctrine of Ends*.

There are two issues, to which I have no very satisfactory resolution, raised by sections 6 and 7, but also by sections 2 and 3. They concern Mill's conception of progress in morality, and indeed in the conduct of life altogether. The first is whether, or perhaps how far, that notion of progress is in the last resort a matter of progress in our understanding of the human psyche, in the nature of social interaction, and the ways in which human beings will live together more or less satisfactorily and lead individually happy lives, which is to say, a matter of progress in scientific understanding rather than something distinctively moral. It may, of course, be an inquiry that yields indeterminate results, and if it does not, the results may be depressing, since we may find that every route to a happier society filled with more flourishing individuals is inaccessible to us. Chapter xii, section 2 suggests that progress may be wholly a matter of scientific progress. It sketches the relationship between science and art in the simplest possible fashion—art proposes an end, science tells us the means—if appropriate, art declares them desirable and enjoins us to achieve them. That account goes a long way toward explaining why Mill suggests that he belongs to the inductive school in ethics, but also lead us back to the familiar problems that beset a consequentialist ethics that makes moral rules rules of thumb. "Give everyone's interests equal consideration" does not look like a rule of thumb; "tell the truth" can be so construed, since it readily becomes "tell the truth except when sufficiently dire consequences would ensue." Even then, it is not obvious that "tell the truth" itself rests on consequentialist considerations; it might be thought that it rests on, for example, the right of an interlocutor to have the truth told to him or her. Your right to hear the truth rather than my duty to tell the truth does the moral work. As to what that right rests on, given Mill's skepticism of ungrounded rights, we might appeal to ideas about reciprocity that would entail that you may not deceive me except under conditions where you could endorse my deceiving you, or principles of equal treatment that would yield the same result. Consequences would not be irrelevant, but would enter via their presumed effect on the (rational) decision-making of the persons involved. Mill does not explore any of these possibilities. Rather, he reverts to an insistence that if advice is to be well-founded, it must be founded on a complete scientific understanding of the relevant phenomena. This seems to be all of a piece with his complaints against Auguste Comte.[34] One complaint is more genuinely related to Mill's thoughts on teleology: because Comte ignores the need for an adequate theory of the human good, his practical advice is informed by a morality that consists of mere commonplaces. But in general, it is a weakness in Comte to believe that we, or more exactly he, know sufficient about the workings of both society and the minds of individuals to lay down prescriptions for the permanent future institutions of society. To say that Mill's notion of moral progress may very substantially be understood as a matter of scientific progress is not to complain. Indeed, it allows us to connect Mill's discussion of the art of life with *Liberty* by a different route from the one I suggested fifty years ago. "Experiments in living," undertaken at the agent's own risk and expense, provide evidence, even if only partial and fragmentary, of what novel avenues to happiness we might explore. This is the moment to emphasize a familiar point; Mill thought, reasonably enough, that we knew a great deal about the more obvious aspects of what made human beings happy and unhappy. The centrality of justice to any theory of ethics reflected the importance of security and predictability, and grounded what is often described as the priority of the right over the good within a consequentialist theory that in its nature prioritizes the good over the right. Mill trod a delicate path between over-emphasizing how much we already knew about human nature and over-emphasizing how much we still had to learn. What we had to learn is not the basic truths about human vulnerability and the elementary sources of human happiness, but the more obscure truths implied in his throwaway remarks in section 7, the penultimate paragraph of the *Logic*. There, Mill's characteristic mixture of bleak disappointment with human existence as it is and boundless optimism about what it might be emerges when he talks of seeking the conditions that might make life such as a person of developed culture would wish to live, rather than the wretched failure that life too often amounts to at present.

That, however, raises the second issue; writing of teleology or the doctrine of ends, Mill suggests that almost everything remains to be discovered. Setting aside my earlier doubts about what discovery involves in a field or discipline whose outcomes emerge in the imperative mood, we may still wonder what Mill has in mind and why he is so emphatic that we have barely started on elaborating an adequate Teleology. There are many connected puzzles, such as Mill's uninterest in Aristotle; he refers to Aristotle as a "judicious utilitarian" in *On Liberty*, but nowhere explores, for instance, Aristotle's discussion of the virtues or the development of a virtuous character.[35] Another is whether the so-called "missing science" of ethology is implicated in the failure to elaborate on what a properly grounded Teleology would look like and why it is so incomplete.[36] Mill's first discussion of the Art of Life included education as one of its branches, and Mill's conception of education was invariably a very broad one, embracing above all the creation of character. In this he was both very Victorian and very Greek. It is at least possible that in the light of his previous account of the way an art pronounces an end to be desirable, passes to science the task of discovering how it is be achieved, and then converts the truths of science into instructions for practice, the inadequacy of any contemporary doctrines of ends lay both in our unclarity about just what the human good consisted in, and in our ignorance about how to achieve it. This is one of those places where it is obvious what "progress" involves if it is a matter of the human sciences and obscures what it involves if it is purely a matter of progress in the understanding of the ends of life. Mill, after all, did not believe in Platonic forms, nor therefore that education was to be understood as *anamnesis* with a final revelation of the true, the good and the beautiful to look forward to. All the same, Mill was a monist to the extent of arguing that an ultimate principle or end is required to bring order to our practical reasoning; moreover, there can be only one ultimate principle, since a multiplicity of principles might yield conflicting injunctions for action and we would need some further principle to resolve the disagreement. In arguing this, of course, Mill puts himself firmly at odds with writers such as Nietzsche in his own day and Bernard

Williams in ours, who regard the pull of equally ultimate and irreconcilable demands on us as a central fact of moral life. The ultimate principle for Mill is the maximization of the happiness of all sentient beings; he says in the 1865 edition that *Utilitarianism* contains his argument for adopting it as the ultimate principle of all practice, but says also, as he does in all editions from the third, that *Logic* is not the place for further elaboration.[37]

The difficulty, as always, is that Mill did not think that we should always, and perhaps that we should rather rarely, be guided by that principle when deciding what to do. Not only was it true that the subordinate arts, such as architecture, had their own ends that could commonly be taken for granted without further reflection, it was more importantly true that individuals ought generally not aim at happiness, whether their own or the general happiness, but at objects pursued for their own sake irrespective of their immediate effect on our happiness. The man who desires to climb Everest because he thinks it really important to do so acts rightly, not only on most views of the matter, but on Mill's view as well. What utilitarianism offers us is a way of understanding why that is the right thing to do. The answer seems to be that only when individuals have and are encouraged to have ideals such as courage, endurance and resistance to oppression against all odds, will human beings be all they should be, and humanity, or sentient creatures generally, be as happy as they can be. Can this happiness be explained as pleasure and absence of pain? Plainly, it can be so at a straightforward level; immunity to ill-treatment, adequate health, nutrition and the like are utilitarian goods and their opposites are utilitarian ills, though not directly *moral* goods and evils. Cruelty, on this view is a very obvious moral evil for good utilitarian reasons; cruel acts are bad, and the frame of mind that leads to them is one to be repressed by all means that are effective and not themselves worse than it. It is what one might call higher-level or reflective goods that present difficulties; the man who must turn back from Everest may suffer simple pains including frostbite and physical injury, but more interestingly suffers pangs of disappointment, perhaps the pain of realizing that his nerve cracked, pains and unhappiness that are genuine, but genuine only because of his commitments. The man who sits quietly on his sofa neither attempts the climb nor suffers the disappointments; it is not "not climbing Everest" that is painful, but the frustration of a project central to the would-be climber's existence. All this is commonplace enough; the problem it presents in the context of the *Logic* is that it leaves it somewhat mysterious just what an adequate "doctrine of ends" would achieve that we presently do without.

This brings us to the final problem. Whether we think of progress as a deeper understanding of psychology and sociology on the basis of which we can build more intelligent practices, whether moral, prudential or aesthetic, or as a deeper understanding of the ends of life organized more intelligently in a developed "teleology or the doctrine of ends," we are left to wonder whether Mill imagines that we shall all converge on one theory of the good life, and whether that theory will yield a determinate, rationally compelling account of how to rank human lives from best to worst, most to least successful, virtuous or admirable, and in the process settle the questions we might raise about—let us say—how far the successful pursuit of artistic excellence justifies neglecting our moral obligations.[38] There are one or two simple points that we might make, and then speculation must take over. The first simple point is that Mill plainly thinks that we shall continue to be born with different aptitudes and temperaments, and that we shall therefore acquire different skills and tastes; if "good" means "good for" it will mean something different for one person and another. That is entirely consistent with there being only one standard, and perhaps enough to launch a utilitarian defense of a substantial degree of individual liberty. Comte's crime in Mill's view was not that he did not know that different people had different tastes and abilities, but that he thought the entire point of human existence was *vivre pour autrui*, which is to say to devote ourselves only to the welfare of others.[39] This was a "liberticide" project, and in any case absurd because it rested only on Comte's conviction that he had found the recipe for the organic society. Whatever else Mill's individualism amounted to, it certainly meant that each person should take his or her own development as a central object of concern, and not equate the point of existence with a life of self-sacrifice. This was not to encourage selfishness, but to repudiate a certain kind of organicism. It was also to embrace a kind of social aestheticism, perhaps another aspect of Mill's enthusiasm for classical Athens and certainly an aspect of Mill's affection for Goethe and von Humboldt. A society in which innumerable flowers bloomed could display the uncoerced harmony of a successful garden: a human contrivance in which nature was liberated as much as constrained.

NOTES

1. See, e.g., Moore (1903:116–26 (ch. III, §39–44)). See also Ryan (1966).
2. See Ryan (1965).
3. See Berlin (1959); Mill (1859, CW: XVIII.224). All references to Mill's works are to the authoritative edition of *Collected Works of John Stuart Mill* (Mill, 1963–1991—cited as CW, followed by volume and page number), unless otherwise indicated.
4. This is hardly a matter for complaint; only in 1865 could Mill refer to his discussion of utilitarianism in the essay of that name (see Mill, 1843, CW: VIII.951n), and there was nothing in the text on which he might have been provoked to hang a reference to *On Liberty* after 1858.
5. See Mill (1852, CW: X.167–201). For a discussion of the Mill-Whewell debate, see *infra*, chapter four.
6. Mill (1865a, CW: IX.ciii); see also Mill (1873, CW: I.233).
7. See Ryan (1995:100ff).
8. "Moral sciences," of course, means the sciences in which the laws of the human mind are involved; they are the *Gesisteswissenschaften*, a term that was introduced into German precisely in order to translate the English expression. In Cambridge, the Moral Sciences Tripos survived until the 1970s.

9. J. Mill (1820); Macaulay (1829).
10. See Loizides (2013: ch. 7).
11. See Hampshire (1983).
12. Mill (1844, CW: IV, 312).
13. See, e.g., Smith (1776: 678–79).
14. Mill (1844, CW: IV.312).
15. Mill (1843, CW: VIII.943–48).
16. Mill (1843, CW: VII.3, 140).
17. Mill (1861, CW: X.207–08 and 234–39).
18. Mill (1843, CW: VII.318–19; 1844, CW: IV.313).
19. See Mill (1844, CW: IV.312; 1843, CW: VIII.943n).
20. Moore (1903: 58–62 (ch. I, §6–10)).
21. Mill (1861, CW: X.234). See also J. S. Mill to H. Jones, 13 Jun. 1868, CW: XVI.1414.
22. Mill (1861, CW: X.207–08). See also, Mill (1843, CW: VII.109).
23. Mill (1843, CW: VII.193, 319–22).
24. Mill (1838, CW: X.110–11). See also Mill (1833, CW: X.29 and 1843, CW: VIII.870).
25. See Rawls (1993: Introduction; lecture IV).
26. Mill (1861, CW: X.208).
27. See Riley (2011).
28. See, e.g., Dworkin (2011).
29. See Mill's introduction to his translation of Plato's "Protagoras" (1834) in CW: XI.39–45.
30. See J. Bentham to J. P. Brissot de Warville, [25] Nov. 1791 (in Bentham, 1968–2006: IV. 341–42); Owen (1813: 19). See Mill (1873, CW: I.163, 175, 177; 1859, CW: XIII.219).
31. See, Mill (1843, CW: VIII.944) and Appendix H (*ibid.*, 1155).
32. Hare (1981:107ff).
33. See Mill (1852, CW: X.167–201).
34. See Mill (1873, CW: I.219, 221).
35. See Mill (1859, CW: XVIII.235).
36. See Mill (1843, CW: VIII.872–73).
37. Mill (1843, CW: VIII.951n) and Appendix H (*ibid.*, 1154ff).
38. Bernard Williams's discussion in *Moral Luck* (Williams, 1982) and Mill's mention of George Barnwell in *Liberty* (Mill, 1859, CW: XVIII.281) suggest it is possible to take very different sides on moral obligations.
39. Mill (1865b, CW: X.336).

REFERENCES

Bentham, J. (1968–2006) *The Correspondence of Jeremy Bentham*, T.L.S. Sprigge (I, II), I. R. Christie (III), A. T. Milne (IV, V), J. R. Dinwiddy (VI, VII), S. Conway (VIII–X), C. Fuller (XI), L. O'Sullivan, C. Fuller (XII) (eds.), 12 vols. (London/ Oxford: Athlone Press/Oxford University Press).
Berlin, I. (1959) "John Stuart Mill and the Ends of Life," reprinted in H. Hardy (ed.) *Liberty* (Oxford: Oxford University Press, 2002): 218–51.
Dworkin, R. (2011) *Justice for Hedgehogs* (Cambridge, MA: Belknap Press).
Hampshire, S. (1983) *Morality and Conflict* (Oxford: Blackwell).
Hare, R. M. (1981) *Moral Thinking: Its Levels, Method, and Point* (Oxford: Oxford University Press).
Loizides, A. (2013) *John Stuart Mill's Platonic Heritage: Happiness through Character* (Lanham, MD: Lexington Books).

Macaulay, T. B. (1829) "Mill's *Essay on Government*: Utilitarian Logic and Politics," *Edinburgh Review* 49 (97): 159–89.

Mill, J. (1820) "Government," in *Supplement to the IV, V, and VI Editions of the Encyclopaedia Britannica*, Macvey Napier (ed.), vol. 4, part 2 (Edinburgh: Archibald Constable and Co.): 491–505.

Mill, J. S. (1833) "Blakey's History of Moral Science," in vol. X (1969) of Mill (1963–1991).

——. (1834) "Plato's *Protagoras*," in vol. XI (1978) of Mill (1963–1991): 39–61

——. (1838) "Bentham," in vol. X (1969) of Mill (1963–1991).

——. (1843) *A System of Logic, Ratiocinative and Inductive: Being a Connected View of the Principles of Evidence and the Methods of Scientific Investigation*, in vols. VII and VIII (1974) of Mill (1963–1991).

——. (1844) *Essays on Some Unsettled Questions of Political Economy*, in vol. VI (1967) of Mill (1963–1991).

——. (1852) "Whewell on Moral Philosophy," in vol. X (1969) of Mill (1963–1991).

——. (1859) *On Liberty*, in vol. XVIII (1977) of Mill (1963–1991).

——. (1861) *Utilitarianism*, in vol. X (1969) of Mill (1963–1991).

——. (1865a) *An Examination of Sir William Hamilton's Philosophy and of the Principal Philosophical Questions Discussed in his Writings*, in vol. IX (1979) of Mill (1963–1991).

——. (1865b) *Auguste Comte and Positivism*, in vol. X (1969) of Mill (1963–1991).

——. (1873) *Autobiography*, in vol. I (1981) of Mill (1963–1991).

——. (1963–1991) *Collected Works of John Stuart Mill*, F.E.L. Priestly (gen. ed.), and subsequently J. M. Robson, 33 vols. (London/Toronto: Routledge and Kegan Paul/University of Toronto Press).

Moore, G. E. (1903) *Principia Ethica*, T. Baldwin (ed.), rev. ed. (Cambridge: Cambridge University Press, 1993).

Owen, R. (1813) *A New View of Society*, 3rd ed. (London: Longman, Hurst, Rees, Orme, Brown, Cadell and Davies, J. Hatchard, Murray., 1817).

Rawls, J. (1993) *Political Liberalism* (New York: Columbia University Press).

Riley, J. (2011) "Optimal Moral Rules and Supererogatory Acts," in B. Eggleston, D. E. Miller and D. Weinstein (eds.) *John Stuart Mill and the Art of Life* (Oxford: Oxford University Press): 119–45.

Ryan, A. (1965) "Mill and the Art of Living," reprinted in J. Gray and G. W. Smith (eds.), *On Liberty in Focus* (London and New York: Routledge, 1991): 162–8.

——. (1966) "Mill and the Naturalistic Fallacy," *Mind* 75 (299): 422–25.

——. (1995) *John Dewey and the High Tide of American Liberalism* (New York: W. W. Norton).

Smith, A. (1776) *An Inquiry into the Nature and Causes of the Wealth of Nations*, R. H. Campbell, A. S. Skinner (gen. eds.), W. B. Todd (text ed.), reprinted in vols. II and III of the *Glasgow Edition of the Works and Correspondence of Adam Smith* (Indianapolis: Liberty Fund, 1981).

Williams, B. (1982) *Moral Luck* (Cambridge: Cambridge University Press).

Contributors

Mark Balaguer is a professor of philosophy at California State University, Los Angeles. Balaguer works on metaphysics, philosophy of mathematics, philosophy of language, philosophy of logic and free will. He is the author of *Free Will as an Open Scientific Problem* (MIT Press, 2010) and *Platonism and Anti-Platonism in Mathematics* (Oxford University Press, 1998).

Bernard Berofsky is an emeritus professor of philosophy at Columbia University. Berofsky has published widely on free will, autonomy, determinism and causality. His most recent monograph is *Nature's Challenge to Free Will* (Oxford University Press, 2012). Other books include: *Liberation from Self: A Theory of Personal Autonomy* (Cambridge University Press, 1995) and *Freedom from Necessity: The Metaphysical Basis of Responsibility* (Routledge & Kegan Paul, 1987).

Steffen Ducheyne is a research professor of philosophy at the Centre for Logic and Philosophy of Science, Vrije Universiteit Brussel. Ducheyne works the history and philosophy of scientific methodology from the seventeenth to the nineteenth century. He is the author of *"The Main Business of Natural Philosophy": Isaac Newton's Natural-Philosophical Methodology* (Springer, 2012).

Hans V. Hansen is a professor of philosophy at the Centre for Research in Reasoning, Argumentation and Rhetoric, University of Windsor. Hansen works on integration of logic, dialectics and rhetoric in argumentation theories, and on John Stuart Mill on argumentation. He is co-editor of *Informal Logic*; he co-edited (with R. C. Pinto) *Reason Reclaimed: Essays in Honor of J. Anthony Blair and Ralph H. Johnson* (Vale Press, 2007) and *Fallacies: Classical and Contemporary Readings* (Penn State Press, 1995).

Antis Loizides teaches at the University of Cyprus. Loizides works on the history of political thought, particularly the moral and political thought of James Mill and John Stuart Mill. He is the author of *John Stuart Mill's*

Platonic Heritage: Happiness through Character (Lexington Books, 2013) and co-editor *of John Stuart Mill: A British Socrates* (Palgrave Macmillan, 2013).

Christopher Macleod is a lecturer at Lancaster University. Macleod works on the philosophy of John Stuart Mill, but has wide a range of interests in philosophy, political theory and the philosophy of international criminal law. He is co-editor (with D. E. Miller) of the *Blackwell Companion to Mill* (Wiley-Blackwell, forthcoming).

John P. McCaskey currently teaches at Brown University. McCaskey researches the history of scientific method and the history of induction. He has presented papers at various conferences in the US and Europe and has published on Aristotelian induction. He is the editor and translator of Jacopo Zabarella's *On Method* and *On Regressus* (I Tatti Renaissance Library by Harvard University Press, forthcoming).

Elijah Millgram is the E. E. Ericksen Professor of Philosophy at the University of Utah. Millgram works on the theory of rationality; he is currently working on a monograph on John Stuart Mill, among other book projects. He is the author of *Hard Truths* (Wiley-Blackwell, 2009), *Ethics Done Right: Practical Reasoning as a Foundation for Moral Theory* (Cambridge University Press, 2005) and *Practical Induction* (Harvard University Press, 1997).

Jonathan Riley is a professor of philosophy at the Murphy Institute of Political Economy at Tulane University. Riley has published widely on the moral and political thought of John Stuart Mill; his research interests include utilitarianism liberalism, democracy and justice. He is the author of *Mill's Radical Liberalism: An Essay in Retrieval* (Routledge, forthcoming), *Mill on Liberty* (Routledge, 1998), *Liberal Utilitarianism: Social Choice Theory and J. S. Mill's Philosophy* (Cambridge University Press, 1988).

Frederick Rosen is an emeritus professor of the history of political thought at University College London. Rosen, former director and joint general editor of the Bentham Project, works on John Stuart Mill's ethical and political thought, Bentham's constitutional law writings and the history of political thought. Rosen is the author of *Mill* (Oxford University Press, 2013). His monographs include, among others, *Classical Utilitarianism from Hume to Mill* (Routledge, 2003) and *Bentham, Byron, and Greece: Constitutionalism, Nationalism, and Early Liberal Political Thought* (Clarendon Press, 1992).

Alan Ryan is a visiting scholar at Princeton University. Ryan has published on the philosophy of John Stuart Mill, John Dewey and the philosophy of the social sciences, democracy and education among others. His most recent books include *On Politics* (Penguin, 2013) and *The Making of Modern Liberalism* (Princeton University Press, 2012). His monographs include, among others, *Liberal Anxieties and Liberal Education* (Hill & Wang, 1998; Profile Books, 1999); *Russell: A Political Life* (Allen Lane/ Hill & Wang, 1988; OUP, 1993).

Stephen P. Schwartz is an emeritus professor of philosophy at Ithaca College. Schwartz works on the philosophy of language and the history of analytic philosophy. He is the author of *A Brief History of Analytic Philosophy: From Russell to Rawls* (Wiley-Blackwell, 2012) and *Fundamentals of Reasoning* (Prentice-Hall, 1993); he is editor of *Naming, Necessity, and Natural Kinds* (Cornell University Press, 1977).

John M. Skorupski is a professor of philosophy at the University of St. Andrews. Skorupski works on moral and political philosophy, metaethics and epistemology, and the history of nineteenth and twentieth century philosophy. His monographs include, among others, *The Domain of Reasons* (Oxford University Press, 2010), *Why Read Mill Today* (Routledge, 2006) and *Ethical Explorations* (Oxford University Press, 1999).

Index

12–3, see also logic; syllogism;
petitio principii; Utility, "Proof" of
psychology 15, 23, 125, 134, 152,
221, 222; see also associationist
psychology
Putnam, Hilary 44, 53, 56, 58, 59;
see also Kripke, Saul; names,
Kripke-Putnam on

qualities 170–2, 179, 181–6; see also
attributes; pleasure(s)

Ramsey, Frank 138, 140, 143
ratiocination see syllogism
Rawls, John 251–2
reason: theoretical 151–4; practical
154–5
regularity theory 137, 138–41, 143,
144–5, 146–8
Reid, Thomas 12, 64
Roberts, John134, 139
rules: and logic as art 8, 10, 12
14, 19, 25, 76; of conduct
222–3; of justice 185–6; rule-
following 155–6; rule-worship
255; and science 22; see also
argumentation; art of life;
Deductive Method; formal logic;
inference; informal logic; Mill's
Methods; law(s); logic; syllogism
Russell, Bertrand: on Mill 44, 47, 54,
59; on proper names 48–50;
Kripke on 51–3

self-development 254
semantic physicalism 92, 94
semantic platonism 92, 94–6; see also
anti-platonism
semantic psychologism 92–4
set theory 87–8, 93
Sidgwick, Henry
Smith, Adam, The Wealth of Nations
Smith, William Henry 19–20
Social Dynamics / Social Statics 233–4;
see also Deductive Method,
Inverse
Society: state of 229, 232, 234; science
of 228, 230, 234; see also Social
Dynamics / Social Statics
Socrates 71, 158, 211, 250; see also
dialectics

species 55, 57, 58, 177–82, 185
Spencer, Herbert 16, 125
spontaneity: in Mill 11, 151, 153,
155–7, 161–2, 164–5; in Kant
158–61
Sterling, John 4, 5, 7, 8
Steward, Dugald 5, 22, 64–7, 125; on
mathematical axioms 68–9
syllogism: cannot lead to new
knowledge charge 63, 66;
inductive 71–3; involving
"interpretation"9–10, 69–70,
75–6, 251; major premise
of, Mill on 9–10, 11; Mill's
originality as regards 19; petitio
principii charge 10, 19–22, 63,
65–8, 197; rules of 10, 76, 200;
as tool 10, 108

Taylor Mill, Harriet 122, 123, 254
Teleology 154, 255, 256, 257, 258
Tocqueville, Alexis de 229–30
Toulmin, Stephen 201–2, 212
transcendental idealism 151, 160, 161–2;
see also Intuitionism; Kant
truth(s): mathematical 84, 98; necessary
6, 19–20, 106, 108, 110, 112;
see also logic; proof

uniformity: and laws 137; of nature 11,
17–18, 73; principle of 70, 72,
75–6; see also regularity theory
utility: principle of 154–6, 171, 172,
246; "Proof" of 156, 246, 250,
251; and security 185, 252–3

Walton, Douglas 203, 208
Ward, William George 17–18
warrants, method of 197–201
Whately, Richard 16, 19–20, 63–4, 76,
196; Elements of Logic 65–8,
70–3, 209; Elements of Rhetoric
203–4, 210, 212; Mill's review
of 64, 72, 195
Whewell, William 5, 11, 16, 17, 19, 55,
73, 76; on argument 109–10; on
deduction 107–8; on induction
104–7; on scientific inference
108–9; "Inductive Tables" 108;
see also Mill-Whewell debate
Woodward, James 144, 147